Teacher's Edition

Vocabulary
for Achievement

Second Course

Margaret Ann Ríchek

GREAT SOURCE
WILMINGTON, MA

Author

Margaret Ann Richek

Professor of Education Emerita, Northeastern Illinois University; consultant in reading and vocabulary study; author of The World of Words *(Houghton Mifflin)*

Classroom Consultants

Beth Gaby
English Chair, Carl Schurz High School, Chicago, Illinois

Chris Hausammann
Teacher of English, Central Mountain High School, Lock Haven, Pennsylvania

Malisa Cannon
Teacher of Language Arts, Desert Sky Middle School, Tucson, Arizona

Patricia Melvin
District Secondary Reading Specialist, Duval County Public Schools, Jacksonville, Florida

Sean Rochester
Teacher of English, Parkway Central High School, St. Louis, Missouri

Acknowledgments

Editorial: Ruth Rothstein, Victoria Fortune, Dan Carsen, Amy Gilbert

Design and Production: Mazer Corporation

Text Design and Production: Mazer Creative Services

Illustrations: Chris Vallo/Mazer Creative Services; Cookie Cook, Susan Aiello of Wilkinson Studios, LLC; David McFeders, George Cathey, Jerry Hoare, Ron Zalme of Langley Creative

Cover Design: Mazer Creative Services

Cover Photo: Stockbyte/Mazer Creative Services

Definitions for the three hundred words taught in this textbook are based on Houghton Mifflin dictionaries—in particular, the *Houghton Mifflin High School Dictionary*—but have been abbreviated and adapted for instructional purposes.

All pronunciations are reproduced by permission from the *American Heritage Dictionary of the English Language, Fourth Edition*, copyright © 2000.

ISBN-13: 978-0-669-51763-7   ISBN-10: 0-669-51763-1

3 4 5 6 7 8 9 10 - DBH - 10 09

Contents

Why Study Vocabulary Systematically?

Teachers and researchers agree on the importance of vocabulary in refining language skills. The greater the store of words we have at our disposal, the better equipped we are to comprehend what we read and express what we think.

Vocabulary for Achievement is a systematic approach to word learning that helps students to

- understand and use words effectively and flexibly
- learn, retain, and apply a core of important words
- independently unlock the meanings of new words
- engage in lifelong vocabulary acquisition
- improve reading comprehension in all curriculum areas
- improve performance on standardized, state, and college entrance tests
- select words forcefully in speaking and writing
- continually increase vocabulary knowledge

A systematic program ensures the development of the large storehouse of words that is critical to achievement, both in the classroom and in the larger world.

Essential features of the program include:
- exercises and features based on changes in the SAT, standardized, and state tests
- a revised, improved word list
- increased concentration on Greek and Latin word elements
- increased review of Greek and Latin word elements
- lesson organization that ensures correspondence between skills and words
- increased assessment
- the addition of exercises that directly apply word usage and comprehension
- increased word enrichment
- illustrations of specific words
- word explanations and teacher notes
- emphasis on related, derivative words

How Were the Words Selected?

The principal source for word lists was SATs published by the College Entrance Examination Board. Authors and editors also consulted numerous scholarly works, including the *Educator's Word Frequency Guide,* the American Heritage *Word Frequency Book, Living Vocabulary,* and many standard thesauruses. Most important, the words were chosen for usefulness, appropriateness to grade level, and applicability to lesson themes and word elements.

Vocabulary for Achievement contains over 80 percent of a well-accepted list of SAT words. The words in *Vocabulary for Achievement* are representative of the difficulty level of vocabulary frequently used in sentence-completion and critical-reading test items on the verbal section of the SAT. Further, most are taught in the Fourth Course or earlier, providing students with ample time to master them before encountering them on the SAT.

Vocabulary for Achievement ensures success, not only on the SAT but in lifelong vocabulary acquisition, by offering students early and engaging instruction with critical and challenging words.

A Tour of the Program

Vocabulary for Achievement is a systematic program of vocabulary development that provides comprehensive instruction and application of word meanings. These four principles guide the program:

- Clearly structured lessons teach best.
- Application of meanings in rich contexts aids retention.
- Learning vocabulary acquisition skills promotes independent learning.
- Vocabulary instruction must be accessible and adaptable to classroom needs.

These four principles are reflected throughout the program, which provides the structure necessary for students to learn new words; to apply them in a variety of practice formats to ensure ownership; and to use dictionary, reasoning, context, test-taking, and word structure skills to independently build and incorporate their growing pool of words.

Teacher-Friendly Elements

- The clear and consistent structure of *Vocabulary for Achievement* makes it ideal for either direct classroom instruction or for independent use, allowing you to direct sound and successful vocabulary instruction.
- **Lessons** provide complete presentation of words, special notes on word usage, carefully scaffolded and abundant practice, numerous contexts, substantial application, and notes for the teacher. Six of the thirty lessons focus on Greek and Latin word roots.
- **Skill Features** facilitate independent vocabulary learning through dictionary skills, reading and reasoning, test-taking, and Greek and Latin word elements.
- **Flash Cards (in student book only)** enable students to review words independently. Each card shows a vocabulary word on one side, and phonetic spelling and definition on the other.
- **Tests** cover each two consecutive lessons. The fifteen reproducible multiple-choice tests (with answers) allow you to monitor student progress.
- **Bonuses** align with tests to provide review on every two lessons. These activities include engaging practice formats such as word searches, crossword puzzles, and scrambled words.
- **Teaching Suggestions** provide concrete ideas to help you extend the range of the program for special classroom needs as well as enrichment.

The Lessons

- There are thirty six-page lessons per level.
- Each theme- or root-related lesson has ten words.
- Entries for words are adapted from the *American Heritage Dictionary* series, and use a dictionary format. They include pronunciations, part-of-speech labels, multiple definitions, etymologies, illustrative sentences, and related words (derivatives) with part-of-speech labels and example sentences.

- There are four scaffolded exercises for practice in writing words that correspond with definitions, completing sentences in an SAT format, writing derived forms in appropriate sentences, and finding examples of the words in varied contexts. Additional word learning is facilitated through illustrations.
- There is an additional challenge exercise using the SAT format of two blanks.
- An engaging reading comprehension passage incorporates each of the ten words, followed by two exercises, one focusing on vocabulary and the other on passage comprehension. The passages cover all areas of the curriculum, and include history, science and nature, the arts, myths and legends, technology, and careers.
- A writing assignment relates to the theme. In alternate lessons, students are asked to use their words in an essay of varied genres or to use words creatively in sentence stems.
- Vocabulary enrichment focuses on word histories and information to spark students' interest as well as to facilitate independent word learning.

Skill Features

- Ten skill features, one following every third lesson.

- Each feature focuses on fostering student independence in word learning.

- Four skill strands that are critical to independent word learning are covered:
  - using the dictionary
  - reading and reasoning
  - taking tests
  - prefixes, roots, and suffixes

- Clear explanation includes examples, tables of information, and strategies for learning and using new words independently.

- Immediate practice is provided to ensure mastery of the information and strategies.

- Review of Greek and Latin word elements are found in both lessons and skill features.

Dictionary Skills

- Lessons emphasize grade-appropriate skills, building on each other.

- Topics include understanding an entry, finding the right definition, using parts of speech, understanding etymologies, using biographical and geographical entries, reading labels and usage notes, differentiating among synonyms, and using a thesaurus.

- Exercises require students to immediately apply their knowledge to dictionary entries.

Reading and Reasoning Skills: Contextual Clues and Analogies

- Lessons focus on guiding students to figure out unknown words as they read.

- Several different strategies—substitution, definition, opposition—are provided for students.

- Specific procedures present methods of reasoning to help students get maximum contextual information in a sentence.

- Students practice deriving word meanings from context and then check their working definitions with a dictionary.

- Skills application is graduated from sentence level in earlier books to passage level in more advanced grades; authentic passages are taken from historical sources and literature.

- To deepen reasoning skills, analogies are provided in Second Course through Sixth Course.

Test-Taking Skills

- Students are given strategies for successfully completing a variety of verbal tests—synonym, antonym, sentence completion, and reading comprehension tests—often found on standardized tests, such as the SAT, ACT, and state tests.

- The two-blank sentence completion items found on the SAT receive focus in Second Course through Sixth Course.

- Guided strategies help students to understand the thought processes required to eliminate inappropriate answer choices and select the correct one.

- Immediate practice provides students the opportunity to apply the strategies they have learned.

Prefixes, Roots, and Suffixes

- Students are given specific cognitive strategies, using illustrative words, to determine meaning from Greek and Latin word roots, prefixes, and suffixes.

- These strategies are first applied in single words, and then in words within a sentence context. Students check their working definitions against dictionary definitions.

- Clear and concise explanation, including possible points of confusion, illuminate the use of word parts in unlocking word meaning.

- The features are carefully sequenced and organized to facilitate cumulative learning and application.

- Lessons featuring Greek and Latin word elements are sequenced near Skill Features on the same subject to provide consistent focus.

- Special review sections cover Greek and Latin word elements in both Word Lessons and Skill Features.

ANNOTATED LESSON

Lessons are **theme-related** or **root-centered** to provide a context in which students can learn new words.

The **Word List** is a convenient reference for both students and teachers.

Introductions are motivational.

Teaching Suggestions provide concrete ideas to extend the range of the program.

Pronunciations, definitions, and **etymologies** are from Houghton Mifflin dictionaries.

Word entries are presented **dictionary-style.**

Illustrations provide extra context for understanding the words.

Sidebars provide tips for using the words correctly or remembering them.

Example sentences illustrate the primary definition of each word.

Related words were chosen for their usefulness and appropriateness to grade level.

Analogies deepen reasoning skills and provide more practice for word use and understanding.

Lesson 23

The Root -pel-

WORD LIST

| appealing | compel | impel | impulse | peal |
| pelt | propulsion | pulsate | repeal | repulse |

The Latin word root *-pel-* means "thrust, strike, drive, or call out." It comes from the Latin verb *pellere* and can be spelled *pel, pulse, peal,* and *pul* in English words. For example, if you are *expelled* from school, you are "thrust out." An *appeal* "calls out" for help. When you are *repelled* by something, you are "driven away" from it.

Discuss the different ways the prefixes *ap-, com-, im-, pro-,* and *re-* can be combined with the root *pel* to form words.

1. **appealing** (ə-pē´lĭng) from Latin *ap-,* "toward" + *pel,* "drive"
   a. *adjective* Having the power to attract or arouse interest
      • Who can resist the charm of these **appealing** little kittens?
   b. *verb* Making a serious or formal request for help
      • After **appealing** to governments for aid for the tsunami survivors, charitable organizations asked the public for donations.

> The word *appeal* also means "a request that a legal decision be reviewed," usually by a Court of Appeals.

2. **compel** (kəm-pĕl´) *verb* from Latin *com-,* "together" + *pel,* drive
   To force someone to do something; to make necessary
      • The law **compels** drivers to carry their license.
   compulsion (kəm-pŭl´shən) Because of her **compulsion** for cleanliness, she spent most of the day cleaning the house.

> *Compel* and *impel* both imply force, but *compel* suggests outside force, and *impel* suggests an inner drive.

3. **impel** (ĭm-pĕl´) *verb* from *in-,* "against" + *pel,* "drive"
   To urge to action, usually through moral pressure; to motivate
      • I wonder what **impels** him to spend all his free time volunteering at the assisted-living home.

4. **impulse** (ĭm´pŭls´) *noun* from *in-,* "against" + *pel,* "drive"
   A strong urge or drive
      • Mom had a sudden **impulse** to rearrange the living-room furniture.
   impulsive *adjective* People who tend to be **impulsive** should stop and think before they act.

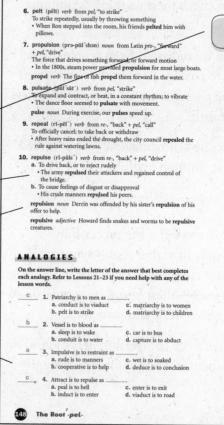
impulse shopping

5. **peal** (pēl) from *pel,* "call out"
   a. *noun* The loud ringing of bells; a loud sound
      • **Peals** of laughter could be heard from the next room.
   b. *verb* To ring or sound loudly
      • The bells **pealed** each hour.

Lesson 23 **147**

©Great Source. DO NOT COPY

---

6. **pelt** (pĕlt) *verb* from *pel,* "to strike"
   To strike repeatedly, usually by throwing something
      • When Ron stepped into the room, his friends **pelted** him with pillows.

> *Pelt* has a homonym that means "the skin of an animal with the fur or hair still on it," as in "the bear's *pelt*."

7. **propulsion** (prə-pŭl´shən) *noun* from Latin *pro-,* "forward" + *pel,* "drive"
   The force that drives something forward; or forward motion
      • In the 1800s, steam power provided **propulsion** for most large boats.
   propel *verb* The fins of fish **propel** them forward in the water.

8. **pulsate** (pŭl´sāt´) *verb* from *pel,* "strike"
   To expand and contract, or beat, in a constant rhythm; to vibrate
      • The dance floor seemed to **pulsate** with movement.
   pulse *noun* During exercise, our **pulses** speed up.

9. **repeal** (rĭ-pēl´) *verb* from *re-,* "back" + *pel,* "call"
   To officially cancel; to take back or withdraw
      • After heavy rains ended the drought, the city council **repealed** the rule against watering lawns.

10. **repulse** (rĭ-pŭls´) *verb* from *re-,* "back" + *pel,* "drive"
    a. To drive back, or to reject rudely
       • The army **repulsed** their attackers and regained control of the bridge.
    b. To cause feelings of disgust or disapproval
       • His crude manners **repulsed** his peers.
   repulsion *noun* Derrin was offended by his sister's **repulsion** of his offer to help.
   repulsive *adjective* Howard finds snakes and worms to be **repulsive** creatures.

ANALOGIES

On the answer line, write the letter of the answer that best completes each analogy. Refer to Lessons 21–23 if you need help with any of the lesson words.

__c__ 1. Patriarchy is to men as _____.
   a. conduct is to viaduct   c. matriarchy is to women
   b. pelt is to strike   d. matriarchy is to children

__b__ 2. Vessel is to blood as _____.
   a. sleep is to wake   c. car is to bus
   b. conduit is to water   d. capture is to abduct

__a__ 3. Impulsive is to restraint as _____.
   a. rude is to manners   c. wet is to soaked
   b. cooperative is to help   d. deduce is to conclusion

__c__ 4. Attract is to repulse as _____.
   a. peal is to bell   c. enter is to exit
   b. induct is to enter   d. viaduct is to road

148 The Root *-pel-*

©Great Source. DO NOT COPY

A variety of **exercise formats** provides practice and aids in **recognition, recall,** and **application** of the words.

A **Write the Correct Word** exercise reinforces definitions and spelling.

A **Complete the Sentence** exercise provides application practice similar to that found on the SAT.

A **Challenge** activity provides practice with the two-blank format found on SATs and other standardized tests.

NAME _____ DATE _____

WRITE THE CORRECT WORD

Write the correct word in the space next to each definition.

repeal	1. to cancel		impulse	6. a strong urge
propulsion	2. forward motion		compel	7. to make someone do something
peal	3. a loud burst of noise		repulse	8. to reject rudely
pelt	4. to hit repeatedly		impel	9. to urge to action
appealing	5. attractive; arousing interest		pulsate	10. to expand and contract

COMPLETE THE SENTENCE

Write the letter for the word that best completes each sentence.

_d_ 1. On the hot day, Sophie felt a(n) _____ to dive into the water.
   a. peal   b. repeal   c. propulsion   d. impulse

_a_ 2. The ultrasound showed her arteries _____ as the blood pumped through them.
   a. pulsating   b. impelling   c. pelting   d. appealing

_a_ 3. Often, simple curiosity is what _____ research scientists to conduct experiments.
   a. impels   b. appeals   c. repeals   d. repulses

_b_ 4. Maureen's perfume _____ Harvey, so he moved to a seat farther away from her.
   a. pelted   b. repulsed   c. compelled   d. propelled

_c_ 5. The boat's engine needed some serious repairs because it provided no _____.
   a. pulse   b. appeal   c. propulsion   d. impulse

_c_ 6. The commission _____ the ban on certain food additives after studies showed they didn't cause serious health problems.
   a. pelted   b. propelled   c. repealed   d. impelled

_b_ 7. The sermon was interrupted by the _____ of church bells.
   a. pelt   b. peal   c. pulse   d. appeal

_a_ 8. After the _____ for donations to the volunteer firefighters' organization, there was enough money to buy a new fire engine.
   a. appeal   b. peal   c. propulsion   d. pulse

_d_ 9. The boys _____ their sister with snowballs.
   a. compelled   b. impelled   c. appealed   d. pelted

_c_ 10. Homeowners are _____ to pay taxes on their property.
   a. pulsated   b. repealed   c. compelled   d. repulsed

Challenge: Although many people are _____ by the thought of eating frogs, in some countries this food is considered quite _____.
_a_   a. repulsed…appealing   b. impelled…compelling   c. propelled…repulsive

Lesson 23 **149**

©Great Source. DO NOT COPY

Reading passages incorporating the vocabulary words reinforce the important link between vocabulary and reading comprehension.

A **follow-up exercise** on the passage tests students' understanding of the vocabulary words in context.

READING COMPREHENSION

The Amazing Cockroach

What creature can eat almost anything, lives almost everywhere, and can survive just about any catastrophe? The cockroach, of course! **(1)** This amazing but not very *appealing* little bug has much to teach us about survival.

(2) Are you *repulsed* by the thought of cockroaches? If so, perhaps some facts about them will change your mind. First, cockroaches are unique individuals who recognize friends and family by using their feelers to smell. Cockroaches also keep themselves very clean. **(3)** That may come as a surprise to the many people who feel *compelled* to clean their homes to get rid of these insects.

Cockroaches spend 75 percent of their time sleeping. When they do move, however, they are speedy. **(4)** With *propulsion* provided by their six legs, they can run at speeds of up to three miles per hour. This is as fast as many humans can walk—and their legs are much shorter than ours!

Cockroaches were probably around more than 100 million years before the first dinosaurs, but, unlike dinosaurs, they still exist. How have these hardy little creatures survived? For one thing, they have early warning systems. **(5)** *Impulses* in their backs tell them when danger is near. They also use the 4,000 separate lenses in their eyes to detect danger.

(6) Also, cockroaches are not *impelled* to eat very much. In fact, a cockroach can live without food for a month. When they do eat, though, they are not picky. They will consume meat, starches, glue, clothes, and paper.

Cockroaches can go without breathing for forty minutes. **(7)** Their hearts can stop *pulsating* temporarily, and they will still survive. Cockroaches can even live for a week without their heads, for their brains are located near their bellies. Eventually, however, they will die from thirst.

(8) Would you break into *peals* of laughter if someone told you that cockroaches make good pets? In fact, they are becoming quite popular. Though there are over 3,500 species to choose from, a favorite pet is the Madagascan Hissing Cockroach. At a length of three inches, it is easy to see, doesn't fly, and won't eat much.

Even after reading all these facts about cockroaches, you may still just want to eliminate them. **(9)** If you have cockroaches in your home, you know that *pelting* them with a shoe won't get rid of them. And many strong chemicals used to combat cockroaches can harm the environment (which includes people) as well as the bugs. **(10)** Laws have been passed against using environmentally harmful chemicals like DDT, although some of these legal restrictions could be *repealed*. Boric acid, however, is effective against pests and harmless to humans. Stewed cucumber peels and okra are also effective cockroach repellents.

Although many people do not want cockroaches anywhere near them, robotics labs are using these resilient bugs more and more in their research. Scientists are now building robots based on cockroach anatomy to reproduce the critters' speed and ability to climb. It is hoped that these robots will not only explore distant planets and underwater volcanoes, but also detect and retrieve land mines. Who knew how valuable cockroaches could be?

Each sentence below refers to a numbered sentence in the passage. Write the letter of the choice that gives the sentence a meaning that is closest to the original sentence.

_a_ 1. This amazing but not very _____ little bug has much to teach us about survival.
   a. attractive   b. large   c. loud   d. quick

_d_ 2. Are you _____ by the thought of cockroaches?
   a. driven forward   b. curious   c. attracted   d. disgusted

_a_ 3. Many people feel _____ to clean their homes to get rid of them.
   a. forced   b. asked   c. urged   d. attracted

150 The Root -pel-

©Great Source. DO NOT COPY

ix

A **Writing Extended Responses** activity, related to the lesson theme or passage topic, lets students apply new words. Assignments are designed to stimulate interest, enthusiasm, and creativity.

A **Write the Derivative** exercise helps students apply related words and provides practice in writing these forms.

A **Find the Example** exercise encourages creative and higher-level thinking.

---

d 4. With _____ provided by their six legs, they can run three miles per hour.
   a. attractiveness   b. loud sounds   c. added force   d. forward motion

a 5. _____ tell them when danger is near.
   a. Strong drives   b. Loud sounds   c. Repeated strikes   d. Regular rhythms

c 6. Cockroaches are not _____ to eat very much.
   a. withdrawn   b. picky eaters   c. urged from within   d. rudely rejected

b 7. Their hearts can stop _____ temporarily, and they will still survive.
   a. breathing   b. beating   c. making sound   d. moving forward

a 8. Would you break into _____ of laughter if someone told you that cockroaches make good pets?
   a. loud sounds   b. sudden action   c. uncontrollable urges   d. rhythmic movements

d 9. You know that _____ them with a shoe won't get rid of them.
   a. forcing   b. entertaining   c. rudely rejecting   d. repeatedly hitting

c 10. Laws have been passed against using chemicals like DDT, although some of these legal restrictions could be _____.
   a. disgusting   b. made stronger   c. withdrawn   d. driven forward

Indicate whether the statements below are TRUE or FALSE according to the passage.

T 1. Cockroaches have been around for hundreds of millions of years.

T 2. Some people enjoy having cockroaches as pets.

T 3. You can get rid of cockroaches without using strong chemicals.

WRITING EXTENDED RESPONSES

The reading passage gives reasons why cockroaches are valuable, or even admirable. On the other hand, many people feel that they are simply disgusting pests. What is your opinion of cockroaches? Defend your point of view in a persuasive essay of at least three paragraphs. Support your position with at least two main points. Use at least three lesson words in your essay and underline them.

WRITE THE DERIVATIVE

Complete the sentence by writing the correct form of the word shown in parentheses. You may not need to change the form that is given.

Peals 1. _____ of thunder broke the silence. *(peal)*

compelling 2. Enrique made a _____ argument for the new safety guidelines. *(compel)*

---

impulsive 3. I was worried that Sasha's _____ behavior would get him into trouble. *(impulse)*

pulsating 4. The tiny animal _____ under the microscope was an amoeba. *(pulsate)*

propelled 5. The wind _____ the sailboat across the lake. *(propulsion)*

repulsive 6. I couldn't stand the _____ smell of dirty sneakers in the locker room. *(repulse)*

Appeals 7. William took his case to the Court of _____. *(appealing)*

impelled 8. Kendra's love for thrills _____ her to take skydiving lessons. *(impel)*

pelting 9. We could hear the pouring rain _____ our roof the whole night. *(pelt)*

repealed 10. The new law cannot be _____ for at least two years. *(repeal)*

FIND THE EXAMPLE

Choose the answer that best describes the action or situation.

c 1. How an *impulsive* person makes decisions.
   a. slowly   b. thoughtfully   c. quickly   d. happily

c 2. A type of sandwich that would *repulse* most people
   a. grilled cheese   b. tuna salad   c. sardine and jelly   d. peanut butter

b 3. Something that would likely be most *appealing* to someone who has spent all morning shoveling snow
   a. ice cream   b. hot chocolate   c. a hard workout   d. a picnic

d 4. Something that might *impel* a person to get to school on time
   a. a sense of humor   b. a bad attitude   c. laziness   d. responsibility

c 5. Someone most likely to be *pelted* with water balloons
   a. police officer   b. your principal   c. circus clown   d. Abraham Lincoln

a 6. Something that has been *repealed* in America
   a. slavery   b. anti-drug laws   c. discrimination laws   d. leash laws

b 7. Something that drivers are NOT *compelled* to do
   a. obey speed limits   b. drive at night   c. have a license   d. obey traffic signals

d 8. A time when you would likely feel your heart *pulsating* rapidly
   a. while sleeping   b. while eating   c. when tired   d. when scared

a 9. Something that is *propelled* by muscle power
   a. a bicycle   b. a helicopter   c. a kite   d. a rocket ship

a 10. Something that *peals*
   a. a bell   b. a mouse   c. a window   d. a snowstorm

Teaching Suggestions

Review and Retention

Resources in *Vocabulary for Achievement* provide many opportunities for review.

1. Have students use **Flash Cards,** located on pages 201–220 of the student books, for individual drill or game-style classroom practice.

2. Assign the **Bonuses** as follow-up activities for the vocabulary lessons.

3. Many motivating and short games help students to both deeply process and gain automaticity with words. These are referenced in Richek, Margaret, (2005) "Words are Wonderful: Interactive, Time-efficient Strategies to Teach Meaning Vocabulary, *The Reading Teacher,* Vol. 58 (5, February). Each can be done in segments as short as five minutes.

- In **Find That Word,** students receive extra credit points for bringing in program words that they have found in their reading, in the media, or in speech. They are required to write the word and its sentence context, correctly spelled and punctuated, before receiving this credit. To encourage use in student speech, double credit can be given if one student overhears another using the word. If desired, students may be given a few minutes per week to read some sentences they found. All sentences, whether read publicly or not, should be posted on a bulletin board. You might prefer to give cumulative class points rather than individual credit.

- In **Two in One,** students may be encouraged to write sentences containing two, three, or four lesson words. I often find it helpful for students to be with partners or in groups of three when doing this.

- In **Connect Two,** the words from several lessons are written in two columns. Students are asked to find a similarity between the words in column one and those in column two. For example, in the following list, students could point out that "renaissance" and "medieval" both refer to time periods. They could also point out that "dynamic" and "static" have opposite senses, as do "unearth" and "inter." Or they could note that a person would be likely to be involved in a "strife" with an "adversary."

belated	medieval
renaissance	subsequent
spendthrift	profusely
dynamic	static
adversary	strife
unearth	inter

- In **Anything Goes,** words are written on a board, overhead, or wall chart. For quick review, the teacher may simply point to a word and ask a question for a class member to answer. Sample questions include: What does _____ mean? What part of speech is _____? How do you spell _____? Use _____ and _____ in the same sentence. What is the difference between _____ and _____?

Students can also be encouraged to make connections among lessons and to prior learning in other areas.

- As you cover new lessons, ask students how particular words relate to ones already studied. Examples include: What elements of meaning do *slander* (Lesson 3) and *chide* (Lesson 5) share, and how are they different? How does *abetting* (Lesson 2) behavior differ from *inducing* (Lesson 22) behavior? In what situations could you use *faux pas* (Lesson 12) and *infraction* (Lesson 25) interchangeably? What is the difference in *deportment* between someone *congenial* (Lesson 4) and someone *benign* (Lesson 8) or between someone *boisterous* (Lesson 17) and someone *subdued* (Lesson 22)? How does *retracting* (Lesson 25) differ in usage from *revoking* (Lesson 27)? Refer to the **Complete Word List** on page xv to aid in making similarly related word pairs.

- Have students periodically review their own or others' writing pieces for word choice. Encourage them to replace overused words or phrases with vocabulary words. For example, in the sentence "The meeting was *friendly,*" students might replace the word *friendly* with *amicable* (Lesson 8).

Vocabulary and Reading

1. To help students realize how naturally they use context clues as they read, review with them some of the more common ways that words are defined in context.

   Formal definition: Named for a character in Greek mythology, a *Sisyphean* task is one which must be repeated endlessly—and unsuccessfully.

   Definition by appositive: The *croissant*—a crescent-shaped roll made of dough or puff pastry—was created by bakers in Vienna to commemorate their city's successful stand against an army of Turks in 1863.

   Definition by example: Mosses and liverworts are examples of *bryophyla*, one of the oldest living groups of plants on Earth.

2. Analogies provide excellent practice in reasoning, as well as in vocabulary study.

   These types of relationships are common:

degree	type of
part/whole	relative size
is used to	place where
characteristic of	part of
antonym	synonym

Challenge students to identify what kind of relationship these word pairs express:

Lens is to *camera* as *door* is to *building*.
Car is to *vehicle* as *spider* is to *animal*.

Students can also write complete analogies that use some vocabulary words, and give them to their classmates to solve. (Examples are found in the Skill Feature on analogies following Lesson 15.)

3. Noting effective word choices can aid students in interpreting literature, as well as in writing effectively. Have students analyze word choice as they read. Good examples to discuss include "a *miniscule* payment," "*judicious* choice of words," and "*lumbering up* the stairs."

Vocabulary, Grammar, and Usage

Correct grammar and usage require vigilance and practice. Support for these important activities is found within *Vocabulary for Achievement*.

1. Lesson 1 deals directly with word *derivatives*. In addition, an exercise called **Write the Derivative** is found in each lesson. Finally, irregularly spelled inflected and derived forms are given special notes in the sidebars found throughout the Second Course.

2. Notes that illustrate nuances of usage are also found in the sidebars throughout the lessons.

3. A number of the lesson words, such as *slander*, *strife*, *throng*, and *conservative* are used as several types of speech. Have students write sentences that illustrate uses for each.

4. When covering conjunctions and prepositions, have students examine the multiple meanings of *for* (because, in place of, in honor of, in spite of, suited to), *since* (from then, until now, because), *yet* (still, nevertheless), *whatever* (exactly what, no matter what, at all), *before* (previously, in front of), and *but* (only, except that, yet). Provide a group of sentences illustrating each use, such as the following.

EXAMPLE The class had a surprise party *for* Erica.

Have students reword the conjunction or preposition.

EXAMPLE The class had a surprise party *in honor of* Erica.

5. Have students write original sentences that illustrate both particular principles of grammar or usage and incorporate vocabulary words. For example, when covering adverbs, ask students to substitute the correct form of these lesson words.

EXAMPLE He approached the abandoned building *(wary)*. Substitute *warily*. The child sat *(forlorn)* on the bench. Substitute *forlornly*.

6. When discussing usage problems, have students examine the likelihood of confusion between pairs of homophones such as the following: *principle/principal, hue/hew, metal/mettle, throws/throes, pray/prey, course/coarse, dual/duel,* and so forth. Then have them look up the definition(s) of each word and write a sentence for each, illustrating its use.

Vocabulary and Composition

An important aim of vocabulary instruction is to enhance writing. Only in this way can word learning be fully applied in a literate context.

Vocabulary for Achievement lessons include both focused composition activities for specific word practice and longer composition opportunities that relate to passages. In **Finish the Thought** (even-numbered lessons), students must complete two sentence starters containing lesson words with illustrative and personalized responses. **Writing Extended Responses** (odd-numbered lessons) requires a (at least) three-paragraph response to a detailed writing assignment that is related to information in the passage. Different assignments call for students to practice descriptive, narrative, expository, and persuasive genres. Every effort has been made to ensure that these responses do not require research.

1. Help students become more aware of word choice by emphasizing the importance of revision. Remind them that revising a rough draft gives them the opportunity to choose the appropriate words and to use concrete or figurative words, depending on the purpose of the assignment.

2. Help students use synonyms to replace common words in descriptions by asking them to brainstorm lists of words within topics.

EXAMPLES *texture: smooth, even, filmy, coarse, harsh, dry, abrasive, gritty, granular, fluffy, uniform, sleek, slick, polished, bumpy, corrugated, rippled, gnarled, jagged, bristly,* and so forth.

3. To help students distinguish shades of meaning of synonyms, give them a list of words and ask them to rank them according to intensity, degree, or amount.

EXAMPLES *bright, shiny, clear, brilliant* or *warm, hot, tepid, lukewarm*

VOCABULARY FOR ACHIEVEMENT
READING COMPREHENSION PASSAGES

An informative and entertaining Reading Comprehension passage appears in each of the thirty vocabulary lessons in each level. The passage contains all ten vocabulary words, giving students an opportunity to understand the new words in reading. The passages also lend depth, length, and variety to the abundant practice. Finally, they provide students with enriching information drawn from a wide variety of subject areas. *Vocabulary for Achievement* passages offer students a chance to read across the curriculum while they deepen understanding of newly learned words. For your convenience, the following is a level-specific list of content areas and passage titles.

Lesson	Area	Title of Passage
1	Language	Dialects from Coast to Coast
2	Social Service	"They Need a Cow"
3	Social Science: History	The Bitter Campaign of 1800
4	Mythology	The Lost Love of Orpheus
5	Sports	Champion Female Wrestler
6	Social Science: History	Treating the Wounds of War
7	Social Service	Helpers—Young and Old
8	Social Science: History	A Dinner Guest
9	Medicine; History	Plague!
10	Social Science: History	Athens and Sparta
11	Environment	Condor Comeback?
12	Sports	Baseball Blunder
13	Social Science: Law	Jury—Service and Trial
14	Mythology	Starving on Gold
15	Career Profile	Animation and Animators
16	The Arts	Murals Lost and Found
17	Medicine	The Spirit Soars
18	Environment; Science	The Shape of Antarctica
19	Social Science: History	Ambassador of the Paiute
20	Language	A New Language—of Silence
21	History; Mythology	Amazons—Fact or Fiction?
22	Popular Culture	Duct Tape Everywhere
23	Science	The Amazing Cockroach
24	Science; Medicine	Hope for Regeneration
25	Social Science; History	Victory at Marathon
26	Social Science; History	A Pirate's Life
27	Popular Culture	The Teenagers of Doo-wop
28	Social Science; Geography	Our Nation's Capital
29	Geography; Science	Discovering Earth from Space
30	Social Science: History	Witness to Pompeii

COMPLETE WORD LIST FOR SECOND COURSE

SCOPE AND SEQUENCE OF SKILLS

	INTRODUCTORY	FIRST	SECOND	THIRD	FOURTH	FIFTH	SIXTH
Using the Dictionary	Parts of Speech and Derivatives (pp. 19–20) Parts of a Dictionary Entry (pp. 39–40) Looking for the Right Definition (pp. 59–60)	Finding the Appropriate Definition (pp. 19–20) Using Parts of Speech Labels (pp. 39–40) Run-on Entries and Inflected Word Forms (pp. 59–60)	Finding the Appropriate Definition (pp. 19–20) Understanding Etymologies, Biographical Entries, and Geographical Entries (pp. 39–40)	Finding the Appropriate Definition (pp. 19–20)	Using Synonym Paragraphs (pp. 19–20)	Usage Notes (pp. 19–20)	Combining the Dictionary Synonym Paragraphs and a Thesaurus (pp. 19–20)
Reading and Reasoning	Context Clues (pp. 79–80)	Context Clues: Definition in the Sentence (pp. 79–80)	Context Clues of Substitution (pp. 59–60) Context Clues of Opposites (pp. 79–80) Analogies (pp. 99–100)	Three Types of Context Clues (pp. 39–40) Context Clues in Literature (pp. 59–60) Analogies (pp. 79–80)	Three Types of Context Clues (pp. 39–40) Using Context Clues to Read Primary Sources (pp. 59–60)	Three Types of Context Clues (pp. 39–40) Using Context Clues to Read Literature (pp. 59–60)	Three Types of Context Clues (pp. 39–40) Using Context Clues to Read Primary Sources (pp. 59–60)
Taking Tests	Synonym Tests (pp. 99–100) Antonym Tests (pp. 119–120)	Sentence-Completion Tests (pp. 99–100) Synonym and Antonym Tests (pp. 119–120)	Sentence-Completion Tests with Two Blanks (pp. 119–120)	Sentence-Completion with Two Blanks (pp. 99–100) SAT Critical Reading Tests (pp. 119–120)	SAT Writing Test (pp. 79–80) SAT Sentence-Completion Items with Two Blanks (pp. 99–100) SAT Critical Reading Tests (pp. 119–120)	SAT Writing Test (pp. 79–80) SAT Sentence-Completion Items with Two Blanks (pp. 99–100) SAT Critical Reading Tests (pp. 119–120)	SAT Writing Test (pp. 79–80) SAT Sentence-Completion Items with Two Blanks (pp. 99–100) SAT Critical Reading Tests (pp. 119–120)
Prefixes, Roots, and Suffixes	Identifying Prefixes, Roots, Suffixes (pp. 139–140) The Prefixes non- and un- (pp. 159–160) The Prefixes pre- and post- (pp. 179–180) The Prefixes sub- and super- (pp. 199–200)	Word Elements (pp. 139–140) The Prefixes in-, im-, ir-, and il- (pp. 159–160) The Prefixes ex- and en- (pp. 179–180) The Prefix trans- (pp. 199–200)	The Prefix re- (pp. 139–140) The Prefixes com-, con-, and cor- (pp. 159–160) Number Prefixes (pp. 179–180) Number Prefixes (pp. 199–200)	The Prefixes a- and an- (pp. 139–140) The Prefixes micro-, macro-, mini-, maxi-, and mega- (pp. 159–160) The Prefix de- (pp. 179–180) The Prefix dis- (pp. 199–200)	The Prefixes circum-, peri-, semi-, and hemi- (pp. 139–140) The Prefixes auto-, equi-, and iso- (pp. 159–160) The Prefixes sym-, syn-, and syl- (pp. 179–180) The Prefixes anti- and counter- (pp. 199–200)	The Prefixes inter- and intra- (pp. 139–140) The Prefixes ambi- and para- (pp. 159–160) The Word Elements astro-, geo-, hydro-, -mar-, and -terra- (pp. 179–180) The Prefixes pan-, extra-, ultra-, and omni- (pp. 199–200)	The Word Elements archy-, -dem-, -ver, and -cracy (pp. 139–140) The Prefixes bene-, eu-, and mal- (pp. 159–160) The Word Elements ante- and -ann- (pp. 179–180) The Word Elements hyper-, hypo-, and -dyn- (pp. 199–200)

Vocabulary
for Achievement
Second Course

Margaret Ann Ríchek

GREAT SOURCE
WILMINGTON, MA

Author

Margaret Ann Richek

Professor of Education Emerita, Northeastern Illinois University; consultant in reading and vocabulary study; author of The World of Words *(Houghton Mifflin)*

Classroom Consultants

Beth Gaby
English Chair, Carl Schurz High School, Chicago, Illinois

Chris Hausammann
Teacher of English, Central Mountain High School, Lock Haven, Pennsylvania

Malisa Cannon
Teacher of Language Arts, Desert Sky Middle School, Tucson, Arizona

Patricia Melvin
District Secondary Reading Specialist, Duval County Public Schools, Jacksonville, Florida

Sean Rochester
Teacher of English, Parkway Central High School, St. Louis, Missouri

Credits

Editorial: Ruth Rothstein, Victoria Fortune, Dan Carsen, Amy Gilbert

Design and Production: Mazer Corporation

Text Design and Production: Mazer Creative Services

Illustrations: Chris Vallo/Mazer Creative Services; Cookie Cook, Susan Aiello of Wilkinson Studios, LLC; David McFeders, George Cathey, Jerry Hoare, Ron Zalme of Langley Creative

Cover Design: Mazer Creative Services

Cover Photo: Stockbyte/Mazer Creative Services

Definitions for the three hundred words taught in this textbook are based on Houghton Mifflin dictionaries—in particular, the *Houghton Mifflin Student Dictionary*—but have been abbreviated and adapted for instructional purposes.

All pronunciations are reproduced by permission from the *American Heritage Dictionary of the English Language, Fourth Edition*, copyright © 2000.

Printed in the United States of America

International Standard Book Number: 0-669-51756-9

1 2 3 4 5 6 7 8 9 10 - DBH - 10 09 08 07 06 05

Contents

COMPLETE WORD LIST FOR SECOND COURSE

Dialect

WORD LIST

accent	articulate	dialect	diction	enunciate
hierarchy	intelligible	peer	stratify	stress

The many varieties of English make it a fascinating language. In England, people talk about the "bonnet," not the "hood," of a car; signs on apartments read "to let" rather than "for rent." Scotland's residents refer to a "wee" job rather than a "small" one. Even within the United States, we find many *dialects,* or language forms, that differ in pronunciation, vocabulary, and grammar.

1. **accent** (ăk´sĕnt´) from Latin *ad-,* "to" + *cantus,* "song"
   a. *noun* A style of pronunciation typical of people from a certain region or country
      • Erin's **accent** showed that she had been raised in Ireland.
   b. *noun* An emphasis on a particular syllable in a word
      • When saying the word *tidy,* we put the **accent** on the first syllable.
   c. *verb* To focus attention on
      • The color of that sweater really **accents** her blue eyes.

2. **articulate** from Latin *articulare,* "say clearly"
   a. *adjective* (är-tĭk´yə-lĭt) Skilled in expressing oneself clearly and effectively
      • The senator was an **articulate** spokesperson for children's rights.
   b. *verb* (är-tĭk´yə-lāt´) To express clearly in words
      • Feelings of love can be difficult to **articulate.**

   articulation *noun* The worker's convincing **articulation** of her accomplishments persuaded the boss to give her a raise.

3. **dialect** (dī´ə-lĕkt´) *noun* from Greek *dialectus,* "form of speech" A unique form of a language, spoken by people from a country, region, or social group
   • In some **dialects** of English, the word *pop* is used to refer to *soda.*

4. **diction** (dĭk´shən) *noun* from Latin *dicee,* "to say" Clearness of speech or pronunciation
   • An actor must have excellent **diction** to perform Shakespearean plays.

5. **enunciate** (ĭ-nŭn´sē-āt´) *verb* from Latin *ex-,* "out" + *nuntiare,* "to announce"
   a. To pronounce, especially in a clear manner
      • The teacher **enunciated** the directions carefully so that students at the back of the large hall could hear her.
   b. To state or set forth clearly
      • In his speech, the president **enunciated** his foreign policy positions.

   enunciation *noun* The lack of **enunciation** of lyrics can make some songs difficult to understand.

To ensure that students understand the entries given below, work through a few of them, pointing out the word, the pronunciation and location of the key, the part of speech, the etymology, the example sentences, and the comments on words. Then, guide them through the exercise formats.

> Definition b of the word *accent* can also be used as a verb: When saying the word *tidy,* we *accent* the first syllable.

dialects

> *Diction* can also refer to one's choice of words.

6. **hierarchy** (hī´ə-rär´kē) *noun* from Greek *hierarkhia,* "rule of high priest"
A group organized according to rank or status
• In the army **hierarchy,** a colonel ranks below a general.

hierarchical (hī´ə-rär´kĭ-kəl) *adjective* Many primates live in societies that are **hierarchical,** so some individuals are dominant and others are subordinate.

7. **intelligible** (ĭn-tĕl´ĭ-jə-bəl) *adjective* from Latin *intellegere,* "to perceive"
Able to be understood
• The two-year-old's speech was only **intelligible** to his parents.

intelligibility *noun* The **intelligibility** of the poem will be greatly increased if you know the myths to which it refers.

> The opposite of *intelligible* is *unintelligible.*

8. **peer** (pîr) *noun* from Latin *par,* "equal"
A person who is equal to another in social standing or age
• Teenagers tend to use the same expressions as their **peers.**

> *Peer* has a homonym that means "to look intently."

9. **stratify** (străt´ə-fī´) *verb* from Latin *stratum,* "covering"
To separate into different levels or layers
• The bowling league was **stratified** into "A" players, with high averages, and "B" players, with lower ones.

stratification *noun* The **stratification** of the earth's rock layers reflects the climate, earthquakes, and volcanic activity over millions of years.

> Often, *stratify* means "to separate people into groups that differ in quality or in power."

stratum *noun* (plural, **strata**) In the Middle Ages, nobles and peasants made up two separate **strata** of society.

10. **stress** (strĕs) from Latin *stringere,* "to draw tight"
   a. *noun* Emphasis in speaking or music
      • The **stress** in the word "impossible" is placed on the second syllable.
   b. *verb* To emphasize
      • The nurse **stressed** the importance of a healthy diet.
   c. *noun* Tension; strain
      • Tests are a source of **stress** to many students.

WORD ENRICHMENT

What is "Standard English"?

English is rich in different dialects, but the pronunciation and grammar that we hear from most newscasters and that we read in most books is called "Standard English." This is the form used by most educated people, especially in the workplace and in more formal settings. Of course, Standard U.S. English is different from the standard form of English used in England.

WRITE THE CORRECT WORD

Write the correct word in the space next to each definition.

diction	**1.** clearness of speech		enunciate	**6.** to pronounce clearly
peer	**2.** an equal in age or position		articulate	**7.** clear and expressive
stress	**3.** pressure or strain		accent	**8.** a style of pronunciation
dialect	**4.** a regional form of a language		stratify	**9.** to separate into layers
hierarchy	**5.** a group organized by rank		intelligible	**10.** understandable

COMPLETE THE SENTENCE

Write the letter for the word that best completes each sentence.

___c___ **1.** The club president _____ the club's reasons for wanting to raise money.
    a. accented   **b.** stratified   **c.** articulated   **d.** enunciated

___b___ **2.** My league is _____ into teams for new golfers and for experienced ones.
    a. stressed   **b.** stratified   **c.** accented   **d.** articulated

___d___ **3.** Most businesses are organized into a(n) _____, with positions ranging from entry level jobs to the CEO of the company.
    a. diction   **b.** accent   **c.** articulation   **d.** hierarchy

___c___ **4.** Large countries often include regions where people speak different _____ of the country's main language.
    a. dictions   **b.** stratifications   **c.** dialects   **d.** peers

___a___ **5.** The speaker's _____ revealed that she probably had grown up in England.
    a. accent   **b.** stratification   **c.** hierarchy   **d.** intelligibility

___a___ **6.** When dictating the spelling test, the teacher carefully _____ each word.
    a. enunciated   **b.** stressed   **c.** stratified   **d.** accented

___d___ **7.** The message on the answering machine was so garbled that it was barely _____.
    a. stressed   **b.** hierarchical   **c.** accented   **d.** intelligible

___b___ **8.** Do you think that choices of clothing are influenced by one's _____?
    a. stresses   **b.** peers   **c.** dialects   **d.** accents

___d___ **9.** It's hard to have good _____ when you talk with food in your mouth.
    a. hierarchy   **b.** stratification   **c.** dialect   **d.** diction

___c___ **10.** Many people experience great nervousness and _____ when speaking in public.
    a. stratification   **b.** diction   **c.** stress   **d.** articulation

Challenge: The _____ of the student club into a many-leveled _____ disappointed some members who had articulated their opposition to the plan.
___b___   **a.** stress…stratification   **b.** stratification…hierarchy   **c.** enunciation…dialect

Dialects from Coast to Coast

Suppose that, while watching the news one evening, you see a report of a flood in another region of the United States. The reporter is interviewing a resident of the area. English subtitles appear on your television screen, so you assume the speaker is using another language. Then, you realize—that person is speaking English!

(1) People who live in different regions of a country often speak different *dialects.* **(2)** Some are so distinct that subtitles—or an interpreter—are needed to help make them *intelligible* to people from other regions. **(3)** This is particularly true when the speaker's *diction* is not very good.

Dialects often have a unique vocabulary, as well. A *hero* sandwich in Philadelphia is a *po'boy* in New Orleans. A *potluck* supper in Tennessee might be called a *pitch-in* in Indiana, and a *scramble* in Illinois. **(4)** If one of your *peers* wanted to play *potsy,* she'd probably be from Manhattan; if he wanted to play *sky blue,* he might be a Chicago boy. Both would be asking you to play a game known in other areas as hopscotch!

(5) Sometimes, vowels are *articulated* in different ways in different dialects. Let's use the word *coffee,* for example. In Seattle, one drinks "cahfee," and in New York City, one drinks "cawfee." **(6)** In Los Angeles, you might be directed to "take a right," but someone with an Atlanta *accent* would tell you to "tick a raht."

(7) The *enunciation* of consonants and syllables also varies from one region to another. A Denver native might visit a relative who lives by the Chesapeake Bay in Baltimore; but that relative would say that she lives by the "Chestpeak" Bay in "Baltmer." In Phoenix, you might be instructed to "park your car in the parking lot"; in Boston, you would probably be told to "pahk yuh cah in the pahking lot."

(8) The *stress* of a word may differ from region to region, as well. A Miami native would use an um-BREL-la in the rain; a person from Cincinnati would use an UM-brell-a.

Dictionaries tend to focus on Standard English usage rather than dialect differences. But *The Dictionary of American Regional English,* or *DARE* for short, references phrases and pronunciations that differ from region to region. The dictionary notes where each term is used and how words are pronounced in different places. **(9)** The experts who put together the first four volumes of *DARE* spent years interviewing people from all over the country and from different *strata* of society.

(10) Some language experts propose a *hierarchy* of dialects, arguing for a preferred standard version of English. On the other hand, the writers of *DARE* strive to document all variations of English spoken in the United States. They want to create a record of the richness and cultural diversity of American society.

Each sentence below refers to a numbered sentence in the passage. Write the letter of the choice that gives the sentence a meaning that is closest to the original sentence.

___d___ **1.** People who live in different regions of a country often speak different _____ .
- **a.** traditions
- **b.** styles of pronunciation
- **c.** local customs
- **d.** forms of language

___a___ **2.** Some are so distinct that subtitles—or an interpreter—are needed to help make them _____ to people from other regions.
- **a.** understandable
- **b.** acceptable
- **c.** appealing
- **d.** emphasized

___c___ **3.** This is particularly true when the speaker's _____ is not very good.
- **a.** appearance
- **b.** use of props
- **c.** clearness of speech
- **d.** skill

___b___ **4.** If one of your _____ wanted to play *potsy,* she'd probably be from Manhattan.
- **a.** two parents
- **b.** friends your age
- **c.** ranked groups
- **d.** distant relatives

_____b_____ **5.** Sometimes, vowels are _____ in different ways in different dialects.
    a. arranged   **b.** pronounced   **c.** layered   **d.** dictated

_____d_____ **6.** In Los Angeles, you might be directed to "take a right," but someone with an Atlanta _____ would tell you to "tick a raht."
    a. form of language   • **b.** spelling   **c.** emphasis   **d.** style of pronunciation

_____a_____ **7.** The _____ of consonants and syllables also varies from one region to another.
    a. pronunciation   **b.** spelling   **c.** punctuation   **d.** hearing

_____d_____ **8.** The _____ of a word may differ from region to region, as well.
    a. written version   **b.** dictation   **c.** vowel sounds   **d.** syllable emphasis

_____a_____ **9.** The experts spent years interviewing people from all over the country and from different _____ of society.
    a. levels   **b.** regions   **c.** age groups   **d.** geographies

_____b_____ **10.** Some language experts propose a(n) _____ of dialects, arguing for a preferred standard version of English.
    a. emphasis   **b.** ranking   **c.** clarity   **d.** collection

Indicate whether the statements below are TRUE or FALSE according to the passage.

_____T_____ **1.** People in different areas of the United States sometimes stress different syllables in the same word.

_____T_____ **2.** Dialect differences may include both different pronunciations of the same words and different words representing the same object.

_____F_____ **3.** The writers of *DARE* believe that some dialects are better than others.

WRITING EXTENDED RESPONSES

As the passage indicates, some people believe that dialect differences are good, and some think that it would be better if we all spoke the same dialect. Consider which of these two positions you agree with. Then write a persuasive essay detailing your point of view. Your essay should contain at least two reasons for your position and should be a minimum of three paragraphs long. If you choose, instead of taking one point of view, you may present arguments from both sides. Use at least three lesson words in your essay and underline them.

WRITE THE DERIVATIVE

Complete the sentence by writing the correct form of the word shown in parentheses. You may not need to change the form that is given.

___intelligibility___ **1.** The teacher told Jeremy that the _____ of his oral report would improve if he spoke more slowly and clearly. *(intelligible)*

_____peers_____ **2.** The accused person was tried by a jury of his _____. *(peer)*

<u>dialect</u>   **3.** The substitute teacher's unfamiliar _____ was confusing to the students. *(dialect)*

<u>diction</u>   **4.** The actor's _____ was so clear that even those in the back row of the auditorium could hear his every word. *(diction)*

<u>stratifications or strata</u>   **5.** Earthquakes are one cause of visible _____ in the earth's surface. *(stratify)*

<u>hierarchies</u>   **6.** Many large organizations have complicated _____. *(hierarchy)*

<u>enunciates</u>   **7.** The English teacher _____ each syllable very deliberately. *(enunciate)*

<u>accents</u>   **8.** Each time he plays that song, the drummer _____ the first and third beats of every measure. *(accent)*

<u>articulated</u>   **9.** Before every game last year, the coach _____ the game plan in detail. *(articulate)*

<u>stressed</u>   **10.** My former math teacher always _____ the importance of doing orderly work when solving problems. *(stress)*

FIND THE EXAMPLE

Choose the answer that best describes the action or situation.

<u>a</u>   **1.** Something arranged in a *hierarchy*
     a. the military   **b.** fruit   **c.** a mall   **d.** a book

<u>b</u>   **2.** A performer who would most likely use regional *dialects*
     a. a pianist   **b.** a storyteller   **c.** a pantomimist   **d.** a ballerina

<u>d</u>   **3.** A common source of *stress*
     a. resting   **b.** sleeping   **c.** eating   **d.** competing

<u>b</u>   **4.** Something you would *accent*
     a. a sentence   **b.** a syllable   **c.** a paragraph   **d.** a letter

<u>a</u>   **5.** Someone who needs to be *articulate*
     a. a politician   **b.** a wrestler   **c.** a painter   **d.** a runner

<u>c</u>   **6.** Something that should NOT be *intelligible* to everyone
     a. a phone message   **b.** a public order   **c.** a secret code   **d.** your handwriting

<u>c</u>   **7.** Someone who would be your ultimate *peer*
     a. a friend   **b.** a parent   **c.** a twin   **d.** a child

<u>b</u>   **8.** A place where you would be most likely to observe *strata*
     a. a rough ocean   **b.** a rock cliff   **c.** a parking lot   **d.** a field of flowers

<u>b</u>   **9.** A performer who needs to have good *diction*
     a. a tap dancer   **b.** a stage actor   **c.** an acrobat   **d.** a violinist

<u>d</u>   **10.** An event at which one should *enunciate* very clearly
     a. a sports event   **b.** a rock concert   **c.** a county fair   **d.** a spelling bee

Help and Improvement

WORD LIST

abet	bestow	deliverance	expedite	haven
intercede	offset	pacify	refurbish	sanctuary

"No man is an island." This famous quotation implies that no one can operate without the help and support of others. The words in this lesson relate to ways that we can give and receive help, and improve the lives of ourselves and others.

1. **abet** (ə-bĕt´) *verb* from Latin *ad-*, "to" + *beter*, "bait"
   To encourage or assist, particularly in doing something wrong
   • A person who **abets** the criminal actions of another may also be found guilty of a crime.

   abettor *noun* The **abettors** of terrorism will be caught and punished.

bestow

2. **bestow** (bĭ-stō´) *verb* from Old English *bi-*, "be" + *stow*, "place"
   To give or present, especially as a gift or an honor
   • The award was **bestowed** upon the artist for her lifetime achievements.

3. **deliverance** (dĭ-lĭv´ər-əns) *noun* from Latin *liberare*, "to free"
   Liberation; rescue from slavery, capture, or danger
   • An 1841 shipwreck meant **deliverance** for Africans on a slave ship, who were freed when they swam ashore to British colonies.

   > *Deliverance* is taken from the verb *deliver*.

4. **expedite** (ĕk´spĭ-dīt´) *verb* from Latin *expedire*, "to set free"
   a. To speed up or help the progress of
      • Our business often uses express mail to **expedite** delivery of packages.
   b. To do quickly and efficiently
      • The company president trusted her assistant to **expedite** her orders.

   expeditious *adjective* During the fire drill, the students filed out of the building in an **expeditious** manner.

   > Point out that both *haven* and *sanctuary* are actual places of refuge or safety.

5. **haven** (hā´vən) *noun*
   A place of refuge or safety
   • During unstable political times, embassies are often **havens** for travelers stranded in foreign countries.

   > A *haven* can also be a port or harbor.

6. **intercede** (ĭn´tər-sēd´) *verb* from Latin *inter-*, "between"+ *cedere*, "to go"

   a. To mediate or help in a problem between others
   - The referee **interceded** when the two coaches started shouting at each other.

   b. To plead for another
   - The relief agency **interceded** on behalf of refugees, calling for additional aid.

   intercession *noun* When the nurse was falsely accused of stealing, the doctor's **intercession** helped prevent the loss of her job.

7. **offset** (ôf´sĕt´) *verb*

   To make up for; to compensate for; to counteract
   - The runner **offset** her slow time in the first lap, by speeding up her pace in the next two.

   > *Offset* can also be used as a noun, as in "The refund was an *offset* for her overpayment."

8. **pacify** (păs´ə-fī´) *verb* from Latin *pax*, "peace"+ *facere*, "to make"

   a. To calm anger
   - When the singer failed to appear at the concert, the management issued refunds to **pacify** the crowd.

   b. To establish peace; to end fighting or violence
   - The treaty **pacified** regions that had been at war for centuries.

   pacification *noun* In the last few years, several nations have been involved in the **pacification** of Northern Ireland.

9. **refurbish** (rē-fûr´bĭsh) *verb*

   To clean, renew, repair, or refresh
   - Anthony made a business of buying used computers, **refurbishing** them, then selling them for profit.

   refurbishment *noun* After its **refurbishment,** the old sofa looked new.

10. **sanctuary** (săngk´chŏŏ-ĕr´ē) *noun* from Latin *sanctus*, "sacred"

    a. Any place of safety or protection
    - The animals roamed freely in the wildlife **sanctuary.**

    b. A holy place; a house of worship
    - The organ was playing as we entered the **sanctuary** to pray.

WORD ENRICHMENT

Words of peace

The word *pacific* comes from the Latin word *pax*, meaning "peace." Other English words come from this root, including *peace* itself. A *pact*, or "agreement," also comes from *pax*, as does *appease*, which means to calm, usually by giving into demands.

The name of one of the world's great oceans comes from *pax*. In 1513, Spanish explorer Vasco Nunez de Balboa crossed the Isthmus of Panama and saw an ocean. So peaceful did it appear, he named it the *Pacific*.

WRITE THE CORRECT WORD

Write the correct word in the space next to each definition.

pacify **1.** to make peace

expedite **2.** to speed up the progress of

deliverance **3.** rescue from danger

sanctuary **4.** a place of worship

abet **5.** to encourage

intercede **6.** to mediate

refurbish **7.** to clean up or repair

haven **8.** a refuge

offset **9.** to counteract

bestow **10.** to present an honor

COMPLETE THE SENTENCE

Write the letter for the word that best completes each sentence.

a **1.** You should probably ———— your rusty bike before you try to sell it.
a. refurbish   b. offset   c. bestow   d. expedite

b **2.** In earlier times, criminals could avoid arrest by seeking ———— in churches.
a. expedition   b. sanctuary   c. pacification   d. refurbishment

d **3.** She ———— the criminal by allowing him to stay in her home.
a. offset   b. refurbished   c. bestowed   d. abetted

d **4.** The queen can reward loyal subjects by ———— honorary titles.
a. expediting   b. abetting   c. offsetting   d. bestowing

c **5.** The ambassador tried to ———— on behalf of the falsely accused travelers.
a. expedite   b. refurbish   c. intercede   d. bestow

a **6.** In winter, a backyard feeder can become a(n) ———— for birds.
a. haven   b. refurbishment   c. pacification   d. intercession

b **7.** Before the U.S. Civil War, the Underground Railroad provided ———— for escaped slaves seeking freedom.
a. pacification   b. deliverance   c. bestowment   d. refurbishment

b **8.** The efficient computer system helped the company to ———— their orders.
a. pacify   b. expedite   c. refurbish   d. offset

c **9.** Nothing but an appearance by their leader could ———— the angry crowd.
a. expedite   b. abet   c. pacify   d. bestow

d **10.** The penalties received by the two teams ———— one another, so the play had to be repeated.
a. pacified   b. bestowed   c. interceded   d. offset

Challenge: In order to ———— the unhappy residents, the director ———— the refurbishment of the recreation room.
c a. abet...offset   b. bestow...pacified   c. pacify...expedited

"They Need a Cow"

"These children don't need a cup, they need a cow," thought Dan West.

West was frustrated that his volunteer efforts during the Spanish Civil War of the 1930s did not seem to be helping enough people. Day after day, hungry children begged for the food that he distributed, but the provisions that he gave to one, he had to deny to another. **(1)** West decided that simply *bestowing* food would not improve lives. **(2)** People needed a way to *refurbish* their own food supplies. Thus, Operation Heifer, now Heifer International, was born.

Heifer International gives livestock—heifers (young cows), goats, and even bees—to people in need. These animals provide renewable sources of food, such as milk and honey. **(3)** However, giving one family a goat, while ignoring another family, would *abet* inequality. So any family that receives livestock is required to give the animal's first born offspring to another needy family. **(4)** Or the family can keep the offspring and *offset* the livestock gift by giving another family enough money to buy its own animal.

Early missions of Heifer International brought cowhands to war-torn Europe, in the 1940s. **(5)** In countries like Poland, the organization provided *deliverance* from poverty, as farmers once again were able to produce their own food. **(6)** At first, animals and volunteers traveled by ship, but the process was *expedited* when they began to travel by plane. In an account of his journey to Korea, cowboy Newton S. Goodridge paints a vivid picture of traveling on a plane with 100 goats, 600 rabbits, and an estimated 1,500,000 bees! Heifer International has helped more than 4.5 million farm families in over a hundred countries to become self-reliant.

A terrible civil war in Mozambique pushed hundreds of thousands of people from their lands. **(7)** These refugees were forced to seek *sanctuary* in neighboring countries. **(8)** Seventeen years after the war began, a treaty *pacified* the country. **(9)** When people returned from their *havens*, they had no livestock and found that years of violence had turned their once-fertile land to dust. **(10)** In 1995, Heifer International *interceded* by supplying goats to families. By 1999, more than 1,600 baby goats had been given to others.

Some aid recipients have achieved such success for themselves that they have been able to increase the required livestock gift. In 2001, Ganga Devi Khanai received two goats from Heifer International. Within a year, she had enough money to pay for her children's schooling and to buy a water buffalo. That animal helped her to farm and provided milk for her to sell. Ganga was required to pass on two goats to others, but in gratitude, she decided to give a third goat. Ganga also helped to found a cooperative business that funds community schooling for women.

The mooing of cows, the bleating of goats, and the buzzing of bees are all signs that Heifer International is on the way. Its volunteers spread dignity and hope to people worldwide.

Each sentence below refers to a numbered sentence in the passage. Write the letter of the choice that gives the sentence a meaning that is closest to the original sentence.

___b___ **1.** West decided that simply _____ food would not improve lives.
   a. removing   **b.** giving   **c.** producing   **d.** rescuing

___a___ **2.** People needed a way to _____ their own food supplies.
   a. renew   **b.** speed up   **c.** store   **d.** consume

___a___ **3.** Giving one family a goat, while ignoring another, would _____ inequality.
   a. encourage   **b.** eliminate   **c.** rescue   **d.** argue for

___d___ **4.** Or the family can keep the offspring and _____ the livestock gift.
   a. encourage   **b.** repair   **c.** plead for   **d.** make up for

_____ c   **5.** In countries like Poland, the organization provided _____ from poverty.
       a. refreshment   **b.** honor   **c.** escape   **d.** peace

_____ d   **6.** The process was _____ when they began to travel by plane.
       a. repaired   **b.** calmed down   **c.** presented   **d.** sped up

_____ c   **7.** These refugees were forced to seek _____ in neighboring countries.
       a. progress   **b.** honors   **c.** safety   **d.** food

_____ b   **8.** Seventeen years after the war began, a treaty _____ the country.
       a. helped to assist   **b.** ended fighting in   **c.** caused hunger in   **d.** frightened

_____ a   **9.** When people returned from their _____, they had no livestock.
       a. protected areas   **b.** places of worship   **c.** former slavery   **d.** retirement homes

_____ b   **10.** In 1995, Heifer International _____ by supplying goats to families.
       a. caused trouble   **b.** provided help   **c.** got in the way   **d.** made peace

Indicate whether the statements below are TRUE or FALSE according to the passage.

_____ T   **1.** A goal of Heifer International is to help families become self-reliant.

_____ F   **2.** Heifer International limits its activities to a few countries in Europe.

_____ T   **3.** Aid recipients are required to donate to another needy family.

FINISH THE THOUGHT

Complete each sentence so that it shows the meaning of the italicized word.

1. One way to *pacify* a baby is to _____ Answers will vary. _____

_____

2. Someone has *interceded* for me when _____ Answers will vary. _____

_____

WRITE THE DERIVATIVE

Complete the sentence by writing the correct form of the word shown in parentheses. You may not need to change the form that is given.

___offsets___   **1.** The money Joe earns working in the convenience store more than _____ his increasing school-activity costs. (*offset*)

___deliverance___   **2.** Most people seek _____ from misfortune at some point in their lives. (*deliverance*)

bestows or bestowed

3. The school principal _____ strong praise on the winners of the achievement awards. *(bestow)*

abetting

4. In the Old West, _____ a cattle rustler could get you in a heap of trouble. *(abet)*

pacified

5. Holding a fair election restored calm and _____ the uprising. *(pacify)*

haven

6. As the gale force winds grew stronger, the ship's captain searched his charts of the Maine seacoast for a _____ where he could ride out the storm. *(haven)*

intercession

7. Were it not for their friend's _____, the quarrel between the brothers might have turned violent. *(intercede)*

expeditious

8. The speedy courier delivered the letter in a manner that can only be described as _____. *(expedite)*

sanctuaries

9. Because of the loss of their natural habitat, many birds and animals are forced to live in wildlife _____. *(sanctuary)*

Refurbishing

10. _____ old appliances can conserve resources. *(refurbish)*

FIND THE EXAMPLE

Choose the answer that best describes the action or situation.

_d_ **1.** Something from which people need *deliverance*
    a. good fortune   **b.** rescuers   **c.** fine weather   **d.** kidnapping

_d_ **2.** Something you might *refurbish*
    a. a school report   **b.** a barrel of trash   **c.** a new house   **d.** an old house

_a_ **3.** Something in need of *pacification*
    a. an angry mob   **b.** a peaceful protest   **c.** a quiet courtroom   **d.** a religious service

_c_ **4.** Something that might *expedite* a carpenter's work
    a. a heavy rain   **b.** noisy onlookers   **c.** power tools   **d.** a tax audit

_b_ **5.** An example of a *haven*
    a. an open field   **b.** a warm shelter   **c.** a cold prison   **d.** a cool breeze

_b_ **6.** Something in which you might *intercede*
    a. a dance   **b.** a disagreement   **c.** a speech   **d.** a party

_a_ **7.** Something that could provide *sanctuary* to birds
    a. a birdhouse   **b.** bird food   **c.** a bird song   **d.** a bird book

_c_ **8.** One way to *abet*
    a. gambling   **b.** discouraging   **c.** giving information   **d.** reading

_d_ **9.** Things that *offset* each other
    a. cooking and singing   **b.** brother and sister   **c.** wind and rain   **d.** savings and expenses

_a_ **10.** Something that could be *bestowed*
    a. a knighthood   **b.** a driver's license   **c.** a water bottle   **d.** a sandwich

Fairness and Unfairness

WORD LIST

amenable	deception	forbearance	objective	partiality
partisanship	preconceived	slander	subjective	tolerate

We have all heard preschoolers shout simply, "That's not fair!" But fairness is actually a range of complex and subtle concepts that have been the subject of much thought and discussion. The words in this lesson help you communicate about these timeless topics.

To encourage students to make connections among words, have them discuss which words have connotations of unfairness, such as *deception, partiality, partisan, slander,* and *subjective.* Students should discuss how each word is connected to the concept of unfairness.

1. **amenable** (ə-mĕn´ə-bəl) *adjective* from Latin *a-*, "against" + *minari,* "to threaten"
   Willing to consider; open to advice or suggestion
   • Meena's parents were **amenable** to extending her curfew, as long as she had her cell phone and called to check in.

2. **deception** (dĭ-sĕp´shən) *noun* from Latin *decipere,* "to deceive"
   A trick; an attempt to make someone believe something that is not true
   • When she didn't do her homework, the child resorted to **deception,** telling her teacher she felt sick and needed to see the nurse.

   deceive *verb* Don't try to **deceive** me; I know you came home late!

   deceptive *adjective* His **deceptive** actions revealed his true intentions.

3. **forbearance** (fôr-bâr´əns) *noun* from Old English *forberan,* "to put up with"
   Patience; not reacting when annoyed or harmed
   • The big dog showed gentle **forbearance** toward the bothersome new kittens.

   forbear *verb* (past tense: **forbore**) The king decided to **forbear** punishing the thief, giving him a chance to reform instead.

We show *forbearance* to people and to situations that annoy or harm us.

4. **objective** (əb-jĕk´tĭv) from Latin *ob-,* "toward" + *iacere,* "to throw"
   a. *adjective* Fair; impartial
      • It is difficult to be **objective** when you are judging a contest that a family member is competing in.
   b. *adjective* Realistic; actual
      • Many prejudices disappear when faced with **objective** facts.
   c. *noun* A goal or purpose
      • Toni's **objective** was to save enough money to buy a piano.

   objectivity *noun* **Objectivity** is essential to making fair decisions.

5. **partiality** (pär´shē-ăl´ĭ-tē) *noun* from Latin *parte,* "part"
   A favorable bias or a prejudice toward something
   • The competition judges' **partiality** to sopranos became clear when we noticed that all the finalists sang in that range.

   partial *adjective* Costa's mother knew he was **partial** to chocolate cake.

a forbearing dog

Lesson 3 13

6. **partisanship** (pär´tĭ-zənshĭp´) *noun* from Latin *pars*, "part"
Very strong, sometimes excessive support for one group, idea, or cause
• Committee members showed their **partisanship** when they approved their party's nominee, despite his lack of qualifications.

partisan *adjective* Driven by **partisan** enthusiasm, Terry placed twenty "Vote for Smith" bumper stickers on her car.

7. **preconceived** (prē´kən-sēvd´) *adjective* from Latin *pre-*, "before" + *concipere*, "to take hold of"
Believed before one has full knowledge or experience
• Sean had a **preconceived** idea that he would hate summer camp.

preconception *noun* Any **preconceptions** we had that short people had trouble with basketball vanished when we saw Gabrielle on the court.

8. **slander** (slăn´dər) from Latin *scaudalum*, "a cause of offense or sin"
   a. *noun* False and harmful statements about someone
      • The man was accused of **slander** because he called his political rival a thief.
   b. *verb* To make false and harmful statements about someone
      • The columnist was sued after she **slandered** her competitor on a talk show.

9. **subjective** (səb-jĕk´tĭv) *adjective* from Latin *sub-*, "under" + *iacere*, "to throw"
Governed by personal thoughts or feelings
• Judgments about art are often **subjective**.

subjectivity *noun* The coach appeared to show **subjectivity** when he picked his favorite student to be team captain.

10. **tolerate** (tŏl´ə-rāt´) *verb* from Latin *tolerare*, "to bear"
To allow; to bear; to endure
• The understanding neighbors tried to **tolerate** the noise from the children who lived upstairs.

tolerance *noun* She showed great **tolerance** for differing viewpoints.

toleration *noun* The principal had no **toleration** for students who ran in the halls.

WORD ENRICHMENT

The prefix meaning "before"

The *pre-* in *preconceived* means "before." We are still using this prefix to form words. Newer ones include *prepay*, *preadolescent*, *pre-op* (before an operation), and *pregame*. Even the word *prefix* contains *pre-*; the word means "fixed before."

WRITE THE CORRECT WORD

Write the correct word in the space next to each definition.

objective 1. fair; not influenced by emotions

partisanship 2. excessive support for a cause or candidate

partiality 3. a preference for something

amenable 4. willing to consider something

tolerate 5. to put up with

deception 6. a trick

slander 7. to tell harmful lies about someone

subjective 8. based on personal feelings

preconceived 9. formed without complete knowledge

forbearance 10. patience

COMPLETE THE SENTENCE

Write the letter for the word that best completes each sentence.

d 1. The TV ads _____ the politician's opponent with false charges of tax evasion.
   a. tolerated   **b.** forebore   **c.** preconceived   **d.** slandered

b 2. It's not always easy to _____ the rude behavior of others.
   a. slander   **b.** tolerate   **c.** deceive   **d.** preconceive

c 3. Sheila always seems _____ to helping her brother take out the garbage.
   a. deceptive   **b.** objective   **c.** amenable   **d.** partisan

c 4. The crowd in the end zone displayed their _____ by wearing their school colors.
   a. deception   **b.** slander   **c.** partisanship   **d.** tolerance

a 5. Mike displays admirable _____ toward his little brother's annoying behavior.
   a. forbearance   **b.** subjectivity   **c.** partisanship   **d.** objective

a 6. The audience showed their _____ for the contestant by giving him loud applause.
   a. partiality   **b.** slander   **c.** deception   **d.** tolerance

d 7. The _____ of the award was to honor the long service of the town's mayor.
   a. deception   **b.** forbearance   **c.** subjective   **d.** objective

b 8. In an act of _____, the man fooled people into believing he was a physician.
   a. subjectivity   **b.** deception   **c.** partisanship   **d.** forbearance

b 9. For many people, _____ ideas can be difficult to change.
   a. tolerant   **b.** preconceived   **c.** amenable   **d.** objective

a 10. The critic's negative movie review was very _____; he clearly just doesn't like science fiction.
   a. subjective   **b.** partial   **c.** amenable   **d.** objective

Challenge: The clever political candidate used _____ to make his criticisms of his opponent appear to be _____.

a   **a.** deception…objective   **b.** slander…preconceived   **c.** partiality…slander

The Bitter Campaign of 1800

Critics complain about today's "negative campaigning." But today's elections can't compare to the presidential election of 1800, in which President John Adams ran against his own vice president, Thomas Jefferson. The bitter campaign resulted in a crisis that ultimately changed the Constitution.

Once fast friends, Jefferson and Adams had become icy antagonists. They were members of opposing political parties: Adams was a Federalist, and Jefferson was a Republican. The campaign reflected the bitterness between the two parties. **(1)** *Slanders* came from everywhere. **(2)** Federalists believed in a strong federal government and had *preconceived* notions of Jefferson as a revolutionary, because he admired the recent French Revolution. They warned that he would unleash terror in the United States. One Federalist critic stated that, if Jefferson won, "the soil will be soaked with blood, and the nation black with crime." **(3)** This was hardly an *objective* assessment of the distinguished vice president.

(4) Republicans were also *partisan*. They accused Adams of trying to marry his daughter to the son of King George III, of England. **(5)** This charge was an attempt to *deceive* people into believing that Adams wanted to be king of the United States. Even Adams's own party proved disloyal. **(6)** A highly *subjective* and very critical letter by fellow Federalist Alexander Hamilton was leaked to the press.

According to the Constitution, candidates running for president and vice president were to be listed on the same ballot with no distinction between them. Members of the Electoral College were instructed to choose two names. The candidate who received the most votes would become president; the candidate with the second most votes would become vice president. When the election results were tallied, Jefferson and his vice-presidential running mate, Aaron Burr, had each won the same number of votes, resulting in a tie for president. Burr refused to step aside—he wanted to be president, too. It was then up to members of the House of Representatives to choose between them. **(7)** Though the Federalists did not like Burr, they were unable to even *tolerate* the thought of Jefferson as president. So the Federalists voted for Burr, and the Republicans voted for Jefferson. The House voted thirty-five times, but the tie remained.

John Adams   Thomas Jefferson

(8) Finally, powerful Alexander Hamilton, who felt some *partiality* toward Jefferson and did not trust Burr, decided to encourage his party to support Jefferson. **(9)** A few Federalists from Delaware, wanting an end to the matter, proved *amenable* to Hamilton's influence. They agreed to hand in blank ballots rather than vote for Burr. On the thirty-sixth ballot, just fifteen days before inauguration day, Jefferson was elected president.

(10) Unable to demonstrate *forbearance* in the face of defeat, Adams left Washington, D.C., before dawn on inauguration day. Although Jefferson and Adams eventually reconciled, Burr and Hamilton became bitter enemies. In 1804, Burr killed Hamilton in a duel.

The most important legacy of the election of 1800 was the creation of the Twelfth Amendment to the Constitution. It states that electors must vote for the president and the vice president separately.

Each sentence below refers to a numbered sentence in the passage. Write the letter of the choice that gives the sentence a meaning that is closest to the original sentence.

__c__ **1.** _____ came from everywhere.
    a. Patience   **b.** Tricks   **c.** False statements   **d.** Fair judgments

__d__ **2.** Federalists had _____ notions of Jefferson as a revolutionary.
    a. accepted without question   **b.** emotional   **c.** willing   **d.** formed without knowledge

__b__ **3.** This was hardly a _____ assessment of the distinguished vice president.
    a. favorable   **b.** fair   **c.** popular   **d.** harmful

__c__ **4.** Republicans were also _____.
    a. willing to trick   **b.** weak in support   **c.** strong in support   **d.** eager to be fair

_____a_____ **5.** This charge was an attempt to ——— people.
    a. trick   **b.** threaten   **c.** consider   **d.** frighten

_____d_____ **6.** A highly ——— and very critical letter was leaked to the press.
    a. detailed   **b.** understanding   **c.** agreeable   **d.** personal

_____b_____ **7.** The Federalists were unable to even ——— the thought of Jefferson as president.
    a. forget   **b.** endure   **c.** favor   **d.** remember

_____c_____ **8.** Alexander Hamilton felt some ——— toward Jefferson.
    a. friendship   **b.** patience   **c.** bias   **d.** dislike

_____a_____ **9.** A few Federalists from Delaware proved ——— to Hamilton's influence.
    a. open   **b.** opposed   **c.** hostile   **d.** resistant

_____d_____ **10.** Unable to demonstrate ——— in the face of defeat, Adams left Washington, D.C., before dawn on inauguration day.
    a. a trick   **b.** certainty   **c.** gratitude   **d.** patience

Indicate whether the statements below are TRUE or FALSE according to the passage.

_____F_____ **1.** Adams and Jefferson were close friends during the election campaign of 1800.

_____T_____ **2.** Jefferson and Burr were members of the same political party.

_____T_____ **3.** As a result of the election of 1800, a constitutional amendment changed the way electors vote in presidential elections.

WRITING EXTENDED RESPONSES

The presidential campaign of 1800 contained several elements of unfairness. We have all witnessed, or at least heard about, other situations or events that seem unfair or unjust. Write an expository essay at least three paragraphs long, detailing an event or a response that seems unfair to you. You may choose an example from your own life, or the life of a friend or family member. Or you may want to choose an example that you have seen or read about in the news. Describe the situation; remember to include reasons why it is unfair. Use at least three lesson words in your essay and underline them.

WRITE THE DERIVATIVE

Complete the sentence by writing the correct form of the word shown in parentheses. You may not need to change the form that is given.

_____deceive_____ **1.** The store owner used false advertising to ——— potential customers. *(deception)*

_____slandering_____ **2.** Citing a series of harmful lies, Congressman Walkowitz accused his opponent of ——— him. *(slander)*

objectivity

3. A judge must make decisions with _____. (*objective*)

partial

4. The students were _____ to the new teacher, who assigned very little homework. (*partiality*)

tolerance or toleration

5. At times, unfair behavior by others may test your _____. (*tolerate*)

amenable

6. Amelie was _____ to the idea of having the meeting at her house. (*amenable*)

partisan

7. Do you think that _____ politics is a part of all democratic systems? (*partisanship*)

preconception

8. The young babysitter's _____ that babies are easy to take care of was shattered when he took care of the one-year old. (*preconceived*)

forbearance

9. The salesclerk showed great _____ toward the rude customer. (*forbearance*)

subjectivity

10. Arguments about which type of music is "best" are pointless because musical tastes involve _____. (*subjective*)

FIND THE EXAMPLE

Choose the answer that best describes the action or situation.

a 1. Something difficult for some people to *tolerate*
   a. criticism   **b.** prizes   **c.** sleep   **d.** awards

c 2. Something most people would be *amenable* to receiving
   a. a fine   **b.** threats   **c.** money   **d.** a punishment

b 3. Something that young children are often *partial* to
   a. asparagus   **b.** sweets   **c.** homework   **d.** sweeping

a 4. Something that is known for bringing out *partisan* behavior
   a. an election   **b.** a disaster   **c.** a jail sentence   **d.** a birthday party

b 5. Something that is NOT a common *objective*
   a. to get promoted   **b.** to lose money   **c.** to pass a test   **d.** to win a game

c 6. Socially acceptable *deceptions*
   a. tax returns   **b.** insensitive jokes   **c.** magic tricks   **d.** vicious lies

c 7. Another word for a *preconceived* idea
   a. a prefix   **b.** a predicament   **c.** a prejudice   **d.** a pretest

d 8. Something *subjective*
   a. strength   **b.** weight   **c.** height   **d.** attractiveness

d 9. An example of *slander*
   a. apologetic note   **b.** overdue bill   **c.** high praise   **d.** false accusation

b 10. A situation requiring *forbearance*
   a. sound sleep   **b.** rude interruption   **c.** warm handshake   **d.** well-balanced meal

Using the Dictionary

Finding the Appropriate Definition

Most dictionary words have more than one definition. When you look up a word, you must decide which definition is most appropriate—that is, which one best fits the way the word is used in the material you are reading.

Strategies

1. *Decide the word's part of speech.* Then concentrate on the definitions for that part of speech. The word *contingent* can be used as both a noun and an adjective. However, in the sentence below, *contingent* appears as an adjective that modifies the noun *launching*. So you need to choose from the adjective definitions.

   > Sentence: The launching of the space shuttle is **contingent** upon the weather.

   > **contingent** (kən-tǐn´jənt) *adj.* **1.** Possible but not certain to occur; uncertain. **2.** Dependent on circumstances not yet known; conditional. **3.** Happening by chance; accidental; unexpected. *n.* **1.** A representative group forming part of a gathering; a delegation. **2.** —**con•tin´gent•ly** *adv.*

2. *Choose the definition that best fits the sentence.* Read all the definitions for that part of speech. There are three adjective definitions to choose from; don't simply choose the first one. Read the sentence to yourself, substituting each definition (in the right part of speech) for the unknown word. You may have to change a definition slightly. Doing this shows that the correct adjective definition is number 2. (The word *conditional* fits perfectly into the sentence.)

   > 2. Dependent on circumstances not yet known; conditional.

3. *If there is more than one entry for a word, consider each entry.* Some words are homographs. This means they are spelled the same, but are completely different in meaning, origin, and sometimes pronunciation. Homographs have separate dictionary entries and each one is printed with a number by the word. For example, *fly[1]* means "to travel through the air;" whereas *fly[2]* is an insect. Be sure to choose the correct entry.

Practice

Using the dictionary entries provided below, find the best definition of the italicized word for each of the sentences. Copy the definitions onto the lines provided.

grill (grĭl) *tr.v.* **grilled, grill•ing, grills 1.** To cook on a grill. **2.** *Informal.* To question closely and relentlessly. —*n.* **1.** A cooking utensil of parallel metal bars; a gridiron. **2.** Food cooked by broiling or grilling. **3.** An informal restaurant where grilled foods are served.

resort (rĭ-zôrt´) *intr.v.* **re•sort•ed, re•sort•ing, re•sorts 1.** To go or turn for help as a means of achieving something. **2.** To go customarily or frequently. —*n.* **1.** A place where people go for relaxation or recreation. **2.** A person or thing turned to for aid or relief. **3.** The act of turning to for aid or relief.

input (ĭn´pŏŏt´) *n.* **1.** Something put into a project or process. **2.** The power supplied to an electronic circuit or device. **3.** The data or programs put into a computer. —*tr.v.* **in•put•ted** or **in•put, in•put•ting, in•puts** To enter (data or a program) into a computer.

fluke¹ (flŏŏk) *n.* Any of various flatfishes, especially the flounder.

fluke² (flŏŏk) *n.* Something happening by chance, especially a stroke of good luck.

1. Desperate to get a laugh, Steve *resorted* to telling very silly jokes.

Definition: ___to go or turn for help as a means of achieving something___

2. We often eat lunch at a *grill*.

Definition: ___an informal restaurant where grilled foods are served___

3. We caught a *fluke* and ate it for dinner.

Definition: ___any of various flatfishes, especially the flounder___

4. Who will *input* the numbers into the computer?

Definition: ___to enter (data or a program) into a computer___

5. Last summer, my parents took a vacation at a *resort* in Wisconsin.

Definition: ___a place where people go for relaxation or recreation___

6. The lawyer *grilled* the witness.

Definition: ___to question closely and relentlessly___

7. Meeting my best friend at the train station was a pure *fluke*.

Definition: ___something happening by chance, especially a stroke of good luck___

8. We *grilled* vegetables outside.

Definition: ___to cook on a grill___

9. A sudden increase in *input* overloaded the electronic circuit.

Definition: ___the power supplied to an electronic circuit or device___

10. We have asked everyone else for help, so you are our last *resort*.

Definition: ___a person or thing turned to for aid or relief___

Happiness and Unhappiness

WORD LIST

anguish	blithe	congenial	defiant	desolate
despondent	disgruntled	disillusion	exuberant	gratification

There are lots of ways to describe how you feel. In this lesson, you will learn words that express happiness and unhappiness.

1. **anguish** (ăng´gwĭsh) from Latin *angustus,* "narrow"
   a. *noun* Great physical or mental pain; torment; torture
      • The thought of their missing child filled the parents with **anguish.**
   b. *verb* To suffer emotional pain
      • The patient **anguished** over which cancer treatment to choose.

> "Filled with *anguish*" and "*anguish* over" are common expressions.

2. **blithe** (blīth) *adjective*
   Cheerful; carefree; lighthearted
   • Unconcerned about onlookers, the **blithe** teens gossiped and giggled as they walked down the street.

   blithely *adverb* The dog played **blithely** with its new toy.

3. **congenial** (kən-jēn´yəl) *adjective*
   Friendly; having a pleasant disposition
   • His boyish charm and **congenial** manner helped him win votes.

   congeniality *noun* The restaurant hostess's **congeniality** made patrons feel at home.

> *Congenial* can describe people with similar personalities or tastes.

4. **defiant** (dĭ-fī´ənt) *adjective* from Old French *desfier,* "to challenge"
   Openly or boldly resisting authority
   • **Defiant** workers gathered in the street to protest unfair treatment.

   defy *verb* Alex **defied** his father by staying out past his curfew.

   defiance *noun* In a show of **defiance,** the crowd refused to disperse.

5. **desolate** (dĕs´ə-lĭt) *adjective* from Latin *desolare,* "to leave all alone"
   a. Lonely and sad
      • When her three best friends moved away, the girl felt **desolate.**
   b. Having little or no life or vegetation; barren
      • The plane flew over a vast and **desolate** desert.

   desolation *noun* Alone on the desert island, he was overcome with feelings of **desolation.**

Point out that the words *defiant, desolate, despondent,* and *dissolution* contain the prefixes *de-* or *dis-,* which usually have a negative meaning.

desolate

6. **despondent** (dǐ-spǒn´dənt) *adjective* from Latin *despondere,*
"to give up"
In low spirits; depressed; dejected
• The artist Vincent Van Gogh became **despondent** when people rejected his paintings.

7. **disgruntled** (dǐs-grǔn´tld) *adjective* from Middle English *grunten,*
"to grunt"
Discontented; resentful
• The **disgruntled** employee complained to the personnel office when he failed to get promoted.

8. **disillusion** (dǐs´ǐ-lōō´zhən) *verb* from Latin *dis-,* "remove" + *ludere,*
"to play"
To disappoint someone by breaking his or her belief in a false ideal
• If you expect the people you admire to be perfect, you may soon be **disillusioned.**

   disillusionment *noun* Young Antonio's **disillusionment,** after meeting the obviously fake Santa Claus, kept him awake all night.

9. **exuberant** (ǐg-zōō´bər-ənt) *adjective* from Latin *exuberare,* "to be abundant"
Filled with enthusiasm and joy
• **Exuberant** after returning from a long tour of duty, the naval officer hugged her family members.

   exuberance *noun* The crowd cheered in wild **exuberance** when their baseball team scored the winning run.

10. **gratification** (grăt´ə-fǐ-kā´shən) *noun* from Latin *gratus,* "pleasing"
Satisfaction; a feeling of being rewarded for one's efforts
• Their son's success brought **gratification** to the parents, who had struggled to put him through school.

   gratify *verb* Dr. Bass was **gratified** that many former students remembered her.

WORD ENRICHMENT

The Latin word for play

The Latin verb *ludere,* meaning "to play," is found in a variety of English words. When we have an *illusion,* we believe something false, as though someone is tricking, or playing, with us. *Disillusion* means "to take away play," bringing someone back to reality. The word *ludicrous* means "ridiculous," as though we are laughing at silly child's play.

WRITE THE CORRECT WORD

Write the correct word in the space next to each definition.

___disgruntled___ **1.** unhappy; resentful

___congenial___ **2.** friendly and sociable

___defiant___ **3.** openly resistant to authority

___anguish___ **4.** great pain

___gratification___ **5.** satisfaction

___disillusion___ **6.** to disappoint

___despondent___ **7.** depressed; in low spirits

___exuberant___ **8.** enthusiastic and joyful

___desolate___ **9.** having no vegetation

___blithe___ **10.** carefree and cheerful

COMPLETE THE SENTENCE

Write the letter for the word that best completes each sentence.

___c___ **1.** I always feel a sense of _____ when I get a thank you note for a gift I sent.
   a. congeniality   **b.** desolation   **c.** gratification   **d.** disillusionment

___b___ **2.** Children may become _____ when they discover that their parents aren't perfect.
   a. desolate   **b.** disillusioned   **c.** congenial   **d.** blithe

___d___ **3.** After winning the state spelling bee, the students were _____.
   a. desolate   **b.** defiant   **c.** despondent   **d.** exuberant

___d___ **4.** With exams over and spring underway, the campus center was filled with _____ students.
   a. anguished   **b.** defiant   **c.** disillusioned   **d.** blithe

___a___ **5.** When everything seems to go wrong, it's easy to become _____.
   a. despondent   **b.** exuberant   **c.** gratified   **d.** congenial

___a___ **6.** The student's _____ behavior was rewarded when he was voted "Most Friendly."
   a. congenial   **b.** disillusioned   **c.** despondent   **d.** blithe

___c___ **7.** The _____ on the faces of the injured crash survivors was plain to see.
   a. gratification   **b.** exuberance   **c.** anguish   **d.** congeniality

___b___ **8.** The _____ protestors continued to block traffic even after being ordered to leave.
   a. gratified   **b.** defiant   **c.** congenial   **d.** blithe

___c___ **9.** The _____ athlete complained to the coach when she wasn't chosen for the team.
   a. congenial   **b.** exuberant   **c.** disgruntled   **d.** gratified

___d___ **10.** After a day lost in the woods, the hiker was beginning to feel _____.
   a. gratified   **b.** blithe   **c.** exuberant   **d.** desolate

Challenge: The injured runner's _____ showed on his twisted face, as he waited _____ for the ambulance.
   ___a___ **a.** anguish…despondently   **b.** congeniality…exuberantly   **c.** gratification…defiantly

The Lost Love of Orpheus

According to Greek mythology, Orpheus was the greatest of all musicians. His beautiful songs brought happiness to the saddest hearts. Humans, animals, and even stones and trees gathered around to hear him sing and play the lyre.

When the adventurer Jason sailed in search of the Golden Fleece, Orpheus traveled on Jason's ship, helping the sailors through the long days and nights. **(1)** When tempers flared, Orpheus's singing restored *congeniality*. **(2)** Sailors, *disgruntled* with the length of the voyage, would feel their spirits lift when Orpheus touched his lyre. **(3)** Those *disillusioned* by the unexpectedly hard conditions at sea would feel contented, once again.

However, Orpheus's great charms could not prevent his own unhappiness. The story began when he fell in love with a beautiful maiden named Eurydice. **(4)** *Exuberant* with happiness, the young couple were married at a joyous ceremony. **(5)** But shortly afterward, as Eurydice was *blithely* walking through a field, a poisonous snake bit and killed her.

(6) Orpheus's *anguish* knew no bounds. He had lost his love on the very day of their wedding. **(7)** He sat by the rocks in *desolation*.

Finally, he decided that he would go to the Underworld and plead for his wife's return. His journey was long and dangerous, but his beautiful music helped convince the monsters who guarded the Underworld to let him pass. Finally, he came to the throne of Hades, the ruler of the Underworld. Charmed by Orpheus's music and his devotion to Eurydice, Hades decided to grant Orpheus's request. He agreed to let Eurydice return with Orpheus to the land of the living. Hades had only one

condition: Orpheus was not to look back at his bride until they had climbed to Earth's surface.

(8) The *gratified* couple began their long journey back to Earth, passing through the gates of the Underworld and traveling ever upward. Orpheus carefully kept his eyes on the path ahead of them. But just as they were about to pass into the sunlight, perhaps to reassure himself that she was really there, Orpheus suddenly looked back. Eurydice, calling out to him, vanished again into the Underworld.

Orpheus was heartbroken. His own carelessness had cost him his love. **(9)** *Defiantly,* he tried to descend into the Underworld again, but this time, even his music couldn't convince the guards to let him through.

From that day on, the joy went out of Orpheus. Abandoning the company of humans, he sat alone, playing his lyre for comfort. **(10)** The uplifting happiness of his music gave way to *despondent,* mournful tunes.

Each sentence below refers to a numbered sentence in the passage. Write the letter of the choice that gives the sentence a meaning that is closest to the original sentence.

___d___ **1.** When tempers flared, Orpheus's singing restored _____ .
    a. hostility   **b.** loneliness   **c.** discontent   **d.** friendliness

___b___ **2.** Sailors, _____ with the length of the voyage, would feel their spirits lift when Orpheus touched his lyre.
    a. tortured   **b.** displeased   **c.** happy   **d.** lighthearted

___a___ **3.** Those _____ the unexpectedly hard conditions at sea would feel contented, once again.
    a. disappointed by   **b.** enthusiastic about   **c.** satisfied with   **d.** tormented by

___c___ **4.** _____ with happiness, the young couple were married at a joyous ceremony.
    a. Resentful   **b.** Satisfied   **c.** Overjoyed   **d.** Annoyed

___c___ **5.** But shortly afterward, as Eurydice was _____ walking through a field, a poisonous snake bit and killed her.
  a. pleasantly   **b.** boldly   **c.** lightheartedly   **d.** sadly

___a___ **6.** Orpheus's _____ knew no bounds.
  a. pain   **b.** cheerfulness   **c.** happiness   **d.** resistance

___b___ **7.** He sat by the rocks in _____ .
  a. great anger   **b.** sad loneliness   **c.** a crowd   **d.** silence

___d___ **8.** The _____ couple began their long journey back to Earth, passing through the gates of the Underworld and traveling ever upward.
  a. irritated   **b.** enthusiastic   **c.** despairing   **d.** grateful

___b___ **9.** _____ , he tried to descend into the Underworld again.
  a. Sadly   **b.** Boldly   **c.** Noisily   **d.** Humbly

___a___ **10.** The uplifting happiness of his music gave way to _____ , mournful tunes.
  a. sad   **b.** quiet   **c.** carefree   **d.** satisfied

Indicate whether the statements below are TRUE or FALSE according to the passage.

___T___ **1.** According to the myth, Orpheus's music had the power to bring happiness.

___T___ **2.** Orpheus lost his love because he did not follow instructions.

___F___ **3.** Orpheus recovered from his grief and was able to make joyful music, once again.

FINISH THE THOUGHT

Complete each sentence so that it shows the meaning of the italicized word.

1. A person might feel *disgruntled* if _____ Answers will vary. _____

_____

2. A *congenial* person would _____ Answers will vary. _____

_____

WRITE THE DERIVATIVE

Complete the sentence by writing the correct form of the word shown in parentheses. You may not need to change the form that is given.

___exuberance___ **1.** The _____ of the cheerleaders spread to the fans. (*exuberant*)

___blithely___ **2.** The children _____ played on the rusty old swing set, unconcerned about getting hurt. (*blithe*)

___disgruntled___ **3.** Though unhappy with their training, the _____ recruits refrained from complaining. (*disgruntled*) disillusionment

4. It will be difficult for voters to overcome their _____ after they were mislead during the last election campaign. *(disillusion)*

Congeniality

5. The friendliest contestant was voted Miss _____. *(congenial)*

defiance

6. Refusing to speak to the police officer was an act of _____ by the suspect. *(defiant)*

despondent

7. After losing the World Series, the team members were _____ as they answered the reporters' questions. *(despondent)*

anguish

8. The mourners' _____ could only be appreciated by others who shared a similar loss. *(anguish)*

desolation

9. Above the timberline, the terrain has a feeling of _____. *(desolate)*

gratified

10. The film director seemed _____ by the lifetime achievement award presented by the academy. *(gratification)*

FIND THE EXAMPLE

Choose the answer that best describes the action or situation.

b **1.** A job that probably would NOT require *congeniality*
   a. restaurant host   **b.** prison guard   **c.** politician   **d.** salesperson

c **2.** Something that might *disillusion* you
   a. a lion's roar   **b.** homework   **c.** a friend's lie   **d.** an enemy's criticism

a **3.** Something most likely to be *desolate*
   a. Mars   **b.** a town   **c.** a huge skyscraper   **d.** a busy highway

b **4.** A cause for *anguish*
   a. a sad movie   **b.** a death in the family   **c.** a cash award   **d.** a torn shirt

d **5.** Something that would be *gratifying*
   a. a toothache   **b.** a tax form   **c.** a grocery bill   **d.** a promotion

d **6.** Someone who is *defiant*
   a. a supporter   **b.** a leader   **c.** a follower   **d.** a rebel

c **7.** A reason to be *despondent*
   a. a new job   **b.** a winning team   **c.** a lost pet   **d.** a minor cut

d **8.** An example of *exuberant* behavior
   a. hoping, praying   **b.** writing, reading   **c.** sitting, standing   **d.** jumping, shouting

b **9.** Someone who usually appears *blithe*
   a. an aid worker   **b.** a cheerleader   **c.** a firefighter   **d.** a police officer

b **10.** Someone who might be *disgruntled*
   a. a popular leader   **b.** a benched player   **c.** a contest winner   **d.** a promoted worker

Disagreement

WORD LIST

adversary	belligerent	chide	contradictory	discord
embroil	haggle	ruse	skirmish	strife

From time to time, everyone has disagreements. Children are *chided* by their parents. We might face *discord* with our friends or become *embroiled* in disagreements between others. The words in this lesson will help you understand and write about different types of conflict, the behavior that leads to them, and how they can be resolved.

1. adversary (ăd´vər-sĕr´ē) *noun* from Latin *ad-*, "toward" + *vertere*, "to turn"
An opponent; an enemy
• His **adversary** had only one rule—to win.

adversarial *adjective* Unfortunately, the two sisters had an **adversarial** relationship.

2. belligerent (bə-lĭj´ər-ənt) *adjective* from Latin *bellum*, "war" + *gerere*, "to make"
Hostile; aggressive; quarrelsome
• The minor argument turned into a **belligerent** shouting match.

belligerence *noun* Because of her **belligerence,** the policemen had to handcuff the woman they had arrested.

3. chide (chīd) *verb* from Old English *cidan*, "strife"
To scold; to express dissatisfaction
• Mom **chided** Alice for leaving her slippers out where the dog could chew them.

4. contradictory (kŏn´trə-dĭk´tə-rē) *adjective* from Latin *contra*, "against" + *dicere*, "to say"
Expressing the opposite; inconsistent
• We were puzzled by the **contradictory** statements of the two witnesses.

contradict *verb* It is not tactful to **contradict** one's coworkers in the presence of others.

contradiction *noun* Bad-tempered at work, yet gentle at home, he was a man of many **contradictions.**

chide

To encourage deeper understanding of the words, discuss which ones have to do with arguments between people. While *adversary, discord, haggle,* and *strife* are certainly relevant, students may be able to defend other choices.

5. **discord** (dĭs´kôrd) *noun* from Latin *dis-*, "apart" + *cord*, "heart"
Lack of agreement or harmony
• The vacation was ruined by **discord** among the campers.

   discordant *adjective* An argument between the two captains set a **discordant** tone for the swim meet.

> *Discordant* sounds, such as those made by orchestra members tuning instruments, lack harmony.

6. **embroil** (ĕm-broil´) *verb* from French *embrouiller*, "to tangle"
To get involved in a conflict, an argument, or confusion
• Try not to get **embroiled** in arguments between other people.

7. **haggle** (hăg´əl) *verb*
To argue or bargain in order to come to favorable terms or a good price
• Some people go to flea markets just for the fun of **haggling** over prices.

   haggler *noun* Six-year-old Eric proved to be a true **haggler,** as he talked his father into letting him stay up later and later.

8. **ruse** (ro͞os) *noun* from Old French *ruser*, "to drive back"
A crafty trick intended to create a false impression
• The **ruse** succeeded, and the escapees disguised as prison guards vanished into the night.

9. **skirmish** (skûr´mĭsh) *noun* from Old French *eskermir*, "to fight with a sword"
A minor battle, sometimes on the fringes of a larger battle
• Six people were killed in the **skirmish** that started a civil war.

10. **strife** (strīf) *noun*
Bitter conflict or struggle
• **Strife** between ethnic groups in Bosnia resulted in the deaths of many thousands of people.

WORD ENRICHMENT

Oxymorons—language contradictions

If you have ever asked for a *plastic glass*, then you have used an *oxymoron*. Oxymorons are combinations of two contradictory words. Perhaps you have eaten *jumbo shrimp* (shrimp sometimes means "small") and have commented that they were *awfully good.*

Did you ever look at your shoes and think they were *pretty ugly?* If so, then maybe you polished them to a *dull shine.* Afterward, they may have looked *extremely average.* As you can see, we use *oxymorons* all the time. Can you think of any others?

WRITE THE CORRECT WORD

Write the correct word in the space next to each definition.

skirmish 1. a minor battle

belligerent 2. aggressive; eager to fight

contradictory 3. inconsistent

strife 4. bitter conflict

ruse 5. a cunning trick

chide 6. to scold

embroil 7. to become involved in a conflict

adversary 8. an opponent

haggle 9. to bargain

discord 10. lack of agreement

COMPLETE THE SENTENCE

Write the letter for the word that best completes each sentence.

a 1. The parents caused _____ between their children by constantly comparing one to the other.
a. strife   b. chiding   c. ruse   d. embroiling

d 2. The _____ between the committee members was finally resolved when they reached a compromise.
a. chiding   b. ruse   c. skirmish   d. discord

c 3. The _____ leader threatened to attack a neighboring country.
a. contradictory   b. haggled   c. belligerent   d. chided

b 4. Tired of _____ with the plumber about when he could fix the problem, Mom called another company.
a. chiding   b. haggling   c. contradicting   d. embroiling

b 5. Our players failed to discover the other team's _____ until it was too late.
a. strife   b. ruse   c. adversary   d. belligerence

b 6. The small country was afraid of being _____ in the struggle between its neighbors.
a. contradicted   b. embroiled   c. chided   d. haggled

c 7. The _____ evidence seemed both to support and to weaken the suspect's alibi.
a. belligerent   b. embroiling   c. contradictory   d. skirmish

a 8. A minor _____ is better than an all-out war.
a. skirmish   b. ruse   c. adversary   d. contradiction

a 9. Sports events are most fun to watch when the _____ are well matched.
a. adversaries   b. ruses   c. contradictions   d. skirmishes

b 10. Tom's grandmother _____ him for his bad table manners.
a. embroiled   b. chided   c. haggled   d. contradicted

Challenge: While traveling with my family, it felt as though we became _____ in a _____ contest every time we went shopping.

c   a. chided…strife   b. haggled…discordant   c. embroiled…haggling

Champion Female Wrestler

For many years, Patricia Miranda had to fight to compete in the sport she loves—wrestling. But today, she is a successful Olympic contender.

As a child, Miranda was always interested in taking on challenges. One day, as she watched a group of boys in a wrestling class, she decided that wrestling was the sport for her.

Unfortunately, there were no girls' wrestling teams, so Miranda learned the sport by competing with the boys. At times, she found it hard. She had to get used to the pain and bruises from a rough sport. **(1)** She had to *haggle* with coaches to be recognized as a team member. **(2)** Some people thought that Miranda's request to join the high-school wrestling team was a *ruse* to get attention, and they didn't treat it seriously. Perhaps most painful were the taunts and mean jokes she had to endure. But Miranda continued her efforts to become a wrestler.

(3) Wrestling is an aggressive sport; at times, opponents and fans can be *belligerent*. Miranda stood five feet tall and weighed just over a hundred pounds. **(4)** She found it challenging to win against stronger *adversaries*. In college, she had trouble even getting a chance to compete in matches. In fact, she had to wait until her senior year to get into the lineup. Even then, she wrestled only after three male teammates were disqualified. She lost far more matches than she won. But finally, one important victory over a male opponent boosted her confidence.

(5) Not all the *skirmishes* Miranda fought were in the ring. **(6)** She became *embroiled* in a dispute with her father, who initially opposed her decision to wrestle. **(7)** The cause of the *strife* was her father's concern about her schoolwork. **(8)** He *chided* her for her interest in wrestling because he worried that it would interfere with her studies. **(9)** The *discord* ended when they made a deal: Miranda promised that she would get all A's if he would let her wrestle. **(10)** When she kept her part of the bargain, her father realized that sports and academic excellence were not *contradictory*. Today, he supports her fully.

Slowly, Miranda's skills developed. She did exceptionally well in women's events, winning the gold at the 2003 Pan American Games and the 2003 World Cup. She also took second place in the World Championships in 2000 and 2003. Then, in 2004, women's wrestling was approved as an Olympic sport. That same year, a proud Patricia Miranda earned a bronze medal for the United States at the Summer Olympic Games in Athens.

Today, Miranda, a Phi Beta Kappa graduate of Stanford, is studying law at Yale University. Not surprisingly, she wants to specialize in conflict mediation. Overcoming barriers that stood in her way—teams without a place for her, family opposition, and long strings of losses—Miranda has proved that women belong in wrestling.

Each sentence below refers to a numbered sentence in the passage. Write the letter of the choice that gives the sentence a meaning that is closest to the original sentence.

_____a_____ **1.** She had to _____ with coaches to be recognized as a team member.
   a. argue   **b.** spend time   **c.** war   **d.** agree

_____b_____ **2.** Some thought that her request to join the wrestling team was a(n) _____.
   a. conflict   **b.** trick   **c.** argument   **d.** struggle

_____c_____ **3.** Wrestling is an aggressive sport; at times, opponents and fans can be _____.
   a. inconsistent   **b.** cooperative   **c.** hostile   **d.** entangled

_____c_____ **4.** She found it challenging to win against stronger _____.
   a. supporters   **b.** battles   **c.** opponents   **d.** friends

_a_   **5.** Not all the _____ Miranda fought were in the ring.

     a. minor battles   **b.** clever tricks   **c.** strong enemies   **d.** hostile people

_d_   **6.** She became _____ in a dispute with her father, who initially opposed her decision to wrestle.

     a. unhappy   **b.** surprised   **c.** dissatisfied   **d.** involved

_b_   **7.** The cause of the _____ was her father's concern about her schoolwork.

     a. war   **b.** conflict   **c.** harmony   **d.** trickery

_b_   **8.** He _____ her for her interest in wrestling because he worried that it would interfere with her studies.

     a. congratulated   **b.** scolded   **c.** opposed   **d.** threatened

_d_   **9.** The _____ ended when they made a deal.

     a. battle   **b.** support   **c.** discussion   **d.** disagreement

_a_   **10.** When she kept her part of the bargain, her father realized that sports and academic excellence were not _____.

     a. in opposition   **b.** in harmony   **c.** important   **d.** involved

Indicate whether the statements below are TRUE or FALSE according to the passage.

_F_   **1.** Success in wrestling came easily to Patricia Miranda.

_T_   **2.** For a time, Patricia Miranda's father was opposed to her wrestling competitively.

_T_   **3.** Patricia Miranda won a bronze medal in the 2004 Summer Olympic Games.

WRITING EXTENDED RESPONSES

Patricia Miranda fought hard to pursue the sport she loved. Think about a struggle that you, someone you know, or someone you have heard about has been through. Then, in a narrative essay, tell the story of the effort. You may describe a success or a failure. In either case, make sure to give a clear sense of the struggle involved. Your piece should be at least three paragraphs long. Use at least three lesson words in your essay and underline them.

WRITE THE DERIVATIVE

Complete the sentence by writing the correct form of the word shown in parentheses. You may not need to change the form that is given.

haggling   **1.** Mom seems to enjoy _____ over meat prices with the butcher. (_haggle_)

Belligerence   **2.** _____ is probably not a quality that will help you make friends. (_belligerent_)

embroiled   **3.** Governments can become _____ in hostile actions when peaceful diplomacy fails. (_embroil_)

ruses   **4.** Faced with a larger and stronger opponent, a smaller force may resort to clever _____ in order to achieve victory. (_ruse_)

skirmishes	5. After starting several _____ in the schoolyard, the girl was suspended. *(skirmish)*
chides or chided	6. Dad always _____ me for eating too fast. *(chide)*
contradiction	7. The phrase "tough love" may seem to be a _____ . *(contradictory)*
strife	8. Political _____ is best settled at the ballot box. *(strife)*
adversarial	9. I'm sorry you took a position that was _____ to mine. *(adversary)*
discordant	10. The _____ feelings within the group spoiled the atmosphere of the party. *(discord)*

FIND THE EXAMPLE

Choose the answer that best describes the action or situation.

__d__ 1. Something your mother might *chide* you for
   a. passing a test   **b.** cleaning up   **c.** winning a prize   **d.** not studying

__c__ 2. Usual goal of a *ruse*
   a. to argue   **b.** to learn   **c.** to deceive   **d.** to reward

__a__ 3. An example of *strife*
   a. a violent riot   **b.** a loud concert   **c.** a card game   **d.** a long parade

__d__ 4. Likely *adversaries*
   a. doctors and patients   **b.** lawyers and clients   **c.** teachers and students   **d.** police and thieves

__a__ 5. Something you might get *embroiled* in
   a. an argument   **b.** an oven   **c.** a microwave   **d.** a test

__b__ 6. A feeling most closely associated with *discord*
   a. hope   **b.** unhappiness   **c.** wonder   **d.** curiosity

__c__ 7. Something a *belligerent* person is most likely to do
   a. nourish   **b.** protect   **c.** attack   **d.** whisper

__d__ 8. Something one would *haggle* about
   a. a feeling   **b.** a cloud   **c.** a dream   **d.** a price

__d__ 9. Something most likely to cause a *skirmish*
   a. peace   **b.** good relations   **c.** good grades   **d.** threats

__a__ 10. Something *contradictory*
   a. opposite opinions   **b.** similar reasons   **c.** unrelated facts   **d.** consistent evidence

Cooperation and Groups

WORD LIST

accompany	accomplice	affiliate	assimilate	communal
complement	congregate	consensus	miscellaneous	throng

The words in this lesson will help you describe interaction in school, clubs, teams, and volunteer organizations. You will be able to talk about people who *complement* your abilities. Or you can describe what it's like to reach a group *consensus*.

1. **accompany** (ə-kŭm´pə-nē) *verb* from Old French *compaignon*, "companion"
   a. To provide vocal or instrumental support for another musical part
      • A saxophonist **accompanied** the blues singer.
   b. To go someplace with another, as a companion
      • My brother **accompanied** me to my soccer tryout.

   accompaniment *noun* The piano teacher provided **accompaniment** as the students auditioned for parts in the musical.

accompany

2. **accomplice** (ə-kŏm´plĭs) *noun* from Latin *complice*, "close associate"
   A person who helps another person carry out a crime
   • The bank robber's **accomplice** hid him in a basement.

3. **affiliate** Latin *ad-*, "to" + *filius*, "son"
   a. *verb* (ə-fĭl´ē-āt´) To join or associate with a larger or more powerful group
      • Members of our local volunteer medical group decided to **affiliate** with the American Red Cross.
   b. *noun* (ə-fĭl´ē-ĭt) Person or group joined with a larger, more powerful group
      • Our insurance agency was an **affiliate** of a larger company.

   affiliation *noun* The actor had an **affiliation** with the Guthrie Theater.

4. **assimilate** (ə-sĭm´ə-lāt´) *verb* from Latin *ad-*, "to" + *similis*, "similar"
   a. To adopt or take on the traditions of the larger or surrounding group
      • The immigrants wanted to **assimilate** while preserving their customs.
   b. To absorb into the larger culture or group
      • The United States has **assimilated** people from all over the world.

   assimilation *noun* The farmer was surprised to see the **assimilation** of two wild ducks into his flock of tame ducks.

Point out that four of these words contain the prefix *com-* (also spelled *con-*), which means "together." These are *communal, complement, congregate,* and *consensus.* Two other lesson words, *accompany* and *accomplice,* have *com* within them. Discuss with students how the meaning of each word is related to "togetherness."

5. **communal** (kə-myoo′nəl) *adjective* from Latin *communis*, "common"
Public; shared commonly by a group
• The campers ate in a **communal** dining hall.

commune *noun* Artists and musicians lived together in a **commune**.

6. **complement** (kŏm′plə-mənt) from Latin *complere*, "to fill out"
a. *noun* Something that harmonizes with or completes something else
• My organizational skills provided the perfect **complement** to my co-chair's ability to get people to volunteer for the project.
b. *verb* To harmonize with or complete something else
• The color of the walls **complements** the furniture perfectly.

complementary *adjective* The soft harp music was **complementary** to the performance of the traditional ballads.

> Be careful: A *compliment* (with an *i*) is praise, as in "My friends *complimented* my new haircut."

7. **congregate** (kŏng′grĭ-gāt′) *verb* from Latin *com-*, "together" + *gregare*, "to assemble"
To gather; to come together
• Community members **congregated** in the hall for a town meeting.

congregation *noun* A **congregation** of ants surrounded the spilled sugar.

> *Congregation* is often used to refer to the members of a religious group.

8. **consensus** (kən-sĕn′səs) *noun* from Latin *com-*, "together" + *sentire*, "to feel"
General agreement among a group of people
• Club members reached a **consensus**: we would work in a homeless shelter.

9. **miscellaneous** (mĭs′ə-lā′nē-əs) *adjective* from Latin *miscere*, "to mix"
Made up of a variety of unrelated items; difficult to categorize
• Juliet had one e-mail folder for work, one for school, and a **miscellaneous** one that included everything else.

miscellany *noun* A **miscellany** of items was sold at the flea market.

10. **throng** (thrông) from Middle English *gethrang*, "a throng"
a. *noun* A large crowd gathered densely together
• A **throng** of fans gathered to meet the hip-hop group.
b. *verb* To gather into a dense crowd
• Sparrows **throng** around the bird feeder each morning.

WORD ENRICHMENT

Breaking bread together

Many words in this lesson begin with or contain *con* or *com*, meaning "together." *Accompany* comes from *companion*. *Companion* comes from the Latin *com-*, "together," and *panis*, "bread." Just as in ancient Rome, friends today often eat with each other, and thus "break bread" together.

WRITE THE CORRECT WORD

Write the correct word in the space next to each definition.

___consensus___ **1.** a general agreement

___miscellaneous___ **2.** made up of a variety of unrelated items

___assimilate___ **3.** to absorb a culture

___complement___ **4.** something that completes

___affiliate___ **5.** to join a larger group

___congregate___ **6.** to gather together

___throng___ **7.** a large, dense crowd

___accomplice___ **8.** a person who helps commit a crime

___accompany___ **9.** to go with another

___communal___ **10.** shared by a group

COMPLETE THE SENTENCE

Write the letter for the word that best completes each sentence.

___a___ **1.** When he helped his friend, he had no idea he was becoming a(n) _____ to a crime.
   a. accomplice   **b.** consensus   **c.** throng   **d.** congregation

___d___ **2.** The red scarf was a nice _____ to the otherwise dull outfit.
   a. consensus   **b.** throng   **c.** congregation   **d.** complement

___b___ **3.** The _____ among the teachers was that the student deserved a second chance.
   a. affiliate   **b.** consensus   **c.** complement   **d.** commune

___c___ **4.** He emptied books, gloves, gum, and other _____ items from his backpack.
   a. congregational   **b.** assimilated   **c.** miscellaneous   **d.** communal

___c___ **5.** It wasn't easy for her parents to _____ when the culture was so different from their own.
   a. congregate   **b.** accompany   **c.** assimilate   **d.** affiliate

___d___ **6.** A(n) _____ of fans surrounded the author, who was graciously signing books.
   a. accomplice   **b.** consensus   **c.** complement   **d.** throng

___a___ **7.** A superb pianist _____ the singer for her final song.
   a. accompanied   **b.** affiliated   **c.** assimilated   **d.** congregated

___b___ **8.** The college students' dorm rooms were arranged around a(n) _____ lounge.
   a. thronged   **b.** communal   **c.** affiliated   **d.** miscellaneous

___d___ **9.** Our school's chapter of Key Club is _____ with the national organization.
   a. congregated   **b.** accompanied   **c.** thronged   **d.** affiliated

___a___ **10.** The students _____ in the hallway to talk between classes.
   a. congregated   **b.** accompanied   **c.** assimilated   **d.** complemented

Challenge: The agenda for the meeting included a large number of _____ items about which the committee needed to come to a _____ .
___c___   **a.** communal…throng   **b.** congregational…commune   **c.** miscellaneous…consensus

Treating the Wounds of War

The year was 1859. A Swiss citizen named Jean-Henri Dunant watched as French and Austrian soldiers battled. He was horrified by the human cost of warfare. When the fighting ended, thousands of wounded soldiers lay helpless in the hot sun. Shocked, Dunant organized efforts to bring medical attention to soldiers and put together a worldwide system to provide medical aid during warfare.

Dunant organized a group of neutral civilians to provide emergency medical aid. They were to help soldiers, regardless of which side the soldiers had fought on. Someone suggested that wearing white armbands with a red cross would make the medical workers easier to identify. The organization soon became known as the "Red Cross." **(1)** Today, the International Committee of the Red Cross (ICRC) has *affiliates* throughout the world.

Dunant also proposed international agreements on warfare. **(2)** In 1864, twelve countries reached a *consensus* when they signed the first Geneva Convention. This agreement guaranteed that hospitals, ambulances, and medical staff would be considered neutral and that all soldiers were entitled to medical treatment. **(3)** Members of the Red Cross believed that it was wrong to try to identify villains or determine which soldiers were *accomplices* of wrongdoers.

The organization extended its efforts to prisoners of war. Today, ICRC volunteers monitor conditions in

prisoner-of-war camps. Workers have helped thousands of families find missing soldiers. **(4)** They have delivered countless cards, letters, and packages of *miscellaneous* items to prisoners. The organization has even developed online courses to help train physicians to work in prison camps.

(5) The ICRC has also helped assure civilian safety by establishing refugee camps where people can *congregate* during times of war. **(6)** When towns and villages are in danger of attack, civilians *throng* to these camps. **(7)** Although they sometimes must live in tents and eat in *communal* dining areas, people are usually safer in these camps than in their homes. **(8)** The Red Cross also helps refugees return to their homes or *assimilate* into host countries.

The ICRC remains a worldwide volunteer organization. Though its workers often face dangers, including gunfire, minefields, and rocket attacks, they do not carry weapons. It is important that they are seen as neutral.

The ICRC has extended its services to helping in peacetime, too. **(9)** Red Cross physicians *accompany* local relief workers as they help people whose communities have been hit by floods, earthquakes, and other natural disasters. The organization also helps improve health and sanitation. In Mozambique, for example, the Red Cross Players combine comic theater with serious lessons about keeping water clean.

(10) Today, many organizations *complement* the ICRC's efforts in providing war and disaster relief. However, the ICRC remains the first and most important aid agency. Jean-Henri Dunant's horror at the bloodshed he witnessed so many years ago resulted in better treatment for countless victims of war and disaster.

Each sentence below refers to a numbered sentence in the passage. Write the letter of the choice that gives the sentence a meaning that is closest to the original sentence.

____d____ **1.** The International Committee of the Red Cross has _____ throughout the world.

    a. supervisors   **b.** victims   **c.** partners in crime   **d.** associates

____c____ **2.** Twelve countries reached a(n) _____ when they signed the first Geneva Convention.

    a. crisis   **b.** variety   **c.** agreement   **d.** gathering

____a____ **3.** Members of the Red Cross believed that it was wrong to try to determine which soldiers were _____ of wrongdoers.

    a. helpers   **b.** members   **c.** crowds   **d.** supervisors

___b___ **4.** They have delivered countless cards, letters, and packages of _____ items.
  a. gathered   **b.** unrelated   **c.** shared   **d.** identical

___a___ **5.** The ICRC established refugee camps where people can _____ during times
     of war.
  a. gather together   **b.** absorb   **c.** help others   **d.** fight

___b___ **6.** When towns and villages are in danger of attack, civilians _____ to these camps.
  a. run   **b.** crowd   **c.** assist   **d.** agree

___d___ **7.** Sometimes they must live in tents and eat in _____ dining areas.
  a. various   **b.** absorbed   **c.** isolated   **d.** shared

___b___ **8.** The Red Cross also helps refugees return to their homes or _____ into host
     countries.
  a. disappear   **b.** fit   **c.** gather   **d.** travel

___a___ **9.** Red Cross physicians _____ local relief workers.
  a. go with   **b.** crowd   **c.** watch over   **d.** inspect

___c___ **10.** Today, many organizations _____ the ICRC's efforts in providing war and
     disaster relief.
  a. threaten   **b.** gather around   **c.** make more complete   **d.** agree heartily with

Indicate whether the statements below are TRUE or FALSE according to the passage.

___F___ **1.** Switzerland and France were the only countries to sign the original
     Geneva Convention.

___F___ **2.** The ICRC arms its volunteers.

___T___ **3.** The ICRC helps improve health and sanitation.

FINISH THE THOUGHT

Complete each sentence so that it shows the meaning of the italicized word.

1. In order to *assimilate*, people must _____ Answers will vary. _____

_____

2. People often *congregate* to _____ Answers will vary. _____

_____

WRITE THE DERIVATIVE

**Complete the sentence by writing the correct form of the word shown in
parentheses. You may not need to change the form that is given.**

___congregated___ **1.** Everyone had _____ in the lobby. (*congregate*)

___throng___ **2.** People will _____ to the store during the big sale. (*throng*)

Lesson 6   37

affiliation **3.** He was happy about his small company's _____ with the larger organization. (*affiliate*)

commune **4.** The camp was just like a _____. (*communal*)

accomplices **5.** There were many _____ to the crime. (*accomplice*)

consensus **6.** The family reached a _____ about where to go on their annual vacation. (*consensus*)

accompaniment **7.** She provided the singers with _____ on her flute. (*accompany*)

Assimilation **8.** _____ can be difficult for immigrants. (*assimilate*)

complementary **9.** Exercising and healthy eating are _____ activities that help a person lose weight. (*complement*)

miscellany **10.** Donors contributed a _____ of items, including books, toys, food, and furniture. (*miscellaneous*)

FIND THE EXAMPLE

Choose the answer that best describes the action or situation.

a **1.** Something immigrants often must learn in order to *assimilate*
   a. language and customs   **b.** eye color and hair   **c.** territory and land   **d.** cartoons and fish

d **2.** A likely *accompaniment* for a choir
   a. a stage   **b.** sheet music   **c.** an encore   **d.** piano music

c **3.** Something in a school that is *communal*
   a. a report card   **b.** a backpack   **c.** the library   **d.** a locker

b **4.** The place you would most likely find a *throng* of fans
   a. grocery store   **b.** stadium   **c.** school   **d.** office building

c **5.** A place you would go to find *miscellaneous* foods
   a. candy shop   **b.** butcher   **c.** grocery store   **d.** bakery

a **6.** Something a student council is most likely *affiliated* with
   a. school   **b.** hospital   **c.** clothing store   **d.** NBA team

d **7.** Where a *consensus* is LEAST necessary
   a. club meeting   **b.** group project   **c.** family trip   **d.** diary entry

a **8.** A place football players are most likely to *congregate*
   a. on a field   **b.** at a store   **c.** at an airport   **d.** on a bridge

c **9.** Something an *accomplice* often does
   a. deposits money   **b.** uses the ATM   **c.** helps break the law   **d.** reports the crime

c **10.** A common *complement* to peanut butter
   a. chili peppers   **b.** coffee   **c.** jelly   **d.** nachos

Using the Dictionary

Etymologies, Biographical Entries, and Geographical Entries

The history of a word is called its *etymology*. Most dictionaries give etymologies within entries, enclosed in square brackets [ ]. They may be found at the beginning or end of entries, and they list the ancestors of a word, beginning with the most recent and ending with the oldest. If the meaning has changed over time, then the original meaning is given.

English words come from many languages; the most common are listed below with their dictionary abbreviations. However, words may come from other languages.

Here is an example:

con·ger (kŏng´gər) *n.* Any of various large scaleless marine eels of the family Congridae, esp. *Conger oceanicus*, native to Atlantic waters. [ME *conger* < OFr., prob. < LLat. *congrus* < Lat. *conger* < Gk. *gongros*.]

The etymology occurs at the end of the entry. It tells you that *conger* can be traced back to ancient Greek. From there it went to Latin, to Late Latin, probably to Old French, to Middle English, and finally to modern English. Notice that the oldest language is listed last. Because no other meanings are listed, you know that the meaning of the word hasn't changed.

Abbreviation	Language
Gk.	Greek
Lat.	Latin
Med. Lat.	Medieval Latin
OE	Old English
ME	Middle English
OFr.	Old French
Fr.	French
Sp.	Spanish

Variations of these also include adding O (for Old) and L (for Late).

Practice Etymologies

Answer the questions below using the dictionary etymologies given. List the full name of languages; do not use abbreviations.

Word	Etymology
hippopotamus	[Lat. < Gk. *hippopotamos*: *hippos*, horse + *potamos*, river.]
sun	[ME < OE *sunne*.]
maize	[Sp. *maiz* < Arawakan *mahiz, mahis*.]
implore	[Lat. *implorare*: *in-*, toward, + *plorare*, to weep.]
dolor	[ME *dolour* < OFr. < Lat. *dolor*, pain < *dolere*, to suffer, feel pain.]

1. In which language did *sun* originate?

Old English

2. Which Latin prefix became part of *implore?*

in-

3. What did the original root words of *hippopotamus* mean?

horse and river

4. Which language did the word *maize* originate in?

Arawakan

5. From which language did Middle English get *dolor?*

Old French

Biographical and Geographical Entries

Biographical entries give information about people of achievement. They give the years of the person's birth and death, as well as facts about his or her historical importance. This entry below tells you that Frank Lloyd Wright lived from 1869–1959 and that he was an American architect. Note that his last name is listed first in the entry.

Wright, Frank Lloyd 1869–1959. Amer. architect whose distinctive style was based on natural forms.

Geographical entries give information about important places:

Par•is (Păr´ĭs) The cap. of France, in the N-central part on the Seine R.; founded as a fishing village on the Ile de la Cité by Hugh Capet in 987. Pop. 2,149,900. –**Pa•ris´ian** (Pə-rē´zhən, -rĭz´ē-ən) *adj. & n.*

This entry is more complex. It gives a derivative for *Paris,* which is *Parisian.* The syllabication and pronunciation of Paris and Parisian also appear. Several abbreviations are used, such as *cap.* (capital), *R* (river), *Pop.* (population). It lists the country containing this city and the fact that it is a capital. It also lists the location, founding date and founder, and population.

Practice Biographical and Geographical Entries

Answer the questions below using the following biographical and geographical entries. Do not use abbreviations in your answers.

Roosevelt, Franklin Delano 1882–1945. The 32nd President of the US (1933–45) whose administration was marked by measures to increase employment and assist recovery from the Depression and by US participation in World War II.

Kelly, Grace Patricia. Princess Grace 1929–82. Amer. actress who appeared in motion pictures such as *Country Girl* (1954) and married Prince Rainier III of Monaco (1956).

O•hi•o (ō-hī´ō) A state of the N-central US in the Great Lakes region; admitted as the 17th state in 1803. Cap. Columbus. Pop. 11,353,140. — **O•hi•o•an** *adj. & n.*

Victoria 1. The cap. of British Columbia, Canada, on SE Vancouver I. at the E end of the Strait of Juan de Fuca; founded in 1843 as a Hudson's Bay Company outpost. Pop. 73,504. **2.** The cap. of Hong Kong, on the NW coast of Hong Kong I. Pop. 1,183,621. **3.** The cap. of Seychelles, on the NE coast of Mahé I. on the Indian Ocean. Pop. 23,000

1. What year was Franklin Delano Roosevelt born?

1882

2. Where in the United States is Ohio located?

North Central region

3. What professional activity did Grace Kelly pursue?

acting; she was an actress

4. How many cities are listed for Victoria?

three

5. Is Victoria the capital of the province of British Columbia?

yes

Maturity and Immaturity

WORD LIST

antiquated	centenarian	fledgling	frail	geriatrics
infantile	longevity	nascent	puerile	venerable

Each of us is surrounded by people of all ages, from infants to senior citizens. The words in this lesson apply to both youth and old age. Some words refer directly to people. Others describe age-related characteristics of people or things.

1. **antiquated** (ăn′tĭ-kwā′tĭd) *adjective* from Latin *antiquus,* "old"
   Too old to be useful or suitable
   • She kept the **antiquated** oven for decoration, but she never tried to cook in it because it was too much trouble to build a fire.

   antique *noun* The chair was an **antique** from the 1700s.

2. **centenarian** (sĕn′tə-nâr′ē-ən) *noun* from Latin *cent-,* "hundred"
   A person who is one hundred years old or older
   • The number of **centenarians** in the United States continues to increase.

3. **fledgling** (flĕj′lĭng)
   a. *adjective* Inexperienced; untried
   • The **fledgling** reporter was eager to receive her first assignment.
   b. *noun* An inexperienced person
   • Fresh from training, the soldier was a **fledgling** in need of guidance.
   c. *noun* A bird that has just grown the feathers needed to fly
   • The mother bird encouraged the **fledgling** to leave the nest.

4. **frail** (frāl) *adjective* from Latin *frangere,* "to break"
   Weak or delicate
   • Although he was **frail,** the senior citizen worked long hours on the political campaign.

   frailty *noun* The **frailty** of Tamara's injured knee kept her from playing high-school softball.

5. **geriatrics** (jĕr′ē-ăt′rĭks) *noun* from Greek *geras,* "old age"
   The medical study of the elderly and their diseases
   • The doctor specializes in **geriatrics** and particularly likes to help people with Alzheimer's, a disease that afflicted his grandmother.

   geriatric *adjective* **Geriatric** studies have shown that exercise is important to the health of senior citizens.

antiquated

Have students classify lesson words into those that refer to maturity and those that refer to immaturity.

Although *geriatrics* ends with an *s,* it is singular and should be paired with a singular verb form.

6. **infantile** (ĭn´fən-tīl´) *adjective* from Latin *infans*, "not able to speak"
   a. Having to do with an infant or with that stage of life
      • Dr. Kearney was an expert in **infantile** diseases.
   b. As immature as an infant
      • Don't you think that screaming fits are rather **infantile** behavior for a twelve-year-old?

7. **longevity** (lŏn-jĕv´ĭ-tē) *noun* from Latin *longus*, "long" + *aevum*, "age"
   Long life or a long time spent at a job or an activity
   • Better medical care is increasing the **longevity** of many Americans.

8. **nascent** (năs´ənt, nās´ənt) *adjective* from Latin *nasci*, "to be born"
   Just coming into existence; emerging
   • The student's **nascent** interest in ecology grew when he joined the park's conservation committee.

9. **puerile** (pyoŏr´əl, pyoŏr´īl) *adjective* from Latin *puer*, "boy, child"
   Childish; immature
   • After her brother was born, Sara exhibited **puerile** behavior for several weeks.

   puerility *noun* Although some adults object to the **puerility** of cartoons, others find them amusing.

10. **venerable** (vĕn´ər-ə-bəl) *adjective* from Latin *vener-*, "love, desire"
    Worthy of great respect because of age or dignity
    • The **venerable** great-grandfather was always consulted about family problems.

    venerate *verb* Many people **venerate** the memory of Mother Theresa, who worked with the poor and the sick in India.

    veneration *noun* The Basilica of Our Lady of Guadalupe shows the **veneration** that the Mexican people have for this important figure.

> Don't confuse *venerable* with *vulnerable*, which means "open to danger or attack; unprotected."

WORD ENRICHMENT

Love and respect

A *venerable* person is worthy of great respect. And when we *venerate* something, we regard it with reverence. These positive feelings may be thought of as something similar to love. So it is not surprising that the Roman name for the goddess of love and beauty was *Venus*.

WRITE THE CORRECT WORD

Write the correct word in the space next to each definition.

___nascent___   **1.** just coming into existence

___frail___   **2.** weak or delicate

___antiquated___   **3.** too old to be useful

___infantile___   **4.** having to do with infants

___geriatrics___   **5.** medical study of the elderly

___fledgling___   **6.** inexperienced; untested

___longevity___   **7.** long length of time

___puerile___   **8.** childish; immature

___venerable___   **9.** worthy of respect due to age or dignity

___centenarian___   **10.** someone at least one hundred years old

COMPLETE THE SENTENCE

Write the letter for the word that best completes each sentence.

___c___   **1.** She stormed off, saying she was too old to play their _____ game of tag.
   a. centenarian   **b.** nascent   **c.** infantile   **d.** venerable

___c___   **2.** The _____ blew out all one hundred candles on his birthday cake.
   a. fledgling   **b.** geriatrics   **c.** centenarian   **d.** veneration

___b___   **3.** The _____ group was formed yesterday; they haven't even chosen a name yet.
   a. frail   **b.** nascent   **c.** puerile   **d.** antiquated

___d___   **4.** Colin's relationship with his sick grandfather made him decide to study _____.
   a. antiques   **b.** fledglings   **c.** puerility   **d.** geriatrics

___a___   **5.** Mara was disappointed with the disposable batteries' lack of _____.
   a. longevity   **b.** antique   **c.** centenarian   **d.** fledgling

___d___   **6.** After surviving a life-threatening illness, my aunt was _____ for many months.
   a. venerable   **b.** geriatric   **c.** nascent   **d.** frail

___b___   **7.** The upperclassmen were each paired with a(n) _____ student on the first day.
   a. venerable   **b.** fledgling   **c.** antiquated   **d.** geriatric

___a___   **8.** My grandfather won't use the cell phone we gave him; he loves slowly dialing each number on his _____ rotary phone.
   a. antiquated   **b.** fledgling   **c.** geriatric   **d.** nascent

___c___   **9.** The athletes showed the coach great _____; she was well known for her successes.
   a. nascence   **b.** centenary   **c.** veneration   **d.** puerility

___b___   **10.** Armand rolled his eyes at his little sister's _____ behavior when she made a volcano out of her mashed potatoes and gravy.
   a. antiquated   **b.** puerile   **c.** nascent   **d.** frail

Challenge: The _____ that fell from the nest was _____ and sickly.

___a___   **a.** fledgling...frail   **b.** antique...puerile   **c.** geriatrics...venerable

Helpers—Young and Old

It's never too late, or too early, to help others. Every day, people of all ages provide food, shelter, advice, and inspiration to their fellow human beings. Here are just a few of the heroes who have quietly devoted their lives to helping others:

Many years ago, Osceola McCarty had to drop out of school to help her elderly aunt. **(1)** At that time, a *nascent* dream began to take shape within her: She wanted to help others achieve the education that she had missed. Earning her living by washing other people's clothes, she managed to save money. Her dream remained her constant companion. **(2)** In 1995, at the *venerable* age of eighty-seven, McCarty donated her $150,000 life savings to the University of Southern Mississippi. It was the largest gift the university had ever received!

Matel "Mat" Dawson moved to Detroit as a teenager. He soon began working for the Ford Motor Company. **(3)** He stayed there for more than sixty years, almost the company record for *longevity*. **(4)** Dawson drove an *antiquated* car, lived in a one-bedroom apartment, and worked all the overtime hours he could get. Much of the money he earned he gave to charity. By the time he passed away in 2002, Dawson had donated more than a million dollars to organizations such as the United Negro College Fund, Louisiana State University, and Wayne State University.

(5) At the age of eighty-nine, with a back brace and a history of emphysema, Doris Haddock could have been admitted to a *geriatric* institution. Instead, she chose to walk across the United States to demonstrate her support for campaign-finance reform. **(6)** She may have looked *frail,* but she kept up a brisk pace. **(7)** No less amazing is the Chicago *centenarian* who worked in a food pantry, bringing nutritious meals to the less fortunate.

This type of unselfishness is not limited to the elderly. **(8)** Children around the world have shown that, although they are young, their concerns need not be *puerile.* Some, like Brandon Keefe, collect books for others. When he was eight years old, Brandon's teacher asked students to come up with a community service idea. **(9)** In his *fledgling* effort, Brandon collected 847 books to start a library for the Hollygrove Home for children. For his next project, he collected over 5,000 books.

At other times, children work for political and social reform. From the age of four, Iqbal Masih worked at a carpet factory. Rescued and allowed to attend school, he never forgot his terrible childhood. He now gives speeches throughout the world to promote an end to child labor.

Like selfishness, the will to be charitable and helpful is found in people of all ages. **(10)** Of course, there are plenty of people who spend their lives focused on *infantile,* selfish concerns. Fortunately, for all of us, there are also remarkable people who find their greatest pleasure in helping others.

Each sentence below refers to a numbered sentence in the passage. Write the letter of the choice that gives the sentence a meaning that is closest to the original sentence.

___b___ **1.** A(n) _____ dream began to take shape within her.
  a. weak   **b.** emerging   **c.** age-old   **d.** recurring

___a___ **2.** At the _____ age of eighty-seven, McCarty donated her $150,000 life savings to the University of Southern Mississippi.
  a. respectable   **b.** embarrassing   **c.** immature   **d.** unsuitable

___a___ **3.** He stayed there for more than sixty years, almost the company record for _____.
  a. length of time   **b.** tardiness   **c.** excellence   **d.** old-age fitness

___c___ **4.** Dawson drove a(n) _____ car.
  a. always working   **b.** broken-down   **c.** out-of-date   **d.** bad-looking

___d___ **5.** Doris Haddock could have been admitted to a(n) _____ institution.
    a. infant   **b.** unusual   **c.** hundred-year-old   **d.** old-age

___b___ **6.** She may have looked _____, but she kept up a brisk pace.
    a. strong   **b.** weak   **c.** childish   **d.** old

___c___ **7.** No less amazing is the Chicago _____ who worked in a food pantry.
    a. four-year-old   **b.** grandmother   **c.** hundred-year-old   **d.** newcomer

___d___ **8.** Children around the world show that their concerns need not be _____.
    a. long-lived   **b.** ignored   **c.** forgotten   **d.** childish

___a___ **9.** In his _____ effort, Brandon collected 847 books.
    a. first   **b.** weak   **c.** experienced   **d.** lengthy

___b___ **10.** Of course, there are plenty of people who spend their lives focused on _____,
selfish concerns.
    a. unsuitable   **b.** immature   **c.** old   **d.** untried

Indicate whether the statements below are TRUE or FALSE according to the passage.

___T___ **1.** Osceola McCarty valued education.

___F___ **2.** Doris Haddock is in excellent health.

___F___ **3.** Brandon Keefe collected over 5,000 books on his first effort.

WRITING EXTENDED RESPONSES

The passage you have read describes the charitable activities of a few people. Choose one person who, in your opinion, makes a positive difference in his or her community. If possible, choose a person who is either older than sixty or younger than twelve. In a descriptive essay, present the activities of this person in a way that will convince the reader that the person makes a positive difference. Your essay should be at least three paragraphs long and should give detailed examples of this person's activities. Use at least three lesson words in your essay and underline them.

WRITE THE DERIVATIVE

Complete the sentence by writing the correct form of the word shown in parentheses. You may not need to change the form that is given.

__longevity__ **1.** With three grandparents who lived to their nineties, Cheryl hoped that _____ is genetic. *(longevity)*

__venerated__ **2.** The students _____ the dedicated teacher. *(venerable)* centenarians

3. When we called my great-aunt on her birthday, she announced that she was going on a special cruise for _____. (*centenarian*)

fledglings

4. Backstage, the _____ were easy to spot; they paced nervously and looked terrified when their curtain call was announced. (*fledgling*)

infantile

5. Not all crying is _____. (*infantile*)

puerility

6. The teenager's _____ infuriated his parents. (*puerile*)

geriatric

7. Arthritis is generally considered a _____ disease. (*geriatrics*)

frailty

8. Everyone in our family was aware of my great-grandfather's _____. (*frail*)

antiques

9. My mother likes to collect _____. (*antiquated*)

nascent

10. His _____ interest in the theater began when he attended the play. (*nascent*)

FIND THE EXAMPLE

Choose the answer that best describes the action or situation.

a   1. Something that generally has great *longevity*
   a. can of soup   **b.** flies   **c.** flowers   **d.** chocolate milk

b   2. Something you should NOT do if you have a *frail* dog
   a. bring it to the vet   **b.** let it chase cars   **c.** help it up the stairs   **d.** walk it slowly

a   3. Something that is *infantile*
   a. a security blanket   **b.** a gold necklace   **c.** a tie   **d.** a car

c   4. An *antiquated* weapon
   a. a rocket   **b.** a gun   **c.** a spear   **d.** a tank

b   5. A good thing to ask a *venerable* person for
   a. help moving   **b.** advice   **c.** a loan   **d.** a haircut

d   6. The most likely place to find *geriatrics* being practiced
   a. zoo   **b.** kindergarten class   **c.** coffee shop   **d.** hospital

a   7. An example of *puerile* behavior
   a. throwing a fit **b.** sharing toys   **c.** listening to others   **d.** taking turns

c   8. A place where you would probably NOT find a *fledgling* athlete playing
   a. school field   **b.** playground   **c.** large stadium   **d.** backyard

a   9. A place where you would be LEAST likely to find a *centenarian*
   a. preschool   **b.** grocery store   **c.** doctor's office   **d.** restaurant

d   10. Something a *nascent* sports team would be LEAST likely to have
   a. hope   **b.** players   **c.** hard-working coach   **d.** championship trophy

Maturity and Immaturity

Kindness

WORD LIST

altruism	amicable	benefactor	benign	bountiful
civility	exemplary	humanitarian	indulge	rectify

Acts of kindness can be as small as thinking about other people's feelings, or as large as dedicating a lifetime to eliminating world hunger. Each act, large or small, is important. The words in this lesson describe the varied ways in which people show care and concern.

1. **altruism** (ăl´trŏŏ-ĭz´əm) *noun* from Latin *alter*, "other"
   Unselfish concern and actions for the welfare of others
   • Andrew Carnegie's **altruism** inspired him to finance libraries across the United States.

   altruistic *adjective* The **altruistic** teacher donated his time to tutor students after class.

2. **amicable** (ăm´ĭ-kə-bəl) *adjective* from Latin *amicus*, "friend"
   Friendly; showing goodwill
   • The teacher had an **amicable** meeting with his student's parents.

   amicability *noun* Known for her **amicability,** the town's mayor always stopped to chat with people.

3. **benefactor** (běn´ə-făk´tər) *noun* from Latin *bene*, "good" + *facere*, "to do"
   A person who gives financial or other aid
   • Jamie received a scholarship from an unknown **benefactor.**

4. **benign** (bĭ-nīn´) *adjective* from Latin *benignus*, "kind"
   a. Kind and gentle
      • Magda's **benign** manner makes her a good kindergarten teacher.
   b. Harmless; not dangerous to health
      • The mole on my arm was **benign** and did not need to be removed.

5. **bountiful** (boun´tə-fəl) *adjective* from Latin *bonitas*, "goodness"
   Abundant; plentiful
   • As people learned that the family's house had burned down, **bountiful** donations of food and other necessities began to pour in.

   bounty *noun* The harvest resulted in a **bounty** of apples, grain, and root vegetables.

6. **civility** (sĭ-vĭl´ĭ-tē) *noun* from Latin *civus*, "citizen"
   Courteous behavior; politeness
   • The committee members treated each other with **civility,** even though they represented opposing interests.

   civil *adjective* "Keep a **civil** tongue," the teacher warned the rude student.

When forming derivatives of *altruistic* and *amicable*, the accented syllable changes. Discuss these changes and have students pronounce each entry word and its derivatives.

amicable

7. **exemplary** (ĭg-zĕm´plə-rē) *adjective* from Middle English *exemplum,* "example"
Worthy of imitation; admirable
   - The great baseball player Lou Gehrig faced his terrible illness with **exemplary** courage.

> Someone whose behavior is *exemplary* sets a good *example* for others.

8. **humanitarian** (hyōō-măn´-ĭ-târ´ē-ən) from Latin *humanus,* "human"
   a. *noun* A person concerned with social reforms and improving human welfare
      - One reason former president Jimmy Carter is considered a great **humanitarian** is his work with Habitat for Humanity.
   b. *adjective* Intended to help humans
      - She reported the crimes against the refugees to a **humanitarian** group.

   humanitarianism *noun* During the American Civil War, Clara Barton demonstrated her **humanitarianism** by working with dying soldiers.

9. **indulge** (ĭn-dŭlj´) *verb* from Latin *indulgere,* "to give way to"
To yield to desires or wishes
   - Cora **indulges** in a nap every afternoon at one o'clock.

   indulgence *noun* Po-Yee considered her husband's antique cars to be an expensive **indulgence.**

   indulgent *adjective* Louis was **indulgent** of his friend's need to be alone, recognizing that he needed time to recover from his trauma.

> *Indulge* is used with reflexives (I *indulge* **myself** by shopping) and with the preposition *in* (I *indulge* **in** bubble baths).

10. **rectify** (rĕk´tə-fī´) *verb* from Latin *rectus,* "right"
To fix or correct; to set right

   - Lydia hoped to **rectify** the town's lack of good facilities for children by organizing a committee to build a playground.

indulge

WORD ENRICHMENT

Civility and citizens

The word *civility* is taken from the Latin word *civitas,* which means "a state that is formed from *citizens.*" The word *city* also comes from this root. The concept of a *citizen* dates back to the city-states of Greece, such as Athens and Sparta. A *citizen* of these cities was entitled to *civic* rights. But each *citizen* was expected to act with *civility,* or good citizenship. In time, the meaning of *civility* came to be associated with politeness. We also get the words *civilization* and *civilized* from this root.

WRITE THE CORRECT WORD

Write the correct word in the space next to each definition.

_____indulge_____ **1.** to give in to wishes

_____benefactor_____ **2.** a person who gives aid

_____rectify_____ **3.** to set right

_____amicable_____ **4.** friendly

_____benign_____ **5.** kind and gentle

_____humanitarian_____ **6.** one who improves human welfare

_____altruism_____ **7.** unselfish concern for others

_____civility_____ **8.** politeness

_____exemplary_____ **9.** worthy of imitation

_____bountiful_____ **10.** abundant

COMPLETE THE SENTENCE

Write the letter for the word that best completes each sentence.

___a___ **1.** Thankfully, the tumor was ———.
a. benign   **b.** altruistic   **c.** bountiful   **d.** exemplary

___d___ **2.** After a long day at work, Celina ——— herself in a nice, hot bath.
a. exemplified   **b.** civilized   **c.** rectified   **d.** indulged

___b___ **3.** The workers brought ——— aid to flood victims.
a. civil   **b.** humanitarian   **c.** indulgent   **d.** rectified

___c___ **4.** Even though the runners were on different track teams, they exchanged ——— handshakes before the race.
a. humanitarian   **b.** bountiful   **c.** amicable   **d.** altruistic

___d___ **5.** The teacher ——— the problem by allowing Gwen to retake the test.
a. civilized   **b.** exemplified   **c.** indulged   **d.** rectified

___a___ **6.** The teacher read a(n) ——— essay so that the students would have a good model.
a. exemplary   **b.** amicable   **c.** bountiful   **d.** indulgent

___c___ **7.** In the spirit of ———, Malcolm volunteered his time at the soup kitchen, even though it meant that he couldn't go to the movie with his friends.
a. bounty   **b.** indulgence   **c.** altruism   **d.** benefactor

___a___ **8.** The contributions were so ——— that there was more than enough money to build the new community center.
a. bountiful   **b.** benign   **c.** amicable   **d.** civilized

___b___ **9.** The new football field had been funded by a wealthy local ———.
a. amicability   **b.** benefactor   **c.** civility   **d.** indulgence

___c___ **10.** The host treated the honored guest with great ———.
a. humanitarianism   **b.** bounty   **c.** civility   **d.** altruism

Challenge: Bethany ——— in the ——— buffet at her friend's party.

___b___   **a.** rectified…altruistic   **b.** indulged…bountiful   **c.** exemplified…benign

A Dinner Guest

Kindness is an endless chain. **(1)** This story, which spans two world wars, shows how one act of *altruism* can bring about another.

In 1917, near the end of World War I, a lonely American soldier named Alex Lurye walked into a synagogue in a small German town. Although Germany and the United States were enemies, the soldier meant no harm. Alex was a Jewish person who simply wanted to attend a service in the local synagogue.

(2) Sensing that Alex's intentions were *benign*, a local man welcomed him. His name was Herr Rosenau. **(3)** After the service, Herr Rosenau invited Alex to enjoy a *bountiful* home-cooked dinner. **(4)** The homesick soldier *indulged* in the most delicious food he had tasted in months. When he returned to the United States, Alex wrote a thank-you note to his German host.

Although Herr Rosenau never answered the letter, he did save it. For twenty-one years, it sat in a drawer in his home. During that time, many things in Europe changed. Germany's aggression toward neighboring countries strained diplomatic relations, and Europe was again on the verge of war. Even worse, Adolph Hitler had come to power and was staging attacks against Jews within Germany itself. Herr Rosenau feared for the lives of his family.

In 1938, while rummaging through one of his grandfather's drawers, Herr Rosenau's grandson noticed a letter with a foreign stamp. He asked if he could take it home and show it to his parents. The boy's mother, Herr Rosenau's daughter, opened the envelope and read Alex's thank-you letter from long ago.

Remembering the young American soldier, Rosenau's daughter had an idea. The family desperately wanted to leave Germany, but unless they had a sponsor, they could not enter the United States. **(5)** She decided to write to Alex and appeal to his *humanitarian* instincts. She asked him to help her family. She did not know his address, so she sent her request addressed simply, "Alex Lurye, Duluth, Minnesota."

Fortunately, Alex Lurye had become a well-known businessman and the post office was able to find him easily. **(6)** He read the letter from the family who had helped him so long ago and responded with *exemplary* kindness. **(7)** He stated that he would be happy to be their *benefactor* and offered to sponsor them. **(8)** Within the year, the family's problem was *rectified* when they all arrived safely in the United States.

Despite initial hardships, the newcomers prospered. Had the Rosenau's stayed in Germany, they may have been one of the millions of families that were killed in the Holocaust. **(9)** Acts of kindness vary from simple *civility* to great gifts. When we perform them, we never know what they will bring in return. **(10)** In this case, an *amicable* dinner invitation saved a family's lives.

Each sentence below refers to a numbered sentence in the passage. Write the letter of the choice that gives the sentence a meaning that is closest to the original sentence.

___d___ **1.** This story, which spans two world wars, shows how one act of _____ can bring about another.

    a. anger   **b.** financial aid   **c.** politeness   **d.** unselfish concern

___b___ **2.** Sensing that Alex's intentions were _____, a local man welcomed him.

    a. plentiful   **b.** harmless   **c.** prosperous   **d.** lifesaving

___a___ **3.** Herr Rosenau invited Alex to enjoy a(n) _____ home-cooked dinner.

    a. abundant   **b.** hot   **c.** delicious   **d.** friendly

___c___ **4.** The homesick soldier _____ the most delicious food he had tasted in months.

    a. wanted to share   **b.** quickly ate   **c.** treated himself to   **d.** hoped to have

_c_ **5.** She decided to write to Alex and appeal to his _____ instincts.
    a. plentiful   **b.** gentle   **c.** helpful   **d.** favorite

_d_ **6.** He responded with _____ kindness.
    a. helpful   **b.** concerned   **c.** unselfish   **d.** admirable

_a_ **7.** He stated that he would be happy to be their _____.
    a. aid-giver   **b.** friend   **c.** partner   **d.** example

_b_ **8.** The family's problem was _____ when they all arrived in the United States.
    a. worsened   **b.** fixed   **c.** pampered   **d.** forgotten

_b_ **9.** Acts of kindness vary from simple _____ to great gifts.
    a. admiration   **b.** politeness   **c.** donation   **d.** wishes

_d_ **10.** In this case, a _____ dinner invitation saved a family's lives.
    a. plentiful   **b.** worthy   **c.** wealthy   **d.** friendly

Indicate whether the statements below are TRUE or FALSE according to the passage.

_F_ **1.** Alex Lurye had never been to Germany when he received the letter from the Rosenau family.

_T_ **2.** Alex Luyre's letter was found by Herr Rosenau's grandson.

_T_ **3.** The Rosenau's might have been killed if Alex Luyre had not helped them.

FINISH THE THOUGHT

Complete each sentence so that is shows the meaning of the italicized word.

1. A *bountiful* meal might consist of _____ Answers will vary.

_____

2. An example of *altruism* would be _____ Answers will vary.

_____

WRITE THE DERIVATIVE

Complete the sentence by writing the correct form of the word shown in parentheses. You may not need to change the form that is given.

benign **1.** Their new stepmother was so _____ that the children loved her instantly. (*benign*)

amicably **2.** The two competitors _____ agreed on the rules of the contest. (*amicable*)

bounty **3.** They gave thanks for the _____ that they had received. (*bountiful*)

benefactor **4.** The _____ preferred not to make his name known. (*benefactor*)

rectified	**5.** He _____ the problem by apologizing and trying again. _(rectify)_
indulgence	**6.** Ice cream is Jonah's greatest _____. _(indulge)_
civil	**7.** Screaming and shouting is not _____ behavior. _(civility)_
humanitarianism	**8.** Albert Schweitzer was known for his great _____. _(humanitarian)_
exemplary	**9.** The children's behavior at the assembly was _____. _(exemplary)_
altruistic	**10.** It is important to promote an _____ society. _(altruism)_

FIND THE EXAMPLE

Choose the answer that best describes the action or situation.

_c_ **1.** What an _exemplary_ student does after school
   a. sleeps   **b.** plays video games   **c.** does homework   **d.** watches television

_d_ **2.** Something you might _indulge_ in on a hot day
   a. warm blanket   **b.** soup   **c.** hot chocolate   **d.** lemonade

_d_ **3.** Something that demonstrates _civility_
   a. cutting in line   **b.** asking for change   **c.** ignoring a friend   **d.** saying please

_c_ **4.** A demonstration of _amicability_
   a. frowning   **b.** running fast   **c.** shaking hands   **d.** sneezing

_b_ **5.** Something that could use a _benefactor_
   a. sports car   **b.** rundown park   **c.** wealthy man   **d.** new book

_a_ **6.** A place you would most likely find a _humanitarian_
   a. crisis center   **b.** zoo   **c.** car dealership   **d.** circus

_d_ **7.** An _altruistic_ act
   a. get a manicure   **b.** buy new clothes   **c.** write a story   **d.** feed the hungry

_a_ **8.** Something you might do to _rectify_ poor grades
   a. study harder   **b.** play a sport   **c.** go shopping   **d.** go out with friends

_c_ **9.** An animal that is thought to be _benign_
   a. lion   **b.** tiger   **c.** sheep   **d.** crocodile

_b_ **10.** A place to find a _bounty_ of fruit
   a. garage   **b.** farm stand   **c.** pharmacy   **d.** dry cleaner

Time and Sequence

WORD LIST

belated	conception	duration	expire	incessantly
medieval	renaissance	respite	simultaneous	subsequently

Have you ever heard the expression "time is money"? We use time to measure everything from historical periods to productivity in the workplace to promptness for a party. The words in this lesson describe various aspects of time.

1. belated (bĭ-lā´tĭd) *adjective* from Old English *late*
Done or sent too late
- On June 14, Lorraine sent a **belated** card to a friend who had celebrated her birthday on June 12.

belated

2. conception (kən-sĕp´shən) *noun* from Latin *concipere*, "to conceive; to start"
a. A beginning or formation of an idea
- From its **conception,** the car design seemed destined for success.
b. A general idea or understanding
- Manuel had only a vague **conception** of how to solve the problem.

3. duration (dōō-rā´shən) *noun* from Latin *durare*, "to last"
The period or length of time during which something exists or persists
- The **duration** of an average movie is about two hours.

4. expire (ĭk-spīr´) *verb* from Latin *ex-*, "out" + *spirare*, "to breathe"
a. To come to an end; to die
- Harold was anxious to renew his magazine subscription before it **expired.**
b. To breathe out; to exhale
- Susan took deep breaths and **expired** as the doctor checked her lungs.

expiration *noun* George checked the **expiration** date on the milk carton.

5. incessantly (ĭn-sĕs´ənt-lē) *adverb* from Latin *in-*, "not" + *cessare*, "to stop"
Constantly; continually, without interruption
- Mark's little sister questioned him **incessantly** throughout the movie.

incessant *adjective* The **incessant** rain continued for seven days.

6. medieval (mĕd´ē´vəl) *adjective* from Latin *medius*, "middle" + *aevum*, "age"
Referring to the Middle Ages, the period in European history from about 475 to 1450
- Numerous castles were built during **medieval** times.

Point out that two of these words, *medieval* and *renaissance*, refer to historical periods. Historically, the period of *antiquity* comes before the *medieval* period.

The word *medieval* is also used informally to mean "old-fashioned or lacking insight."

7. **renaissance** (rĕn´ĭ-säns´) *noun* from Latin *re-*, "again" + *nasci,*
   "to be born"
   a. **Renaissance** The historical European period from about 1400 to
      1600, during which classical art, literature, architecture, and learning
      were revived in Europe
      • The **Renaissance** produced great artists and thinkers such as
        Leonardo da Vinci and Michelangelo.
   b. **renaissance** A rebirth or revival
      • Fashion trends often undergo a **renaissance,** when styles from
        previous decades become fashionable once again.

8. **respite** (rĕs´pĭt) *noun* from Latin *respectus,* "a refuge"
   A short time of rest or relief; a break
   • The half-hour break provided a welcome **respite** from studying.

9. **simultaneous** (sī´məl-tā´nē-əs) *adjective* from Latin *simul,*
   "at the same time"
   Happening, existing, or done at the same time
   • The rebels launched **simultaneous** attacks on two major cities.

   simultaneously *adverb* The race was a tie because the bicyclists
   crossed the finish line **simultaneously.**

10. **subsequently** (sŭb´sĭ-kwĕnt´-lē) *adverb* from Latin *subsequi,*
    "to follow close after"
    Later on; at a later time
    • Singer Diana Ross started with the group The Supremes and
      subsequently performed as a solo act.

    subsequent *adjective* Heavy rains and **subsequent** floods caused a
    great deal of damage to the town.

WORD ENRICHMENT

Historical eras

History is often divided into major historical eras. The era of the
ancient Egyptians, Babylonians, Greeks, and Roman Empire is called
antiquity. This period ends with the fall of Rome to the "barbarians"
(or Germanic tribes) in 476.

In 476, the capital of the Roman Empire moved to Constantinople
(present-day Istanbul), and the Middle Ages, or *medieval* age, began. This
lasted until Constantinople was conquered in 1453.

Then, the *Renaissance* began. This era takes its name from the "rebirth"
of interest in scientific learning and classical (ancient Greek and Roman)
heritage. The Renaissance lasted until about 1600.

These eras are associated with common modern words. Something
antique is old. In informal use, *medieval* means old-fashioned and
backward. Finally, a *renaissance* is a rebirth or revival.

WRITE THE CORRECT WORD

Write the correct word in the space next to each definition.

incessantly	1. constantly
subsequently	2. later on
expire	3. to come to an end; to die
respite	4. a short period of rest
renaissance	5. a rebirth or revival

belated	6. too late
simultaneous	7. done at the same time
conception	8. a general idea
duration	9. the length of time that something exists
medieval	10. referring to the Middle Ages

COMPLETE THE SENTENCE

Write the letter for the word that best completes each sentence.

c   1. Mara's _____ requests to use the computer annoyed her dad, who was working on it.
   a. belated   b. subsequent   c. incessant   d. simultaneous

d   2. Seth missed the lesson because he slept for the entire _____ of the class.
   a. renaissance   b. expiration   c. conception   d. duration

b   3. The teacher allowed us a(n) _____ before we began the second part of the exam.
   a. duration   b. respite   c. renaissance   d. expiration

a   4. The dancers moved _____ as if they were mirror images of each other.
   a. simultaneously   b. subsequently   c. belatedly   d. conceptually

b   5. The antique dealer was thrilled when she found a sword from _____ times.
   a. incessant   b. medieval   c. simultaneous   d. subsequent

d   6. The gift certificate was useless, since the _____ date had passed.
   a. respite   b. renaissance   c. conception   d. expiration

c   7. I have no _____ of what you are talking about; please explain.
   a. respite   b. expiration   c. conception   d. duration

a   8. She sent the couple a(n) _____ gift, two weeks after their anniversary.
   a. belated   b. incessant   c. medieval   d. simultaneous

b   9. Carl joined the baseball team in 2005, and his younger brother signed up the _____ year.
   a. medieval   b. subsequent   c. incessant   d. belated

d   10. We are studying paintings from the _____ period in art class.
   a. conception   b. expiration   c. respite   d. Renaissance

Challenge: The child's _____ interruptions lasted for the _____ of the play.

c   a. medieval...expiration   b. belated...conception   c. incessant...duration

Plague!

The bubonic plague is a horrible disease that had killed millions of people worldwide, until a cure was found in the twentieth century. People called it the Black Death, because victims turned a dark gray color from blood clotted under their skin. It was quick and deadly. **(1)** The *duration* of the disease was often less than a week. **(2)** More than 90 percent of the victims *expired*. **(3)** It is no wonder that people lived in *incessant* fear of the bubonic plague.

The plague is usually associated with rats, which carry the disease. Yet it is most likely spread by fleas that picked it up from the rats. Bacteria attack the gut of a flea, then multiply and interfere with the flea's digestion. **(4)** *Subsequently,* the hungry flea seeks food. Each time it bites, the flea can transmit bacteria to the victim.

The origin of the bubonic plague is still disputed. Some think it began in China. **(5)** Others feel that the disease's *conception* can be traced to Egypt. One researcher found evidence of plague bacteria in the 4,000-year-old remains of Egyptian fleas. The animals that carried the fleas are native to the Nile area, and Egyptian writings of almost 3,500 years ago mention a similar disease.

The plague is believed to have first hit Europe in about the year AD 500. Weakened by a series of crop failures due to cold, dry weather, the population was already weak and close to starvation when the disease began to spread. **(6)** There are not many records of this early *medieval* plague in western Europe. **(7)** However, the disease *simultaneously* hit the Byzantine Empire, where the terrible suffering was better documented.

The devastating European pandemic, which began in 1347, may have originated with Italian sailors returning from the Black Sea. Within five years, more than 25 million Europeans, about one-third of the population, had died. **(8)** People experienced a *respite* from the disease each winter, but each summer it renewed its deadly attack. It spread so fast that some scientists feel it must have been the very deadly pneumonic form of the disease, which attacks the lungs and is spread by coughing, sneezing, and even talking.

(9) The last major European outbreak of the plague was after the *Renaissance,* in 1665. Once again, it struck a population weakened by freezing weather. It is estimated that more than 65,000 died in England alone. The houses of infected people were marked with a red cross and guarded, so that no one left or entered. In the 1600s, physicians wore suits with huge beaks that were filled with vinegar, hoping that the strong smell would ward off infection.

(10) It was only *belatedly,* after the worst epidemics had passed, that the cause of the horrible disease was discovered. The bubonic plague is now curable with antibiotics. Modern outbreaks are rare, but not unknown. The island of Madagascar experienced an outbreak of the plague in the late 1990s. But science has ended the terrible fears that haunted Medieval and Renaissance Europe.

Each sentence below refers to a numbered sentence in the passage. Write the letter of the choice that gives the sentence a meaning that is closest to the original sentence.

___d___ **1.** The _____ of the disease was often less than a week.
  a. survival   **b.** death   **c.** strength   **d.** length

___a___ **2.** More than 90 percent of the victims _____ .
  a. died   **b.** recovered   **c.** rested   **d.** persisted

___b___ **3.** It is no wonder that people lived in _____ fear of the bubonic plague.
  a. deathly   **b.** constant   **c.** intense   **d.** late

___c___ **4.** _____ , the hungry flea seeks food.
  a. Often   **b.** Finally   **c.** Later on   **d.** Too late

___b___ **5.** Others feel that the disease's _____ can be traced to Egypt.
  a. length   **b.** beginning   **c.** relief   **d.** cure

_d_ **6.** There are not many records of this early _____ plague in western Europe.
    a. continual   **b.** deadly   **c.** revival   **d.** from the Middle Ages

_c_ **7.** However, the disease _____ hit the Byzantine Empire.
    a. constantly   **b.** later on   **c.** at the same time   **d.** immediately after

_a_ **8.** People experienced a _____ from the disease each winter.
    a. relief   **b.** rebirth   **c.** death   **d.** pain

_d_ **9.** The last major European outbreak of the plague was after the _____ , in 1665.
    a. relief   **b.** Middle Ages   **c.** same time   **d.** period from 1400–1600

_b_ **10.** It was only _____ that the cause of the horrible disease was discovered.
    a. a general idea   **b.** too late   **c.** by chance   **d.** by an accident

Indicate whether the statements below are TRUE or FALSE according to the passage.

_T_ **1.** It is unclear where the bubonic plague first appeared.

_T_ **2.** The houses of infected people were marked with a red cross so that no one left or entered.

_F_ **3.** There is still no cure for the plague.

WRITING EXTENDED RESPONSES

The passage you have read traces the bubonic plague through several time periods, including ancient times, the Middle Ages, and the Renaissance. Choose one of these time periods and, in an expository essay, write what you know about it. Your essay should be at least three paragraphs long and should cover at least two aspects. You might choose to describe clothes, housing, transportation, customs, or other things. Use at least three lesson words in your essay and underline them.

WRITE THE DERIVATIVE

Complete the sentence by writing the correct form of the word shown in parentheses. You may not need to change the form that is given.

expiration   **1.** Check the _____ date on that orange-juice carton. *(expire)*

subsequent   **2.** The team lost their first game but won the _____ one. *(subsequently)*

renaissance   **3.** The beehive hairstyle isn't likely to have a _____ . *(renaissance)*

medieval   **4.** The book was set during _____ times. *(medieval)*

simultaneously   **5.** The two spoke _____ and sounded as though they had one voice. *(simultaneous)*

belated   **6.** I ate a _____ dinner, long after the others had finished. *(belated)*

incessant   **7.** The dog's _____ barking annoyed our neighbors. *(incessantly)*

<u>_____duration_____</u>   **8.** She was nervous for the _____ of the interview. *(duration)*

<u>____conception____</u>   **9.** From its _____, we could see that the idea would be a success. *(conception)*

<u>respite or respites</u>   **10.** I need frequent _____ in the country, to bear the stress of city life. *(respite)*

FIND THE EXAMPLE

Choose the answer that best describes the action or situation.

<u>___a___</u>   **1.** Something you might use to determine the *duration* of a speech
    a. a stopwatch   **b.** a critic   **c.** a microphone   **d.** a tape measure

<u>___c___</u>   **2.** Something that would cause a *belated* arrival at school
    a. singing a song   **b.** good traffic   **c.** oversleeping   **d.** waking up early

<u>___b___</u>   **3.** Something you would NOT find in *medieval* times
    a. swords   **b.** cell phones   **c.** homes   **d.** knights

<u>___d___</u>   **4.** Two things that can't happen *simultaneously*
    a. eat/watch TV   **b.** sing/walk   **c.** run/breathe   **d.** drive/shower

<u>___b___</u>   **5.** What you have if you come up with a *conception*
    a. a sickness   **b.** an idea   **c.** a plant   **d.** a problem

<u>___a___</u>   **6.** The *subsequent* step after going to bed
    a. falling asleep   **b.** brushing teeth   **c.** eating lunch   **d.** putting on pajamas

<u>___c___</u>   **7.** Something you would NOT need a *respite* from
    a. running   **b.** climbing   **c.** breathing   **d.** homework

<u>___d___</u>   **8.** Something that was NOT produced in the *Renaissance*
    a. paintings   **b.** books   **c.** sculpture   **d.** movies

<u>___d___</u>   **9.** Something a refrigerator does *incessantly*
    a. lights   **b.** reads   **c.** eats   **d.** cools

<u>___a___</u>   **10.** Something that is likely to *expire*
    a. a coupon   **b.** a rock   **c.** a chair   **d.** music

Reading and Reasoning

Context Clues: Substitution

The sentence or group of sentences that surrounds an unfamiliar word often provides clues to the meaning of that word. These *context clues* can be very helpful in figuring out unknown words.

Strategies

Often, you can simply substitute another word that makes sense in the sentence; that word will be the (approximate) meaning of the word you need to define. Here are some ways that this type of substitution works.

1. *Read the surrounding sentence and paragraph completely.* Hints to meaning can be found both before and after a word.

2. *Look for clues that would be suitable to substitute for the unknown word.*

   • At times, a *synonym* for the unknown word is provided in the sentence:

     Three **raconteurs** left the party early, but the fourth storyteller stayed to entertain us.

     In this sentence, the word **raconteur** is defined by its common synonym, **storyteller.**

   • At other times, hints to the word's meaning are given in a longer form:

     Three dogs were having a noisy fight, but the fourth would not join in the **fray.**

     The phrase "a noisy fight" gives the approximate meaning of **fray.**

3. *Make an intelligent guess about the meaning of the word.* Reread the sentence substituting that meaning to see if it makes sense.

4. *Check your definition by looking the word up in the dictionary.* Remember that context clues only provide approximate meanings.

Practice

Read each sentence and use context clues of substitution to determine the meaning of the italicized word. After making an intelligent guess about the meaning, write your definition of the italicized word. Then look up the word in the dictionary and write the formal definition that best fits the use of the word.

1. The *stipend* was enough to live on, but this payment allowed no luxuries.

   My definition _____ payment _____

   Dictionary definition _____ a fixed and/or regular payment _____

2. The other academic meeting was dull, but our *symposium* was informative.

   My definition _____ academic meeting _____

   Dictionary definition _____ meeting or conference for discussion of a topic _____

3. Please don't *divulge* my secret. I would be horrified if you revealed it.

My definition _____ tell, reveal, "give away" _____

Dictionary definition _____ to make known, reveal, tell _____

4. The team's *exuberant* behavior was matched by the enthusiasm of the spectators.

My definition _____ enthusiastic _____

Dictionary definition _____ full of unrestrained enthusiasm or joy _____

5. She threw the food wrapper in the garbage and also *jettisoned* her cup.

My definition _____ threw away _____

Dictionary definition _____ to discard; throw away _____

6. Alone on the stage, the actor delivered a *soliloquy*.

My definition _____ a performance of one person _____

Dictionary definition _____ speech in which a lone character reveals thoughts _____

7. Glenda was quiet, and her sister was also rather *taciturn*.

My definition _____ quiet _____

Dictionary definition _____ not inclined to talk; untalkative _____

8. I'd have to say that, with your moods varying every few minutes, you are *mercurial*.

My definition _____ changeable in mood or temperament _____

Dictionary definition _____ changeable, fickle _____

9. The pleasant smell of baking cookies *emanated* from the kitchen.

My definition _____ came out from _____

Dictionary definition _____ to come or send forth, as from a source _____

10. I walked one way up the hill and my friend made a *trek* in the other direction.

My definition _____ journey, climb _____

Dictionary definition _____ a journey, especially a long and difficult one _____

Government and Control

WORD LIST

anarchy	authoritarian	conservative	delegate	dominion
impeach	inaugurate	liberal	Spartan	tyrant

Government affects many aspects of our lives. While people living in a democracy can choose their representatives and speak their opinions freely, those in a dictatorship are ruled by one person who makes decisions for them. The words in this lesson deal with forms of government, ranging from *authoritarian*—exercising complete control over people, to *anarchy*—total lack of government.

1. **anarchy** (ăn′ər-kē) *noun* from Greek *an-*, "without" + *arkhos*, "ruler"
   a. A lack of government
      • Some libertarians see **anarchy** as the ideal form of society.
   b. Disorder and confusion
      • Dropping cash from a skyscraper window might cause **anarchy** in the streets below.

   anarchic *adjective* The streets became **anarchic** during the riot.

   anarchist *noun* The **anarchist** preached against the government.

2. **authoritarian** (ə-thôr′ĭ-târ′ē-ən) *adjective* from Greek *auctor*, "creator"
   Requiring complete obedience to a single ruler or group
   • Under Joseph Stalin's **authoritarian** rule, citizens of the Soviet Union were often thrown into prison with no chance to defend themselves.

   > *Authoritarian* comes from the common word *authority*.

3. **conservative** (kən-sûr′və-tĭv) from Latin *conservare*, "to preserve"
   a. *adjective* Favoring traditional values and institutions; resistant to change; cautious
      • The **conservative** senator opposed any changes in procedures.
   b. *adjective* Traditional in style; not showy
      • Ned's colorful tie was a contrast to his **conservative** business suit.
   c. *noun* A person favoring traditional values and institutions
      • As a **conservative,** I favor lower taxes.

   conservatism *noun* Despite her **conservatism,** May rode a motorcycle.

   > *Conservative* comes from the word *conserve*, or "save."

4. **delegate** from Latin *de-*, "out" + *legare*, "to send"
   a. *noun* (dĕl′ĭ-gĭt′) A representative chosen to speak or act for others
      • A new **delegate** to the convention was elected last April.
   b. *verb* (dĕl′ĭ-gāt′) To give out power, responsibility, or tasks
      • The new manager was overwhelmed with work and needed to **delegate** more tasks to his employees.

   delegation *noun* Ann was part of her school's **delegation** to the conference.

delegate

5. **dominion** (də-mĭnʹyən) *noun* from Latin *dominus,* "lord"
   a. Control
      • Some parts of the Americas were once under Dutch **dominion.**
   b. The territory or realm that one controls
      • All the lands of the king's **dominion** were peaceful and prosperous.

6. **impeach** (ĭm-pēchʹ) *verb* from Latin *impedicare,* "to entangle"
   To accuse a public official of unacceptable conduct
   • Two U.S. presidents have been **impeached** by the House of
   Representatives; neither has been convicted by the Senate.

   impeachment *noun* The **impeachment** proceedings were covered by
   hundreds of news reporters.

Impeach can also mean "to challenge someone's truthfulness."

7. **inaugurate** (ĭn-ôʹgyə-rātʹ) *verb*
   To install in office by formal ceremony
   • The club will **inaugurate** the new officers on New Years Day.

   inaugural *adjective* John Kennedy's **inaugural** address stated: "Ask
   not what your country can do for you; ask what you can do for your
   country."

8. **liberal** (lĭbʹər-əl, lĭbʹrəl) from Latin *liber,* "free"
   a. *adjective* Favoring social progress, democratic reform, and civil
      liberties
      • Many **liberal** politicians favor extending health care to all citizens.
   b. *adjective* Tolerant; generous
      • The college's **liberal** rules allowed students to live off campus.
   c. *noun* A person who favors social progress, democratic reform, and
      civil liberties
      • As a **liberal,** the senator supported laws assuring those accused of
      crimes the right to a jury trial.

   liberally *adverb* She ate the sweets **liberally.**

Liberal is the opposite of *conservative. Liberal* also means "generous," as in "She could buy a lot with her *liberal* allowance."

9. **Spartan** (spärʹtn) *adjective* from the ancient Greek city of *Sparta*
   a. Self-disciplined
      • Practicing more than five hours per day, the acrobats followed a
      Spartan training routine.
   b. Simple; lacking in comfort
      • Living quarters on a submarine are known to be **Spartan.**

Because it comes from the name of a city, *Spartan* is capitalized.

10. **tyrant** (tīrʹənt) *noun*
    A ruler who exercises absolute power in a harsh, cruel manner
    • No one could leave the country without the **tyrant's** permission.

    tyrannical *adjective* People worldwide protested the **tyrannical**
    behavior of the general who seized control of the country.

    tyrannize *verb* The playground bully **tyrannized** younger children.

    tyranny *noun* Philosopher John Locke (1632–1704) said, "Wherever
    law ends, **tyranny** begins . . ."

WRITE THE CORRECT WORD

Write the correct word in the space next to each definition.

impeach	**1.** to accuse of wrongdoing
anarchy	**2.** a lack of government
inaugurate	**3.** to install in office by formal ceremony
tyrant	**4.** a harsh, cruel ruler
dominion	**5.** control

delegate	**6.** to assign power or tasks to others
Spartan	**7.** lacking comfort
authoritarian	**8.** ruled by one person or group
conservative	**9.** cautious; traditional
liberal	**10.** favoring reform

COMPLETE THE SENTENCE

Write the letter for the word that best completes each sentence.

b **1.** The _____ celebration for the new class president was well attended.
   a. authoritarian   **b.** inaugural   **c.** tyrannical   **d.** conservative

c **2.** Parents generally have _____ over their children.
   a. conservatism   **b.** impeachment   **c.** dominion   **d.** anarchy

d **3.** Being used to luxury, Tara was unhappy with the _____ dorm room.
   a. inaugural   **b.** authoritarian   **c.** liberal   **d.** Spartan

a **4.** It was a surprise to see the _____ librarian wearing jeans.
   a. conservative   **b.** liberal   **c.** authoritarian   **d.** impeached

d **5.** Her parents were _____; they always made decisions for her.
   a. anarchic   **b.** liberal   **c.** inaugural   **d.** authoritarian

b **6.** With no teacher to control the fifth graders, _____ broke loose in the classroom.
   a. delegate   **b.** anarchy   **c.** dominion   **d.** conservatism

c **7.** Surprisingly, the little Chihuahua _____ the huge golden retriever.
   a. impeached   **b.** delegated   **c.** tyrannized   **d.** liberalized

c **8.** The club chose a(n) _____ to represent them at the regional conference.
   a. dominion   **b.** tyrant   **c.** delegate   **d.** impeachment

a **9.** The conspirators decided to _____ the president in the hopes that he would resign if accused.
   a. impeach   **b.** delegate   **c.** conserve   **d.** inaugurate

d **10.** As a(n) _____, I favor extending voting rights whenever possible.
   a. tyrannical   **b.** authoritarian   **c.** conservative   **d.** liberal

Challenge: Only a year after the corrupt governor was _____, he was _____ for stealing money from the treasury.
b   **a.** impeached...delegated   **b.** inaugurated...impeached   **c.** tyrannized...liberalized

Athens and Sparta

Perhaps you have heard that the first large-scale democracy was in ancient Greece. **(1)** That is true, but Greece was also home to a very *authoritarian* military state. **(2)** Ancient Greece was made up of city-states, each with its separate *dominion*. Athens and Sparta were two of the largest and most important city-states.

In Athens, a long process of political change brought about democracy. Before democracy was established, the Greeks were ruled by a series of dictators. **(3)** Although many of these rulers were destructive *tyrants*, some actually improved conditions in Athens. **(4)** For example, in 594 BC, Athens hovered on the brink of *anarchy*. **(5)** To avoid this danger, the Athenians *inaugurated* Solon, giving him complete power over the city-state. He went on to establish reforms that improved the lives of Athenians and laid the groundwork for democracy.

By 502 BC, the Athenians had removed all tyrants and established a democracy. Their constitution, the first in the world, established nine rulers, ten generals, a 500-person council divided into separate committees, and a citizen assembly. **(6)** The rulers and the *delegates* to the council were chosen annually by drawing lots. The generals in charge of military decisions were the only elected officials. **(7)** There was also a provision for *impeaching* ineffective leaders. If the majority of citizens voted against an official, he was banished from Athens for ten years.

The assembly, which voted on laws drawn up by the council, consisted of all the adult citizens of Athens. However, the Athenian idea of citizenship was narrowly defined: Only free males born in Athens had the rights and privileges of citizenship; non-Athenians, women, freed slaves, and slaves could neither vote nor participate in government.

Unlike Athens, ancient Sparta never developed into a democracy. Under the tightly controlled rule of two kings, most Spartans did not participate in government. Their system was authoritarian, but orderly. From age seven, male children were expected to live in camps and receive military training; only boys trained in these camps could become citizens. Military service, which was required of all Sparta's citizens, began at age twenty. **(8)** The *Spartan* lifestyle was designed to serve the government of the city-state. Warlike Sparta eventually felt the need to establish itself as the strongest city-state. This led to several decades of war that weakened Greece.

What were the contributions of Sparta and Athens? **(9)** *Conservative* Sparta, having concentrated on developing military strength and personal endurance, made few contributions to culture. **(10)** *Liberal* Athens, however, with its devotion to democracy and its openness to new ideas, made important advances in the arts and sciences. Athenians built beautiful temples on the Acropolis. The city was also the home of the philosophers Plato and Socrates. Playwrights such as Aristophanes and Euripides developed the first comedies and tragedies there. In fact, most of what we think of as the glories of ancient Greece came from the city-state of Athens.

Each sentence below refers to a numbered sentence in the passage. Write the letter of the choice that gives the sentence a meaning that is closest to the original sentence.

_____ a **1.** Greece was also home to a very _____ military state.
   a. strictly controlled   **b.** weak   **c.** open-minded   **d.** self-disciplined

_____ c **2.** Ancient Greece was made up of city-states, each with its separate _____.
   a. king   **b.** traditional values   **c.** area of control   **d.** usefulness

_____ d **3.** Although many of these rulers were _____, some actually improved conditions.
   a. open-minded people   **b.** gods   **c.** traditional people   **d.** harsh rulers

_____ c **4.** In 594 BC, Athens hovered on the brink of _____.
   a. disagreements   **b.** hunger   **c.** disorder   **d.** tolerance

b   **5.** To avoid this danger, the Athenians _____ Solon.
     a. discussed   **b.** installed in office   **c.** removed from office   **d.** disciplined

a   **6.** The rulers and the _____ to the council were chosen annually by drawing lots.
     a. representatives   **b.** harsh rulers   **c.** witnesses   **d.** directions

d   **7.** There was also a provision for _____ ineffective leaders.
     a. supporting   **b.** disciplining   **c.** installing   **d.** accusing

b   **8.** The _____ lifestyle was designed to serve the government of the city-state.
     a. luxurious   **b.** disciplined   **c.** pleasant   **d.** tolerant

d   **9.** _____ Sparta, having concentrated on developing military strength and personal endurance, made few contributions to culture.
     a. Military   **b.** Democratic   **c.** Ancient and chaotic   **d.** Traditional and rigid

a   **10.** _____ Athens, however, made important advances in the arts and sciences.
     a. Tolerant   **b.** Peaceful   **c.** Firm   **d.** Fearful

Indicate whether the statements below are TRUE or FALSE according to the passage.

T   **1.** Generals were the only elected officials in Athens.

F   **2.** The citizen assembly in Athens was made up of soldiers.

F   **3.** Sparta had the first democratic government.

FINISH THE THOUGHT

Complete each sentence so that it shows the meaning of the italicized word.

1. *Spartan* living conditions probably would not include _____   Answers will vary.

_____

2. A *liberal* person would probably _____   Answers will vary.

_____

WRITE THE DERIVATIVE

Complete the sentence by writing the correct form of the word shown in parentheses. You may not need to change the form that is given.

impeachment   **1.** When the official was accused of taking bribes, the legislature started an _____ process. *(impeach)*

anarchic   **2.** As the holiday shoppers rushed in, the store became _____. *(anarchy)*

tyrannical   **3.** Jeff's mother didn't believe that his teacher was _____. *(tyrant)*

Spartan   **4.** Grant's _____ diet included only brown rice and vegetables. *(Spartan)* _conservatism_   **5.** Marina disagreed with her neighbor's _____. *(conservative)*

delegating   **6.** The team leader began by _____ various tasks to members. *(delegate)*

dominion   **7.** Britain once considered its _____ over the seas to be its best defense. *(dominion)*

liberally   **8.** Max _____ covered his salad with dressing. *(liberal)*

inauguration   **9.** They went to Washington, D.C., to attend the _____. *(inaugurate)*

authoritarian   **10.** Some tourists choose not to travel to countries that have _____ governments. *(authoritarian)*

FIND THE EXAMPLE

Choose the answer that best describes the action or situation.

_d_   **1.** Something a stingy person is NOT likely to do *liberally*
     a. walk   **b.** sleep   **c.** save time   **d.** spend money

_a_   **2.** A word that a *tyrant* is NOT likely to use
     a. please   **b.** come   **c.** go   **d.** immediately

_d_   **3.** An *authoritarian* person's worst enemy
     a. employee   **b.** assistant   **c.** servant   **d.** rebel

_c_   **4.** Something you would be LEAST likely to find in a *Spartan* bedroom
     a. bed   **b.** dresser   **c.** lots of pillows   **d.** wooden chair

_b_   **5.** Someone an *anarchist* would most likely oppose
     a. cowboy   **b.** president   **c.** chef   **d.** antique collector

_b_   **6.** Something a *conservative* person would probably NOT wear
     a. watch   **b.** spiked hair   **c.** socks   **d.** suit

_d_   **7.** A task you could NOT *delegate* to someone else
     a. vacuuming   **b.** taking out trash   **c.** washing dishes   **d.** taking a test

_c_   **8.** An *impeachable* offense
     a. working   **b.** eating   **c.** stealing   **d.** sleeping

_d_   **9.** A person who is NOT likely to be *inaugurated*
     a. mayor   **b.** governor   **c.** president   **d.** barber

_c_   **10.** A chef's *dominion*
     a. garage   **b.** bathroom   **c.** kitchen   **d.** basement

Harm and Criticism

WORD LIST

admonish	alienate	censure	detriment	imperil
incapacitate	injurious	malign	scoff	subvert

Harm and criticism are usually negative, but they can also be seen in a positive light. We need to identify and understand harmful things in order to protect ourselves from them. Although criticism can cause harm, it can also be appropriate—or even helpful.

1. **admonish** (ăd-mŏn´ĭsh) *verb* from Latin *ad-*, "to" + *monere*, "to warn"
   a. To criticize mildly
   • Brad's father **admonished** the boys for playing music too loudly.
   b. To warn or advise against something; to caution
   • "Don't go outside without your umbrella," **admonished** Mom.

   admonition *noun* The manager's **admonition** against speeding reminded the cab drivers to drive safely.

   admonishment *noun* The referee issued an **admonishment** to the two players who fought over the ball.

2. **alienate** (āl´yə-nāt´, āl´ē-ə-nāt´) *verb* from Latin *alius*, "other" To cause a person to become distant, unfriendly, or hostile; to lose the friendship or support of
   • Constant showing off and bragging tends to **alienate** people.

   alienation *noun* Disagreement over a proposed law led to **alienation** between the two state senators.

3. **censure** (sĕn´shər) from Latin *censura*, "severe judgment"
   a. *noun* An expression of harsh criticism
   • Japan issued an official **censure** of several foreign companies that were illegally operating fishing fleets in Japan's waters.
   b. *verb* To criticize severely
   • The United Nations **censured** the violence against civilians in Sudan.

4. **detriment** (dĕt´rə-mənt) *noun* from Latin *de-*, "away" + *terere*, "to rub"
   Damage; harm; something that causes damage or harm
   • A criminal record is a **detriment** to anyone seeking public office.

   detrimental *adjective* Inhaling smoke of any kind is **detrimental** to one's health.

5. **imperil** (ĭm-pĕr´əl) *verb*
   To endanger
   • The oil spill **imperiled** local marine life.

admonish

Keep your hat on. It's cold out there!

Admonition and *admonishment* have the same meaning.

Point out that some of the lesson words have a meaning that is more negative than others. *Subvert* and *malign*, for example, are very negative words. *Admonish* is only mildly negative.

6. **incapacitate** (ĭn´kə-păs´ĭ-tāt´) *verb* from Latin *in-*, "not"
+ *capacitare*, "to lead"
To disable; to deprive of power or ability
• The backup electrical systems of hospitals ensure that a loss of power will not **incapacitate** any hospital functions.

incapacitation *noun* A severe stroke led to the man's **incapacitation**.

> *Incapacitate* comes from the word *capacity*. *Injurious* comes from *injury*.

7. **injurious** (ĭn-jŏŏr´ē-əs) *adjective* from Latin *iniuria*, "a wrong or injustice"
Causing injury or damage
• Eating large quantities of sweets is usually **injurious** to your teeth.

8. **malign** (mə-līn´) from Latin *mal-*, "bad"
   a. *verb* To speak evil of; to slander
   • How dare you **malign** my reputation by calling me a thief!
   b. *adjective* Evil; harmful
   • The evil adviser was a **malign** influence on the king.

malignant (mə-lĭg´nənt) *adjective* The **malignant** villain devised a plot to kidnap the hero.

> *Malignant* is often used to describe a cancerous tumor. The opposite of *malignant* is *benign*.

9. **scoff** (skŏf) *verb* from Middle English *scoff*, "mockery"
To make fun of; to mock; to ridicule
• People **scoffed** at the awkward professor—until he won the Nobel Prize.

> *Scoff* is usually used with the preposition *at*, as in "The commentator *scoffed at* all theories different from his."

10. **subvert** (səb-vûrt´) *verb* from Latin *sub-*, "under" + *vertere*, "to turn"
To undermine, weaken, or destroy an established institution
• Despite the rebel's attempts to **subvert** the country's elections, by blocking routes to the polls, citizens participated in the balloting.

subversion *noun* Under the dictator's rule, simply being charged with "attempted **subversion** of the government" resulted in severe punishment.

WORD ENRICHMENT

The "bad" prefix

Malign, "to speak evil about," contains the prefix *mal-*, meaning "bad." *Mal-* is used in many English words. *Maladjusted* means "badly adjusted;" *malfunctioning* means "functioning badly." The complicated-looking word *malodorous* simply means "bad smelling." At one time, people thought that "bad air" around swamps caused a dangerous disease, so they named the disease *malaria*. Today, we know that mosquitoes, which are often found around swamps, spread the disease.

WRITE THE CORRECT WORD

Write the correct word in the space next to each definition.

_____censure_____ **1.** a severe criticism   _____detriment_____ **6.** harm; injury

_____imperil_____ **2.** to endanger   _____admonish_____ **7.** to criticize mildly

_____malign_____ **3.** to speak evil of   _____injurious_____ **8.** causing injury

_____subvert_____ **4.** to undermine or destroy   _____alienate_____ **9.** to lose support of

_____scoff_____ **5.** to make fun of   _____incapacitate_____ **10.** to disable or make ineffective

COMPLETE THE SENTENCE

Write the letter for the word that best completes each sentence.

___a___ **1.** _____ a person behind his back is the act of a coward.
     a. Maligning   **b.** Admonishing   **c.** Alienating   **d.** Incapacitating

___a___ **2.** Ingesting harmful chemicals can result in total or near-total _____.
     a. incapacitation   **b.** scoffing   **c.** alienation   **d.** censure

___b___ **3.** Your loud, annoying music is _____ to my concentration.
     a. admonishing   **b.** detrimental   **c.** alienated   **d.** incapacitated

___d___ **4.** The agent was secretly working to _____ the government of the foreign country.
     a. scoff   **b.** admonish   **c.** alienate   **d.** subvert

___a___ **5.** Which is more _____ to people, smoking or car accidents?
     a. injurious   **b.** subverted   **c.** incapacitated   **d.** scoffed

___b___ **6.** The wild, unexpected storm _____ the crew of the aging fishing boat.
     a. censured   **b.** imperiled   **c.** scoffed   **d.** admonished

___d___ **7.** Sara _____ her sister not to wander away from the campsite.
     a. imperiled   **b.** alienated   **c.** maligned   **d.** admonished

___c___ **8.** Congress issued a(n) _____ of the lawmaker who had been caught stealing.
     a. scoff   **b.** detriment   **c.** censure   **d.** injury

___b___ **9.** Darcy _____ many of her classmates with her rudeness.
     a. imperiled   **b.** alienated   **c.** maligned   **d.** scoffed

___d___ **10.** The shallow boy _____ at Sasha for not wearing the "right" brand of expensive shoes.
     a. imperiled   **b.** subverted   **c.** admonished   **d.** scoffed

Challenge: Many parents _____ their children not to _____ themselves by doing dangerous or foolish things.
___c___   **a.** subvert…censure   **b.** malign…admonish   **c.** admonish…imperil

Condor Comeback?

One of the world's largest birds often soars miles above California, Arizona, and Mexico. Against the sky, its nine-foot wing span projects power and glory. The California condor, a sharp-eyed scavenger that once lived along much of the east and west coasts of North America, is now an endangered species. **(1)** What could *imperil* a bird that was once so widespread? As with other endangered species, there are many answers to this question.

(2) Perhaps the most important factor still *subverting* the survival of the California condor is habitat loss. Additionally, they are hampered by a very slow reproductive rate, the dangers of power lines, and illegal shooting. **(3)** Also, condors accidentally eat *injurious* substances. Harmful pesticides and other chemicals are now found in the animals that condors eat. Sometimes, ranchers poison the carcasses of dead livestock in attempts to kill predators. Because condors—like vultures—eat dead animals, condors are often accidental victims. Finally, some hunters still use lead ammunition. Animals killed by lead ammunition and left behind can poison condors that later eat the carcass. **(4)** Lead poisoning can *incapacitate* or kill condors.

The birds face more subtle problems, too. **(5)** Condors have been *maligned* for their eating habits because they eat dead or rotting meat. They actually are relatively neat eaters that provide a valuable service. (One expert called them "nature's clean-up crew!") But many people find it hard to care about condors. **(6)** Also, the birds' unattractive, bald-headed appearance tends to *alienate* people. Right or wrong, people find it easier to rally around cute, cuddly creatures than around less attractive ones like the condor.

Additionally, early efforts to capture and breed condors were ineffective. **(7)** One program, started in the 1950s, was so unsuccessful that the National Audubon Society and other groups publicly *censured* it, claiming it was harming the birds. **(8)** The failure of this program and others like it led some experts to *scoff* at the idea of captive breeding. By 1982, there were fewer than twenty-five wild California condors. Five years later, experts could confirm the existence of only one. That male was captured and bred with captive females.

At that point, the fate of the entire condor species was in human hands. Unfortunately, the birds' handlers made some early mistakes. They allowed the birds to get too accustomed to people. When the birds were released, their natural fear of humans was gone. They got too close to humans, even perching on hot tubs. When the condors came into contact with humans, they didn't fly away in fear. **(9)** This was *detrimental* to the condors. Some people attacked condors that had found their way inside buildings. Many of the birds died.

(10) After *admonishments* from experts, breeding programs began to improve. Condor chicks have been raised differently, and their survival rates have increased. In late 2004, there were more than 200 California condors flying free in our southwestern skies. The future of this enormous bird is far from certain, but at least for now, there is hope.

Each sentence below refers to a numbered sentence in the passage. Write the letter of the choice that gives the sentence a meaning that is closest to the original sentence.

_c_ **1.** What could _____ a bird that was once so widespread?
   a. criticize   **b.** ridicule   **c.** endanger   **d.** disable

_a_ **2.** Perhaps the most important factor still _____ the survival of the California condor is habitat loss.
   a. weakening   **b.** warning   **c.** causing hunger to   **d.** making hostile

_b_ **3.** Condors accidentally eat _____ substances.
   a. necessary   **b.** damaging   **c.** evil   **d.** spoiled

_____d_____ **4.** Lead poisoning can _____ or kill condors.
    a. put off   **b.** mock   **c.** criticize   **d.** disable

_____d_____ **5.** Condors have been _____ for their eating habits.
    a. killed   **b.** warned   **c.** admired   **d.** criticized

_____a_____ **6.** The birds' unattractive, bald-headed appearance tends to _____ people.
    a. lose the support of   **b.** cause to criticize   **c.** make sick   **d.** warn against

_____c_____ **7.** The National Audubon Society and other groups publicly _____ it.
    a. praised   **b.** warned   **c.** criticized   **d.** spied on

_____b_____ **8.** The failure of this program and others like it led some experts to _____ the idea of captive breeding.
    a. be afraid of   **b.** make fun of   **c.** cause harm to   **d.** work to stop

_____b_____ **9.** This was _____ to the condors.
    a. evil   **b.** harmful   **c.** dangerous   **d.** critical

_____c_____ **10.** After _____ from experts, breeding programs began to improve.
    a. war cries   **b.** painful shots   **c.** mild criticism   **d.** bad reports

Indicate whether the statements below are TRUE or FALSE according to the passage.

_____F_____ **1.** California condors serve no useful purpose in nature.

_____F_____ **2.** California condors tend to appear attractive to human beings.

_____F_____ **3.** Experts are now certain the condor species will survive.

WRITING EXTENDED RESPONSES

The passage you just read shows that disagreement and criticism arise even among people who share common goals. Think of an issue that has caused disagreement. You may choose an issue that directly affects you or someone you know, or one that you have learned about through the news. In an expository essay, explain both (or all) sides of the issue. Include criticisms that are made by opposing sides. Your essay should be at least three paragraphs long. Use at least three lesson words in your essay and underline them.

WRITE THE DERIVATIVE

Complete the sentence by writing the correct form of the word shown in parentheses. You may not need to change the form that is given.

_____malignant_____ **1.** We were all relieved to learn that Grandmother's tumor was not _____. (*malign*)

_____imperiling_____ **2.** Loss of habitat is _____ many species of birds. (*imperil*)

_____scoffing_____ **3.** Stop _____ at what you don't understand! (*scoff*)

<u>censured</u>   **4.** The scientist who misrepresented the data was _____ by the university's administration. *(censure)*

<u>admonishment or admonition</u>   **5.** Though the father meant his words to be a mild _____, his son burst into tears. *(admonish)*

<u>subversion</u>   **6.** One person's _____ is another person's "fighting for freedom." *(subvert)*

<u>injuriousness</u>   **7.** The _____ of smoking is no longer in question. *(injurious)*

<u>incapacitation</u>   **8.** One symptom of hypothermia, or abnormally low body temperature, is mental _____. *(incapacitate)*

<u>detrimental</u>   **9.** The loss of so many animal species is _____ to us all. *(detriment)*

<u>alienation</u>   **10.** Your _____ was obvious from your scowl and cold manner. *(alienate)*

FIND THE EXAMPLE

Choose the answer that best describes the action or situation.

<u>b</u>   **1.** Something that is most likely to *incapacitate* firefighters
  a. food   **b.** smoke   **c.** reading   **d.** sirens

<u>d</u>   **2.** An *admonishment*
  a. Goodbye.   **b.** Well done.   **c.** My leg hurts.   **d.** I wouldn't do that.

<u>d</u>   **3.** Someone who is likely to attempt *subversion*
  a. infant   **b.** dog groomer   **c.** sculptor   **d.** opponent

<u>d</u>   **4.** An example of *scoffing*
  a. I love rice.   **b.** You're wrong.   **c.** Nice job!   **d.** What a fool you are!

<u>a</u>   **5.** Something likely to be *injurious*
  a. a sunburn   **b.** light stretching   **c.** enough rest   **d.** soft cushions

<u>c</u>   **6.** Something *detrimental* to an endangered species
  a. legal protection   **b.** wildlife preserves   **c.** habitat destruction   **d.** breeding

<u>b</u>   **7.** Something that is likely to *alienate* teammates
  a. shaking hands   **b.** hogging the ball   **c.** working hard   **d.** eating pizza

<u>a</u>   **8.** Likely result of an official *censure*
  a. embarrassment   **b.** raise   **c.** promotion   **d.** election

<u>b</u>   **9.** People frequently *imperiled* on the job
  a. accountants   **b.** police officers   **c.** professors   **d.** editors

<u>a</u>   **10.** A likely reaction from someone who has been *maligned*
  a. anger   **b.** gladness   **c.** gratitude   **d.** giggles

Error and Confusion

WORD LIST

amiss	bewilderment	blunder	erroneous	fallible
faux pas	flustered	miscalculation	misinterpret	predicament

People generally try to do their best, but everybody makes errors. As Alexander Pope commented, "To err is human." Occasionally, errors have positive consequences. When Alexander Fleming accidentally let mold grow on his bacteria cultures, he discovered penicillin. The words in this lesson will help you describe errors and confusion.

1. **amiss** (ə-mĭs´) from Old Norse *a-*, "on" + *mis*, "missing"
   a. *adjective* Wrong; faulty; out of proper order
   • Jake's mother knew that something was **amiss** when he didn't come home from school on time.
   b. *adverb* In a bad, defective, or improper way
   • The roller-coaster accident was caused by controls that went **amiss**.

2. **bewilderment** (bĭ-wĭl´dər-mənt) *noun* from English *wilder*, "to lead astray"
   The state of being puzzled or confused
   • The crowd looked on in **bewilderment** when the referee called a foul.

   bewilder *verb* It **bewildered** the history teacher that his students were not interested in politics.

3. **blunder** (blŭn´dər) from Middle English *blunderen*, "to go blindly"
   a. *noun* A foolish or careless mistake
   • Buying the worthless car was a **blunder** that cost Malcolm several thousand dollars.
   b. *verb* To move in a clumsy way
   • Caroline **blundered** around her room in the dark until she found the lamp.

4. **erroneous** (ĭ-rō´nē-əs) *adjective* from Latin *errare*, "to err; wander"
   Wrong; mistaken; false
   • There were several **erroneous** conclusions in the detective's sloppy report.

5. **fallible** (făl´ə-bəl) *adjective* from Latin *fallere*, "to deceive"
   Able to be mistaken, wrong, or in error
   • All human beings are **fallible;** no one is perfect.

   fallibility *noun* Political polls demonstrate their **fallibility** when they incorrectly predict election results.

> *Went* amiss and *something is* amiss are common phrases.

bewilderment

Have students think of examples of how each word relates to their lives. For example, when have they realized that something was *amiss*? When have they made a *blunder*?

6. **faux pas** (fō pä´) *noun* from French phrase *faux pas*, "false step"
   A minor social error that may cause embarrassment
   - Anna committed a **faux pas** when she ate her salad with a dinner fork.

7. **flustered** (flŭs´tərd) *adjective*
   Nervous and confused
   - After he missed an easy shot, the basketball player became **flustered** and started to make even more mistakes.

   fluster *verb* Lila did not let the arrival of unexpected guests **fluster** her.

   fluster *noun* The teacher's question put the student in a **fluster.**

8. **miscalculation** (mĭs-kăl´kyə-lā´shən) *noun* from Latin *mis-*, "wrong" + *calculus*, "stone used for counting"
   a. An error in math or in estimation
      - A **miscalculation** in the recipe prevented the bread from rising.
   b. A bad judgment
      - The producer made a **miscalculation** about the appeal of the new TV show.

   miscalculate *verb* The teacher was embarrassed when she realized that she had **miscalculated** the math problem.

9. **misinterpret** (mĭs´ĭn-tûr´prĭt) *verb* from Latin *mis-*, "wrong" + *interpres*, "explainer"
   To understand incorrectly
   - After Lionel **misinterpreted** the word's definition, he proceeded to write a faulty sentence.

   misinterpretation *noun* Greg's **misinterpretation** of the map led him to take a wrong turn.

10. **predicament** (prĭ-dĭk´ə-mənt) *noun*
    A difficult or unpleasant situation
    - Latoya found herself in a **predicament** when she wanted to invite two friends who were not speaking to each other to the same party.

WORD ENRICHMENT

It came from French

English has borrowed many words from French, including *faux pas*, which is defined in this lesson. A *faux pas* has to do with manners (really a lack of them), and many other French words also apply to situations where manners are important, including meals.

The French concern with table manners is understandable, considering that food is such a central part of French culture. The French are known for their excellent *cuisine*, or style of cooking. When you eat an *omelet*, remember to think of the French. And think of them also when you put *mayonnaise* on your sandwich. Perhaps you have been to France and eaten fine food worthy of a *gourmet*, a person who knows and appreciates fine cooking.

WRITE THE CORRECT WORD

Write the correct word in the space next to each definition.

miscalculation	1. a math error	fallible	6. able to be wrong
erroneous	2. mistaken	amiss	7. out of order
faux pas	3. a minor, embarrassing error	bewilderment	8. the state of being puzzled
predicament	4. a difficult situation	blunder	9. a careless mistake
misinterpret	5. to understand incorrectly	flustered	10. nervous and confused

COMPLETE THE SENTENCE

Write the letter for the word that best completes each sentence.

__a__ 1. George found himself in the _____ of either putting up with his noisy neighbor or making an unfriendly call to the police.
a. predicament   b. misinterpretation   c. blunder   d. fluster

__c__ 2. José was _____ by all the attention he received after scoring the winning goal.
a. amiss   b. misinterpreted   c. flustered   d. miscalculated

__d__ 3. The police searched the room carefully, but found nothing _____.
a. erroneous   b. fallible   c. misinterpreted   d. amiss

__b__ 4. The ads showed a(n) _____ start time for the play, so audience members arrived late.
a. bewildered   b. erroneous   c. flustered   d. fallible

__b__ 5. Michael made a _____ by forgetting to introduce his mother to his friends.
a. bewilderment   b. faux pas   c. misinterpretation   d. fluster

__d__ 6. Because we are all _____, it is important to admit when we have made mistakes.
a. misinterpreted   b. bewildered   c. flustered   d. fallible

__a__ 7. When they realized they were lost, the hikers exchanged looks of _____.
a. bewilderment   b. fluster   c. faux pas   d. blunder

__c__ 8. The sailor's _____ caused his boat to hit the rock beneath the shallow water.
a. predicament   b. fluster   c. miscalculation   d. faux pas

__d__ 9. Researchers who _____ their data will likely draw conclusions that are false.
a. blunder   b. fluster   c. bewilder   d. misinterpret

__c__ 10. When Johnny reached home, he discovered that splashing through the mud with his new leather shoes was a silly _____.
a. fluster   b. predicament   c. blunder   d. misinterpretation

Challenge: If we _____ another person's facial expressions, we may draw _____ conclusions about their thoughts and feelings.
__a__ a. misinterpret...erroneous   b. miscalculate...flustered   c. fluster...fallible

Baseball Blunder

Was it the fan who caught the ball? **(1)** Was it the *blunders* made during play? Whatever the cause, something terrible happened to the Chicago Cubs in the sixth game of the National League Championship Series (NLCS) on October 15, 2003.

In Major League Baseball, each team competes for its league's pennant in a championship series. The two teams that win pennants then compete in the World Series. The Chicago Cubs hadn't won a pennant since 1945 and hadn't won a World Series since 1908. But in 2003, it looked like they were on their way to victory.

The Florida Marlins and the Cubs met in the 2003 NLCS; one team needed to win four out of seven games, and the Cubs had already won three. They were close to taking their fourth, leading 3–0 near the end of the game. Then it happened.

Marlins player Luis Castillo hit a foul ball, outside the field of play. But if a Cub outfielder could catch the ball, even though it was in foul territory, Castillo would be out.

Left fielder Moises Alou chased the ball to the edge of the field and toward the crowded stands. **(2)** He lifted his glove to catch the ball, but he was *bewildered* when his glove came back empty. **(3)** Alou soon realized what was *amiss*. A fan had reached up and grabbed the ball just as it was about to land in Alou's glove. A Cubs fan had interfered with the success of his team!

(4) The fan had the souvenir he wanted, but he found himself in a *predicament*. Angry bystanders started shouting at him, "You cost us the World Series!" Within minutes, security guards had thrown a jacket over the fan's face and escorted him out of the ballpark.

(5) After the incident, the *flustered* Cubs began making errors. In the end, they lost the game 8-3, tying the series at three games each. The NLCS went into the seventh game, which the Marlins won, sending them to the World Series.

Would Alou have caught the ball if the fan hadn't interfered? **(6)** Alou knows ballplayers are *fallible* but said he was fairly sure he would have caught it. At the same time, he said he felt bad for the fan because he knows that everyone who comes to the ballpark wants a ball.

There is good reason to feel sorry for the fan. **(7)** In the excitement of the moment, he may have *miscalculated* the strength of the public's reaction to his catch. The next day, newspapers carried headlines like "FAN ROBS CUBS!" Faced with many threats, he left Chicago.

(8) Some Cubs fans, however, were *misinterpreting* baseball rules. The rules state that once the ball flies into the stands, fans are allowed to catch it. Photos show that other people had their hands up, too. **(9)** Furthermore, it would be *erroneous* to state that the fan lost the game for the Cubs; the truth is that the team made several bad plays that contributed to the loss that night.

So, Cubs fans will have to wait a little longer for another chance to go to the World Series. But they are not surprised. In 1945, a Cubs fan brought a goat into the stadium with him to cheer for his team. Both he and his goat were promptly ejected. **(10)** Angered by what he considered to be a *faux pas,* the fan predicted that the Cubs would never play a World Series in Wrigley Stadium. So far, he has been correct.

Each sentence below refers to a numbered sentence in the passage. Write the letter of the choice that gives the sentence a meaning that is closest to the original sentence.

___a___ **1.** Was it the _____ made during play?
a. mistakes   b. base hits   c. foul balls   d. puzzles

___d___ **2.** He was _____ when his glove came back empty.
a. angry   b. pleased   c. relieved   d. confused

___c___ **3.** Alou soon realized what was _____.
a. in doubt   b. confused   c. wrong   d. difficult

b **4.** The fan had the souvenir he wanted, but he found himself in a(n) _____.
   a. good situation   **b.** difficult situation   **c.** angry crowd   **d.** need to leave

b **5.** After the incident, the _____ Cubs began making errors.
   a. puzzled   **b.** nervous   **c.** unaware   **d.** saddened

a **6.** Alou knows ballplayers are _____, but said he was fairly sure he would have caught it.
   a. capable of errors   **b.** usually perfect   **c.** able to change   **d.** always winners

c **7.** He may have _____ the strength of the public's reaction.
   a. not known about   **b.** not seen   **c.** badly judged   **d.** guessed right

d **8.** Some Cubs fans, however, were _____ baseball rules.
   a. ignoring   **b.** changing   **c.** thinking about   **d.** misunderstanding

c **9.** Furthermore, it would be _____ to state that the fan lost the game for the Cubs.
   a. exaggerated   **b.** foolish   **c.** incorrect   **d.** humble

b **10.** He was angered by what he considered to be a _____.
   a. huge mistake   **b.** social error   **c.** bad estimate   **d.** near miss

Indicate whether the statements below are TRUE or FALSE according to the passage.

T **1.** Public reaction went against the fan that caught the ball.

F **2.** The Cubs have recently won numerous World Series games.

T **3.** The rules of baseball state that once the ball flies into the stands, fans are allowed to catch it.

FINISH THE THOUGHT

Complete each sentence so that it shows the meaning of the italicized word.

1. One example of a *faux pas* is _____ Answers will vary. _____

2. I found myself in a *predicament* when _____ Answers will vary. _____

WRITE THE DERIVATIVE

Complete the sentence by writing the correct form of the word shown in parentheses. You may not need to change the form that is given.

fluster   **1.** People often _____ easily during job interviews. (*flustered*)

Erroneous   **2.** _____ data cannot lead to sound conclusions. (*erroneous*)

__amiss__ 3. As he checked the gears of his bike, Jaime knew that something was _____. *(amiss)*

__predicament__ 4. The phrase "stuck between a rock and a hard place" describes a _____. *(predicament)*

__miscalculated__ 5. The manager _____ the demand for American flags, so the shop ran out of them several days before the July 4 holiday. *(miscalculation)*

__blundered__ 6. After the fact, she recognized that she had _____. *(blunder)*

__faux pas__ 7. He blushed when he realized he'd committed a _____. *(faux pas)*

__bewildered__ 8. The _____ looks on the faces of the concertgoers suggested that they were in shock after the lead singer was carried offstage by paramedics. *(bewilderment)*

__fallibility__ 9. The weather forecaster cheerfully admitted his _____ after being wrong several days in a row. *(fallible)*

__misinterpretation__ 10. Statements that are unclear lend themselves to _____. *(misinterpret)*

FIND THE EXAMPLE

Choose the answer that best describes the action or situation.

__d__ 1. Something that might go *amiss*
  a. gravity   **b.** an earring   **c.** a tree   **d.** plans

__c__ 2. The thing that is most *fallible*
  a. research   **b.** evidence   **c.** a guess   **d.** good advice

__b__ 3. Something that is most likely to be *misinterpreted*
  a. first name   **b.** messy writing   **c.** nursery rhyme   **d.** magazine subscription

__a__ 4. Something that is most likely to make you *flustered*
  a. giving a speech   **b.** sitting in an assembly   **c.** calling a friend   **d.** eating a sandwich

__b__ 5. Example of a *faux pas* when done in public
  a. eating an apple   **b.** picking your teeth   **c.** singing in a choir   **d.** cheering your team

__c__ 6. Something that is NOT a common *predicament*
  a. too little time   **b.** what to do   **c.** too much money   **d.** what to wear

__a__ 7. Cause for *bewilderment*
  a. too many choices   **b.** clear directions   **c.** everyone agrees   **d.** just enough choices

__d__ 8. Example of a *blunder*
  a. buying breakfast   **b.** eating lunch   **c.** serving a salad   **d.** sitting on a cake

__b__ 9. Statement that is NOT *erroneous*
  a. Earth is flat.   **b.** Sun is hot.   **c.** Moon is cheese.   **d.** Universe is small.

__b__ 10. Something that could be *miscalculated*
  a. a road   **b.** a restaurant bill   **c.** spelling   **d.** artwork

78 **Error and Confusion**

Reading and Reasoning

Context Clues: Opposites and Negatives

Context clues are hints about the meaning of an unfamiliar word. Some clues help you understand the meaning of the word by telling you its opposites. For example:

> The soup was not hot, but **frigid.**

In this sentence, the word *not* signals that *hot* is the opposite of **frigid,** which means "extremely cold."

Strategies

1. *Read the surrounding sentence and paragraph completely.* Hints to meaning are found both before and after a word.

2. *Look for opposite clue words.* Look for the use of negative words and expressions.

   • These may be *not* or *no*. Some less common ways to signal an opposite are *but, rather than, unless, is not,* and *although:*

   > Although there was **enmity** between the two men, their sisters were friends.

   From this sentence, you can see that **enmity** means "a bad feeling," or "hatred."

   • Other words, such as *merely, barely, rarely, never, nothing,* and *only,* indicate opposites:

   > I am merely a beginning student, but Jon is a **savant.**

   Savant means the opposite of *beginning student;* it is a wise, knowing person.

   • Some words contain negative prefixes. These include *non-, un-,* and *in-:*

   > The hospital administration fired the **unqualified** nurse.

   Unqualified is the opposite of *qualified.*

3. *Make an intelligent guess about the meaning of the word.* Reread the sentence substituting that meaning to see if it makes sense.

4. *Check your definition by looking the word up in the dictionary.* Remember that context clues only provide approximate meanings.

Practice

Read each sentence and use context clues to determine the meaning of the italicized word. After making an intelligent guess about the meaning, write your definition of the italicized word. Then look up the word in the dictionary and write the formal definition that best fits the use of the word.

1. The *meticulous* proofreader never missed an error.

   My definition _____ never missing an error; very careful _____

   Dictionary definition _____ extremely or excessively careful or precise _____

2. The code breaker was not able to understand the *cryptic* message.

My definition _____ secret; unable to be understood _____

Dictionary definition _____ having a hidden meaning; puzzling _____

3. The picture was anything but clear; all I could see were *nebulous* shapes.

My definition _____ unclear _____

Dictionary definition _____ lacking definite form; unclear _____

4. This *diminutive* bug hardly ever grows more than a few millimeters long.

My definition _____ small; very small _____

Dictionary definition _____ extremely small in size _____

5. It is an *indisputable* fact that the world is round.

My definition _____ true; not disputable; not able to be argued about _____

Dictionary definition _____ beyond doubt; unquestionable _____

6. This movie is about to *commence*, but the other one is ending.

My definition _____ start _____

Dictionary definition _____ to begin; start _____

7. Since I never write *convoluted* sentences, my constructions are simple and clear.

My definition _____ complicated; unclear _____

Dictionary definition _____ complicated; intricate _____

8. There are *innumerable* grains of sand on the beach.

My definition _____ without number; too many to count _____

Dictionary definition _____ too numerous to be counted _____

9. In contrast to the harmful, polluted city air, country air is *salubrious*.

My definition _____ good; healthy _____

Dictionary definition _____ good for the health _____

10. Rather than take a limousine, the bride and groom decided to *promenade* through the park to the reception.

My definition _____ walk _____

Dictionary definition _____ to go on a leisurely walk; stroll _____

Crime and Justice

WORD LIST

acquit	arson	corruption	counterfeit	culprit
felony	incarcerate	incriminate	jurisdiction	swindle

The words in this lesson deal with criminal acts and the prosecution of criminals. Some words, like *swindle* and *counterfeit,* refer to actual criminal offenses. Other words, like *jurisdiction, incarcerate,* and *acquit,* are terms that might be mentioned in a trial. These words are common in the news as well as in fiction.

Ask students to consider places they might encounter these words (such as news stories, crime novels, and so on).

1. **acquit** (ə-kwĭt´) *verb* from Latin *ad-,* "to" + French *quite,* "free; clear"
To declare not guilty
   • We wondered whether the jury would convict the man or **acquit** him.

   acquittal *noun* After her **acquittal,** the woman was free to leave.

2. **arson** (är´sən) *noun* from Latin *adere,* "to burn"
The crime of deliberately setting fire to something
   • Detectives searched the burned building for signs of **arson.**

   arsonist *noun* The **arsonist** was sentenced to several years in prison.

3. **corruption** (kə-rŭp´shən) *noun* from Latin *rumpere,* "to break"
Dishonesty or improper behavior in a person of authority
   • The mayor was accused of **corruption** after he accepted gifts in return for changing the zoning laws.

   corrupt *verb* It is said that power **corrupts.**

   corrupt *adjective* The **corrupt** jury member changed his vote after the defendant's relatives promised him a high-paying job.

   corruptible *adjective* We hope that police officers are not **corruptible.**

4. **counterfeit** (koun´tər-fĭt´) from Latin *contra,* "opposite" + *facere,* "to make"
   a. *verb* To make a fake or misleading copy of
      • It is a crime to **counterfeit** money.
   b. *adjective* Made in false imitation
      • A **counterfeit** Picasso painting was removed from the museum display.
   c. *noun* Something made in false imitation
      • That hundred dollar bill is a **counterfeit.**

   counterfeiter *noun* The **counterfeiter** was arrested.

> Although it can apply to other things, the word *counterfeit* usually applies to phony money.

counterfeit

5. **culprit** (kŭl´prĭt) *noun*
A guilty person
• Simone was the **culprit** who broke the window.

6. **felony** (fĕl´ə-nē) *noun* from Latin *fello,* "wicked person"
A serious crime
• Armed robbery is a **felony.**

   felon *noun* The convicted **felon** served ten years in prison.

   felonious *adjective* The trial proved that the man had **felonious** intent.

> Serious crimes, like arson, are *felonies.* Less serious crimes are called *misdemeanors.*

7. **incarcerate** (ĭn-kär´sə-rāt´) *verb* from Latin *in-,* "in" + *carcer,* "prison"
To put in prison
• The violent criminal was **incarcerated** in a maximum-security prison.

   incarceration *noun* After her **incarceration** ended, the woman became a model citizen.

8. **incriminate** (ĭn-krĭm´ə-nāt´) *verb* from Latin *in-,* "put in" + *crimen,* "crime"
To cause to appear guilty; to give evidence of guilt
• The testimony of three witnesses **incriminated** the man on trial.

   incrimination *noun* The Fifth Amendment of the U.S. Constitution protects citizens against self-**incrimination.**

9. **jurisdiction** (jŏŏr´ĭs-dĭk´shən) *noun* from Latin *ius,* "law" + *dicere,* "to say"
The extent or range of authority; control
• Federal courts have **jurisdiction** in bankruptcy cases.

10. **swindle** (swĭn´dl) from Old High German *swintan,* "to disappear"
    a. *verb* To cheat someone out of money or property
    • The salesman **swindled** people by convincing them to invest in a phony retirement fund.
    b. *noun* A scheme cheating someone out of money or property
    • We knew we were victims of a **swindle** when we saw that our vacation property was in the middle of a swamp.

    swindler *noun* The police pursued the **swindler** who had fled town.

WORD ENRICHMENT

An abbreviation of guilt

When William the Conqueror became king of England in 1066, he ordered that trials were to be conducted in French. If an accused person pleaded innocent, the prosecutor said the words *culpable, prest,* meaning "guilty: ready." This was an abbreviation for *he is guilty and we are ready to prove it.* After French was abandoned for English, the expression was shortened to *culprit.* Used first in 1678, the word now means "a guilty person."

WRITE THE CORRECT WORD

Write the correct word in the space next to each definition.

arson	**1.** the crime of setting fire	
incriminate	**2.** to cause to appear guilty	
corruption	**3.** improper behavior of an authority figure	
culprit	**4.** a guilty person	
felony	**5.** a serious crime	

swindle	**6.** to cheat of money	
counterfeit	**7.** to make a fake copy intended to deceive	
jurisdiction	**8.** the extent of authority	
acquit	**9.** to declare not guilty	
incarcerate	**10.** to put in prison	

COMPLETE THE SENTENCE

Write the letter for the word that best completes each sentence.

d **1.** Conviction for a(n) _____ usually carries a severe sentence.
    a. corruption   **b.** acquittal   **c.** culprit   **d.** felony

b **2.** A(n) _____ is a form of stealing.
    a. culprit   **b.** swindle   **c.** acquittal   **d.** jurisdiction

a **3.** The innocent man heaved a sigh of relief after the jury _____ him.
    a. acquitted   **b.** incriminated   **c.** incarcerated   **d.** corrupted

c **4.** The bank manager discovered several _____ twenty-dollar bills in the ATM.
    a. acquitted   **b.** corrupt   **c.** counterfeit   **d.** felonious

c **5.** The police captured the _____, using a description from a witness.
    a. arson   **b.** corruption   **c.** culprit   **d.** swindle

b **6.** While on school property, all students are under the principal's _____.
    a. corruption   **b.** jurisdiction   **c.** incrimination   **d.** incarceration

d **7.** The _____ burned his own car, in an illegal attempt to collect insurance money.
    a. counterfeiter   **b.** felony   **c.** corruption   **d.** arsonist

a **8.** _____ behavior by a public official, though not always criminal, is never proper.
    a. Corrupt   **b.** Counterfeit   **c.** Acquitted   **d.** Arsonist

d **9.** The man's unusual shoes left unique footprints at the crime scene, which _____ him in the robbery.
    a. corrupted   **b.** incarcerated   **c.** swindled   **d.** incriminated

b **10.** Because the judge thought he might flee, the accused man was _____ in the local jail until his trial.
    a. incriminated   **b.** incarcerated   **c.** acquitted   **d.** swindled

Challenge: The _____ elected official _____ himself when he was overheard accepting a bribe.
c   **a.** felonious...corrupted   **b.** acquitted...swindled   **c.** corrupt...incriminated

Jury—Service and Trial

One of the most important protections included in the U.S. Constitution is the right to a trial by jury. This provision ensures that U.S. citizens who have been accused of crimes have the ability to defend themselves in front of a jury of their peers.

(1) In the early Middle Ages in England, three ways were used to convict or *acquit* an accused person: One was compurgation, in which the accused swore an oath of innocence and got others to say that he had good character. If the person had enough believable witnesses, he was acquitted. In trial by battle, people fought, or chose others to fight for them. If the accused's side won, the person was considered innocent. Finally, there was trial by ordeal. For example, the accused might have had to take a stone out of a pot of boiling water. If the wounds healed within three days, the person was acquitted. (2) Unhealed wounds would *incriminate* a person. As you can see, justice has come a long way.

William the Conqueror created the first juries in England, around 1085. These juries did not preside over criminal cases, but rather determined what land and property belonged to whom. William's grandson, King Henry II, created the first criminal jury trials in England, in the mid-1100s. (3) Although not perfect, this system stopped the worst forms of *corruption*. (4) Before it was in place, people could bribe officials to *incarcerate* unfortunate victims who had no chance to defend themselves. (5) By creating a jury system, England's

kings helped to establish the crown's *jurisdiction* over the courts.

(6) By the end of the 1200s, juries had assumed their modern role of determining whether an accused person was the *culprit* of a crime. Every person had a right to a jury of social equals. In 1302, an accused knight objected to a jury member because the juror was not a knight.

The concept of a person's right to a trial by jury was brought to America by the early English settlers. However, the British kings did not always honor that right with their colonists. In the Declaration of Independence, Thomas Jefferson accused the king of "depriving us in many cases of the benefit of trial by jury."

It is not surprising, then, that the Founding Fathers wanted to assure the right of a jury trial to all U.S. citizens. Ten amendments, called the Bill of Rights, were added to the original Constitution to guarantee certain basic rights to all citizens. The Sixth and Seventh Amendments establish "the right to a trial by jury." (7) These amendments ensure that people accused of *felonies* can come before "a jury of their peers," or fellow citizens. Almost all adult citizens are, at one time or another, called to serve on a jury.

In the United States, a person may be on either a federal or a state jury. (8) Because the U.S. government prints our money, *counterfeiting* is a federal crime, tried before a federal jury. (9) In contrast, most cases of *arson* are tried in state courts. However, when a federal building is set on fire, the trial is held in a federal court. (10) Like arson, cases of *swindling* are usually tried in state courts.

Citizens' right to a jury trial and their willingness to serve on a jury are important safeguards of freedom and justice in the United States. When you read about or watch trials in the future, think back to the days of "trial by hot water." Then, you will appreciate today's justice system.

Each sentence below refers to a numbered sentence in the passage. Write the letter of the choice that gives the sentence a meaning that is closest to the original sentence.

___b___ **1.** Three ways were used to convict or _____ an accused person.
    a. punish   **b.** free   **c.** celebrate   **d.** trick

___d___ **2.** Unhealed wounds would _____ a person.
    a. astonish   **b.** examine in detail   **c.** imprison   **d.** show guilt of

___a___ **3.** Although not perfect, this system stopped the worst forms of _____ .
    a. dishonesty   **b.** government   **c.** imprisonment   **d.** authority

_c_ **4.** People could bribe officials to _____ unfortunate victims.
    a. admonish   **b.** free   **c.** imprison   **d.** insult

_a_ **5.** England's kings helped to establish the crown's _____ over the courts.
    a. authority   **b.** protection   **c.** taxation   **d.** threats

_a_ **6.** By the end of the 1200s, juries had assumed their modern role of determining whether an accused person was the _____ of a crime.
    a. guilty one   **b.** bystander   **c.** witness   **d.** victim

_c_ **7.** These amendments ensure that people accused of _____ can come before "a jury of their peers."
    a. minor offenses   **b.** telling lies   **c.** serious crimes   **d.** withholding evidence

_d_ **8.** Because the U.S. government prints our money, _____ is a federal crime.
    a. cheating on taxes   **b.** lying to judges   **c.** starting fires   **d.** making fakes

_b_ **9.** In contrast, most cases of _____ are tried in state courts.
    a. stealing money   **b.** fire setting   **c.** faking money   **d.** cheating

_c_ **10.** Like arson, cases of _____ are usually tried in state courts.
    a. serious crimes   **b.** burning   **c.** cheating   **d.** improper conduct

Indicate whether the statements below are TRUE or FALSE according to the passage.

_F_ **1.** During the Middle Ages, ways of deciding innocence or guilt were very accurate.

_T_ **2.** The Bill of Rights added the right to a jury trial to the U.S. Constitution.

_F_ **3.** Jury trials are rare and outdated in modern America.

WRITING EXTENDED RESPONSES

Crimes are often reported on TV and radio news, as well as written about in newspapers. Identify the lesson words that refer to specific crimes. Suppose that one of these crimes has been committed and you are the reporter writing about the case. Write a newspaper article about how the crime was allegedly committed and how the case against the accused is playing out in the courtroom. Your article should be at least three paragraphs long. Use at least three lesson words and underline them.

WRITE THE DERIVATIVE

Complete the sentence by writing the correct form of the word shown in parentheses. You may not need to change the form that is given.

incarceration   **1.** When the _____ ended, the prisoner was released. (*incarcerate*)

culprits   **2.** The two _____ escaped by disguising themselves. (*culprit*)

Corrupt   **3.** _____ leaders have a negative impact throughout a society. (*corruption*)

felonious   4. After the brutal fight, all participants were arrested and charged with _____ assault. (*felony*)

acquitted   5. There was not enough evidence to convict the thief, so he was _____. (*acquit*)

jurisdiction   6. The state police wanted to arrest the jewel thief before she could flee their _____. (*jurisdiction*)

swindled   7. The man _____ his business partners out of their share of the profits. (*swindle*)

counterfeit   8. The quality of the _____ stamp was high enough to fool most experts. (*counterfeit*)

incrimination   9. The anonymous tip led to the _____ of the suspect. (*incriminate*)

arsonist   10. The identity of the _____ was discovered soon after the fire was extinguished. (*arson*)

FIND THE EXAMPLE

Choose the answer that best describes the action or situation.

_b_   1. Something you probably can't do if you are *incarcerated*
   a. sleep   **b.** drive   **c.** eat   **d.** talk

_a_   2. Your ice-cream sandwich is missing—the most likely *culprit*
   a. hungry little sister   **b.** very tired lawyer   **c.** good pastry chef   **d.** experienced taxi driver

_b_   3. An example of a *felony*
   a. jaywalking   **b.** bank robbery   **c.** lifesaving   **d.** death

_d_   4. Most likely reason for *acquittal*
   a. lack of judges   **b.** lack of lawyers   **c.** lack of interest   **d.** lack of evidence

_c_   5. Something an *arsonist* probably will NOT need
   a. intent to burn   **b.** matches   **c.** water   **d.** flammable material

_c_   6. An example of *corruption*
   a. paying a bill late   **b.** refusing a favor   **c.** accepting a bribe   **d.** showing honesty

_a_   7. *Incriminating* evidence that someone ate a cookie
   a. crumbs on desk   **b.** full cookie tin   **c.** cookie on desk   **d.** walking away

_a_   8. Something that is LEAST likely to be *counterfeit*
   a. your reflection   **b.** a painting   **c.** money   **d.** a document

_d_   9. An example of a *jurisdiction*
   a. a month   **b.** a dinner   **c.** a planet   **d.** a city

_b_   10. Something likely to be *swindled* from someone
   a. reputation   **b.** property   **c.** opinion   **d.** promise

Abundance and Extravagance

WORD LIST

amass	embellish	extravagance	glut	inexhaustible
lavish	outrageous	profusely	spendthrift	voracious

Have you ever *embellished* the truth? Gone to a *lavish* party? Been *voraciously* hungry? The words in this lesson deal with concepts related to large or excessive amounts. Studying these words will help you to write more expressively.

1. amass (ə-măs´) *verb* from Latin *massa*, "lump; mass"
To gather or collect a large quantity
• Saving her small change enabled her to **amass** enough money to take a cruise.

2. embellish (ĕm-bĕl´ĭsh) *verb* from Latin *in-*, "to" + *bellus*, "beautiful"
To add decorative details or ornaments
• She **embellished** her handwriting with fancy swirls and dots.

embellishment *noun* The wooden lace on Victorian houses was a nineteenth-century **embellishment**.

> *To embellish the truth* means "to exaggerate" or "to lie."

embellish

3. extravagance (ĭk-străv´ə-gəns) *noun* from Latin *extra*, "outside" + *vagary*, "to wander"
An expense or effort that is great or excessive
• The expensive gown was an **extravagance** that she couldn't afford.

extravagant *adjective* They filled their yard with an **extravagant** display of decorations.

4. glut (glŭt) *verb* from Latin *gluttire*, "to eat greedily"
To fill or eat beyond capacity; to flood with an excess of goods
• When I **glut** myself on candy, I feel sick to my stomach.

glutton *noun* The giant in the fairy tale was a **glutton**, eating everything in sight.

gluttony *noun* **Gluttony** was once called one of the "Seven Deadly Sins."

5. inexhaustible (ĭn´ĭg-zô´stə-bəl) *adjective* from Latin *in-*, "not" + *exhaurire*, "to exhaust"
Unlimited; unable to be used up or tired out
• The restaurant seemed to have an **inexhaustible** supply of hamburgers.

Point out that many of these words have negative connotations (such as *glut* and *outrageous*.) Can the students identify a few? Allow them to defend their choices.

6. **lavish** (lăv´ĭsh) from Old French *lavesse,* "downpour"
   a. *adjective* Extremely plentiful and luxurious; generous in amount
     • Collin was impressed by the **lavish** furnishings in the hotel room.
   b. *verb* To give in great abundance
     • The mother **lavished** attention on her sick child.

   lavishness *noun* Barry was embarrassed by the **lavishness** of his friend's praise.

7. **outrageous** (out-rā´jəs) *adjective* from Old French *outre,* "beyond"
   Going beyond proper limits
   • It is **outrageous** for photographers to follow a celebrity's every move.

   outrage *noun* Customers considered the sudden price increase an **outrage.**

8. **profusely** (prə-fyo̅o̅s´lē) *adverb* from Latin *pro-,* "forward"
   + *fundere,* "to pour"
   Abundantly; generously
   • The daffodils grew **profusely** on the hillside.

   profuse *adjective* Your **profuse** use of exclamation points is inappropriate in a formal essay.

   profusion *noun* A **profusion** of stars appeared in the sky, soon after the sun went down.

9. **spendthrift** (spĕnd´thrĭft´)
   a. *noun* A person who spends money wastefully or carelessly
     • The **spendthrift** won the lottery—and squandered all the money in a month.
   b. *adjective* Wasteful or extravagant
     • His **spendthrift** habits resulted in outrageous credit card debt.

10. **voracious** (vô-rā´shəs) *adjective* from Latin *vorare,* "to devour"
    Extremely hungry for large amounts of food; extremely greedy
    • I had a **voracious** appetite after running the marathon.

    voracity *noun* The teenagers **voracity** made it difficult for their mother to keep the pantry stocked with food.

> *Voracious* can also mean "inexhaustible appetite for an activity," as in "a *voracious* antique collector."

WORD ENRICHMENT

A royal spendthríft

According to legend, Cleopatra, the last Egyptian queen, threw *lavish* parties. In one story, she claimed that she could throw the most expensive dinner party in history. The next night, when the second course arrived—a cup of vinegar—she took off an enormous pearl earring, crushed it, and dropped it in the cup. The solution fizzed and popped as the vinegar dissolved the pearl. Cleopatra then drank the *extravagant* mixture!

WRITE THE CORRECT WORD

Write the correct word in the space next to each definition.

profusely	**1.** abundantly	voracious	**6.** extremely greedy
embellish	**2.** to add decorations	amass	**7.** to collect or gather
glut	**3.** to eat beyond capacity	inexhaustible	**8.** not able to be used up
spendthrift	**4.** one who spends wastefully	extravagance	**9.** an excessive expense or effort
lavish	**5.** plentiful and luxurious	outrageous	**10.** beyond proper limits

COMPLETE THE SENTENCE

Write the letter for the word that best completes each sentence.

d **1.** The _____ hiker easily continued up the mountain while the others rested.
 a. glutted   **b.** lavished   **c.** embellished   **d.** inexhaustible

c **2.** The protestors' demands for tax reductions seemed _____ to the administration.
 a. lavish   **b.** embellished   **c.** outrageous   **d.** gluttonous

a **3.** Maggie, who read a book every day, was considered a(n) _____ reader.
 a. voracious   **b.** lavish   **c.** embellished   **d.** outrageous

a **4.** Going the extra mile, Hannah added numerous _____ to her presentation.
 a. embellishments   **b.** amassments   **c.** profusions   **d.** outrages

b **5.** The roommates _____ an enormous CD collection over the years.
 a. glutted   **b.** amassed   **c.** outraged   **d.** lavished

b **6.** Building too many new coffee shops _____ the market.
 a. outraged   **b.** glutted   **c.** amassed   **d.** embellished

d **7.** The customer orders were so _____ that the manufacturer couldn't keep up with them.
 a. extravagant   **b.** lavish   **c.** embellished   **d.** profuse

c **8.** The _____ of the decor seemed in keeping with the rich history of the mansion.
 a. profusion   **b.** gluttony   **c.** lavishness   **d.** spendthrift

d **9.** Our family vacation each summer was the one _____ we could afford.
 a. voracity   **b.** gluttony   **c.** outrage   **d.** extravagance

a **10.** A(n) _____ and his money are soon separated.
 a. spendthrift   **b.** outrage   **c.** amassment   **d.** extravagance

Challenge: The bride and groom _____ a large collection of _____ gifts from their wealthy relatives.
a **a.** amassed…lavish   **b.** glutted…voracious   **c.** outraged…extravagant

Starving on Gold

"Be careful what you wish for" is an adage that King Midas should have heeded. Instead, his greatest wish almost brought his death.

According to Greek mythology, Midas was king of Phrygia, located in present-day Turkey. **(1)** Phrygia was the land of roses, and these fragrant flowers *embellished* his gardens. **(2)** Midas lived in an elegant castle, where he *amassed* rich tapestries and expensive furniture. But all of these riches were not enough to satisfy him.

One day, Silenus, the former schoolmaster of the god Bacchus, wandered away, got lost, and fell asleep. Some Phrygian peasants found him and carried him to their king. **(3)** Recognizing him, Midas gave Silenus a warm welcome and spared no *extravagance* for his entertainment. The finest delicacies were served up on gold plates; the best poets, singers, and dancers performed for him. **(4)** Silenus ate *voraciously* and amused himself mightily. **(5)** After ten days, *glutted* and entertained, Silenus was ready to return to Bacchus's home. Midas accompanied him on the journey. Bacchus was thrilled to see his former teacher and was so grateful to Midas that he offered to grant him any wish.

Now, Midas was a greedy person. **(6)** "Wouldn't it be nice," thought he, "to have an *inexhaustible* supply of gold?"

So he asked Bacchus to make everything he touched turn to gold. Bacchus sadly granted Midas's wish, disappointed that the king had not made a wiser choice. **(7)** Thanking him *profusely*, Midas rushed out to test his new powers. A twig, a stone, and even a clump of soil instantly became gold as he touched them. He pocketed his newfound wealth and hurried home.

(8) To celebrate, he ordered a *lavish* feast. But as he reached to take some bread, it too turned to metal. The food he raised to his mouth, and the drink in his cup, all turned to gold as soon as he touched them. **(9)** Realizing what he had done, he rushed back to Bacchus, begging to be released from the *outrageous* fate of starving on golden food.

In his mercy, Bacchus revealed that Midas's wish could be reversed if he bathed in the Pactolus River. Midas followed the god's orders. He had hardly touched the water's surface, when his gold-producing powers left him. But in that fraction of a second, the river's sands turned to gold. Even today, traces of gold can be found on the banks of the Pactolus River.

(10) It is said that Midas then came to regret being a *spendthrift*. He spent the rest of his life wandering through the woods and living a simple life.

Each sentence below refers to a numbered sentence in the passage. Write the letter of the choice that gives the sentence a meaning that is closest to the original sentence.

___a___ **1.** Phrygia was the land of roses, and these fragrant flowers _____ his gardens.
  a. decorated   **b.** perfumed   **c.** gathered   **d.** grew in

___b___ **2.** Midas lived in an elegant castle, where he _____ rich tapestries and expensive furniture.
  a. examined   **b.** collected   **c.** wasted   **d.** decorated

___a___ **3.** Midas gave Silenus a warm welcome and spared no _____ for his entertainment.
  a. great expense   **b.** exaggeration   **c.** singer or dancer   **d.** decoration

90 **Abundance and Extravagance**

___d___ **4.** Silenus ate _____ and amused himself mightily.
    a. decoratively   **b.** quietly   **c.** politely   **d.** greedily

___c___ **5.** After ten days, _____ and entertained, Silenus was ready to return to Bacchus's home.
    a. hungry   **b.** generous   **c.** stuffed   **d.** broke

___c___ **6.** "Wouldn't it be nice," thought he, "to have an _____ supply of gold?"
    a. ample   **b.** unusual   **c.** unlimited   **d.** extra

___d___ **7.** Thanking him _____, Midas rushed out to test his new powers.
    a. sincerely   **b.** loudly   **c.** politely   **d.** abundantly

___a___ **8.** To celebrate, he ordered a(n) _____ feast.
    a. plentiful   **b.** small   **c.** decorative   **d.** unlimited

___b___ **9.** Realizing what he had done, he rushed back to Bacchus, begging to be released from the _____ fate of starving on golden food.
    a. tragic human   **b.** beyond limits   **c.** excessive   **d.** very unusual

___b___ **10.** It is said that Midas then came to regret being a(n) _____.
    a. bad friend   **b.** wasteful spender   **c.** overeater   **d.** evil ruler

Indicate whether the statements below are TRUE or FALSE according to the passage.

___T___ **1.** Before receiving his "golden touch," Midas preferred to live richly in expensive surroundings.

___T___ **2.** Midas did not think through the consequences of his wish.

___F___ **3.** With nothing to eat, Midas starved to death.

FINISH THE THOUGHT

Complete each sentence so that it shows the meaning of the italicized word.

1. It would be an *extravagance* to _____ Answers will vary. _____

_____

2. I thanked her *profusely* by _____ Answers will vary. _____

_____

WRITE THE DERIVATIVE

Complete the sentence by writing the correct form of the word shown in parentheses. You may not need to change the form that is given.

___extravagant___ **1.** Some people are annoyed by the _____ purchases of others. *(extravagance)*

___outrage___ **2.** At the press conference, the senator considered the news reporter's interruption to be an _____. *(outrageous)*

amassing	3. Both candidates are _____ a large number of votes. (amass)
spendthrift	4. Mark was no _____, but he found saving money very difficult. (spendthrift)
lavishness	5. The expense and effort that went into preparations were reflected in the _____ of the party. (lavish)
inexhaustible	6. The students complained about the seemingly _____ amount of homework assignments. (inexhaustible)
embellishments	7. The musicians added _____ to the melody, which made their performance unique. (embellish)
voracity	8. If you watch Grace eat once, you will never again question her _____. (voracious)
Gluttony	9. _____ is unhealthy behavior. (glut)
profusion	10. Throughout the pasture, a _____ of daisies shimmered in the summer breeze. (profusely)

FIND THE EXAMPLE

Choose the answer that best describes the action or situation.

d   **1.** Something that would be most difficult for a *glutton* to resist
   a. island vacation   **b.** science fiction   **c.** sports car   **d.** fried chicken

a   **2.** Something a *spendthrift* needs lots of
   a. money   **b.** food   **c.** paper   **d.** friends

c   **3.** Something that is usually NOT *embellished*
   a. music   **b.** artwork   **c.** nature   **d.** carved furniture

a   **4.** Something a library is NOT likely to *amass*
   a. bikes   **b.** books   **c.** magazines   **d.** CDs

d   **5.** A *voracious* person's favorite spot
   a. bed   **b.** dentist's office   **c.** laundrymat   **d.** all-you-can-eat buffet

b   **6.** Something that is most likely to be considered a *lavish* gift
   a. a blanket   **b.** a house   **c.** a DVD   **d.** a new shirt

b   **7.** Something that you usually see in *profusion*
   a. UFOs   **b.** raindrops   **c.** lottery winners   **d.** fire hydrants

a   **8.** The situation most likely to be *extravagant*
   a. wedding   **b.** bus ride   **c.** luncheon   **d.** parent-teacher meeting

b   **9.** Something most likely to be an *outrage*
   a. homework   **b.** cheating   **c.** helping   **d.** exercising

c   **10.** Something that is most likely to be *inexhaustible*
   a. song   **b.** milk   **c.** air   **d.** batteries

Planning and Action

WORD LIST

administration	animation	apportion	concoct	devise
dogged	endeavor	execute	reactivate	render

Good planning is often a key to success, even if our plans don't always go the way we expect. These words help you describe planning—and what happens when those plans get put into action.

1. **administration** (ăd-mĭn´ĭ-strā´shən) *noun* from Latin *ad-,* "to" + *ministrare,* "to manage"
   a. Management or control of a business or political unit
      • The large company had several levels of **administration.**
   b. The giving of; the distribution of
      • The head nurse oversaw the **administration** of medicine.

   administer *verb* Relief workers **administered** aid to flood victims.

   administrator *noun* Mrs. Smith was the **administrator** of social security services in the county.

2. **animation** (ăn´ə-mā´shən) *noun* from Latin *anima,* "life" or "soul" The process or result of giving life or motion to
   • The Web site designer added **animation** to the home page.

   animate *verb* In a famous myth, Aphrodite **animates** Pygmalion's beautiful statue, creating the woman Galatea.

   animator *noun* The **animator** created a new character for the short film.

> The adjective *animated* means "lively," as in "an *animated* performance."

animation

3. **apportion** (ə-pôr´shən) *verb* from Old French *a-,* "to" + *portionner,* "to divide" To measure out or assign something to different people, according to a plan
   • The Constitution **apportions** representatives by state population.

   apportionment *noun* The family members all seemed content with the **apportionment** of the land as described in the will.

4. **concoct** (kən-kŏkt´) *verb* from Latin *com-,* "with" + *coquere,* "to cook"
   a. To make up or invent
      • The rock group **concocted** lyrics from nonsense words.
   b. To make by mixing ingredients
      • Without using a recipe, my mother often **concocts** delicious meals.

   concoction *noun* The boys dined on a **concoction** made from all the candy, cookies, and ice cream they could find.

Point out that *concoct* and *devise* have to do with planning. In contrast, *execute* and *render* deal with actual action.

5. **devise** (dĭ-vīz´) *verb* from Latin *dis-*, "apart" + *videre*, "to separate"
To create by arranging or inventing
• Max **devised** a program that allowed the two computer languages to communicate.

6. **dogged** (dô´gĭd) *adjective* from English *dog*
Stubbornly pursuing a goal
• It took years, but the detective's **dogged** efforts finally solved the crime.

doggedness *noun* We admired the mother's **doggedness** in insisting on the best medical treatment for her sick child.

7. **endeavor** (ĕn-dĕv´ər) from Old French *devoir*, "duty"
a. *noun* An attempt or effort to do something
• The whole family took part in the new business **endeavor.**
b. *verb* To try to do something
• We always **endeavor** to be on time, but sometimes we fail.

8. **execute** (ĕk´sĭ-kyoot´) *verb* from Latin *ex-*, "out" + *sequi*, "sequence"
To do; to put into effect; to carry out
• Moira **executed** the dance routine on skates.

execution *noun* The piano soloist practiced the piece often so that his **execution** of it, at the concert, would be flawless.

> *Execute* can also mean "to kill."

9. **reactivate** (rē-ăk´tə-vāt´) *verb* from Latin *re-*, "again" + *agree*, "to do"
To restore the ability to function; to make active again
• Once repairs were complete, a technician used the control box to **reactivate** the electronic scoreboard.

reactivation *noun* After his injury had completely healed, the player was ready for **reactivation** by the team.

10. **render** (rĕn´dər) *verb* from Latin *re-*, "back" + *dare*, "to give"
a. To give or to make available
• The doctors will **render** medical treatment to all those who come to the clinic.
b. To cause to become; make
• The beautiful ballet **rendered** the audience completely speechless.

WORD ENRICHMENT

Doggie words and phrases

The word *dogged* is taken from the stubborn determination of dogs that are following a scent to locate its source. Other phrases show how many ways we view an animal that has often been called "man's best friend."

Putting on the dog means "to show off one's wealth, elegance, or knowledge." *Going to the dogs* means "to deteriorate or go to ruin." *To rain cats and dogs* means "to rain very hard," and *dog tired* means "extremely tired."

WRITE THE CORRECT WORD

Write the correct word in the space next to each definition.

___render___ **1.** to cause to become; make

___endeavor___ **2.** to try to do something

___devise___ **3.** to create by inventing

___reactivate___ **4.** to make active again

___apportion___ **5.** to measure out or to allot

___administration___ **6.** management

___concoct___ **7.** to make by mixing ingredients

___dogged___ **8.** stubborn

___execute___ **9.** to carry out

___animation___ **10.** the process of giving life or motion to

COMPLETE THE SENTENCE

Write the letter for the word that best completes each sentence.

__c__ **1.** The committee wanted to _____ a foolproof plan for winning the election.
   a. apportion   **b.** reactivate   **c.** devise   **d.** endeavor

__b__ **2.** The new _____ wanted to improve voters' image of their party.
   a. animation   **b.** administration   **c.** concoction   **d.** reactivation

__d__ **3.** The paramedics _____ medical assistance to everyone injured in the accident.
   a. devised   **b.** concocted   **c.** animated   **d.** rendered

__a__ **4.** The three friends _____ an elaborate excuse for being late to school.
   a. concocted   **b.** endeavored   **c.** executed   **d.** administered

__a__ **5.** The virus had to be removed from the whole system before the Web site could be _____.
   a. reactivated   **b.** animated   **c.** apportioned   **d.** administered

__d__ **6.** The building plan required that the land be _____ equally among the house lots.
   a. endeavored   **b.** concocted   **c.** animated   **d.** apportioned

__b__ **7.** The quarterback _____ the play perfectly, making the coach very proud.
   a. apportioned   **b.** executed   **c.** reactivated   **d.** animated

__c__ **8.** The writer's _____ paid off when the book was finally published.
   a. apportionment   **b.** concoction   **c.** doggedness   **d.** reactivation

__c__ **9.** Carla's _____ cartoon received an award of special merit at the art show.
   a. reactivated   **b.** apportioned   **c.** animated   **d.** dogged

__d__ **10.** The young inventor _____ to find people to invest in his new company.
   a. devised   **b.** apportioned   **c.** reactivated   **d.** endeavored

Challenge: The advertising scheme _____ by the music producer was one of the most creative ever _____.
__c__   **a.** rendered…dogged   **b.** animated…reactivated   **c.** concocted…devised

Animation and Animators

You have probably seen many cartoons, but how often do you think about the people who make them? To animate means to give life, or at least movement, to something that can't act by itself. **(1)** *Animation* is achieved through the use of a series of still images. There are many such images, and each one is like a unique snapshot. When they are presented in a quick sequence, the human brain sees them as continuous motion.

(2) Animation was actually *devised* in the 1800s, when people looked into moving cylinders and saw what we would consider very crude cartoons. Later, cameras were used to take pictures of moving objects. One early animation pioneer, Winsor McCay, created films in which he actually performed with his cartoon characters. **(3)** The silly nature of the stories hid the *dogged* effort needed to produce these works. **(4)** At times, it took McKay more than a year to *execute* a five-minute cartoon. From these beginnings, the Walt Disney Studios brought animation to new heights. **(5)** Beginning in the 1920s, they *concocted* longer movies with interesting story lines and characters. In 1937, *Snow White and the Seven Dwarfs* became the first full-length animated film.

(6) Although these films were highly artistic, the Disney *administration* turned production into almost factory-like work. **(7)** Thousands of cartoon images were *apportioned* among different artists. **(8)** The artists *rendered* each image by hand, and the results were put together into works of stunning beauty.

Today, many cartoons are created by using computers. In 1995, Pixar was the first company to create a completely computer-generated full-length animated film, *Toy Story*. **(9)** These computer-generated films have *reactivated* interest in animation. In fact, computer-generated animation has also been integrated into many live-action movies that have special effects.

What would it be like to be an animator? Anne Awh studied art, including drawing, in college. She then attended Sheridan College in Ontario, Canada, where she learned the basics of animation. These basics included drawing the human figure and creating motion.

At her first job, Awh made animated portions of commercials. After that, she helped create children's CD-ROM games, including an adaptation of the Disney movie *101 Dalmatians*. In these two jobs, Awh hand-created art that was scanned into a computer and colored in. Now she works from home, making animated greeting cards. At times, she draws on paper. Or she may use a graphics tablet and stylus to create the images on a computer. The greeting cards include sound effects as well as visual images.

(10) One of Awh's favorite *endeavors* was making her own animated film. She created more than 2,000 drawings, scanned them into a computer, and added sound. The result was a three-minute film! Although many of her friends work at big studios, Awh enjoys the independence of a job that allows her to work on her own projects.

Each sentence below refers to a numbered sentence in the passage. Write the letter of the choice that gives the sentence a meaning that is closest to the original sentence.

_a_ 1. _____ is achieved through the use of a series of still images.
   a. A moving image   **b.** Control   **c.** A computer   **d.** A photograph

_d_ 2. Animation was actually _____ in the 1800s.
   a. abandoned   **b.** revisited   **c.** given out   **d.** created

_b_ 3. The silly nature of the stories hid the _____ effort needed to produce these works.
   a. allotted   **b.** stubborn   **c.** made-up   **d.** controlled

_c_ 4. At times, it took McKay more than a year to _____ a five-minute cartoon.
   a. eliminate   **b.** design   **c.** do   **d.** publish

___d___ **5.** They _____ longer movies with interesting story lines and characters.
    a. canceled   **b.** revised   **c.** activated   **d.** made up

___c___ **6.** The Disney _____ turned production into almost factory-like work.
    a. sales plan   **b.** theater network   **c.** management   **d.** investment

___a___ **7.** Thousands of cartoon images were _____ among different artists.
    a. spread   **b.** preserved   **c.** cataloged   **d.** eliminated

___b___ **8.** The artists _____ each image by hand, and the results were put together into works of stunning beauty.
    a. photographed   **b.** made   **c.** stenciled   **d.** erased

___d___ **9.** These computer-generated films have _____ interest in animation.
    a. eliminated   **b.** maintained   **c.** killed off   **d.** restored

___b___ **10.** One of Awh's favorite _____ was making her own animated film.
    a. drawings   **b.** efforts   **c.** portions   **d.** hobbies

Indicate whether the statements below are TRUE or FALSE according to the passage.

___F___ **1.** Animation did not exist until computers became available.

___T___ **2.** Feature-length animations, such as those from Disney, require a team of artists to produce.

___T___ **3.** Successful animators like Anne Awh work long and hard to learn their craft.

WRITING EXTENDED RESPONSES

Suppose that you are an animator like Anne Awh. You are preparing to produce a ten-minute cartoon. Write a descriptive essay about your cartoon. Describe the subject you would choose and why you would select this subject. You may also choose to describe the process you would go through to make your animation. Your essay should be at least three paragraphs long. Use at least three lesson words in your essay and underline them.

WRITE THE DERIVATIVE

Complete the sentence by writing the correct form of the word shown in parentheses. You may not need to change the form that is given.

endeavored   **1.** Although the job was difficult, I _____ to do my best work. (*endeavor*)

doggedly   **2.** The tracker followed the animal's trail _____, day after day, without giving up. (*dogged*)

devised   **3.** Last year, the club members _____ a secret handshake. (*devise*)

rendered   **4.** After several days of deliberation, the jury _____ its verdict. (*render*)

administrators **5.** All the _____ wanted to improve the school's academic reputation. (*administration*)

reactivated **6.** The old power plant was _____ once its restoration was complete. (*reactivate*)

apportioned **7.** The moderator _____ time equally among the candidates so that each one had a fair chance to speak. (*apportion*)

concoction **8.** The _____ for removing stains was the basis of a multimillion-dollar business venture. (*concoct*)

animators **9.** Some _____ always use a consistent style. (*animation*)

execution **10.** Planning a task is important, but its _____ is the final measure of its success. (*execute*)

FIND THE EXAMPLE

Choose the answer that best describes the action or situation.

a **1.** Something one could *execute*
  a. a plan   **b.** a banana   **c.** a book   **d.** a car

c **2.** An uncommon *concoction*
  a. fruit salad   **b.** stew   **c.** broccoli muffins   **d.** peanut butter and jelly

b **3.** A quality required for *doggedness*
  a. daydreaming   **b.** determination   **c.** sleepiness   **d.** intelligence

b **4.** Something that could be *reactivated*
  a. a falling apple   **b.** a stopped clock   **c.** a sandy beach   **d.** a running nose

a **5.** Something that requires *administration*
  a. a department   **b.** a bike   **c.** a stroll   **d.** a dog

d **6.** A service commonly *rendered* to customers at a restaurant
  a. floor is cleaned   **b.** shirts are washed   **c.** teeth are brushed   **d.** food is served

d **7.** An *endeavor* most athletes find important
  a. sing well   **b.** keep shoes clean   **c.** watch TV   **d.** stay in shape

b **8.** Something an architect would most likely *devise*
  a. stylish haircut   **b.** house blueprints   **c.** new recipe   **d.** plan for peace

c **9.** Something you are likely to *apportion* at dinner
  a. salt shakers   **b.** land   **c.** pizza slices   **d.** a napkin

a **10.** Something that often uses *animation*
  a. a computer game   **b.** a photograph   **c.** a public speech   **d.** a statue

Reading and Reasoning

Analogies

Words can be related in many different ways. One formal way to explore the relationships between words is called an *analogy*. An analogy, which is a comparison between two things, can help you develop your reasoning powers. A word analogy is usually given in this form: Word A is to word B as word C is to word D.

Strategies

1. *Determine the relationship between the first two words.* In the following example, you must understand the relationship between **scrap** and **paper** before you can answer the item.

   Scrap is to paper as _____.
   a. edge is to knife
   b. wall is to brick
   c. dust is to broom
   d. shoe is to heel
   e. splinter is to wood

   Think of a short sentence that describes the relationship between the two words. The relationship between **scrap** and **paper** can best be stated as, "A scrap is a small piece of paper." This sentence is short and specific; avoid long sentences.

2. *Apply your sentence to each of the answer choices.*
   a. edge is to knife: Is an edge a small piece of knife? No
   b. wall is to brick: Is a wall a small piece of brick? No
   c. dust is to broom: Is dust a small piece of a broom? No
   d. shoe is to heel: Is a shoe a small piece of heel? No
   e. splinter is to wood: Is a splinter a small piece of wood? Yes

3. *Select the answer that best matches the relationship between the original pair of words.* In this example, the answer is (e) since, "A scrap is a small piece of paper, and a splinter is a small piece of wood."

Practice

Find the relationship between the first pair of words for each item. Then choose the answer that shows the same relationship or a similar one. Write the letter of your choice on the answer line. Use your dictionary as needed.

___d___ 1. Tyrant is to democracy as _____.
   a. conservative is to change
   b. liberal is to rights
   c. Spartan is to disciplined
   d. anarchist is to laws
   e. delegate is to representation

___c___ 2. Consensus is to agreement as _____.
   a. anguished is to cheerful
   b. blithe is to dejected
   c. momentous is to noteworthy
   d. friendly is to afraid
   e. amicable is to hostile

_____a_____ **3.** Slow is to expedite as _____.
         a. dense is to penetrate   **d.** friendly is to afraid
         b. distinct is to hear   **e.** fragrant is to smell
         c. erroneous is to criticize

_____a_____ **4.** Accompanist is to piano as _____.
         a. surgeon is to scalpel   **d.** actor is to stage
         b. artist is to painting   **e.** watchmaker is to time
         c. archeologist is to pottery

_____a_____ **5.** Aquatic is to water as _____.
         a. terrestrial is to land   **d.** isolated is to island
         b. solar is to energy   **e.** scientific is to experiments
         c. vegetarian is to plants

_____b_____ **6.** Altruism is to benefactor as _____.
         a. plagiarism is to ideas   **d.** young is to centenarian
         b. drama is to actor   **e.** zoology is to animals
         c. etymology is to insects

_____d_____ **7.** Belligerent is to fight as _____.
         a. durable is to deteriorate   **d.** perishable is to spoil
         b. eternal is to end   **e.** perpetual is to stop
         c. heavy is to bounce

_____c_____ **8.** Inauguration is to president as _____.
         a. demotion is to employee   **d.** decoration is to soldier
         b. divorce is to spouse   **e.** maturation is to teenager
         c. coronation is to king

_____e_____ **9.** Despondent is to unhappy as _____.
         a. flower is to seed   **d.** breeze is to wind
         b. muscle is to bone   **e.** eminence is to importance
         c. dryness is to rain

_____a_____ **10.** Peer is to unequal as _____.
         a. throng is to alone   **d.** temporary is to fame
         b. formal is to style   **e.** related is to parallel
         c. contagious is to disease

Secrecy and Openness

WORD LIST

access	cache	conspicuous	elusive	inter
intrigue	obscurity	seclude	unavailable	unearth

We live in a society with free and open communication. Yet we all have personal secrets, combinations to locks, and secret codes for entry. Important secrets can be a risk, however. Identity theft and fraud occur when criminals gain access to our credit card and bank account numbers. The words in this lesson are related to secrecy and openness.

Have students identify some lesson words that relate to the concepts of secrecy (such as *unavailable* and *cache*) or openness (such as *unearth* and *access*). Allow them to discuss and defend their choices.

1. **access** (ăk´sĕs) from Latin *acedere,* "to arrive"
   a. *noun* Entry; a means of getting to something
   • This key provides **access** to my apartment.
   b. *verb* To enter or make available
   • You will need a password to **access** those computer files.

   accessibility *noun* The store improved **accessibility** to fire escapes by widening the aisles.

access

   accessible *adjective* The Internet makes huge amounts of information **accessible** to people around the world.

2. **cache** (kăsh) *noun* from Vulgar Latin *coacticare,* "to store"
   a. A hiding place for supplies or provisions
   • A badger was sleeping in the hollow log that the trapper used as a **cache** for his tools.
   b. A hidden supply of goods or valuables
   • The secret panel in the library concealed a **cache** of jewels.

> In computer science, a *cache*, or *cache memory*, is a way to store frequently used instructions or data.

3. **conspicuous** (kən-spĭk´yōō-əs) *adjective* from Latin *conspicere,* "to look"
   Noticeable; attracting attention
   • Jeremy felt **conspicuous** in the bright orange mechanic's jumper.

   conspicuously *adverb* The large statue stood **conspicuously** in the middle of the small town.

   conspicuousness *noun* The **conspicuousness** of extra guards at the bank helped discourage theft.

4. **elusive** (ĭ-lōō´sĭv) *adjective* from Latin *eludere,* "to elude"
   Hard to grasp or capture
   • He thought he had seen someone, but the **elusive** image vanished into the fog.

   elude *verb* The meaning of that poem simply **eludes** me.

   elusiveness *noun* The **elusiveness** of butterflies helps them to survive.

5. **inter** (ĭn-tûr´) *verb* from Latin *in-*, "in" + *terra,* "earth"
To bury; to place in a grave
• It was Mark's job to **inter** the time capsule, not knowing if he would ever see it again.

interment *noun* After a military service, the **interment** of the general's body will take place at Arlington National Cemetery.

6. **intrigue** from Latin *intricare,* "to entangle"
a. *noun* (ĭn´trēg´) A secret plot
• The nobles' **intrigue** ended with the king losing his throne.
b. *verb* (ĭn-trēg´) To plot secretly
• The spies **intrigued** to obtain the valuable document.
c. *verb* (ĭn-trēg´) To fascinate
• Although I didn't fully understand it, I was **intrigued** by the poem.

7. **obscurity** (ŏb-skyŏor´ĭ-tē) *noun* from Latin *obscurus,* "dark"
a. Darkness
• The child cried in fear, as she entered the **obscurity** of the cave.
b. The condition of being difficult to understand
• The **obscurity** of the literary references baffled most of the novel's readers.
c. The condition of being unknown or not famous
• Many important inventors have lived in poverty and **obscurity.**

obscure *adjective* The instructions for filling out the government form were too **obscure** for Jesse to follow.

8. **seclude** (sĭ-klood´) *verb* from Latin *se-,* "apart" + *claudere,* "to shut"
To set apart; to hide from view
• Ling often **secludes** herself in her room to study for exams.

secluded *adjective* The corporation's headquarters were tucked away in a **secluded** wooded area, miles from any town.

seclusion *noun* The scholar spent many hours studying in **seclusion.**

9. **unavailable** (ŭn´ə-vā´lə-bəl) *adjective* from Old English *un-,* "not" + Latin *valere,* "to be strong"
Not at hand or not capable of being gotten; not ready for use
• Because hot water was **unavailable,** we had to take cold showers.

unavailability *noun* Because of the **unavailability** of high-quality turkeys, Mom made chicken for Thanksgiving dinner.

10. **unearth** (ŭn-ûrth´) *verb* from Old English *un-,* "not" + *eorthe,* "earth"
To bring up out of the earth or from an unknown storage place; to uncover
• The office staff searched all day, hoping to **unearth** the lost file.

WRITE THE CORRECT WORD

Write the correct word in the space next to each definition.

conspicuous	**1.** noticeable		cache	**6.** a hiding place
unavailable	**2.** not capable of being gotten		access	**7.** to enter or make available
seclude	**3.** set apart		unearth	**8.** to dig up or uncover
inter	**4.** to bury		obscurity	**9.** darkness
elusive	**5.** hard to capture		intrigue	**10.** a secret plot

COMPLETE THE SENTENCE

Write the letter for the word that best completes each sentence.

a **1.** During our hike, Katherine pointed out a(n) _____ variety of plant, which none of us had ever seen before.
    a. obscure   **b.** accessible   **c.** accessed   **d.** unavailable

c **2.** The airport is easily _____ from the city; you can get there by train, bus, or car.
    a. conspicuous   **b.** obscure   **c.** accessible   **d.** unavailable

b **3.** Rescued miners joined the struggle to _____ those still trapped underground.
    a. cache   **b.** unearth   **c.** intrigue   **d.** seclude

b **4.** Arianna's large, colorful hat was so _____ that Jill spotted her right away.
    a. elusive   **b.** conspicuous   **c.** unavailable   **d.** secluded

d **5.** Sylvia avoided the beach by the lake because it was lonely and _____.
    a. accessible   **b.** elusive   **c.** unavailable   **d.** secluded

c **6.** Some pharaohs of ancient Egypt were _____ in pyramids, along with many precious possessions.
    a. intrigued   **b.** eluded   **c.** interred   **d.** obscured

d **7.** My brother enjoys movies that involve complex _____.
    a. conspicuousness   **b.** access   **c.** unavailability   **d.** intrigues

a **8.** Lars had a(n) _____ of money under his mattress for emergencies.
    a. cache   **b.** obscurity   **c.** intrigue   **d.** access

d **9.** Since the movie we wanted was _____ at the video store, we rented another one.
    a. interred   **b.** conspicuous   **c.** accessible   **d.** unavailable

a **10.** The _____ robber escaped capture for years.
    a. elusive   **b.** accessible   **c.** unearthed   **d.** conspicuous

Challenge: The _____ senator always seemed to be _____ to comment on the scandal.
b
    a. accessible…obscure   **b.** elusive…unavailable   **c.** intriguing…conspicuous

Murals Lost and Found

The Chicago public schools are home to a valuable collection of beautiful murals that decorate school walls. But for years, these murals were neglected, painted over, or put into storage and forgotten. Many murals had begun to deteriorate. **(1)** The rescue of these murals from *obscurity* restores a precious artistic and historical heritage to the citizens of Chicago.

Although some were painted as early as 1904, many of the school system's murals were painted in the 1930s and 1940s. The Great Depression of the 1930s caused artists, whose income is often unstable, to suffer greatly. In response, President Franklin Delano Roosevelt created an employment program that benefited the artists and the public. Through the Works Progress Administration, or WPA, gifted artists were hired to decorate public places, such as post offices, park buildings, and, most of all, schools.

In the largest effort of the time, murals were painted in numerous Chicago public schools. **(2)** In the 1930s and 1940s, they hung *conspicuously* in halls, auditoriums, and lunchrooms. As time went on, however, the murals were dimmed by dirt, painted over, or removed.

(3) In at least one case, *intrigue* played a part in a mural's decline. In 1940, Edward Millman completed a huge mural for Lucy Flower Vocational High School (now Al Raby). **(4)** Located in a *secluded* place off the main hall, it was a tribute to American women, including reformer Jane Adams, voting-rights advocate Susan B. Anthony, and leader of the Underground Railroad, Harriet Tubman. The mural also showed the suffering of poor, working women. But the realistic images of oppression and misery upset some board of education members. **(5)** They felt that students should not have *access* to this controversial content. They ordered the mural painted over, only eighteen months after it was completed. **(6)** For more than half a century, the beautiful paintings remained *unavailable* for viewing.

When Flower High Principal Dorothy Williams heard stories of murals that were hidden under white paint, she tried to generate interest in their restoration. At first, this proved difficult; many people doubted they even existed. But, in 1995, the Chicago Conservation Center determined that the white paint was covering the murals, and that the murals could be restored.

(7) In 1996, at Flower High School, the Center began to *unearth* the precious works from beneath coats of oil paint and whitewash. Amazed staff and students watched as white walls gave way to brilliant colors.

Teacher Flora Doody, at nearby Lane Tech High School, helped raise money so that the Chicago Conservation Center could restore the wonderful collection of hidden murals at her school.

Soon, a full-scale effort was underway to restore murals throughout the city schools. Some only needed to be cleaned and repaired. **(8)** Others proved more *elusive*. **(9)** Acting as detectives, the conservation team found *caches* of old murals hidden in storage rooms. **(10)** Some were *interred* beneath piles of cartons. At one suburban school, murals had been taken off the wall but saved, in case anyone needed some plywood!

Although about fifty are lost, hundreds of murals have been restored to their former glory. The work continues, as Chicago rescues its precious artistic heritage.

Each sentence below refers to a numbered sentence in the passage. Write the letter of the choice that gives the sentence a meaning that is closest to the original sentence.

___a___ **1.** The rescue of these murals from _____ restores a precious artistic heritage.
   a. being unknown   **b.** hidden burial   **c.** students   **d.** storerooms

___d___ **2.** In the 1930s and 1940s, they hung _____ in halls, auditoriums, and lunchrooms.
   a. mysteriously   **b.** hidden   **c.** secretly   **d.** noticeably

___c___ **3.** In at least one case, _____ played a part in a mural's decline.
   a. a hidden supply   **b.** an entry   **c.** a secret plot   **d.** a villain

_____d_____ **4.** Located in a(n) _____ place off the main hall, it was a tribute to American women.
    a. popular   **b.** obvious   **c.** burial   **d.** set-apart

_____b_____ **5.** They felt that students should not have _____ this controversial content.
    a. attention on   **b.** permission to see   **c.** obstacles to   **d.** a hiding place for

_____c_____ **6.** For more than half a century, the beautiful paintings remained _____ for viewing.
    a. unfinished   **b.** not noticeable   **c.** not at hand   **d.** unknown

_____a_____ **7.** In 1996, at Flower High School, the Center began to _____ the precious works from beneath coats of oil paint and whitewash.
    a. uncover   **b.** bury   **c.** categorize   **d.** lift

_____d_____ **8.** Others proved more _____.
    a. obvious   **b.** ready for use   **c.** set apart   **d.** hard to find

_____d_____ **9.** The conservation team found _____ of old murals hidden in storage rooms.
    a. evidence   **b.** secret plots   **c.** passwords   **d.** supplies of valuables

_____a_____ **10.** Some were _____ beneath piles of cartons.
    a. buried   **b.** hidden   **c.** forgotten   **d.** dug up

Indicate whether the statements below are TRUE or FALSE according to the passage.

_____T_____ **1.** One result of the Works Progress Administration was that it brought art to public buildings.

_____T_____ **2.** Edward Millman painted a tribute to American women.

_____F_____ **3.** Hundreds of Chicago public school murals are still lost.

FINISH THE THOUGHT

Complete each sentence so that it shows the meaning of the italicized word.

1. Something that I find *elusive* is _____ Answers will vary. _____

_____

2. An example of a *secluded* place would be _____ Answers will vary. _____

_____

WRITE THE DERIVATIVE

Complete the sentence by writing the correct form of the word shown in parentheses. You may not need to change the form that is given.

___conspicuously___ **1.** Spies avoid behaving _____. (*conspicuous*)

___intriguing___ **2.** Cyndi found the mystery _____. (*intrigue*) unearthed

3. While he was digging a hole for the tree, Finn _____ many worms. (unearth)

seclusion

4. After a period of _____, the widower felt like socializing again. (seclude)

interment

5. The emperor's _____ was a solemn affair. (inter)

accessible

6. The photography darkroom is only _____ by going through the art room. (access)

cache

7. Fiona accidentally discovered her mom's _____ of holiday gifts. (cache)

unavailability

8. The _____ of citrus from Florida is due to hurricane damage. (unavailable)

obscure

9. My friend's remark was so _____ that no one at the meeting understood her. (obscurity)

elusiveness

10. The hummingbird is an animal of great _____. (elusive)

FIND THE EXAMPLE

Choose the answer that best describes the action or situation.

c   1. Something that is NOT *accessible* to a fourteen-year-old
   a. school   b. TV   c. driver's license   d. PG movie

b   2. Something that might be *unearthed* at a construction site
   a. a skyscraper   b. a fossil   c. a house   d. a cloud

d   3. Someone who would be *conspicuous* in an elementary school
   a. second-grade student   b. custodian   c. teacher   d. pro basketball player

a   4. Something you would most likely prefer to do in a *secluded* place
   a. take a nap   b. see a ball game   c. attend a concert   d. go to a parade

c   5. Something a dog might *inter*
   a. a walk   b. a dog bed   c. a bone   d. some water

d   6. Something a cat is most likely to find *intriguing*
   a. rocks   b. grass   c. clouds   d. birds

b   7. An object that is usually *elusive*
   a. coat   b. bird   c. rock   d. tree

c   8. A time when you are most likely *unavailable* to take a phone call
   a. watching ice melt   b. reading a book   c. taking a shower   d. waiting by the phone

d   9. Something that would be useful in the *obscurity* of an attic
   a. a visor   b. sunglasses   c. blinds   d. a flashlight

a   10. Something you would NOT be likely to find in a camper's *cache*
   a. a bathtub   b. a pocketknife   c. bug spray   d. snacks

Activity and Inactivity

WORD LIST

boisterousness	chaotic	complacency	dynamic	monotony
restive	static	steadfast	tranquility	velocity

The words in this lesson identify states of activity and inactivity, as well as the feelings and values that we attach to them. You might use these words to describe a *boisterous* game, a rocket with great *velocity,* or a *tranquil* moment.

1. **boisterousness** (boi´stər-əs-nəs) *noun* from Middle English *boistres,* "rude; rough"
Noisy, rough, and undisciplined behavior
   • The local fans were known for their **boisterousness** on game days.

   boisterous *adjective* The neighbors called the police to stop the **boisterous** party.

2. **chaotic** (kā-ŏt´ĭk) *adjective* from Greek *khaos,* "disorder; confusion"
Totally confused and lacking in order
   • The crowd became **chaotic** as people rushed to take shelter from the sudden storm.

   chaos *noun* The wild little cousins turned Keri's neat bedroom into **chaos.**

chaotic

3. **complacency** (kəm-plā´sən-sē) *noun* from Latin *complacere,* "to please"
Self-satisfaction without awareness of danger or trouble
   • As a result of the manager's **complacency,** competitors were able to take away much of the store's business.

   complacent *adjective* After Brad made the honor roll, he became **complacent** and stopped studying.

4. **dynamic** (dī-năm´ĭk) *adjective* from Greek *dunamis,* "power"
Energetic; vigorous; quick moving
   • The young couple made a **dynamic** team in the tango competition.

   dynamo *noun* The new president was a **dynamo,** who doubled the company's sales within a year.

5. **monotony** (mə-nŏt´n-ē) *noun* from Greek *mono-,* "one" + *tonus,* "tone"
Boring repetition or sameness
   • Bryan disliked the **monotony** of practicing scales on the piano.

   monotonous *adjective* Susie and Ben took on the **monotonous** task of polishing the silverware before the holidays.

Have students think of words that imply movement (such as *boisterousness* and *velocity*) and those that imply a state of inactivity (such as *static* and *monotony*). Allow them to discuss and defend their choices.

6. **restive** (rĕs´tĭv) *adjective* from Latin *stare*, "to stand"
Uneasy; impatient under restriction
• Living under a strict military curfew, people became **restive**.

restiveness *noun* Grandmother noticed Joan's **restiveness** when bad weather kept her from playing outside for almost a month.

7. **static** (stăt´ĭk) *adjective* from Greek *statikos*, "causing to stand"
Still; without motion
• It is difficult to assume a **static** posture for more than a few minutes.

8. **steadfast** (stĕd´făst´) *adjective* from Old English *stede*, "place" + *faest*, "fixed"
Steady; firmly loyal; constant
• The **steadfast** ally did not desert the king, even during times of great trouble.

steadfastness *noun* **Steadfastness** of purpose helps us to accomplish big and small goals.

9. **tranquility** (trăng-kwĭl´ĭ-tē) *noun* from Latin *tranquillus*, "peaceful"
Calm; peace and quiet
• The pond in the willow grove had a magical air of peace and **tranquility**.

tranquil *adjective* Blessed with a **tranquil** temperament, she rarely lost her temper.

tranquilize *verb* To quiet or calm, often by giving medicine
• The veterinarian said it would be best to **tranquilize** the cat before taking it on an airplane.

10. **velocity** (və-lŏs´ĭ-tē) *noun* from Latin *velocitas*, "fast"
Swiftness; speedy motion
• Light travels at an astonishing **velocity**.

> *Static* is electricity that makes clothes cling and causes slight shocks. It is also interference on a TV set. *To get static* means "to get complaints."

ANALOGIES

On the answer line, write the letter of the answer that best completes each analogy. Refer to Lessons 15–17 if you need help with any of the lesson words.

_b_ 1. Execute is to order as _____.
   a. walk is to hop
   b. accomplish is to task
   c. hope is to believe
   d. monotonous is to dull

_a_ 2. Unearth is to inter as _____.
   a. open is to close
   b. dynamic is to chaotic
   c. car is to velocity
   d. plan is to apportion

_a_ 3. Secluded is to hidden as _____.
   a. intrigued is to fascinated
   b. comfortable is to restive
   c. silent is to boisterous
   d. hot is to cold

_c_ 4. Running is to vigorous as _____.
   a. cow is to milk
   b. foot is to shoe
   c. reading is to tranquil
   d. speaking is to mouth

WRITE THE CORRECT WORD

Write the correct word in the space next to each definition.

chaotic	**1.** lacking order	
restive	**2.** impatient	
tranquility	**3.** peace and quiet	
steadfast	**4.** firmly loyal	
velocity	**5.** swiftness	

complacency	**6.** self-satisfaction	
static	**7.** still; without motion	
boisterousness	**8.** rough, loud behavior	
monotony	**9.** boring repetition	
dynamic	**10.** energetic; vigorous	

COMPLETE THE SENTENCE

Write the letter for the word that best completes each sentence.

___d___ **1.** There was total _____ after the fox entered the hen house.
    a. restiveness   **b.** velocity   **c.** tranquility   **d.** chaos

___b___ **2.** Lara became _____ after waiting an hour in the dentist's chair.
    a. complacent   **b.** restive   **c.** monotonous   **d.** static

___d___ **3.** Alaine does yoga in the early mornings, the most _____ part of her day.
    a. boisterous   **b.** steadfast   **c.** dynamic   **d.** tranquil

___c___ **4.** Because of the friction caused by their high _____ as they enter the atmosphere, meteors often burn up before they reach the earth.
    a. chaos   **b.** tranquility   **c.** velocity   **d.** steadfastness

___b___ **5.** Margaret could easily study her reflection in the _____ lake water.
    a. dynamic   **b.** static   **c.** chaotic   **d.** boisterous

___a___ **6.** Luther was so bored by the _____ landscape that he fell asleep in the car.
    a. monotonous   **b.** chaotic   **c.** restive   **d.** boisterous

___a___ **7.** Tricia's _____ personality and exciting speeches helped her win the election.
    a. dynamic   **b.** static   **c.** chaotic   **d.** restive

___c___ **8.** The soldiers pledged _____ allegiance to their country.
    a. complacent   **b.** chaotic   **c.** steadfast   **d.** monotonous

___d___ **9.** The angry students became loud and _____ during the assembly.
    a. static   **b.** complacent   **c.** tranquil   **d.** boisterous

___b___ **10.** Unfortunately, once Mr. Donnelly got elected mayor, he relaxed, became _____, and did not keep his promises to reform city government.
    a. chaotic   **b.** complacent   **c.** dynamic   **d.** steadfast

Challenge: Jon rolled his eyes at the _____ of the slow, _____ piano piece that his sister played over and over again.
___c___   **a.** static...boisterous   **b.** velocity...chaotic   **c.** monotony...tranquil

The Spirit Soars

(1) In 1995, French journalist Jean-Dominique Bauby had every reason to view life with *complacency.* As the editor of a popular magazine, he was known for his wit and style. Then one day, while driving with his son, he began to feel sick. Within minutes, he was paralyzed by a stroke.

(2) Although his body remained almost totally *static,* his mind continued to create. Using only his left eyelid, Bauby was able to dictate a 137-page book, *The Diving Bell and the Butterfly,* a tale of what it is like to be locked in a body that cannot move.

How did Bauby get the idea? Before his illness, he had been commissioned to write an updated version of Alexander Dumas's classic *The Count of Monte Cristo.* In this book, a paralyzed character uses blinks to communicate. **(3)** When tragedy struck Bauby, he decided to combat the *monotony* of his life by using the same method.

(4) At first, Bauby's eye movements must have seemed like random, *chaotic* blinks to those around him. Soon, however, his assistant realized that they had meaning. Each set of blinks was an attempt to communicate. Bauby and his assistant worked out a system that allowed him to dictate his memoir to her: The assistant would recite the alphabet, and Bauby would blink once for "yes," when she came to the correct letter. **(5)** This took great *steadfastness* of purpose, for writing the book required hundreds of thousands of blinks.

(6) Even writers who use word processors find that their thoughts move at a greater *velocity* than their fingers can type. Using this code, it took Bauby two minutes to blink out an average word! He could not work from notes or revise his writing. Instead, he had to compose passages entirely in his head.

(7) Bauby's book described the experiences of a mind made *restive* by the inability to move the body that contained it. He wrote that his body was confined in a "diving bell," but his mind escaped like a "butterfly." **(8)** He dreamt about *dynamic* activities, such as climbing mountains or driving on a racecourse. **(9)** He remembered sensations: eating delicious meals, *boisterous* shouting. **(10)** He recalled the *tranquility* of family life, stroking the hair of his children and helping his elderly father.

Just two days after the publication of his book, Bauby died. Yet *The Diving Bell and the Butterfly* remains an inspiring example of the power of the human mind.

Many medical advances have been made since Bauby's death in 1997. People paralyzed by such diseases as ALS (or Lou Gehrig's disease) now use computerized devices to communicate. Neuroscientists have developed machines that can be triggered with the slightest movements. One instrument, the Thought-Translation Device, is operated by brain waves, giving even those who are completely paralyzed the ability to communicate with the outside world.

Most of us take for granted the ability to walk and talk, to taste our food, and hug our loved ones. Bauby's story reminds us that even when we lose these things, the human spirit can soar.

Each sentence below refers to a numbered sentence in the passage. Write the letter of the choice that gives the sentence a meaning that is closest to the original sentence.

___b___ **1.** Jean-Dominique Bauby had every reason to view life with _____.
    a. happy expectations   **b.** self-satisfaction   **c.** great confusion   **d.** great longing

___b___ **2.** Although his body remained almost totally _____, his mind continued to create.
    a. helpless   **b.** still   **c.** active   **d.** uneasy

___a___ **3.** He decided to combat the _____ of his life by using the same method.
    a. boredom   **b.** hopelessness   **c.** stillness   **d.** confusion

c **4.** At first, Bauby's eye movements must have seemed like random, _____ blinks.
    a. swift   **b.** impatient   **c.** confused   **d.** meaningless

d **5.** This took great _____ of purpose.
    a. peace   **b.** stillness   **c.** effort   **d.** steadiness

c **6.** Even writers who use word processors find that their thoughts move at a greater _____ than their fingers can type.
    a. awareness   **b.** noise   **c.** speed   **d.** force

b **7.** Bauby's book described the experiences of a mind made _____ by the inability to move the body that contained it.
    a. still   **b.** impatient   **c.** uncertain   **d.** calm

c **8.** He dreamt about _____ activities.
    a. swift   **b.** outdoor   **c.** energetic   **d.** ambitious

d **9.** He remembered sensations: eating delicious meals, _____ shouting.
    a. constant   **b.** tiring   **c.** bitter   **d.** noisy

a **10.** He recalled the _____ of family life.
    a. calm   **b.** happiness   **c.** confusion   **d.** loyalty

Indicate whether the statements below are TRUE or FALSE according to the passage.

F **1.** Bauby was paralyzed by ALS, or Lou Gehrig's disease.

T **2.** Bauby's assistant helped him write his memoir, using an eye-blinking code.

T **3.** Using this code, it took Bauby two minutes to blink out an average word.

WRITING EXTENDED RESPONSES

You have read a passage about a man who found a way to do something that he loved, despite overwhelming challenges. Write a narrative essay about a time when you worked hard for something you really wanted. Your essay should be at least three paragraphs long. Use at least three lesson words in your essay and underline them.

WRITE THE DERIVATIVE

Complete the sentence by writing the correct form of the word shown in parentheses. You may not need to change the form that is given.

complacent **1.** People who become _____ about their health and do not get checkups put themselves at risk. (*complacency*)

boisterously **2.** The hockey players _____ protested their team's disqualification from the tournament. (*boisterousness*)

dynamo **3.** Alicia is such a _____ that she was able to produce, direct, and star in the same school play. (*dynamic*) _restiveness_ **4.** Brandon could not identify a reason for his _____. _(restive)_

chaos **5.** The sudden snowstorm threw the region into _____. _(chaotic)_

monotonous **6.** Sophia amused herself on the long, _____ bus ride by reading a book. _(monotony)_

velocity **7.** For a rocket to escape the earth's gravity, it must travel at a very high _____. _(velocity)_

tranquil **8.** English artists of the 1800s painted _____ landscapes as well as violent scenes of sea storms and battles. _(tranquility)_

static **9.** Terrified of the growling dog, Ella remained in a _____ position. _(static)_

Steadfastness **10.** _____ is an admirable quality in a friend. _(steadfast)_

FIND THE EXAMPLE

Choose the answer that best describes the action or situation.

_d_ **1.** An animal known for _steadfastness_
  a. mouse   **b.** crow   **c.** butterfly   **d.** dog

_c_ **2.** A place where you might feel _restive_
  a. living room   **b.** shower   **c.** waiting room   **d.** swimming pool

_c_ **3.** A profession that attracts _dynamic_ people
  a. tailor   **b.** writer   **c.** tap dancer   **d.** accountant

_b_ **4.** Something that is rarely _static_
  a. a fence   **b.** a hummingbird   **c.** a rock   **d.** a house

_a_ **5.** A place where you are NOT likely to find _tranquility_
  a. a crowded mall   **b.** your bedroom   **c.** a deserted island   **d.** a hot bath

_a_ **6.** A likely place to find a _boisterous_ crowd
  a. a protest rally   **b.** a library   **c.** a study hall   **d.** a computer room

_c_ **7.** An animal that does NOT travel at great _velocity_
  a. eagle   **b.** rabbit   **c.** snail   **d.** cheetah

_b_ **8.** Something that might cause _complacency_
  a. desire for a promotion   **b.** a winning season   **c.** a rabid wolf   **d.** constant failure

_d_ **9.** An activity that most people would consider _monotonous_
  a. singing   **b.** playing a game   **c.** watching a movie   **d.** watching paint dry

_c_ **10.** A scene that would NOT usually be described as _chaotic_
  a. mall before holidays   **b.** earthquake   **c.** a chemistry lab   **d.** a car accident

Forms and Boundaries

WORD LIST

confines	delineate	demarcation	distend	embody
gerrymander	impinge	omnipresent	penetrate	proximity

The words in this lesson refer to forms and boundaries. Some of the words, such as *distend,* refer to physical shapes; others, like *gerrymander,* have political meanings. As you study these words, try to imagine the actions, shapes, or relationships they describe.

1. **confines** (kŏn´fīns´) *noun* from Latin *com-,* "with" + *fines,* "limits"
The boundaries; the limits of a space or an area
   • The preschoolers were kept within the **confines** of the playground.

   confine *verb* Protestors were **confined** to an area roped off by the police.

2. **delineate** (dĭ-lĭn´ē-āt´) *verb* from Latin *de-,* "from" + *linea,* "line"
   a. To draw or trace an outline
   • In carefully rendered drawings, the architect **delineated** the slant of the roof and the placement of columns for the new house.
   b. To describe in words or gestures
   • The manual clearly **delineates** each employee's duties.

   delineation *noun* Sienna, who ended up with most of the work, thought the **delineation** of tasks was unfair.

Have students discuss which of these words refer to borders (such as *confines, delineate, demarcation,* and *gerrymander*). Allow students to explain their choices.

3. **demarcation** (dē´mär-kā´shən) *noun* from Latin *de-,* "off" + *marcar,* "to mark"
   a. The marking of boundaries or limits
   • Before we could build the fence, we needed the surveyor to complete the **demarcation** of our property.
   b. A separation; a distinction
   • There are clear lines of **demarcation** between the different climate zones on many large mountains.

   demarcate *verb* White lines **demarcate** the right side, or shoulder, of U.S. highways.

demarcation

4. **distend** (dĭ-stĕnd´) *verb* from Latin *dis-,* "apart" + *tendere,* "to stretch"
To swell or expand, as if from internal pressure
   • The snake was **distended** because it had just eaten a rat.

   distention *noun* **Distension** of the belly is often a sign of severe protein deficiency.

5. embody (ĕm-bŏd´ē) *verb*

   a. To give concrete form to an idea; to be a perfect example of
a concept
- Olympic athletes **embody** the vigor of youth.

   b. To include; to make part of a system or whole
- Our Constitution **embodies** the values of the Founding Fathers,
values that most Americans have come to share.

   embodiment *noun* Shakespeare's works are considered by many to be
the **embodiment** of great literature.

6. gerrymander (jĕr´ē-măn´dər) *verb*

   To divide voting districts so as to give unfair advantage to one
political party
- After the map of the new voting districts was released, Democrats
accused the Republican majority of **gerrymandering** to gain more
votes for their party's candidates in the next election.

7. impinge (ĭm-pĭnj´) *verb* from Latin *in-*, "against" + *pangere*,
"to fasten"

   To intrude upon; to have an effect, often negative, on something
- Do you feel airport security measures **impinge** upon citizens' privacy?

> *Impinge* can also mean "to strike or collide," as in "Light waves *impinge* on retinas."

8. omnipresent (ŏm´nĭ-prĕz´nt) *adjective* from Latin *omnis*, "all"
+ *praesens*, "present"

   Existing everywhere at the same time
- The **omnipresent** desert sand found its way into our sleeping bags,
food, and water supply.

   omnipresence *noun* Her **omnipresence** on the basketball court was a
testament to her quickness and endurance.

9. penetrate (pĕn´ĭ-trāt´) *verb* from Latin *penitus*, "deeply"

   To enter into or go through something; to pierce
- Sunlight **penetrated** the sheer curtains hanging in the dining room.

   penetration *noun* Bullet-proof vests prevent **penetration** of the body.

10. proximity (prŏk-sĭm´ĭ-tē) *noun* from Latin *proximare*,
"to come near"

   Closeness of location; nearness
- The couple wanted to buy a house in close **proximity** to the school.

> While *proximity* refers to being close in space, *proximate* can refer to space, time, or order.

WORD ENRICHMENT

Where does gerrymander come from?

   In 1812, Massachusetts Governor Elbridge Gerry decided to redraw
the boundaries of congressional districts to favor his party. This resulted in
a district that had such a strange shape that it looked like a salamander—a
small amphibian. Mocking him, a painter actually turned the district's
outline into a picture of a salamander, labeled it a *gerrymander,* and a
word was born.

WRITE THE CORRECT WORD

Write the correct word in the space next to each definition.

delineate	**1.** to draw or trace an outline	distend	**6.** to swell or expand
penetrate	**2.** to enter into or go through	omnipresent	**7.** everywhere at the same time
demarcation	**3.** the markings of a boundary	embody	**8.** to exemplify
proximity	**4.** closeness in location	confines	**9.** the boundaries of an area
impinge	**5.** to intrude upon	gerrymander	**10.** to divide voting districts unfairly

COMPLETE THE SENTENCE

Write the letter for the word that best completes each sentence.

b **1.** When the ball passes beyond the _____ of the field, the referee calls, "Out of bounds!"
   a. distention   **b.** confines   **c.** gerrymandering   **d.** embodiment

c **2.** The Industrial Arts teacher carefully _____ the procedure for welding.
   a. embodied   **b.** distended   **c.** delineated   **d.** confined

d **3.** Classical Greek architecture _____ the principles of proportion and beauty.
   a. impinges   **b.** gerrymanders   **c.** distends   **d.** embodies

d **4.** The archaeologist found a way to _____ the tomb and extract the contents without damaging the structure.
   a. embody   **b.** distend   **c.** confine   **d.** penetrate

c **5.** The homeowners argued about the line of _____ between their properties.
   a. penetration   **b.** confines   **c.** demarcation   **d.** embodiment

c **6.** The child was alarmed by the bulging, _____ throat of the croaking bullfrog.
   a. omnipresent   **b.** delineated   **c.** distended   **d.** embodied

a **7.** Because I live near a swamp, mosquitoes seem to be _____ in the summer.
   a. omnipresent   **b.** gerrymandered   **c.** delineated   **d.** confined

d **8.** The _____ of the open soda can to the computer made me nervous.
   a. demarcation   **b.** delineation   **c.** embodiment   **d.** proximity

a **9.** The annoying neighbor was always _____ on their privacy.
   a. impinging   **b.** gerrymandering   **c.** embodying   **d.** delineating

d **10.** The Supreme Court decided that the legislature had _____ the voting districts.
   a. distended   **b.** embodied   **c.** impinged   **d.** gerrymandered

Challenge: The _____ of the factory forced the employees to work in close _____ to one another.
a **a.** confines...proximity   **b.** distention...omnipresence   **c.** proximity...demarcation

The Shape of Antarctica

At the far southern tip of Earth, in an area as dry as any sandy desert and colder than Alaska, lies Antarctica. **(1)** The ever-changing *confines* of this continent are of great interest to those who study our global climate.

(2) Antarctica is a continent of rock and ice, inhabited by penguins, seals, and other animals that can survive the extreme cold that reigns in the *proximity* of the South Pole. They are joined by the human inhabitants of some forty scientific stations. These chilly outposts were established so scientists could study Antarctica's important role in the world's atmospheric and oceanic conditions. More than twenty-seven nations participate in this scientific research.

One important concern is the increased rate at which Antarctica's glaciers are melting. **(3)** This melting can be observed by *delineating* glaciers, ice shelves, and ice tongues, and by examining how they change over time. Ice shelves and ice tongues form as gravity and melting cause glacial ice to move very slowly toward the sea. **(4)** Through years of growth, they *distend* the shoreline and reach out over the sea. Wave action gradually weakens them. At times, large ice masses "calve," or break off, and fall into the ocean, becoming icebergs. In recent years, global warming has sped up this process. Recently, melting ice shelves along the coasts have changed the very outline of Antarctica.

(5) As the glaciers that are *omnipresent* in the Antarctic move gradually out to the coastlines, great portions of the ice shelves break off, affecting ocean temperature, salt concentration, and global sea levels. Within a hundred years, massive melting could cause the sea to rise twenty feet.

(6) Another concern is preserving the deep layers of Antarctic ice that contain ancient air bubbles which *embody* a geological history of the earth. Scientists want to preserve this valuable store of ice, without contamination, so they can study the progression of Earth's industrial air pollution and other chemical and biological changes.

International agreement currently provides some protection against profit-making from Antarctic research. **(7)** It is hoped that future legislation will be enacted without interference by private interest groups or political *gerrymandering* so that the continent will remain protected. **(8)** However, tourism has recently begun to *penetrate* this once-remote land. **(9)** In an effort to control pollution, clear *demarcations* of very limited tourist areas are being established. **(10)** Even small increases in the number of tour boats could *impinge* on scientists' ability to do valuable research.

Scientists across the world are watching Antarctica closely. What happens there has implications for our global environment.

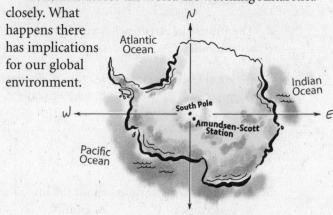

Each sentence below refers to a numbered sentence in the passage. Write the letter of the choice that gives the sentence a meaning that is closest to the original sentence.

____c____ **1.** The ever-changing _____ of this continent are of great interest to those who study our global climate.
a. ideas   **b.** plants   **c.** boundaries   **d.** districts

____d____ **2.** It is inhabited by animals that can survive the extreme cold that reigns in the _____ the South Pole.
a. strange continent of   **b.** changing form of   **c.** icy glaciers of   **d.** area near to

____a____ **3.** This melting can be observed by _____ the glaciers, ice shelves, and ice tongues.
a. outlining   **b.** studying   **c.** heating   **d.** examining

____c____ **4.** Through years of growth, they _____ the shoreline and reach out over the sea.
a. trace   **b.** demolish   **c.** expand   **d.** enter

_d_   **5.** As the glaciers that are _____ in the Antarctic move gradually out to the coastlines, great portions of the ice shelves break off, affecting global sea levels.
     a. smaller   **b.** slow   **c.** found only   **d.** everywhere

_c_   **6.** Another concern is preserving the deep layers of Antarctic ice that contain ancient air bubbles which _____ a geological history of the earth.
     a. explain   **b.** simulate   **c.** include   **d.** hide

_a_   **7.** It is hoped that future legislation will be enacted without interference by private interest groups or political _____.
     a. unfair division   **b.** corruption   **c.** mistakes   **d.** distinction

_c_   **8.** However, tourism has recently begun to _____ this once-remote land.
     a. expand   **b.** limit   **c.** enter   **d.** divide

_d_   **9.** Clear _____ of very limited tourist areas are being established.
     a. agreements   **b.** voting districts   **c.** nearby areas   **d.** marked boundaries

_b_   **10.** Even small increases in the number of tour boats could _____ on scientists' ability to do valuable research.
     a. cooperate   **b.** intrude   **c.** reflect   **d.** include

Indicate whether the statements below are TRUE or FALSE according to the passage.

_F_   **1.** There are no humans in Antarctica.

_T_   **2.** Bubbles in the ice that covers the Antarctic gives a geologic history of the earth.

_T_   **3.** Tourism can affect the Antarctic environment.

FINISH THE THOUGHT

Complete each sentence so that it shows the meaning of the italicized word.

1. If you _impinge_ on my study time, _____ Answers will vary. _____

_____

2. I live in _proximity_ to _____ Answers will vary. _____

_____

WRITE THE DERIVATIVE

Complete the sentence by writing the correct form of the word shown in parentheses. You may not need to change the form that is given.

___delineation___   **1.** Eleanor's teacher praised her for including a _____ of the mountain range on her map. _(delineate)_

___embodiment___   **2.** George Washington is considered the _____ of patriotism. _(embody)_

<u>penetrated</u> 3. The forward _____ the opponents' defense and scored a goal. (*penetrate*)

<u>omnipresence</u> 4. The students noticed the _____ of the chaperones at the dance. (*omnipresent*)

<u>distended</u> 5. The tire was oddly _____ and did not look safe to drive on. (*distend*)

<u>demarcates</u> 6. This map _____ all the national parks in the southwestern United States. (*demarcation*)

<u>confined</u> 7. Before being _____ to quarters, the lieutenant surrendered his weekend pass. (*confines*)

<u>proximity</u> 8. The _____ of the cookies made it difficult for Maggie to resist them. (*proximity*)

<u>gerrymandering</u> 9. Many people in the state were furious with the governor's _____. (*gerrymander*)

<u>impinging</u> 10. The loud television was _____ on Greg's ability to concentrate on his homework. (*impinge*)

FIND THE EXAMPLE

Choose the answer that best describes the action or situation.

<u>a</u> **1.** A common *demarcation* between two rooms
   a. wall   **b.** grass   **c.** swing   **d.** boat

<u>d</u> **2.** The object that is most difficult to *penetrate*
   a. glass   **b.** plank of wood   **c.** paper   **d.** steel vault

<u>c</u> **3.** Something that might *delineate* how to prepare chicken cordon bleu
   a. farmer's almanac   **b.** biography   **c.** cookbook   **d.** grocery store

<u>a</u> **4.** Something often found in close *proximity* to a bus stop
   a. bench   **b.** cow   **c.** balloon   **d.** nurse

<u>b</u> **5.** The thing that *embodies* the ideas of an artist
   a. her brushes   **b.** a painting   **c.** oil paint   **d.** a frame

<u>c</u> **6.** Something that might be *distended* after a large meal
   a. dishes   **b.** table   **c.** stomach   **d.** conversation

<u>d</u> **7.** Something that is *omnipresent* in our air
   a. trees   **b.** fire   **c.** snow   **d.** oxygen

<u>b</u> **8.** Something that might *impinge* on the enjoyment of watching a movie
   a. comfortable seat   **b.** ringing cell phone   **c.** buttered popcorn   **d.** cold soda

<u>d</u> **9.** Something you would NOT be likely to find in the *confines* of a gym locker
   a. T-shirt   **b.** sneakers   **c.** towel   **d.** bicycle

<u>c</u> **10.** A reason someone might decide to *gerrymander*
   a. get more land   **b.** buy a new car   **c.** get more votes   **d.** make new friends

Taking Tests

Sentence Completion with Two Blanks

Standardized tests may contain sentence completion items with either one or two blanks. You practice answering two-blank items in this book when you do the Challenge that is found in each lesson.

Strategies

You can apply what you have already learned about context clues to sentence-completion test items. Following these steps will help you to choose answers for two-blank items.

1. *Read the directions carefully.* You can lose credit if you don't follow the directions.

2. *Read the sentence completely.* Because "two-blank" items involve different parts of the sentence, it is wise to get an overview by carefully reading the entire sentence. Substitute the word blank for the empty spaces as you read.

3. *Look for words that fit the first blank.* To start, try to narrow your choices down to words that fit the first empty space. Make sure the word is the correct part of speech and fits in the context. Eliminate the other choices. Here is an example:

    Although just about everyone was _____ to the agreement, one political party remained _____ and refused to cooperate.

    a. steadfast...objective   **d.** desolate...altruistic
    b. preconceived...tranquil   **e.** amenable...defiant
    c. indifferent...pacified

    By focusing on the first blank, you can eliminate choices (b) and (d); neither *preconceived* nor *desolate* will fit.

4. *From the remaining choices, look for words that fit into the second blank.* Eliminate any remaining choices in which the second word doesn't fit in the second blank. In the example above, try the second word for choices (a), (c), and (e) in the second blank. The second portion of the sentence gives a context clue about the missing word: "refused to cooperate." Only *defiant* is synonymous with "refused to cooperate," so you can now eliminate choices (a) and (c).

5. *Reread the sentence with your choices inserted.* Two-item tests are difficult. Make certain to check your choices. At times, a few choices may fit, and you must choose the one that fits best.

    Although just about everyone was <u>amenable</u> to the agreement, one political party remained <u>defiant</u> and refused to cooperate.

Notice that in the example above, the two missing words are related. The word *although* signals that the first blank and the second blank are opposites in some way. So you can check your answer by making sure that the two words you've chosen are opposing. Some other key words that might indicate a relationship include:

- *not, but, never, hardly, and in spite of* (signaling opposites)
- *and, as well as, or in addition to* (signaling agreement)

Practice

Each sentence below has two blanks, each blank indicating that a word has been omitted. Beneath the sentence are five lettered sets of words labeled a through e. Choose the pair of words that, when inserted in the sentence, **best** fits the meaning of the sentence as a whole.

_d_ **1.** The members of the club quickly came to a _____ about the candidate, and the new president was _____ the following day.
  a. delineation…gerrymandered
  b. conception…bewildered
  c. cache…defied
  d. consensus…inaugurated
  e. misinterpretation…maligned

_c_ **2.** The _____ seized control of the country and initiated a harsh _____ rule.
  a. delegate…censured
  b. centenarian…benign
  c. tyrant…authoritarian
  d. conservative…monotonous
  e. benefactor…puerile

_a_ **3.** Realizing that she had made a(n) _____ while being presented to the prince, she became quite _____.
  a. faux pas…flustered
  b. scoff…abetted
  c. enunciation…incapacitated
  d. embellishment…imperiled
  e. miscalculation…tranquil

_c_ **4.** We weren't surprised that he ate _____ at the party, for he was known to have a(n) _____ appetite.
  a. animatedly…steadfast
  b. superficially…momentous
  c. immoderately…voracious
  d. boisterously…outrageous
  e. conspicuously…exemplary

_e_ **5.** Often people find that it takes a great deal of _____ to accomplish a worthy _____.
  a. gratification…sanctuary
  b. altruism…infantile
  c. strife…communal
  d. steadfastness…fledgling
  e. forbearance…objective

_b_ **6.** We don't want to see any _____; economy is of _____ importance.
  a. philanthropy…superficial
  b. extravagance…paramount
  c. boisterousness…outrageous
  d. refurbishment…indubitable
  e. discord…nascent

_d_ **7.** The researcher's years of _____ effort resulted in a discovery that won him an award of great _____.
  a. indispensable…partisanship
  b. noteworthy…miscellany
  c. tranquil…altruism
  d. dogged…prestige
  e. confined…omnipresence

_c_ **8.** When the lawyer _____ his associate in public, we gathered that there was _____ amongst the team members.
  a. slandered…exuberance
  b. complemented…velocity
  c. chided…discord
  d. indulged…alienation
  e. demarcated…anguish

Strength and Defense

WORD LIST

blockade	coup	indestructibility	martial	omnipotent
robust	stable	staunch	vulnerability	withstand

In addition to requiring food, clothing, and shelter, people need to feel secure. For this reason, many societies establish and maintain armed forces that protect and defend their country. The words in this lesson, which describe aspects of strength and defense, will help you better understand how individuals and groups try to assure their own safety.

a blockade

1. **blockade** (blŏ-kād´)
   a. *noun* The closing off of an area to prevent people and supplies from leaving or entering
   • The troops set up a **blockade** to prevent enemy ships from entering the harbor.
   b. *verb* To set up a barrier that prevents exit or entrance
   • The police tried to **blockade** the area surrounding the car accident.

2. **coup** (ko͞o) *noun* from Latin *colpus,* "blow"
   a. A brilliantly executed action that brings success
   • The new mayor scored a **coup** by coming from behind to win the election.
   b. A sudden takeover that overthrows the existing power
   • The generals established their rule in a **coup.**

Coup comes from the French *coup d'etat,* "blow to a state."

3. **indestructibility** (ĭn´dĭ-strŭk´tə-bəl´ĭ-tē) *noun* from Latin *in-,* "not" + *destruere,* "to destroy"
   The quality of being impossible to destroy
   • Many superheroes are known for their **indestructibility.**

   indestructible *adjective* The massive stone pillars of the ancient building seemed **indestructible.**

4. **martial** (mär´shəl) *adjective* from Latin *Mars,* Roman god of war
   Warlike; relating to war or the military
   • The army band was well known for its performances of **martial** music.

5. **omnipotent** (ŏm-nĭp´ə-tənt) *adjective* from Latin *omni-,* "all" + *posse,* "to be able"
   Having unlimited power, authority, or force
   • Ancient Romans considered their emperors to be **omnipotent.**

   omnipotence *noun* Most young children do not question their parents' **omnipotence.**

Point out that *indestructibility* contains the prefix *in-,* meaning "not," and that *omnipotent* contains the prefix *omni-,* meaning "all." Can students think of other words with these prefixes?

6. **robust** (rō-bŭst´) *adjective* from Latin *robustus*, "of oak"
Healthy, strong, and vigorous; sturdily built
• People who climb the mountains of Tibet must be **robust.**

robustness *noun* To maintain his **robustness,** Grandpa followed a strict, year-round fitness routine.

7. **stable** (stā´bəl) *adjective* from Latin *staulum*, "standing place"
Not easily changed; relatively permanent
• Although it decreased for many years, the African elephant population is now **stable.**

stability *noun* After moving every year or two for much of her life, Nicole longed for the **stability** of living in one place.

> *Stable, staunch,* and the *stand* in *withstand* all contain the root *sta,* "to stand."

8. **staunch** (stônch) *adjective*
Firm; steadfast in support; loyal
• The judge was a **staunch** defender of equal rights.

staunchness *noun* The **staunchness** of the army's defense prevented the enemy from advancing.

9. **vulnerability** (vŭl´nər-ə-bĭl´ĭ-tē) *noun* from Latin *vulnerare,* "to wound"
The quality of being open to injury, disease, attack or criticism; weakness
• The events of September 11 revealed the United States' **vulnerability** to terrorism.

vulnerable *adjective* The **vulnerable** teenager cried when she was not picked for the team.

> Don't confuse *vulnerable* with *venerable,* which means "worthy of respect due to age or dignity."

10. **withstand** (wĭth-stănd´) *verb* from Old English *with,* "against" + *standan,* "to stand"
To successfully resist or oppose something; to survive without damage
• The sand castle could not **withstand** the powerful ocean waves.

> The past tense of *withstand* is *withstood.*

WORD ENRICHMENT

Warlike words

Believe it or not, many of our words come from Mars—not the planet, but the Roman god of war, for whom the red planet is named. As you read earlier, *martial* is an adjective that can describe many things related to war or the military. For example, *martial law* is rule imposed by military authorities. The phrase *martial arts* refers to any of several Asian arts of combat or self-defense, including kung fu, karate, and tae kwon do. In ancient Rome, weapons were cleaned during the month of March, which the Romans had named for this violent, feared god.

WRITE THE CORRECT WORD

Write the correct word in the space next to each definition.

blockade   **1.** the closing off of an area   _vulnerability_   **6.** openness to attack

withstand   **2.** to resist successfully   _robust_   **7.** healthy; strong; vigorous

omnipotent   **3.** having unlimited power or authority   _indestructibility_   **8.** being impossible to harm

martial   **4.** relating to war   _stable_   **9.** not easily changed

staunch   **5.** firm; loyal   _coup_   **10.** a brilliant and successful action

COMPLETE THE SENTENCE

Write the letter for the word that best completes each sentence.

c 1. The ship was able to _____ the strong winds and heavy rain.
a. blockade   **b.** staunch   **c.** withstand   **d.** stabilize

a 2. Being a cautious man, Mr. Oro would invest only in countries with _____ governments.
a. stable   **b.** vulnerable   **c.** omnipotent   **d.** indestructible

b 3. Karate became a popular _____ art in Japan when weapons were banned, creating a need for unarmed fighting techniques.
a. stable   **b.** martial   **c.** blockade   **d.** vulnerable

a 4. For two hours, the _____ camper chopped wood for the campfire.
a. robust   **b.** vulnerable   **c.** martial   **d.** omnipotent

d 5. After he won every fight, his trainer boasted that the boxer was _____.
a. blockaded   **b.** martial   **c.** vulnerable   **d.** indestructible

b 6. The small rebel group overthrew the dictator in a(n) _____.
a. blockade   **b.** coup   **c.** indestructibility   **d.** vulnerability

c 7. No one could leave or enter the town because of the enemy's _____.
a. stability   **b.** vulnerability   **c.** blockade   **d.** staunchness

d 8. Michaela has several _____ supporters who attend all her performances.
a. martial   **b.** vulnerable   **c.** omnipotent   **d.** staunch

d 9. The old wooden house on the cliff was _____ to hurricanes.
a. omnipotent   **b.** robust   **c.** martial   **d.** vulnerable

b 10. As dictator of Russia, Joseph Stalin was very nearly _____.
a. vulnerable   **b.** omnipotent   **c.** stable   **d.** withstood

Challenge: The _____ supporters of the candidate set up a _____ to protect him from protesters.
a a. staunch…blockade   **b.** vulnerable…coup   **c.** martial…robustness

Ambassador of the Paiute

By any reckoning in any age, Sarah Winnemucca, known as Thoc-me-tony, or "Shell Flower," in her native language, was an astonishing and courageous figure. She lived through government forced migrations and wars that left most of her people dead or imprisoned. As one of only two Paiutes who spoke English, she became an articulate interpreter, guide, diplomat, and educator. She changed public opinion, influenced legislation, and founded schools. **(1)** She also wrote a bestselling book—a *coup* that brought great attention to her people's cause. Her achievements are especially impressive considering she lived in an era when both women and Native Americans faced much discrimination.

Sarah was born about 1844, in an area that is now known as Nevada. She was the daughter of Chief Winnemucca II, of the Paiute tribe. At that time, the peaceful Paiute nation was still free, though they had some contact with the endless tide of white soldiers and civilians flooding the West. **(2)** The Paiute, who had once believed their way of life was *indestructible,* began to feel threatened by the newcomers. Sarah's grandfather, a famous guide, predicted, "Someday all Paiutes will live as the whites do."

In 1860, violent outbreaks escalated into the Paiute War. **(3)** The U.S. military instituted *martial* law over the Paiute people. **(4)** They installed the first of the nearly *omnipotent* white overseers, called Indian agents. Many of these agents were horribly cruel and corrupt.

Sarah, only seventeen, was horrified by the war. She tried to stop the bloodshed by intervening with both the Paiute and the U.S. military. Tragically, she lost several family members before the violence ended.

(5) Sarah continued to work for a *stable* peace. **(6)** When her people were put on reservations far from their Nevada home, the *robust* young woman traveled to Washington, D.C., and other cities, making speeches to gain the Paiutes' release. **(7)** Her intelligent arguments gained her the *staunch* support of influential people. With their help, Sarah wrote an autobiography called *Life Among the Paiutes: Their Wrongs and Claims.* The book documented the wrongs that government agents and others had inflicted upon her people. Newspapers began speaking out about the injustices that Sarah described. Her efforts led to many promises from the U.S. government for better treatment of the Paiutes, but few of these promises were kept.

(8) Despite their best efforts, the Paiute and other Native American nations could not *withstand* the white conquest. **(9)** They were often *blockaded* into ever-smaller and more barren pieces of land, where they faced starvation, disease, and the destruction of their way of life. **(10)** Sarah became convinced that only through education could her people overcome their *vulnerability* to white dominance, so she set up schools for Native Americans.

Eventually, the years of struggle took their toll, and Sarah became ill. She died of tuberculosis in 1892. Sarah Winnemucca's memory is honored in stories and monuments throughout Nevada.

Each sentence below refers to a numbered sentence in the passage. Write the letter of the choice that gives the sentence a meaning that is closest to the original sentence.

_____ d 1. She also wrote a bestselling book—a _____ that brought great attention to her people's cause.
    a. breaking barrier   **b.** simple task   **c.** tricky attack   **d.** successful action

_____ c 2. The Paiute, who had once believed their way of life was _____, began to feel threatened by the newcomers.
    a. unlimited in power   **b.** closed off   **c.** impossible to destroy   **d.** healthy and strong

_____ a 3. The U.S. military instituted _____ law.
    a. war-related   **b.** cruel and unusual   **c.** unlimited   **d.** permanent

____d____ **4.** They installed the first of the nearly _____ white overseers, called
Indian agents.
   a. intelligent   **b.** impossible-to-harm   **c.** loyal   **d.** all-powerful

____c____ **5.** Sarah continued to work for a _____ peace.
   a. just   **b.** loyal   **c.** permanent   **d.** warlike

____b____ **6.** The _____ young woman traveled to Washington, D.C., and other cities,
making speeches to gain the Paiutes' release.
   a. brilliant   **b.** strong   **c.** loyal   **d.** desperate

____a____ **7.** Her intelligent arguments gained her the _____ support of influential people.
   a. firm   **b.** angry   **c.** forceful   **d.** resistant

____d____ **8.** Despite their best efforts, the Paiute and other Native American nations could
not _____ the white conquest.
   a. close off   **b.** attack   **c.** destroy   **d.** resist

____c____ **9.** They were often _____ into ever-smaller and more barren pieces of land.
   a. persuaded   **b.** easily changed   **c.** closed off   **d.** sent

____d____ **10.** Sarah became convinced that only through education could her people
overcome their _____ to white dominance.
   a. barriers   **b.** threats   **c.** fear   **d.** weakness

Indicate whether the statements below are TRUE or FALSE according to the passage.

____T____ **1.** Sarah Winnemucca was the daughter of a Paiute chief.

____T____ **2.** Although healthy at first, she became sickly as she aged.

____F____ **3.** Several of her family members died of tuberculosis.

WRITING EXTENDED RESPONSES

Suppose that you heard Sarah Winnemucca speak. Write a letter to a
member of Congress, in Washington, D.C., to convince him or her that
the Paiute nation should be released from the reservation and given
back their former lands. In a persuasive letter, give at least two reasons
why the Paiute people should be released. Your letter should be at least
three paragraphs long. Use at least three lesson words in your letter and
underline them.

WRITE THE DERIVATIVE

Complete the sentence by writing the correct form of the word shown in
parentheses. You may not need to change the form that is given.

_____coup_____ **1.** Getting an interview with the famous sports star was a major _____ for the
young reporter. (*coup*)

___withstood___ **2.** In the last storm, the old barn _____ the hurricane's winds. (*withstand*)

vulnerable	**3.** The falcon could sense that the rabbit was _____. *(vulnerability)*
blockading	**4.** The police are _____ the avenue so that the ambassadors can leave safely. *(blockade)*
indestructible	**5.** The ad said the toy was _____, but mine broke the first day I had it. *(indestructibility)*
staunchly	**6.** Lynn's family _____ supported her decision to go to law school. *(staunch)*
Robustness	**7.** _____ is an essential quality in a furniture mover. *(robust)*
stability	**8.** Before the painter climbed the ladder, he checked its _____. *(stable)*
martial	**9.** The candidate in favor of _____ law lost the election by a landslide. *(martial)*
omnipotence	**10.** In Greek mythology, Zeus's _____ gave him full power over all other gods and goddesses. *(omnipotent)*

FIND THE EXAMPLE

Choose the answer that best describes the action or situation.

_c_ **1.** Something that is most likely to be *blockaded*
  a. dry cleaner   **b.** tree   **c.** road   **d.** garden

_c_ **2.** A person LEAST likely to be a *staunch* supporter of hamburgers
  a. football player   **b.** child   **c.** vegetarian   **d.** fast-food chef

_a_ **3.** Something you do NOT need if you are *omnipotent*
  a. permission   **b.** servants   **c.** assistants   **d.** sleep

_c_ **4.** The place where you might find *martial* law
  a. preschool   **b.** cafeteria   **c.** military base   **d.** courtroom

_b_ **5.** Something you are most *vulnerable* to in the summer
  a. blizzard   **b.** sunburn   **c.** catching a cold   **d.** slipping on ice

_a_ **6.** A job to avoid if you are NOT in *robust* health
  a. firefighter   **b.** librarian   **c.** accountant   **d.** writer

_b_ **7.** Something that is clearly NOT *indestructible*
  a. marble   **b.** glass   **c.** concrete   **d.** steel

_d_ **8.** Something that most easily *withstands* the effects of water
  a. feather   **b.** dust   **c.** leaf   **d.** brick wall

_d_ **9.** A *coup* for a writer
  a. new pen   **b.** bad review   **c.** typewriter   **d.** bestseller

_a_ **10.** Something that is NOT *stable*
  a. tower of cards   **b.** tall high-rise   **c.** large boulder   **d.** marble statue

Importance

WORD LIST

eminence	inconsequential	indispensable	indubitably	momentous
noteworthy	paramount	pettiness	prestige	superficial

The words in this lesson deal with different aspects of importance—and the lack of it. After you learn this vocabulary, you can decide whether an event is *noteworthy* or how *pettiness* may be avoided. Since setting priorities is something we constantly do, this vocabulary will be useful in many activities.

1. **eminence** (ĕm´ə-nəns) *noun* from Latin *eminare*, "to stand out"
   A position of fame, superiority, and distinction
   • Albert Einstein was a physicist of great **eminence.**

   eminent *adjective* The college invited an **eminent** authority on the global economy to speak at the graduation ceremony.

2. **inconsequential** (ĭn-kŏn´sĭ-kwĕn´shəl) *adjective* from Latin *in-*, "not" + *consequi*, "following closely"
   Lacking importance; trivial
   • Although the volunteer task of delivering flowers to patients may seem **inconsequential,** it really helps cheer the patients up.

3. **indispensable** (ĭn´dĭ-spĕn´sə-bəl) *adjective* from Latin *in-*, "not" + *dispensare*, "to distribute"
   Required; essential; necessary
   • The new quarterback was **indispensable** to the team's success.

   indispensability *noun* If you prove your **indispensability,** you can guarantee your job.

4. **indubitably** (ĭn-dōō´bĭ-tə-blē) *adverb* from Latin *in-*, "not" + *dubitere*, "to doubt"
   Clearly; unquestionably; without a doubt
   • George Washington was **indubitably** a great U.S. president.

5. **momentous** (mō-mĕn´təs) *adjective* from Latin *momentere*, "to matter"
   Greatly important or significant
   • The defeat of Hitler in 1945 was a **momentous** event in European and world history.

   momentousness *noun* He was overwhelmed by the **momentousness** of his college graduation.

6. **noteworthy** (nōt´wûr´thē) *adjective* from Latin *notare*, "to notice"
   Deserving notice or attention
   • Richard Axel and Linda Buck won a 2004 Nobel Prize for their **noteworthy** contributions to the understanding of the sense of smell.

Albert Einstein, *eminent* physicist

Have students distinguish between the words that signal importance (such as *eminence*) and those that signal unimportance (such as *inconsequential*).

7. **paramount** (păr´ə-mount´) *adjective* from Anglo-Norman
paramount, "above"
Most important
- Safety is the airline's **paramount** concern.

8. **pettiness** (pĕt´tē-nəs) *noun* from Old French *peti,* "little"
Concern with things of little importance
- Showing her **pettiness,** Angela refused to help rescue the cat buried in the rubble because she was worried about breaking a nail.

petty *adjective* Morgan was **petty** enough to resent having to help clean up after the party.

9. **prestige** (prĕ-stēzh´) *noun*
High status; respect and admiration from others
- A university president has a position of great **prestige.**

prestigious *adjective* A Pulitzer is a **prestigious** writing award.

10. **superficial** (sōō´pər-fĭsh´əl) *adjective* from Latin *super,* "above"
+ *facies,* "face"
a. Near the surface
- Fortunately, the cut was only **superficial.**
b. Not deep; trivial; unimportant
- You need to make more than **superficial** changes in your paper if you want a better grade.

superficiality *noun* The teacher was disappointed with the **superficiality** of the student's essay.

ANALOGIES

On the answer line, write the letter of the answer that best completes each analogy. Refer to Lessons 18–20 if you need help with any of the lesson words.

___d___ **1.** Delineate is to duties as _____.
- a. robust is to weak
- c. teacher is to student
- b. noteworthy is to unimportant
- d. demarcate is to boundaries

___c___ **2.** Paramount is to petty as _____.
- a. staunch is to loyal
- c. excellent is to awful
- b. close is to proximity
- d. hungry is to dinner

___a___ **3.** Coup is to government as _____.
- a. wave is to sandcastle
- c. omnipresent is to omnipotent
- b. vote is to election
- d. vulnerable is to stable

___b___ **4.** Trivial is to significance as _____.
- a. prestige is to momentous
- b. superficial is to depth
- c. books are to learning
- d. embody is to idea

NAME _____ DATE _____

WRITE THE CORRECT WORD

Write the correct word in the space next to each definition.

momentous 1. greatly important; significant
prestige 2. high status
eminence 3. a position of fame and superiority
inconsequential 4. lacking importance; trivial
noteworthy 5. deserving attention
indispensable 6. required; essential; necessary
indubitably 7. unquestionably
superficial 8. near the surface
paramount 9. most important
pettiness 10. of small importance

COMPLETE THE SENTENCE

Write the letter for the word that best completes each sentence.

a 1. Most of the essay was insignificant; the only _____ part was the introduction.
a. noteworthy b. superficial c. petty d. inconsequential

d 2. Dr. Lovinsky earned her _____ by writing numerous articles for well-respected scientific journals.
a. pettiness b. momentousness c. superficiality d. prestige

b 3. Mr. Braddock proudly explained that he had made his daughter vice president because she was _____ to his business.
a. superficial b. indispensable c. inconsequential d. petty

b 4. The use of the computer has had a(n) _____ effect on our lives.
a. inconsequential b. momentous c. superficial d. petty

c 5. The weekly food column in the national paper is written by a(n) _____ chef.
a. petty b. inconsequential c. eminent d. superficial

d 6. The evidence proved to be _____, as it had nothing to do with the crime.
a. prestigious b. paramount c. momentous d. inconsequential

c 7. The children were unanimous; the cookies were _____ delicious.
a. superficially b. inconsequentially c. indubitably d. indispensably

a 8. The strangers engaged in _____ conversation while they waited for the bus.
a. superficial b. eminent c. indispensable d. momentous

d 9. Samantha was upset by her friend's _____ comments about her artwork.
a. paramount b. momentous c. prestigious d. petty

a 10. Saving lives is _____ to firefighters.
a. paramount b. inconsequential c. petty d. superficial

Challenge: The _____ writer published yet another _____ book that made it to the top of the bestseller lists.
b a. petty…momentous b. eminent…noteworthy c. superficial…paramount

©Great Source. DO NOT COPY

Lesson 20 129

A New Language—of Silence

Until the late 1970s, deaf Nicaraguan children had few resources available to them. They stayed at home and communicated using crude signs. Even when schools were started for them, the teaching methods used were slow and largely ineffective. However, when about fifty deaf children came together, something amazing happened: They started to develop their own language— Nicaraguan Sign Language (NSL).

(1) To scientists, this event was *momentous,* for it proved that children, even those who have not been exposed to language, have the ability to create it. **(2)** The factor that seems to be *indispensable* for language development is having a community of speakers. **(3)** The ability to hear language, however, is *inconsequential,* for these children developed a silent language.

The first "speakers" of NSL used relatively simple signs. "To talk" was expressed by opening and closing the thumb and index finger in front of one's mouth. Soon, however, the signs became more subtle. The place where one's fingers opened and closed began to communicate past, present, or future verb tense. Directions, such as up or down, became distinguished from actions, like rolling or walking. For example, *Roll, down, roll* means "to roll down," but *roll down* means "to roll and then go down."

As more deaf children came of school age, the community of language users grew. **(4)** In a *noteworthy* development, people found that younger children used more complex language forms. This was partially because they were refining the first inventions and partially because younger children are more flexible as they learn—and create—language.

(5) *Superficially,* NSL can look like random hand movements. **(6)** However, its "speakers" can communicate messages that are *indubitably* complex. An article in the *New York Times* reported one child signing, "I live with my grandmother. It's way over there in the barrio. We sit around, and we're bored all the time. We do a lot of laundry. But at school, everyone's deaf, so I can talk to them. And I can read a book about Babar."

(7) When staff members at the Nicaraguan school first realized what was happening, they called in *eminent* scholars to investigate the language. **(8)** Realizing the importance of what they had seen, these linguists published articles about NSL in *prestigious* journals. Now the language has become the object of research. Some scholars want to protect the new language by not teaching the children a more standard form of communication, such as American Sign Language. **(9)** To others, this seems *petty,* or even unethical. **(10)** They believe *paramount* concern should be the best interests of the children.

Whatever NSL's eventual fate, it remains the miraculous invention of a few impaired individuals. It is not surprising that the world's newest language was created by the world's most linguistically inventive people— children!

Each sentence below refers to a numbered sentence in the passage. Write the letter of the choice that gives the sentence a meaning that is closest to the original sentence.

___c___ **1.** To scientists, this event was _____ .
  a. beautiful **b.** necessary **c.** significant **d.** unimportant

___d___ **2.** The factor that seems to be _____ for language development is having a community of speakers.
  a. intelligent **b.** lacking **c.** unquestionable **d.** required

___a___ **3.** The ability to hear language, however, is _____ .
  a. not important **b.** absolutely crucial **c.** on the surface **d.** impossible

___d___ **4.** In a _____ development, people found that younger children used more complex language forms.
  a. high-status **b.** recent **c.** respected **d.** deserving attention

_____c_____ 5. _____, NSL can look like random hand movements.
    a. Frequently   **b.** At first   **c.** On the surface   **d.** Unquestionably

_____b_____ 6. However, its "speakers" can communicate messages that are _____ complex.
    a. considered   **b.** unquestionably   **c.** essentially   **d.** hardly

_____b_____ 7. When staff members at the Nicaraguan school first realized what was happening, they called in _____ scholars to investigate the language.
    a. numerous   **b.** famous   **c.** unimportant   **d.** intelligent

_____a_____ 8. Realizing the importance of what they had seen, these linguists published articles about NSL in _____ journals.
    a. respected   **b.** scientific   **c.** insignificant   **d.** numerous

_____a_____ 9. To others, this seems _____, or even unethical.
    a. trivial   **b.** unquestionable   **c.** irresponsible   **d.** wrong

_____c_____ 10. They believe the _____ concern should be the best interests of the children.
    a. without a doubt   **b.** most noticeable   **c.** most important   **d.** near the surface

Indicate whether the statements below are TRUE or FALSE according to the passage.

_____F_____ 1. NSL was developed by linguists at a university in Nicaragua.

_____T_____ 2. The development of NSL proves that children don't have to hear language to be able to create it.

_____T_____ 3. Some scholars think the children shouldn't be taught conventional sign language.

FINISH THE THOUGHT

Complete each sentence so that it shows the meaning of the italicized word.

1. *Indubitably,* _____ Answers will vary.

_____

2. A *petty* remark might be _____ Answers will vary.

_____

WRITE THE DERIVATIVE

Complete the sentence by writing the correct form of the word shown in parentheses. You may not need to change the form that is given.

____eminent____ 1. The _____ artist received many requests to paint portraits. *(eminence)*

__inconsequential__ 2. The fact that she forgot to put pepper in the stew was _____. *(inconsequential)*

petty   **3.** The _____ argument between the five-year-olds was soon over. (*pettiness*)

paramount   **4.** Brushing your teeth is _____ to keeping them healthy. (*paramount*)

superficiality   **5.** The _____ of our new neighbor's friendliness was apparent to us all. (*superficial*)

noteworthy   **6.** Many _____ athletes attended the pitcher's induction into the hall of fame. (*noteworthy*)

momentousness   **7.** Kevin's announcement added to the _____ of the occasion. (*momentous*)

indubitably   **8.** A giraffe's neck is _____ long. (*indubitably*)

indispensability   **9.** Finding his pockets empty, Tom thought about the _____ of money. (*indispensable*)

prestigious   **10.** Liam's parents were so proud when he won the _____ state chess championship! (*prestige*)

FIND THE EXAMPLE

Choose the answer that best describes the action or situation.

d   **1.** A place you would most likely find *eminent* actors
    a. small theater   **b.** Alaska   **c.** grocery store   **d.** Hollywood

c   **2.** Something that is *indubitably* powerful
    a. snowflake   **b.** kitten   **c.** bear   **d.** fly

c   **3.** Something that would most likely be considered a *petty* loss
    a. a car   **b.** a job   **c.** a penny   **d.** a pet

d   **4.** Something that is likely to be *inconsequential* to a baker
    a. sugar   **b.** eggs   **c.** flour   **d.** clay

a   **5.** Something that gives a professional football player *prestige*
    a. Super Bowl ring   **b.** helmet   **c.** shoulder pads   **d.** jersey

d   **6.** Something a *superficial* person might spend a lot of time thinking about
    a. relationships   **b.** education   **c.** culture   **d.** appearances

b   **7.** An *indispensable* tool to a carpenter
    a. keyboard   **b.** hammer   **c.** scissors   **d.** eraser

d   **8.** Something of *paramount* importance to an orchestra
    a. towels   **b.** cups   **c.** trees   **d.** instruments

a   **9.** Where you would most likely go to find *noteworthy* artwork
    a. museum   **b.** dumpster   **c.** post office   **d.** bus station

c   **10.** A *momentous* occasion for most teenagers
    a. taking a pop quiz   **b.** retirement   **c.** getting a license   **d.** saying first words

Families

WORD LIST

brood	cohesive	descendant	dynasty	inheritance
maternal	matriarch	patriarch	posterity	sibling

Few things are more important than family relationships. As the poet William Ross Wallace wrote, " . . . the hand that rocks the cradle / Is the hand that rules the world." Yet family relationships come in many different forms. The words in this lesson deal with the many varieties of families.

1. brood (brood)
   a. *noun* The young of certain animals, especially birds; the children in one family
   • All four children in the Fazio **brood** graduated with honors from college.
   b. *verb* To worry; to think about negatively for a long time
   • Anthony spent the weekend **brooding** over the low score he got on a math test.

2. cohesive (kō-hē´sĭv) *adjective* from Latin *cohaerere*, "to cling together"
Sticking together
• Psychologists say that talking together during dinner every night promotes a **cohesive** family.

cohesion *noun* The **cohesion** of mercury atoms causes them to form droplets.

3. descendant (dĭ-sĕn´dənt) *noun* from Latin *de-*, "down" + *scandere*, "to climb"
An individual who can be traced to one ancestor or a group of ancestors
• John claims to be a **descendant** of George Washington.

descend *verb* I am **descended** from Navajo Native Americans.

descent *noun* A movement downward
• The plane's rapid **descent** caused my ears to pop.

4. dynasty (dī´nə-stē) *noun* from Greek *dunasteia*, "lord"
   a. A series of rulers from the same family
   • The Ming **dynasty** ruled China for almost three centuries.
   b. A group or family that maintains power or success for several generations
   • The Bush family could be considered a political **dynasty.**

dynastic *adjective* The scholar was studying Egyptian **dynastic** history.

When a bird sits on its eggs, it is also said to *brood.*

brood of birds

Point out that some of these words refer to parents (such as *matriarch* and *patriarch*). Others refer to offspring (such as *brood, sibling, descendant,* and *posterity*).

5. **inheritance** (ĭn-hĕr´ĭ-təns) *noun* from Latin *in-*, "in" + *heres*, "heirs"
Property or money willed to a person
   • An **inheritance** from her grandmother funded her college education.

   inherit *verb* To receive from an ancestor
   • Allie hoped her baby would **inherit** his father's blue eyes.

   inheritor *noun* Hallie was the **inheritor** of her father's business.

6. **maternal** (mə-tûr´nəl) *adjective* from Latin *mater*, "mother"
   a. Referring to a mother or motherhood
      • Babysitting brought out Joan's **maternal** side.
   b. Related to one's mother
      • Mr. Finch is Emma's **maternal** grandfather.

7. **matriarch** (mā´trē-ärk´) *noun* from Latin *mater*, "mother" + Greek *arkhos*, "ruler"
A highly respected older woman; a mother who is head of a family or group
   • Queen Elizabeth I was considered the **matriarch** of sixteenth-century England.

   matriarchal or **matriarchic** *adjective* Traditional Algonquin society was **matriarchal**.

   matriarchy *noun* A bee hive is a **matriarchy**.

8. **patriarch** (pā´trē-ärk´) *noun* from Greek *pater*, "father" + *arkhos*, "ruler"
A highly respected older man; a man who is head of a family or group
   • Young family members often consulted the wise **patriarch** for advice.

   patriarchal or **patriarchic** *adjective* Anthropologists have found that most human societies are **patriarchal**.

   patriarchy *noun* The Catholic church is a **patriarchy** headed by the pope.

9. **posterity** (pŏ-stĕr´ĭ-tē) *noun* from Latin *post-*, "after"
   a. Future generations
      • The famous artist's daughter donated a large portion of his work to the museum so that it would be preserved for **posterity**.
   b. All of a person's descendants
      • Lena kept old family photos for the sake of her **posterity**.

10. **sibling** (sĭb´lĭng) *noun* from Old English *sibb*, "kinsman"
A brother or sister; one of a group of children of the same parents
   • **Siblings** often look similar to one another.

> *Matriarchal* and *patriarchal* refer to families, groups, societies, or countries.

WORD ENRICHMENT

Matriarchal and patriarchal

Many traditional human societies are *patriarchal*. Men serve as leaders, inherit property, and have control of their families. A few societies are *matriarchal*, in which women have control of resources and provide leadership. Note that the alternative forms of these words are *patriarchic* and *matriarchic*.

WRITE THE CORRECT WORD

Write the correct word in the space next to each definition.

cohesive	1. sticking together	posterity	6. future generations
inheritance	2. property or money willed to a person	dynasty	7. a series of rulers from one family
patriarch	3. a man who is head of a family	matriarch	8. a woman who is head of the family
brood	4. the children in one family	descendant	9. one who comes from a particular ancestor
maternal	5. referring to a mother or motherhood	sibling	10. a brother or sister

COMPLETE THE SENTENCE

Write the letter for the word that best completes each sentence.

a 1. Over generations, the family formed a(n) _____ of famous writers.
   a. dynasty   **b.** sibling   **c.** inheritance   **d.** posterity

b 2. The cat's _____ treatment of the abandoned kitten made us think it was her own.
   a. cohesive   **b.** maternal   **c.** dynastic   **d.** patriarchal

d 3. I am a _____ of people who came to this country on the Mayflower.
   a. brood   **b.** cohesion   **c.** matriarch   **d.** descendant

c 4. A strong leader, Grandma Doris is the _____ of the Hogan family.
   a. descendant   **b.** patriarch   **c.** matriarch   **d.** inheritance

b 5. My great-grandmother saved many letters for _____, so I have a wonderful collection of first-person accounts of the California gold rush.
   a. patriarchy   **b.** posterity   **c.** dynasty   **d.** descent

a 6. Important U.S. holidays help encourage a _____ national identity.
   a. cohesive   **b.** descendant   **c.** maternal   **d.** patriarchal

c 7. When we met Kathy's twin, we were surprised that the _____ looked nothing alike.
   a. patriarchs   **b.** posterities   **c.** siblings   **d.** broods

d 8. Esther received a large _____ after her great-uncle's death.
   a. descent   **b.** matriarch   **c.** dynasty   **d.** inheritance

a 9. The father collected his _____ and drove them all to the movies.
   a. brood   **b.** sibling   **c.** inheritance   **d.** patriarch

b 10. At family reunions, Uncle Charlie is the acknowledged _____.
   a. matriarch   **b.** patriarch   **c.** brood   **d.** dynasty

Challenge: When the family _____ passed away, she left a large _____ to her only grandson.
c **a.** dynasty…cohesion   **b.** patriarch…inheritance   **c.** matriarch…inheritance

Amazons—Fact or Fiction?

The mythical Amazons had an unusual family structure. **(1)** Most societies, both present and past, have been *patriarchal.* **(2)** In contrast, the Amazons were a *matriarchal* society. According to legend, the women controlled politics and went to battle, among other things. Their societies were composed entirely of females, with only occasional contacts with men. **(3)** If a boy was born to an Amazon woman, he was separated from his female *siblings* immediately and sent to a neighboring tribe.

(4) According to the Greek myth, the Amazons were the *descendants* of the war god, Ares, and the sea nymph, Harmonia. **(5)** The Amazon tribe was warlike, and it was considered a *maternal* duty to train one's daughters for combat. **(6)** Women, together with their all-female *brood,* went charging into battle, carrying bows, spears, and double-sided axes. **(7)** The leadership of inspiring queens encouraged *cohesion* within the tribe.

Stories of the Amazons suggest that they were the first human beings to tame and ride horses. The Greek writer Homer mentioned Amazon soldiers in the *Iliad.* Greek historian Herodotus believed that they came from Russia. He wrote that the Amazons once found themselves shipwrecked on an island, where they engaged the Scythians in warfare. When the battle was over, the Scythians were amazed to find that their fearsome enemies were women. **(8)** The men were enchanted by the prospect of fathering children who would *inherit* such bravery. **(9)** They immediately proposed marriage so they could begin creating a *dynasty* of warriors. The Amazons accepted, but refused to take on traditional female roles.

Recent archaeological excavations have revealed that there may have been some truth to the legends of women warriors. One investigator, Jeannine Davis-Kimball, has uncovered burial sites in present-day Russia that date from about 300 to 100 BC. The graves contain women who were buried with swords, daggers, and an array of beautiful objects. In contrast, the fewer objects found in the surrounding men's tombs suggest that they were of lower status than the women.

(10) Whether or not there were actually Amazon-like tribes, Amazons have left their mark on *posterity.* The magnificent Amazon River was named to honor them. According to many accounts, Spanish explorer Francisco de Orellana gave the river its name in 1541, in honor of the female warriors he met on his journey through South America.

Another important name has a more indirect relationship to the Amazons. In 1510, Spanish writer Garcia Ordonez de Montalvo wrote a romance about a race of warrior women ruled by Queen Califia, of the island of California. When Spanish explorers landed in what is now lower California, in the early 1500s, they thought they had found an island. Perhaps in hopes of finding an earthly paradise with beautiful women and gold, they called it "California," in honor of the Ordonez de Montalvo book.

Each sentence below refers to a numbered sentence in the passage. Write the letter of the choice that gives the sentence a meaning that is closest to the original sentence.

____c____ **1.** Most societies, both present and past, have been _____.
   a. religious   **b.** led by women   **c.** led by men   **d.** ancient

____d____ **2.** In contrast, the Amazons were a _____ society.
   a. male-controlled   **b.** modern   **c.** peaceful   **d.** female-controlled

____b____ **3.** He was separated from his female _____ immediately.
   a. friends   **b.** sisters   **c.** head of family   **d.** future generations

____a____ **4.** The Amazons were the _____ of Ares and Harmonia.
   a. offspring   **b.** superiors   **c.** helpers   **d.** brothers and sisters

_____d_____ 5. It was considered a(n) _____ duty to train one's daughters for combat.
       a. respected   **b.** important   **c.** fatherly   **d.** motherly

_____b_____ 6. Women, together with their all-female _____ went charging into battle.
       a. soldiers   **b.** children   **c.** series of rulers   **d.** supporters

_____d_____ 7. The leadership of inspiring queens encouraged _____ within the tribe.
       a. brave fighting   **b.** devoted respect   **c.** willed money   **d.** sticking together

_____a_____ 8. The men were enchanted by the prospect of fathering children who would _____ such bravery.
       a. get from ancestors   **b.** think well of   **c.** highly respect   **d.** completely ignore

_____d_____ 9. They immediately proposed marriage so they could begin creating a _____ of warriors.
       a. small number   **b.** father   **c.** new type   **d.** powerful group

_____d_____ 10. Amazons have left their mark on _____.
       a. sisters and brothers   **b.** property   **c.** parents   **d.** future generations

Indicate whether the statements below are TRUE or FALSE according to the passage.

_____F_____ 1. Amazon warriors could be male or female.

_____T_____ 2. Recent archaeological excavations support the idea that women warriors may have existed.

_____T_____ 3. The name of the state of California was taken from a Spanish novel.

WRITING EXTENDED RESPONSES

In the passage you have read, the family structure of the Amazons is described. Of course, there are many different types of families. Write about your family or a family you know about from TV, a movie, or a book. Be sure to list and describe the family members. You may also write about what their personalities are like, what role they play in the family, activities they do, traditions they have, notable ancestors, and so on. Your descriptive essay should be at least three paragraphs long, and should detail a few aspects of this family. Use at least three lesson words in your essay and underline them.

WRITE THE DERIVATIVE

Complete the sentence by writing the correct form of the word shown in parentheses. You may not need to change the form that is given.

_____inherited_____ 1. Donald _____ his grandfather's antique car. *(inheritance)*

_____descended_____ 2. Blair discovered that she _____ from Abraham Lincoln. *(descendant)*

matriarchal or matriarchic	**3.** The explorers found a _____ family group while exploring the islands. (*matriarch*)
siblings	**4.** The two _____ shared a bedroom. (*sibling*)
patriarchal or patriarchic	**5.** In early Scottish history, clans ruled through a _____ system. (*patriarch*)
brooded	**6.** Sandra _____ about the argument all day. (*brood*)
dynasty	**7.** Over the years, the family had become a famous _____ of jewelers. (*dynasty*)
cohesion	**8.** They studied _____ in physics class. (*cohesive*)
maternally	**9.** The young girl cradled the doll _____ in her arms. (*maternal*)
posterity	**10.** The park system was created both for current residents and for _____. (*posterity*)

FIND THE EXAMPLE

Choose the answer that best describes the action or situation.

a **1.** Something that can create *cohesion* in a group
    a. cooperation   **b.** alienation   **c.** arguments   **d.** dishonesty

c **2.** A grandfather's *descendant*
    a. his aunt   **b.** his sister   **c.** his grandson   **d.** his mother

d **3.** Someone who can never become a *patriarch* of a family
    a. an uncle   **b.** a father   **c.** a brother   **d.** a niece

b **4.** Something you would NOT be likely to preserve for *posterity*
    a. jewelry   **b.** tissues   **c.** letters   **d.** photos

a **5.** Something *siblings* always share
    a. a parent   **b.** a sandwich   **c.** a car   **d.** a pair of socks

b **6.** Something you would most likely *brood* about
    a. your favorite dinner   **b.** a missed goal   **c.** a friendly e-mail   **d.** a vacation

c **7.** A likely *matriarch*
    a. younger cousin   **b.** nephew   **c.** grandmother   **d.** brother

d **8.** Something members of a *dynasty* are LEAST likely to have in common
    a. history   **b.** ancestors   **c.** last name   **d.** tastes

a **9.** A common *maternal* instinct
    a. protect   **b.** push away   **c.** ignore   **d.** restrict

b **10.** An item commonly *inherited*
    a. apple   **b.** house   **c.** glasses   **d.** wood

Prefixes, Roots, and Suffixes

The Prefixes *co-, col-, com-, con-,* and *cor-*

If you encounter an unknown word, you can use two types of clues to determine its meaning. First, *context clues* are found in the sentence or paragraph surrounding a word.

A second type of clue is found inside words. Known as *word elements,* these clues consist of *prefixes* (which come before a word or root), *roots* (the main part of a word) and *suffixes* (which come after a word or root). Some roots, known as *base words* can stand alone. Others, known as *combining roots* must be combined with other word elements to become English words.

The Latin *prefixes co-, col-, com-, con-,* and *cor-* mean "together." They occur in hundreds of English words, including *coordinate, cooperate,* and *collide.* Can you see how each of these words contains a sense of being together?

This prefix can attach to a base word or a combining part. Here are examples of the prefix with a base word.

Prefix	Base Word	Word	Meaning
co-	author	coauthor	a person who writes together with another
co-	exist	coexist	to exist together

Words that are formed with combining roots are often taken from Latin.

Prefix	Latin Verb and Meaning	Word	Meaning
con-	gregare, "to assemble"	congregate	to assemble together
con-	tempor, "time"	contemporary	happening at the same time
com-	pati, "to suffer"	compassion	suffering together, feeling sorry for another

When do you use each prefix spelling? Here are some guidelines to help you.

col- occurs before the letter *l,* as in *collect*
cor- occurs before the letter *r,* as in *corroborate*
com- occurs before letters *m, p, b,* as in *command, compass, combat*
co- occurs before vowels and also some consonants, as in *coequal, cognate*
con- occurs before many consonants, as in *conduct, confide*

Practice

You can combine the use of context clues with your knowledge of this prefix to make intelligent guesses about the meanings of words. All of the sentences below contain a word formed with the prefixes *co-, col-, com-, con-,* or *cor-*. Read the sentences and write down what you think the word in italics means. Then check your definition with the one you find in the dictionary, remembering to choose the definition that best fits the sentence.

1. Many different streams *converged* to form the river.

   My definition _____ come together _____

   Dictionary definition _____ meet; come together in one place _____

2. As it started to snow harder, flakes *cohered* to the windshield.

My definition _____ stuck together _____

Dictionary definition _____ to stick or hold together in a mass _____

3. The physician operated on the infant to correct the *congenital* heart problem. (*gen* means "birth")

My definition _____ condition present from birth _____

Dictionary definition _____ existing before or at the time of birth _____

4. Eduardo's sixteenth birthday *coincided* with his parents' twentieth anniversary.

My definition _____ happened at the same time _____

Dictionary definition _____ to occur at the same time _____

5. After they copied the loose sheets, the assistants had to *collate* them into packets.

My definition _____ put them together _____

Dictionary definition _____ to arrange in proper sequence _____

6. Adela sought a salary *commensurate* with her abilities. (*mensura* means "measure")

My definition _____ equal to; measuring with _____

Dictionary definition _____ of the same size, corresponding in size _____

7. It is against the law to *collude* to fix prices.

My definition _____ plot together _____

Dictionary definition _____ having secret meetings to deceive or cheat _____

8. The musical medley was a *composite* of many songs.

My definition _____ mixture _____

Dictionary definition _____ something made by combining different parts _____

The Root -duce-

WORD LIST

abduct	conduct	conduit	deduce	duke
inducement	induction	reduction	subdue	viaduct

The words in this lesson are formed from the Latin word *ducere,* which means, "to lead." In English, the root *-duce-* can also be spelled *duct, duk,* and *duit.* Many common words contain this root. For example, a *duct* leads air or water somewhere. To *introduce* can be thought of as "to lead someone or something to another." In this lesson, you will learn ten useful words that come from this root.

Discuss how the idea of "leading" is present in the meaning of each lesson word. Point out the following prefix meanings: *re-,* "back"; *in-,* "in"; *de-,* "away, down, from"; *via-,* "through"; *ab-,* "away"; and *con-,* "with."

1. **abduct** (ăb-dŭkt´) *verb* from Latin *ab-,* "away" + *duct,* "lead"
   To carry off by force; to kidnap
   • The breeder was devastated when two of her prize show dogs were **abducted.**

   abduction *noun* The **abduction** of the Prime Minister's daughter gripped the nation for weeks.

2. **conduct** from Latin *con-,* "together" + *duct,* "lead"
   a. *verb* (kən-dŭkt´) To lead, guide, run, or manage
   • The manager **conducted** the sales meeting with great efficiency and skill, making sure that all items on the agenda were covered.
   b. *noun* (kŏn´dŭkt´) The way a person acts
   • Teachers expect better **conduct** from eighth-graders than from kindergarteners.

   conductor *noun* The **conductor** sets the tempo for the orchestra.

   > Notice that the verb *conduct* is pronounced differently from the noun.

3. **conduit** (kŏn´dōō-ĭt) *noun* from Latin *con-,* "together" + *duit,* "lead"
   a. A pipe or channel for transporting or enclosing fluids, gases, or wires
   • The electrical **conduit's** fireproof insulation prevented a blaze from starting inside the wall.
   b. A means of getting or communicating something
   • The diplomat was a **conduit** for messages between the two leaders.

conduct

4. **deduce** (dĭ-dōōs´) *verb* from Latin *de-,* "away" + *duce,* "lead"
   To reach a conclusion through logical reasoning
   • When Derek saw a food-covered picnic table, he **deduced** that the campers were nearby.

   deduction *noun* The character Sherlock Holmes was a master of using **deduction** to solve crimes.

   deductive *adjective* Many geometry proofs are based on **deductive** reasoning.

   > *Deduction* can also mean, "an amount subtracted," as in "a price *deduction.*"

5. duke (do͞ok) *noun* from Latin *duk,* "lead"
A nobleman of the highest rank other than prince or king
• William, **Duke** of Normandy, conquered England in 1066.

duchess *noun* The wife of a duke is called a **duchess.**

duchy *noun* The **Duchy** of Cornwall is one of the largest in Britain.

> A *duchy* is the territory ruled by a duke or duchess; it is also known as a *dukedom.*

6. inducement (ĭn-do͞os´mənt) *noun* from Latin *in-,* "in" + *duce,* "lead"
Something that tempts or persuades; an incentive
• The bank offered a free CD player as **inducement** for opening an account there.

induce *verb* Warm milk helps to **induce** sleep.

7. induction (ĭn-dŭk´shən) *noun* from Latin *in-,* "in" + *duce,* "lead"
Placement or entry into a club or an office
• As both a soldier and a great athlete, Art Donovan's **induction** into the U.S. Marine Corps Sports Hall of Fame was well deserved.

induct *verb* Derrick was **inducted** into the National Honor Society.

8. reduction (rĭ-dŭk´shən) *noun* from Latin *re-,* "back" + *duct,* "lead"
a. An amount subtracted; the amount that something is lessened
• Many citizens appreciated the **reduction** in their property taxes.
b. The act of making something less, smaller, or less significant
• A fever can lead to a serious **reduction** in strength and endurance.

reduce *verb* Please **reduce** the noise level in this class!

9. subdue (səb-do͞o´) *verb* from Latin *sub-,* "under" + *duct,* "lead"
a. To conquer or bring under control
• After championship games, police may be called upon to **subdue** dangerous and destructive rioters.
b. To make less intense or prominent; to tone down
• The fashion company decided to **subdue** their featured colors, changing them from bright red and yellow to gray and beige.

> *Subdued* is also an adjective, meaning "understated or mild in appearance or behavior."

10. viaduct (vī´ə-dŭkt´) *noun* from Latin *via,* "road" + *duct,* "lead"
A structure of spans or arches carrying a road or railroad over a wide valley or other road or railroad
• The **viaduct** supported the expressway, enabling the street to go beneath it.

> The word *viaduct* was formed from Latin *via* ("road") and the second part of the English word *aqueduct.*

WORD ENRICHMENT

Leading dukes

The word *duke* is taken from *duk,* meaning "lead," because, historically, a duke led soldiers into battle.

WRITE THE CORRECT WORD

Write the correct word in the space next to each definition.

conduit   **1.** pipe or channel

induction   **2.** entry into a group

subdue   **3.** to conquer or bring under control

abduct   **4.** to kidnap

duke   **5.** high-ranking nobleman

reduction   **6.** an amount subtracted

conduct   **7.** one's behavior

deduce   **8.** to conclude logically

viaduct   **9.** bridge carrying a road or railroad

inducement   **10.** an incentive

COMPLETE THE SENTENCE

Write the letter for the word that best completes each sentence.

a   **1.** Working fewer hours per week will result in a pay _____.
a. reduction   b. abduction   c. conduction   d. induction

c   **2.** If the pipeline were to burst, one of the main oil _____ on the continent could become an environmental disaster.
a. inducements   b. dukes   c. conduits   d. viaducts

b   **3.** In football, "unsportsmanlike _____" will result in a penalty.
a. deduction   b. conduct   c. inducement   d. abduction

d   **4.** Her _____ into the Spanish Honor Society was no surprise.
a. abduction   b. reduction   c. conduction   d. induction

c   **5.** The _____ had secret plans to become king one day.
a. conduit   b. viaduct   c. duke   d. induction

a   **6.** _____ people who begin to sympathize with their captors are said to suffer from "Stockholm Syndrome."
a. Abducted   b. Conducted   c. Reduced   d. Induced

d   **7.** _____ allow many different highways to crisscross the city.
a. Inducements   b. Inductions   c. Conduits   d. Viaducts

b   **8.** No matter what _____ you offer me, I will never sell out my ideals.
a. deductions   b. inducements   c. viaducts   d. dukes

b   **9.** We'll need some sort of tranquilizer to _____ the rhino before we tag it.
a. deduce   b. subdue   c. reduce   d. induct

d   **10.** From the mess in the room, we _____ that the children had been playing in it.
a. reduced   b. conducted   c. induced   d. deduced

Challenge: The engineer _____ that the _____ would have to be made of reinforced steel.
c   a. induced…conduit   b. reduced…duke   c. deduced…viaduct

Duct Tape Everywhere

Want to give a red rose to your beloved? Decorate a room? Catch bugs? Reinforce a book bag? Well, my friend, if you want to do all those things, what you need is duct tape.

What we now call "duct tape" was invented in the 1940s, during World War II, to keep water out of ammunition cases. The tape is waterproof and remarkably strong, but can be torn by hand, making it convenient and easy to use. It has three parts: a synthetic, waterproof layer (often plastic or polyethylene); a cloth mesh layer (often made from cotton); and a film of sticky glue.

(1) Military personnel soon *deduced* that there were many uses for this product. It helped fix guns and jeeps. One soldier reportedly used it to seal bullet holes in a plane. **(2)** In these and other ways, duct tape has actually helped America's military to *subdue* its foes.

Duct tape has many peacetime uses, too. **(3)** People building houses began using the tape to connect heating ducts and other *conduits*. This is where "duct tape" got its name. But it is so versatile that its uses are almost limitless. And as with anything that has many uses, it is not always used for good. **(4)** *Abducted* people have been tied up with it.

But duct tape is most often used to help solve problems. **(5)** For example, the presence of fragile knick-knacks on tabletops seems to be an *inducement* for cats to jump up on them, but cat owners report that putting duct tape (sticky-side-up) on tabletops discourages that behavior. Other people have put duct tape on the floor and caught insect pests.

(6) To preserve the decorations on a guardrail above a *viaduct,* workers in Birmingham, Alabama, simply covered them in duct tape. This won them praise for finding an affordable solution to a common problem.

(7) Duct tape has even been *inducted* into the arsenal of wart-removal techniques. **(8)** Researchers *conducted* a study of wart removal and found that covering a wart with duct tape for six days is the first step of a highly effective treatment. **(9)** The technique *reduced* the number of warts on test subjects while causing very little pain.

Finally, clothes and accessories like backpacks, belts, visors, hats, and guitar straps can be repaired, or even made from scratch, with duct tape. The tape now comes in many colors. Several Web sites have instructions for making red roses and other pretty gifts out of duct tape. One company even gives college scholarships to the best duct-tape-dressed couple at a prom! **(10)** Perhaps duct-tape outfits haven't been worn to parties with *dukes,* kings, and queens, but believe it or not, they are starting to be seen just about everywhere else.

If you want to learn more about creative ways to use duct tape, try *www.ducttapefashion.com* and *www.octanecreative.com/ducttape,* or just do an Internet search on "duct tape." Hopefully, the information you get will stick with you.

Each sentence below refers to a numbered sentence in the passage. Write the letter of the choice that gives the sentence a meaning that is closest to the original sentence.

___d___ **1.** Military personnel soon _____ that there were many uses for this product.
 a. convinced them **b.** communicated **c.** carried off **d.** figured out

___b___ **2.** Duct tape has actually helped America's military to _____ its foes.
 a. kidnap **b.** conquer **c.** install **d.** reason with

___a___ **3.** People building houses began using the tape to connect heating ducts and other _____.
 a. pipes **b.** subtractions **c.** nobles **d.** entries

___c___ **4.** _____ people have been tied up with it.
 a. Tempted **b.** Noble **c.** Kidnapped **d.** Logical

_____d_____ **5.** The presence of fragile knick-knacks on tabletops seems to be a _____ for cats to jump up on them.
     a. formal entry   **b.** subtracted amount   **c.** means of communicating   **d.** temptation

_____a_____ **6.** To preserve the decorations on a guardrail above a(n) _____, workers in Birmingham, Alabama, simply covered them in duct tape.
     a. road bridge   **b.** entry to a club   **c.** tempting stimulus   **d.** logical conclusion

_____c_____ **7.** Duct tape has even been _____ into the arsenal of wart-removal techniques.
     a. kidnapped   **b.** triggered   **c.** entered   **d.** defeated

_____b_____ **8.** Researchers _____ a study of wart removal.
     a. reasoned   **b.** ran   **c.** lessened   **d.** entered

_____d_____ **9.** The technique _____ the number of warts on test subjects.
     a. kidnapped   **b.** led   **c.** persuaded   **d.** lessened

_____b_____ **10.** Perhaps duct-tape outfits haven't been worn to parties with _____.
     a. arches   **b.** high-ranking nobles   **c.** guides   **d.** alien kidnappers

Indicate whether the statements below are TRUE or FALSE according to the passage.

_____F_____ **1.** Duct tape was first used to connect heating ducts and pipes.

_____T_____ **2.** Duct tape has been used for medical purposes and to make clothes.

_____F_____ **3.** In 1836, the Duke of Windsor enjoyed dressing in duct-tape smoking jackets.

FINISH THE THOUGHT

Complete each sentence so that it shows the meaning of the italicized word.

1. From the wonderful smell in the room, I *deduced* that _____ Answers will vary. _____

_____

2. The business offered prospective employees *inducements* such as _____ Answers will vary. _____

_____

WRITE THE DERIVATIVE

Complete the sentence by writing the correct form of the word shown in parentheses. You may not need to change the form that is given.

_____duchy_____ **1.** Fauntleroy ruled his _____ with kindness and generosity. *(duke)*

_____subdued_____ **2.** Don't you think you should wear something a bit more _____ to the funeral? *(subdue)*

_____reduced_____ **3.** The heat of the sun _____ the snowman to a small lump of snow. *(reduction)* inducted

4. To be _____ into the secret club, Jesse would have to do something embarrassing. *(induction)*

viaduct

5. Though more costly to build, a _____ is often safer and more convenient for drivers than a huge intersection would be. *(viaduct)*

induced

6. The promise of large campaign contributions _____ the senator to look at the issue in a different light. *(inducement)*

abduction

7. The man on the park bench described in detail his _____ by aliens. *(abduct)*

Deductive

8. _____ reasoning is a key part of both science methodology and common sense. *(deduce)*

conduit

9. After a heavy rain, the huge drainpipe was a _____ for millions of gallons of water. *(conduit)*

conductor

10. Was she the _____ of a train or of an orchestra? *(conduct)*

FIND THE EXAMPLE

Choose the answer that best describes the action or situation.

c **1.** Most likely to be found under a *viaduct*
    a. ocean   **b.** rabbits   **c.** road   **d.** electricity

a **2.** Time and place where *dukes* were in power
    a. old England   **b.** 1990's America   **c.** modern Africa   **d.** Ohio, last week

c **3.** A *subdued* statement
    a. Oh no!   **b.** EEK!   **c.** Okay.   **d.** Never.

b **4.** Career in which *deductive* reasoning is most important
    a. ditch digger   **b.** detective   **c.** burger flipper   **d.** field-goal kicker

d **5.** Example of a *conduit*
    a. allen wrench   **b.** baseball bat   **c.** cirrus cloud   **d.** sewer pipe

d **6.** Something likely to result in weight *reduction*
    a. more ice cream   **b.** more television   **c.** more soda   **d.** more exercise

a **7.** Something a museum employee would be most likely to *conduct*
    a. tour   **b.** orchestra   **c.** wrestling clinic   **d.** investment seminar

b **8.** An organization into which people would want to be *inducted*
    a. Cellblock D-8   **b.** Hall of Fame   **c.** Fools of America   **d.** Fungus Anonymous

c **9.** Likely goal of a criminal who *abducts* someone
    a. healthy diet   **b.** new friends   **c.** ransom money   **d.** free duct tape

d **10.** An *inducement* to do well in school
    a. stress and anger   **b.** louder music   **c.** less free time   **d.** better career choices

The Root -pel-

WORD LIST

appealing	compel	impel	impulse	peal
pelt	propulsion	pulsate	repeal	repulse

The Latin word root *-pel-* means "thrust, strike, drive, or call out." It comes from the Latin verb *pellere* and can be spelled *pel, pulse, peal,* and *pul* in English words. For example, if you are *expelled* from school, you are "thrust out." An *appeal* "calls out" for help. When you are *repelled* by something, you are "driven away" from it.

Discuss the different ways the prefixes *ap-, com-, im-, pro-,* and *re-* can be combined with the root *pel* to form words.

1. **appealing** (ə-pē´lĭng) from Latin *ap-*, "toward" + *pel*, "drive"
   a. *adjective* Having the power to attract or arouse interest
   • Who can resist the charm of these **appealing** little kittens?
   b. *verb* Making a serious or formal request for help
   • After **appealing** to governments for aid for the tsunami survivors, charitable organizations asked the public for donations.

> The word *appeal* also means "a request that a legal decision be reviewed," usually by a Court of Appeals.

2. **compel** (kəm-pĕl´) *verb* from Latin *com-*, "together" + *pel*, drive
   To force someone to do something; to make necessary
   • The law **compels** drivers to carry their license.

   compulsion (kəm-pŭl´shən) Because of her **compulsion** for cleanliness, she spent most of the day cleaning the house.

> *Compel* and *impel* both imply force, but *compel* suggests outside force, and *impel* suggests an inner drive.

3. **impel** (ĭm-pĕl´) *verb* from *in-*, "against" + *pel*, "drive"
   To urge to action, usually through moral pressure; to motivate
   • I wonder what **impels** him to spend all his free time volunteering at the assisted-living home.

4. **impulse** (ĭm´pŭls´) *noun* from *in-*, "against" + *pel*, "drive"
   A strong urge or drive
   • Mom had a sudden **impulse** to rearrange the living-room furniture.

   impulsive *adjective* People who tend to be **impulsive** should stop and think before they act.

impulse shopping

5. **peal** (pēl) from *pel*, "call out"
   a. *noun* The loud ringing of bells; a loud sound
   • **Peals** of laughter could be heard from the next room.
   b. *verb* To ring or sound loudly
   • The bells **pealed** each hour.

6. **pelt** (pĕlt) *verb* from *pel,* "to strike"
   To strike repeatedly, usually by throwing something
   • When Ron stepped into the room, his friends **pelted** him with pillows.

Pelt has a homonym that means "the skin of an animal with the fur or hair still on it," as in "the bear's *pelt.*"

7. **propulsion** (prə-pŭl´shən) *noun* from Latin *pro-,* "forward" + *pel,* "drive"
   The force that drives something forward, or forward motion
   • In the 1800s, steam power provided **propulsion** for most large boats.

   propel *verb* The fins of fish **propel** them forward in the water.

8. **pulsate** (pŭl´sāt´) *verb* from *pel,* "strike"
   To expand and contract, or beat, in a constant rhythm; to vibrate
   • The dance floor seemed to **pulsate** with movement.

   pulse *noun* During exercise, our **pulses** speed up.

9. **repeal** (rĭ-pēl´) *verb* from *re-,* "back" + *pel,* "call"
   To officially cancel; to take back or withdraw
   • After heavy rains ended the drought, the city council **repealed** the rule against watering lawns.

10. **repulse** (rĭ-pŭls´) *verb* from *re-,* "back" + *pel,* "drive"
    a. To drive back, or to reject rudely
       • The army **repulsed** their attackers and regained control of the bridge.
    b. To cause feelings of disgust or disapproval
       • His crude manners **repulsed** his peers.

    repulsion *noun* Derrin was offended by his sister's **repulsion** of his offer to help.

    repulsive *adjective* Howard finds snakes and worms to be **repulsive** creatures.

ANALOGIES

On the answer line, write the letter of the answer that best completes each analogy. Refer to Lessons 21–23 if you need help with any of the lesson words.

  c   1. Patriarchy is to men as _____.
- a. conduct is to viaduct
- c. matriarchy is to women
- b. pelt is to strike
- d. matriarchy is to children

  b   2. Vessel is to blood as _____.
- a. sleep is to wake
- c. car is to bus
- b. conduit is to water
- d. capture is to abduct

  a   3. Impulsive is to restraint as _____.
- a. rude is to manners
- c. wet is to soaked
- b. cooperative is to help
- d. deduce is to conclusion

  c   4. Attract is to repulse as _____.
- a. peal is to bell
- c. enter is to exit
- b. induct is to enter
- d. viaduct is to road

The Root *-pel-*

WRITE THE CORRECT WORD

Write the correct word in the space next to each definition.

repeal   **1.** to cancel

propulsion   **2.** forward motion

peal   **3.** a loud burst of noise

pelt   **4.** to hit repeatedly

appealing   **5.** attractive; arousing interest

impulse   **6.** a strong urge

compel   **7.** to make someone do something

repulse   **8.** to reject rudely

impel   **9.** to urge to action

pulsate   **10.** to expand and contract

COMPLETE THE SENTENCE

Write the letter for the word that best completes each sentence.

_d_   **1.** On the hot day, Sophie felt a(n) _____ to dive into the water.
     a. peal   **b.** repeal   **c.** propulsion   **d.** impulse

_a_   **2.** The ultrasound showed her arteries _____ as the blood pumped through them.
     a. pulsating   **b.** impelling   **c.** pelting   **d.** appealing

_a_   **3.** Often, simple curiosity is what _____ research scientists to conduct experiments.
     a. impels   **b.** appeals   **c.** repeals   **d.** repulses

_b_   **4.** Maureen's perfume _____ Harvey, so he moved to a seat farther away from her.
     a. pelted   **b.** repulsed   **c.** compelled   **d.** propelled

_c_   **5.** The boat's engine needed some serious repairs because it provided no _____.
     a. pulse   **b.** appeal   **c.** propulsion   **d.** impulse

_c_   **6.** The commission _____ the ban on certain food additives after studies showed they didn't cause serious health problems.
     a. pelted   **b.** propelled   **c.** repealed   **d.** impelled

_b_   **7.** The sermon was interrupted by the _____ of church bells.
     a. pelt   **b.** peal   **c.** pulse   **d.** appeal

_a_   **8.** After the _____ for donations to the volunteer firefighters' organization, there was enough money to buy a new fire engine.
     a. appeal   **b.** peal   **c.** propulsion   **d.** pulse

_d_   **9.** The boys _____ their sister with snowballs.
     a. compelled   **b.** impelled   **c.** appealed   **d.** pelted

_c_   **10.** Homeowners are _____ to pay taxes on their property.
     a. pulsated   **b.** repealed   **c.** compelled   **d.** repulsed

Challenge: Although many people are _____ by the thought of eating frogs, in some countries this food is considered quite _____.
_a_   **a.** repulsed…appealing   **b.** impelled…compelling   **c.** propelled…repulsive

The Amazing Cockroach

What creature can eat almost anything, lives almost everywhere, and can survive just about any catastrophe? The cockroach, of course! **(1)** This amazing but not very *appealing* little bug has much to teach us about survival.

(2) Are you *repulsed* by the thought of cockroaches? If so, perhaps some facts about them will change your mind. First, cockroaches are unique individuals who recognize friends and family by using their feelers to smell. Cockroaches also keep themselves very clean. **(3)** That may come as a surprise to the many people who feel *compelled* to clean their homes to get rid of these insects.

Cockroaches spend 75 percent of their time sleeping. When they do move, however, they are speedy. **(4)** With *propulsion* provided by their six legs, they can run at speeds of up to three miles per hour. This is as fast as many humans can walk—and their legs are much shorter than ours!

Cockroaches were probably around more than 100 million years before the first dinosaurs, but, unlike dinosaurs, they still exist. How have these hardy little creatures survived? For one thing, they have early warning systems. **(5)** *Impulses* in their backs tell them when danger is near. They also use the 4,000 separate lenses in their eyes to detect danger.

(6) Also, cockroaches are not *impelled* to eat very much. In fact, a cockroach can live without food for a month. When they do eat, though, they are not picky. They will consume meat, starches, glue, clothes, and paper.

Cockroaches can go without breathing for forty minutes. **(7)** Their hearts can stop *pulsating* temporarily, and they will still survive. Cockroaches can even live for a week without their heads, for their brains are located near their bellies. Eventually, however, they will die from thirst.

(8) Would you break into *peals* of laughter if someone told you that cockroaches make good pets? In fact, they are becoming quite popular. Though there are over 3,500 species to choose from, a favorite pet is the Madagascan Hissing Cockroach. At a length of three inches, it is easy to see, doesn't fly, and won't eat much.

Even after reading all these facts about cockroaches, you may still just want to eliminate them. **(9)** If you have cockroaches in your home, you know that *pelting* them with a shoe won't get rid of them. And many strong chemicals used to combat cockroaches can harm the environment (which includes people) as well as the bugs. **(10)** Laws have been passed against using environmentally harmful chemicals like DDT, although some of these legal restrictions could be *repealed.* Boric acid, however, is effective against pests and harmless to humans. Stewed cucumber peels and okra are also effective cockroach repellents.

Although many people do not want cockroaches anywhere near them, robotics labs are using these resilient bugs more and more in their research. Scientists are now building robots based on cockroach anatomy to reproduce the critters' speed and ability to climb. It is hoped that these robots will not only explore distant planets and underwater volcanoes, but also detect and retrieve land mines. Who knew how valuable cockroaches could be?

Each sentence below refers to a numbered sentence in the passage. Write the letter of the choice that gives the sentence a meaning that is closest to the original sentence.

____a____ **1.** This amazing but not very _____ little bug has much to teach us about survival.

    a. attractive   **b.** large   **c.** loud   **d.** quick

____d____ **2.** Are you _____ by the thought of cockroaches?

    a. driven forward   **b.** curious   **c.** attracted   **d.** disgusted

____a____ **3.** Many people feel _____ to clean their homes to get rid of them.

    a. forced   **b.** asked   **c.** urged   **d.** attracted

_____d_____ **4.** With _____ provided by their six legs, they can run three miles per hour.
    a. attractiveness   **b.** loud sounds   **c.** added force   **d.** forward motion

_____a_____ **5.** _____ tell them when danger is near.
    a. Strong drives   **b.** Loud sounds   **c.** Repeated strikes   **d.** Regular rhythms

_____c_____ **6.** Cockroaches are not _____ to eat very much.
    a. withdrawn   **b.** picky eaters   **c.** urged from within   **d.** rudely rejected

_____b_____ **7.** Their hearts can stop _____ temporarily, and they will still survive.
    a. breathing   **b.** beating   **c.** making sound   **d.** moving forward

_____a_____ **8.** Would you break into _____ of laughter if someone told you that cockroaches make good pets?
    a. loud sounds   **b.** sudden action   **c.** uncontrollable urges   **d.** rhythmic movements

_____d_____ **9.** You know that _____ them with a shoe won't get rid of them.
    a. forcing   **b.** entertaining   **c.** rudely rejecting   **d.** repeatedly hitting

_____c_____ **10.** Laws have been passed against using chemicals like DDT, although some of these legal restrictions could be _____ .
    a. disgusting   **b.** made stronger   **c.** withdrawn   **d.** driven forward

Indicate whether the statements below are TRUE or FALSE according to the passage.

_____T_____ **1.** Cockroaches have been around for hundreds of millions of years.

_____T_____ **2.** Some people enjoy having cockroaches as pets.

_____T_____ **3.** You can get rid of cockroaches without using strong chemicals.

WRITING EXTENDED RESPONSES

The reading passage gives reasons why cockroaches are valuable, or even admirable. On the other hand, many people feel that they are simply disgusting pests. What is your opinion of cockroaches? Defend your point of view in a persuasive essay of at least three paragraphs. Support your position with at least two main points. Use at least three lesson words in your essay and underline them.

WRITE THE DERIVATIVE

Complete the sentence by writing the correct form of the word shown in parentheses. You may not need to change the form that is given.

_____Peals_____ **1.** _____ of thunder broke the silence. (*peal*)

_____compelling_____ **2.** Enrique made a _____ argument for the new safety guidelines. (*compel*) impulsive   **3.** I was worried that Sasha's _____ behavior would get him into trouble. (*impulse*)

pulsating   **4.** The tiny animal _____ under the microscope was an amoeba. (*pulsate*)

propelled   **5.** The wind _____ the sailboat across the lake. (*propulsion*)

repulsive   **6.** I couldn't stand the _____ smell of dirty sneakers in the locker room. (*repulse*)

Appeals   **7.** William took his case to the Court of _____. (*appealing*)

impelled   **8.** Kendra's love for thrills _____ her to take skydiving lessons. (*impel*)

pelting   **9.** We could hear the pouring rain _____ our roof the whole night. (*pelt*)

repealed   **10.** The new law cannot be _____ for at least two years. (*repeal*)

FIND THE EXAMPLE

Choose the answer that best describes the action or situation.

c   **1.** How an *impulsive* person makes decisions.
     a. slowly   **b.** thoughtfully   **c.** quickly   **d.** happily

c   **2.** A type of sandwich that would *repulse* most people
     a. grilled cheese   **b.** tuna salad   **c.** sardine and jelly   **d.** peanut butter

b   **3.** Something that would likely be most *appealing* to someone who has spent all morning shoveling snow
     a. ice cream   **b.** hot chocolate   **c.** a hard workout   **d.** a picnic

d   **4.** Something that might *impel* a person to get to school on time
     a. a sense of humor   **b.** a bad attitude   **c.** laziness   **d.** responsibility

c   **5.** Someone most likely to be *pelted* with water balloons
     a. police officer   **b.** your principal   **c.** circus clown   **d.** Abraham Lincoln

a   **6.** Something that has been *repealed* in America
     a. slavery   **b.** anti-drug laws   **c.** discrimination laws   **d.** leash laws

b   **7.** Something that drivers are NOT *compelled* to do
     a. obey speed limits   **b.** drive at night   **c.** have a license   **d.** obey traffic signals

d   **8.** A time when you would likely feel your heart *pulsating* rapidly
     a. while sleeping   **b.** while eating   **c.** when tired   **d.** when scared

a   **9.** Something that is *propelled* by muscle power
     a. a bicycle   **b.** a helicopter   **c.** a kite   **d.** a rocket ship

a   **10.** Something that *peals*
     a. a bell   **b.** a mouse   **c.** a window   **d.** a snowstorm

The Root -gen-

WORD LIST

congenital	degenerate	engender	gender	genealogy
generic	genesis	gentry	progeny	regenerate

The root *-gen-*, which comes from both Greek *(genos)* and Latin *(genus),* is used in hundreds of words. Although it originally conveyed the meaning "birth," it now carries several meanings, including "type," "family," "birth," "produce," and "origin." However, all these meanings have something to do with birth or creation. A person is born with *genes* inherited from parents. A *generator* produces electricity.

1. **congenital** (kən-jĕn´ĭ-tl) *adjective* from Latin *com-*, "together" + *gen*, "birth"
   a. Existing at the time of birth; inborn
      • Surgeons operated to correct the baby's **congenital** heart defect.
   b. Occurring in the nature of a person
      • The man almost never told the truth; he seemed to be a **congenital** liar.

> The root *gen* has many meanings. Discuss which of these is found in the definitions of each lesson word.

2. **degenerate** from Latin *de-*, "worsen" + *gen*, "type"
   a. *verb* (dĭ-jĕn´ə-rāt´) To become worse
      • The calm meeting **degenerated** into a bitter shouting match.
   b. *adjective* (dĭ-jĕn´ər-ĭt) Deteriorated; worse; having declined
      • The patient's **degenerate** condition was attributed to a long history of heart disease.

   degeneration *noun* Macular **degeneration** causes loss of vision.

   degenerative *adjective* Parkinson's disease is a **degenerative** disorder.

> As an adjective, *degenerate* can mean "immoral." As a noun, *degenerate* can mean "an immoral person."

3. **engender** (ĕn-jĕn´dər) *verb* from Latin *in-*, "in" + *gen*, "produce"
   To start; to bring into existence
      • Violent acts often **engender** a cycle of violence.

4. **gender** (jĕn´dər) *noun* from *gen*, "type"
   The categories of male, female, or neuter
      • A deer of the female **gender** is called a doe.

5. **genealogy** (jē´nē-ŏl´ə-jē) *noun* from *gen*, "birth; family" + Greek *-logy,* "study"
   The record of a person's ancestors; a family tree
      • Roy's **genealogy** showed that his ancestors included King Henry VIII.

   genealogical *adjective* **Genealogical** research of public records gave Marlena evidence of her family's African origins.

   genealogist *noun* Shawn, our family **genealogist,** keeps track of all our births, marriages, and deaths.

genealogy

6. **generic** (jə-nĕr´ĭk) *adjective* from *gen*, "type"
General; referring to an entire group or class; not specific
   • The **generic** word *cats* includes tigers, jaguars, and house cats.

7. **genesis** (jĕn´ĭ-sĭs) *noun* from *gen*, "beginning"
The origin or beginning
   • Complex ideas often have their **genesis** in a simple observation.

8. **gentry** (jĕn´trē) *noun* from *gen*, "nobly born"
People of high social standing; the ruling class
   • Jane Austen's novels are often set in the country homes of the
   English **gentry.**

9. **progeny** (prŏj´ə-nē) *noun* from *pro-*, "in front of" + *gen*, "born"
A group of children or descendants
   • The **progeny** of the great composer Johann Sebastian Bach included
   several musicians.

10. **regenerate** (rĭ-jĕn´ə-rāt´) *verb* from *Latin re-*, "again" + *gen*, "born"
   a. To give new life to; to energize
      • A million dollar grant **regenerated** the school's music and art
      programs.
   b. To replace by growing new tissue
      • Starfish can sometimes **regenerate** from only one arm.

   regeneration *noun* The construction of Chicago's Millennium Park
   resulted in the **regeneration** of the downtown area.

   regenerative *adjective* The human liver is an organ that has
   some **regenerative** capacity.

> *Genesis* is also the first book of the Judeo-Christian Bible.

> To *gentrify* is to change a poor area into a richer one.

WORD ENRICHMENT

The many senses of *gen*

Words like *gene* and *genetic* relate to birth, so it is easy to see how they
relate to the root *gen*. Other words, however, have less direct relationships to
the root's meaning.

In the Middle Ages, the word *generosity* meant "having a noble birth." It
was believed that those born into nobility would have noble traits, such as
generosity. Similarly, *gentle* meant "high born," a status assumed to lead
automatically to courteous and noble behavior.

Genius comes from a Latin word that meant "a guiding spirit, present
at birth." From there, the definition of genius became "ability one is born
with," and eventually, it came to mean "great natural ability."

WRITE THE CORRECT WORD

Write the correct word in the space next to each definition.

degenerate 1. to deteriorate

progeny 2. descendants

gender 3. male, female, or neuter

congenital 4. present at birth

regenerate 5. to give new life

generic 6. general; not specific

genealogy 7. family history

genesis 8. origin

engender 9. to bring into being

gentry 10. upper social class

COMPLETE THE SENTENCE

Write the letter for the word that best completes each sentence.

a 1. The _____ of the project was a few good friends talking in a basement.
   a. genesis   b. progeny   c. gentry   d. gender

b 2. The diplomats believe that relations between the opposing countries will
   _____, perhaps resulting in war.
   a. engender   b. degenerate   c. regenerate   d. gentrify

d 3. The _____ of the famous author met to discuss how to restore his estate.
   a. gender   b. genealogy   c. genesis   d. progeny

d 4. Though the parents-to-be knew the baby's _____, they told no one.
   a. gentry   b. progeny   c. generic   d. gender

b 5. Scientists believe they will eventually be able to eliminate many _____ defects.
   a. generic   b. congenital   c. engendered   d. regenerative

c 6. _____ prescription medicines often cost less than those with popular
   brand names.
   a. Congenital   b. Degenerative   c. Generic   d. Regenerative

c 7. The new principal's upbeat manner _____ the enthusiasm that had
   disappeared from the school.
   a. degenerated   b. gentrified   c. regenerated   d. generic

a 8. While looking at our _____, I discovered names like Ezekiel and Ebenezer.
   a. genealogy   b. gender   c. regeneration   d. degeneration

d 9. In earlier times, members of the _____ usually were born into their high social
   positions.
   a. gender   b. genealogy   c. progeny   d. gentry

a 10. Beethoven's innovative compositions _____ a whole new style of music.
   a. engendered   b. degenerated   c. gentrified   d. regenerated

Challenge: The _____ helped families identify when _____ defects were likely to occur
   in their offspring.
c   a. gentry...genealogy   b. gender...generic   c. genealogist...congenital

Hope for Regeneration

Salamanders are interesting little creatures. They are cold-blooded amphibians; they can walk and swim; and if they lose their legs, they simply grow new ones. **(1)** That's right—salamanders are masters of *regeneration*.

Scientists have been conducting research on this amazing ability. Not only can salamanders grow new legs, but they also grow new tails, retinas, and parts of their hearts. **(2)** The scientists hope that their studies will lead to the *genesis* of new treatments for human ailments.

(3) Imagine that a person with heart failure could grow a new, healthy heart or that a person suffering from macular *degeneration* (an eye condition that leads to blindness) could grow a new retina. Scientists argue that regenerating new organs could be easier and safer than organ transplants.

(4) Until recently, the idea of regeneration in humans has not *engendered* much support. This is because people have been studying regeneration for more than 200 years and haven't come up with practical applications for humans. But today, due to new advances in the field of genetics, scientists are starting to better understand the mechanisms involved.

Regeneration involves a process called "cell de-differentiation." **(5)** This means that cells become *generic*. These cells have the ability to change into the specific type of cell needed to regrow a specific body part. In humans, this ability does not yet exist. Humans can regenerate some types of tissues, such as skin, liver, and bone. But unlike salamanders, we are limited to regenerating these types of tissue. This means that we cannot grow a new arm, which would involve many types of tissue (including bone, muscle, and skin). Scientists are searching for breakthroughs that will allow human cells to grow into many different types of tissue.

If salamander research yields practical applications, the benefit to people could be enormous. **(6)** Just examine your own *genealogy*. **(7)** You might discover that family members of both *genders* have suffered from the same diseases. **(8)** If, one day, people can regenerate body parts, someone with a *congenital* disease might be able to regrow the affected organs. **(9)** Such treatments would also help one's *progeny* who may have the same ailments. **(10)** These treatments could benefit people all over the world and from all social classes, from the *gentry* to the very poor.

The next time you see a little salamander sunning itself on a rock, think about its amazing regenerative abilities. Imagine the possibilities and the hope that this intriguing creature has provided for human beings.

Each sentence below refers to a numbered sentence in the passage. Write the letter of the choice that gives the sentence a meaning that is closest to the original sentence.

____d____ **1.** Salamanders are masters of _____.
a. birth defects   **b.** family history   **c.** avoiding disease   **d.** regrowing tissue

____c____ **2.** The scientists hope that their studies will lead to the _____ of new treatments.
a. fulfillment   **b.** improvement   **c.** beginning   **d.** popularity

____b____ **3.** Imagine that a person suffering from macular _____ could grow a new retina.
a. improvement   **b.** worsening   **c.** recreation   **d.** disappearance

____a____ **4.** Until recently, the idea of regeneration in humans has not _____ much support.
a. produced   **b.** eliminated   **c.** reduced   **d.** popularized

__b__ **5.** This means that cells become _____.
   a. specialized   **b.** general   **c.** small   **d.** diseased

__a__ **6.** Just examine your own _____.
   a. family history   **b.** health condition   **c.** past experience   **d.** future goals

__c__ **7.** You might discover that family members of both _____ have suffered from the same diseases.
   a. rich and poor   **b.** defects   **c.** sexes   **d.** sides of the family

__d__ **8.** If, one day, people can regenerate body parts, someone with a _____ disease might be able to regrow the affected organ.
   a. serious   **b.** painful   **c.** minor   **d.** inborn

__a__ **9.** Such treatments would also help one's _____ who may have the same ailments.
   a. descendants   **b.** neighbors   **c.** ancestors   **d.** friends

__c__ **10.** These treatments could benefit people all over the world and from all social classes, from the _____ to the very poor.
   a. famous   **b.** unknown   **c.** upper class   **d.** lower class

Indicate whether the statements below are TRUE or FALSE according to the passage.

__T__ **1.** Salamanders can regrow some of their body parts.

__T__ **2.** Regeneration depends upon generic cells that can develop into specialized cells.

__F__ **3.** Humans can't regenerate any kind of tissue at all.

FINISH THE THOUGHT

Complete each sentence so that it shows the meaning of the italicized word.

1. The family dinner *degenerated* into _____ Answers will vary. _____

_____

2. As a member of the *gentry*, _____ Answers will vary. _____

_____

WRITE THE DERIVATIVE

Complete the sentence by writing the correct form of the word shown in parentheses. You may not need to change the form that is given.

__generic__ **1.** The physician wrote a prescription for a _____ medication. (*generic*)

__progeny__ **2.** Morris was honored by three generations of his _____ at the family reunion. (*progeny*) regeneration 3. Even after the recession ended, the permanent loss of many local jobs slowed the _____ of the town's economy. (*regenerate*)

gender 4. Birds of the same species can look very different, depending on their _____. (*gender*)

genesis 5. The historian gave a lecture on the _____ of coal mining. (*genesis*)

congenital 6. The friendly con man was a _____ liar. (*congenital*)

genealogist 7. Her interest in family history led her to become a _____. (*genealogy*)

gentry 8. The local _____ had considerable influence over town affairs. (*gentry*)

degenerative 9. The patient's _____ disease caused great heartache to her family and friends. (*degenerate*)

engendered 10. Deceitful behavior has never _____ trust. (*engender*)

FIND THE EXAMPLE

Choose the answer that best describes the action or situation.

b 1. Someone who would NOT be included among your parents' *progeny*
    a. you   **b.** your aunt   **c.** your children   **d.** your siblings

a 2. Describes a member of the *gentry*
    a. privileged   **b.** underprivileged   **c.** very poor   **d.** middle class

d 3. An example of a *generic* product
    a. Dirt Be-Gone!   **b.** Scrub-Away   **c.** Polly's Polish   **d.** toothpaste

c 4. Someplace that is usually *gender*-specific
    a. cars   **b.** waiting rooms   **c.** public restrooms   **d.** cafeterias

a 5. An example of a *congenital* condition
    a. colorblindness   **b.** a broken leg   **c.** a bad cold   **d.** the flu

b 6. Something that is most likely to *degenerate* over time
    a. a rock   **b.** a battery's charge   **c.** plastic   **d.** a song

c 7. Something NOT usually included in a *genealogy*
    a. births   **b.** marriages   **c.** wealth   **d.** deaths

c 8. Something that usually *regenerates* people
    a. electricity   **b.** loud noises   **c.** plenty of sleep   **d.** too much work

d 9. A figurative synonym for *genesis*
    a. noon   **b.** twilight   **c.** evening   **d.** dawn

b 10. Something you would be most likely to *engender*
    a. the universe   **b.** a creative idea   **c.** a car   **d.** global warming

Prefixes, Roots, and Suffixes

The Prefix *re-*

The Latin prefix *re-* actually has two common meanings. It means both "back" and "again." Like many prefixes, *re-* can combine with both *base words* (which can stand alone) and with *combining roots* (which need elements added to make words). In general—although not always—*re-* means "again" when it is combined with a root word. Here are some examples:

Prefix	Base Word	Word	Word Meaning
re-	do	redo	to do again
re-	fill	refill	to fill again

When *re-* combines with combining roots, some interesting word stories result.

Recalcitrant, meaning "stubborn," comes from "back" and "heel." We might imagine a stubborn mule kicking back its heels.

Revelation, meaning "shocking disclosure," comes from "back" and "veil." We might imagine a person lifting a veil off of to reveal something shocking.

Renowned, meaning "famous," comes from "again" and "name." When a person is named repeatedly, he or she becomes famous. Note that, in this word, *re-* means "again."

Practice

You can combine the use of context clues with your knowledge of this prefix to make intelligent guesses about the meanings of words. All of the sentences below contain a word formed with the prefix *re-*. Read the sentences and write down what you think the word in italics means. Then check your definition with the one you find in the dictionary, remembering to choose the definition that best fits the sentence. Finally, write whether *re-* seems to mean "again" or "back" in the word.

1. The troops *repelled* the invaders.

   My definition _____ pushed back _____

   Dictionary definition _____ to drive off, force back _____

   Meaning of *re-*: ("back" or "again") _____ back _____

2. The used professional sports equipment was *refitted* for poor children to use.

   My definition _____ to change for use again _____

   Dictionary definition _____ to prepare and equip for additional use _____

   Meaning of *re-*: ("back" or "again") _____ again _____

3. The turtle *retracted* its head into its shell.

My definition _____ drew back _____

Dictionary definition _____ to pull back or in _____

Meaning of *re-:* ("back" or "again") _____ back _____

4. During the procession, the wedding party walked into the hall; after the ceremony, there was a *recession*.

My definition _____ walking back out _____

Dictionary definition _____ the act of withdrawing or going back _____

Meaning of *re-:* ("back" or "again") _____ back _____

5. Can I *refill* your glass of water?

My definition _____ fill again _____

Dictionary definition _____ fill again _____

Meaning of *re-:* ("back" or "again") _____ again _____

6. After Vickie improved her grades, her privileges were *reinstated*.

My definition _____ put in place again; implemented again _____

Dictionary definition _____ to restore to a previous condition _____

Meaning of *re-:* ("back" or "again") _____ again _____

7. Water *revived* the dying flowers.

My definition _____ brought to life again _____

Dictionary definition _____ to bring back to life or consciousness _____

Meaning of *re-:* ("back" or "again") _____ again _____

8. The ball *rebounded* off the wall.

My definition _____ bounced back _____

Dictionary definition _____ to spring or bounce back _____

Meaning of *re-:* ("back" or "again") _____ back _____

Review Word Elements

Reviewing word elements helps you to remember them and use them in your reading. Below, write the meaning of the word elements you have studied. Each one appears italicized in a word.

Word	Word Element	Type of Element	Meaning of Word Element
*com*patible	*com-*	prefix	together
*gen*erate	*gen*	root	birth; beginning
via*duct*	*duce*	root	lead
*pel*t	*pel*	root	strike; thrust

The Roots -rupt- and -fract-

WORD LIST

abrupt	disrupt	eruption	fractious	fragmentary
infraction	refract	refractory	rout	rupture

Has anyone ever *interrupted* you, or broken into your conversation? Do you know someone who has *fractured,* or broken, a bone? The Latin words *ruptus* and *fractus* mean "broken." In modern English, they appear as the roots *-rupt-* and *-fract-,* which mean "break."

1. **abrupt** (ə-brŭpt´) *adjective* from Latin *ab-*, "off" + *rupt,* "break"
   a. Sudden; unexpected
      • At the Halloween haunted house, the ghost's **abrupt** appearance made many of the children scream.
   b. Rude in its shortness
      • After a friendly conversation, I was amazed by her **abrupt** goodbye.

   abruptness *noun* A rain or snow shower comes on with **abruptness** and lasts for a short time.

2. **disrupt** (dĭs-rŭpt´) *verb* from Latin *dis-*, "apart" + *rupt,* "break"
   To throw into confusion and disorder
   • Alice's laughter **disrupted** the other students' concentration.

   disruption *noun* We lost power because of a **disruption** in electrical service.

   disruptive *adjective* **Disruptive** students are sent to the principal's office.

3. **eruption** (ĭ-rŭp´shən) *noun* from Latin *e-*, "out" + *rupt,* "break"
   A sudden, violent movement or occurrence
   • The **eruption** of screams from the stadium told us the home team had won the game.

   erupt *verb* When a volcano **erupts,** people who live nearby flee to safety.

4. **fractious** (frăk´shəs) *adjective* from *fract,* "break"
   Likely to make trouble; irritable
   • The company president tried to get the **fractious** divisions to cooperate.

   fractiousness *noun* We were annoyed by the **fractiousness** of the neighbor, who accused us of being too loud when we were playing a quiet board game.

Have students use the roots of each word to try to determine the meaning. Discuss ways students arrive at their definitions.

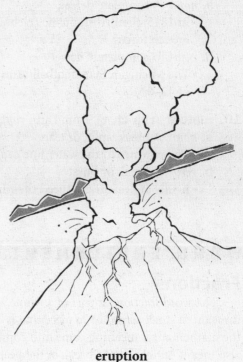

eruption

5. fragmentary (frăg´mən-tĕr´ē) *adjective* from *fract*, "break"
Partial; having only small parts of
• Scientists were able to reconstruct the appearance of the dinosaur from only **fragmentary** pieces of its skeleton.

fragment *verb* The brittle stone **fragmented** when a hammer hit it.

fragment *noun* Due to careless packaging, the glass bowl broke into **fragments.**

fragmentation *noun* The **fragmentation** of the political party into several different parts decreased its power.

6. infraction (ĭn-frăk´shən) *noun* from *fract*, "break"
A breaking of a law or rule
• Parking next to a fire hydrant is an **infraction** of the law.

7. refract (rĭ-frăkt´) *verb* from Latin *re-*, "back" + *fract*, "break"
To cause the path of light to bend
• The window is made of thick glass blocks that **refract** light and block the view.

refraction *noun* A rainbow is created by a **refraction** of light caused by moisture in the air.

8. refractory (rĭ-frăk´tə-rē) *adjective* from Latin *re-*, "back" + *fract*, "break"
Stubborn and difficult to control
• The **refractory** private refused to carry out the sergeant's orders.

> A *refractory* metal is difficult to melt or work with because it is resistant to heat.

9. rout (rout) from Latin *rupt*, "break"
a. *noun* A complete defeat
• In 1815, the British public celebrated after the **rout** of Napoleon's French forces.
b. *verb* To completely defeat
• The Michigan State football team **routed** Ohio State by a score of 42–0.

> *Rout* can also mean "a chaotic, panicked retreat following a terrible defeat."

10. rupture (rŭp´chər) from Latin *rupt*, "break"
a. *noun* A break, split, or tear
• The **rupture** in the water line caused our basement to flood.
b. *verb* To break or burst
• A silly argument **ruptured** their friendship.

WORD ENRICHMENT

Fractions

The word *fraction*, "a part of a whole," also comes from *fract*. Originally, it meant "a small scrap" or "a piece that is broken off." Then, around 1400, the mathematical meaning came into common use. At one time, *fraction* also meant "a fight," or "a break in the peace." The word *fractious* descends from this meaning of *fraction*. The word *fragile*, or "easily broken," also comes from the same root, *fract*.

WRITE THE CORRECT WORD

Write the correct word in the space next to each definition.

infraction   **1.** a breaking of a law

rupture   **2.** to burst

disrupt   **3.** to cause disorder

fractious   **4.** likely to stir up trouble

refract   **5.** to cause the path of light to bend

fragmentary   **6.** partial

abrupt   **7.** unexpected; sudden

rout   **8.** to utterly defeat

refractory   **9.** difficult to control

eruption   **10.** sudden, violent movement

COMPLETE THE SENTENCE

Write the letter for the word that best completes each sentence.

c **1.** The _____ horse would not allow a saddle to be put on his back.
 a. fragmentary   **b.** abrupt   **c.** fractious   **d.** refracted

b **2.** The prism _____ the white light into different colors.
 a. disrupted   **b.** refracted   **c.** infracted   **d.** routed

b **3.** He slammed on the brakes when the car ahead made a(n) _____ stop.
 a. refracted   **b.** abrupt   **c.** fragmentary   **d.** routed

a **4.** The huge snowstorm _____ morning traffic.
 a. disrupted   **b.** refracted   **c.** ruptured   **d.** erupted

a **5.** At the end of the play, the main character reacts to her husband's betrayal with a(n) _____ of anger.
 a. eruption   **b.** rout   **c.** abruptness   **d.** refraction

d **6.** Because dogs are legally required to be on a leash, letting your dog run free in the park is a(n) _____.
 a. fragment   **b.** eruption   **c.** rout   **d.** infraction

d **7.** Although the reports from the remote area are still _____, it is clear that the earthquake has done much damage.
 a. refractory   **b.** fractious   **c.** abrupt   **d.** fragmentary

b **8.** The election was a complete _____; the senator won 90 percent of the votes.
 a. infraction   **b.** rout   **c.** fractiousness   **d.** rupture

c **9.** Don't overfill the water balloon or it might _____!
 a. rout   **b.** refract   **c.** rupture   **d.** disrupt

c **10.** The _____ child refused to obey his mother's rules.
 a. routed   **b.** fragmentary   **c.** refractory   **d.** abrupt

Challenge: The _____ in the main water pipe _____ the water pressure throughout the apartment complex.
a   **a.** rupture…disrupted   **b.** eruption…routed   **c.** fragmentary…refracted

Victory at Marathon

In 490 BC, the world's earliest known democracy defeated a powerful empire. **(1)** Our accounts of ancient wars are often *fragmentary,* but historian Herodotus left us the full account of the Athenian victory over the Persians at Marathon.

(2) Darius, king of the great Persian Empire, wanted to expand his kingdom, but the Greek city-state of Athens *disrupted* his plans to conquer Ionia, a region located in what is now Turkey, by providing military aid to the Ionians. The Persian king was furious and decided that Greece must be conquered.

In 492 BC, Darius launched an attack on Greece. **(3)** But a strong storm came up *abruptly,* wrecking many ships in the Persian fleet. The Persian army retreated, but the Greeks knew they would be back.

As expected, two years later, Darius left Persia with 25,000 soldiers and 600 ships. Conquering cities in their path, the Persian army finally landed near the town of Marathon, about twenty-six miles northeast of Athens. Assisting them was Hippias, a former tyrant of Athens, who sought to regain his power.

General Militades and 10,000 Athenian men marched to Marathon to meet the enemy. They sent their fastest runner, Pheidippides, to beg the city of Sparta for aid. **(4)** But the *refractory* Spartans refused to help. **(5)** They told the Athenians that joining the battle before the full moon would be an *infraction* of Spartan religious customs. The Athenians were surprised and grateful, though, when 1,000 soldiers from the city of Plataea joined them.

Although greatly outnumbered, the Greek forces were unified in this fight. They shared a common language and culture. Most important, they were defending their own families, homes, and governments. In contrast, the Persian forces spoke many different languages and were made up of many men who had been captured and forced into serving in Darius' army.

Militades knew that the Persian cavalry (warriors on horseback) hadn't landed yet, so he chose to charge immediately. **(6)** The Athenians *erupted* in attack, charging toward the enemy. In close combat, the usually superior Persian bows and arrows were useless, as the men were forced into hand-to-hand combat. **(7)** The Athenians surrounded the mass of Persian soldiers and *ruptured* their lines from the sides. **(8)** The result was a *rout* of the once mighty Persian forces.

The Athenian army had to get news of the victory back to Athens as well as warn the citizens of a possible attack by Persian survivors. Pheidippides raced to warn the Athenians. After delivering the news, "Rejoice, we conquer," he died from exhaustion. But because he delivered his message, the Athenians had enough time to prepare to defend their city. Today, a marathon is an endurance race of twenty-six miles, the distance from Marathon to Athens, which honors Pheidippides' heroism.

(9) At times, citizens of early democracies were *fractious* as they boldly exercised their political freedoms. But the victory at Marathon shows that the Greek citizens were unified in their desire to defend their freedoms. The city-state of Athens went on to develop and advance science, art, and government. **(10)** In the next few centuries, Greek culture became like a light that *refracted* across the Western world.

Each sentence below refers to a numbered sentence in the passage. Write the letter of the choice that gives the sentence a meaning that is closest to the original sentence.

_____d_____ **1.** Our accounts of ancient wars are often _____.
  a. thorough **b.** unexpected **c.** exciting **d.** partial

_____d_____ **2.** But the Greek city-state of Athens _____ his plans to conquer Ionia.
  a. suddenly moved **b.** broke the rule of **c.** tried to defeat **d.** threw into disorder

_____a_____ **3.** A strong storm came up _____.
  a. quickly **b.** violently **c.** brokenly **d.** darkly

_____ a **4.** But the _____ Spartans refused to help.
  a. stubborn **b.** disorderly **c.** loyal and helpful **d.** completely defeated

_____ b **5.** They told the Athenians that joining the battle before the full moon would be
  a(n) _____ of Spartan religious customs.
  a. attack **b.** violation **c.** defeat **d.** break

_____ c **6.** The Athenians _____ in attack, charging toward the enemy.
  a. ran away **b.** broke a law **c.** burst suddenly **d.** defeated

_____ d **7.** The Athenians surrounded the mass of Persian soldiers and _____ their lines
  from the sides.
  a. carried **b.** killed **c.** controlled **d.** broke up

_____ b **8.** The result was a _____ of the once mighty Persian forces.
  a. sudden movement **b.** complete defeat **c.** disorder **d.** panic

_____ d **9.** At times, citizens of early democracies, like Athens, were _____.
  a. broken into pieces **b.** lawbreakers **c.** ready to run **d.** likely to cause trouble

_____ c **10.** In the next few centuries, Greek culture became like a light that _____ across
  the Western world.
  a. caused trouble **b.** turned off **c.** bent into rays **d.** were difficult to control

Indicate whether the statements below are TRUE or FALSE according to the passage.

_____ F **1.** The Athenian soldiers were more numerous than the Persian soldiers.

_____ T **2.** The battle at Marathon had long-lasting effects.

_____ F **3.** Persian fighters were more dedicated to their cause than the Athenian fighters.

WRITING EXTENDED RESPONSES

Suppose that you are a witness to the Persian invasion and the Battle
of Marathon. In addition, you speak several languages and have had an
opportunity to talk to soldiers from both sides. In a descriptive essay,
provide a picture of the events. Your description should be vivid and
should contain at least three paragraphs. Use at least three lesson words
in your essay and underline them.

WRITE THE DERIVATIVE

Complete the sentence by writing the correct form of the word shown in
parentheses. You may not need to change the form that is given.

refraction **1.** The stained glass window caused _____ of the sunlight. (*refract*)

refractory **2.** The _____ student was sent to the principal's office. (*refractory*)

erupting **3.** The photograph was taken as Mt. Etna was _____. (*eruption*)

fractiousness **4.** I can't stand the _____ of those meetings! (*fractious*)

<u>rupture</u>   5. The demonstration threatened to _____ the peace between the two groups. *(rupture)*

<u>disruptive</u>   6. Clicking your pen in class is _____ to the concentration of other students. *(disrupt)*

<u>infraction</u>   7. Biting during a boxing match is an _____. *(infraction)*

<u>fragments</u>   8. The child cried when he saw the _____ of his favorite toy in the driveway. *(fragmentary)*

<u>routed</u>   9. Our math team _____ all competitors at the championship match last year. *(rout)*

<u>abruptness</u>   10. Knowing that she couldn't stand long goodbyes, I was not surprised by the _____ of her departure. *(abrupt)*

FIND THE EXAMPLE

Choose the answer that best describes the action or situation.

<u>d</u>   **1.** Something that might cause light to *refract*
   a. pavement   **b.** brick   **c.** chalkboard   **d.** water

<u>b</u>   **2.** An animal with a reputation for being *refractory*
   a. owl   **b.** mule   **c.** lion   **d.** mouse

<u>c</u>   **3.** Something that would *disrupt* a party
   a. decorations   **b.** music   **c.** fire alarm   **d.** snacks

<u>a</u>   **4.** Something that is *fragmentary* has this quality
   a. incompleteness   **b.** helpfulness   **c.** prettiness   **d.** completeness

<u>c</u>   **5.** An *infraction* of school rules
   a. playing on a team   **b.** behaving honestly   **c.** skipping class   **d.** studying hard

<u>b</u>   **6.** Something that is most likely to *rupture* a friendship
   a. a secret   **b.** a fight   **c.** a party   **d.** an agreement

<u>d</u>   **7.** A final sports score that best shows a *rout*
   a. 48–46   **b.** 34–34   **c.** 32–23   **d.** 67–12

<u>a</u>   **8.** A person who is *abrupt* is usually also described this way
   a. unfriendly   **b.** happy   **c.** generous   **d.** selfish

<u>a</u>   **9.** A person most likely to be fascinated by volcanic *eruptions*
   a. geologist   **b.** biologist   **c.** chemist   **d.** botanist

<u>c</u>   **10.** What a *fractious* person might do if something doesn't go exactly her way
   a. laugh it off   **b.** smile graciously   **c.** get angry   **d.** tell a friend

166 **The Roots** *-rupt-* **and** *-fract-*

©Great Source. DO NOT COPY

The Root -*port*-

comport	deport	deportment	disport	export
import	insupportable	portable	portage	portfolio

The root -*port*- comes from the Latin word *portare*, which means "to carry." This root is the basis of many English words. For example, when we *transport* something, we carry it from one place to another. A *port* is a place into which goods are carried. The words in this lesson all refer, in some way, to the idea or action of carrying.

Point out that some of these words refer to carrying actual things from one place to another, such as *import*, *export*, and *portage*. Others refer to the way people "carry" themselves or behave, such as *comport* and *deportment*.

1. **comport** (kəm-pôrt´) *verb* from Latin *com-*, "together" + *port,* "carry"
   To behave oneself in a certain way
   • When in the presence of the king, please **comport** yourself with dignity.

2. **deport** (dĭ-pôrt´) *verb* from Latin *de-* "out" + *port,* "carry"
   To force out of a country; to expel
   • In the 1700s, England **deported** prisoners to Australia.

   deportation *noun* The judge ordered the **deportation** of the man who falsified his passport.

3. **deportment** (dĭ-pôrt´mənt) *noun* from Latin *de-* "out" + *port,* "carry"
   Manner of personal conduct
   • The students' excellent **deportment** earned their class a pizza party.

4. **disport** (dĭ-spôrt´) *verb* from Latin *dis-,* "apart" + port, "carry"
   To play; to entertain oneself by sport or play
   • At recess, the children **disported** themselves by playing tag.

disport

5. **export** from Latin *ex-*, "out" + *port,* "carry"
   a. *verb* (ĭk-spôrt´) To send products out of the country for sale
   • China **exports** much clothing to the United States.
   b. *noun* (ĕk´spôrt´) A product that is sent out of the country for sale
   • Many of the fruits and vegetables that Americans eat are **exports** from other countries.

   exportation *noun* These grapes are for **exportation**.

   exporter *noun* The French **exporter** sent perfume to the United States.

In the verb forms of *export* and *import*, either the first or second syllable can be accented; in the noun forms, the first syllable is accented.

6. import from *im-*, "in" + *port*, "carry"
  a. *verb* (ĭm-pôrt´) To bring in products from another country
  • The United States **imports** many cars from Japan.
  b. *noun* (ĭm´pôrt´) A product brought in from another country
  • Europe **imports** citrus fruit from Florida and California.

  importation *noun* The United States stopped the **importation** of an unsafe vaccine.

  importer *noun* Mr. Honigberg was an **importer** of Mexican produce.

7. insupportable (ĭn´sə-pôr´tə-bəl) *adjective* from Latin *in-*, "not" + *sub-*, "below" + port, "carry"
  Unbearable; intolerable; unable to be tolerated
  • The **insupportable** heat made some people faint.

8. portable (pôr´tə-bəl) *adjective* from *port*, "carry"
  Able to be easily carried
  • The **portable** DVD player was so small I could hold it in the palm of my hand.

9. portage (pôr´tĭj) *noun* from *port*, "carry"
  The carrying of boats and supplies overland between two waterways or around an obstacle
  • The light canoes made for easy **portage,** as the campers carried their food and boats from one stream to another.

> *Portage* also means "the act of carrying" and "a fee for carrying."

10. portfolio (pôrt-fō´lē-ō´) *noun* from Latin *port*, "carry" + *foglio*, "sheet"
  a. A carrying case for holding loose papers or drawings
  • Kelsey's **portfolio** fell, spilling her architectural plans on the floor.
  b. A collection of one's best or most representative writing or drawings
  • The designer brought his **portfolio** of sketches to the interview.
  c. A collection of investments
  • My **portfolio** includes common stocks and bonds.

> A *portfolio* can also refer to the office of a cabinet member or minister of state.

ANALOGIES

On the answer line, write the letter of the answer that best completes each analogy. Refer to Lessons 24–26 if you need help with any of the lesson words.

  __b__ **1.** Improve is to degenerate as _____.
    a. ice cream is to cone   **c.** social is to gentry
    b. happy is to miserable   **d.** fire is to match

  __b__ **2.** Genesis is to beginning as _____.
    a. high is to low   **c.** bearable is to insupportable
    b. generic is to unspecific **d.** veterinarian is to pet

  __a__ **3.** Thoughtful is to slowly as _____.
    a. abrupt is to suddenly   **c.** bottle is to liquid
    b. volcano is to erupt   **d.** hateful is to lovingly

  __d__ **4.** Portfolio is to papers as _____.
    a. bush is to tree   **c.** comportment is to behavior
    b. dog is to leash   **d.** album is to photographs

WRITE THE CORRECT WORD

Write the correct word in the space next to each definition.

portfolio	**1.** a case for holding papers
portable	**2.** easily carried
deportment	**3.** manner of personal conduct
portage	**4.** carrying of supplies between waterways
comport	**5.** to behave oneself in a certain manner

deport	**6.** to force out of a country
insupportable	**7.** intolerable; unbearable
disport	**8.** to entertain oneself by sport or play
import	**9.** to bring in goods from another country
export	**10.** a product sent to another country

COMPLETE THE SENTENCE

Write the letter for the word that best completes each sentence.

___a___ **1.** The illegal immigrants were _____ back to their country of origin.
a. deported   b. exported   c. imported   d. disported

___d___ **2.** For her interview, Jessa brought a _____ of her best writing samples.
a. comportment   b. disport   c. portage   d. portfolio

___b___ **3.** Louis bought a laptop so that he would have a(n) _____ computer to bring with him any time he traveled.
a. imported   b. portable   c. insupportable   d. deported

___a___ **4.** Israel _____ oranges and artichokes to countries all over the world.
a. exports   b. deports   c. disports   d. imports

___a___ **5.** Shelley always _____ herself with kindness and grace.
a. comports   b. exports   c. disports   d. imports

___d___ **6.** Henry _____ himself by practicing his juggling tricks.
a. imported   b. comported   c. exported   d. disported

___d___ **7.** Throughout the crisis, Lai maintained a calm _____.
a. portage   b. export   c. portfolio   d. deportment

___a___ **8.** The _____ of our canoe over the rocks was difficult.
a. portage   b. deportation   c. department   d. comport

___c___ **9.** Was this chocolate made in this country, or was it _____?
a. deported   b. disported   c. imported   d. comported

___b___ **10.** In the Middle Ages, living conditions were _____ for many people.
a. imported   b. insupportable   c. portable   d. disported

Challenge: When the spy was discovered, he was _____ for his treacherous _____.

___c___ a. imported...portage   b. exported...portfolio   c. deported...deportment

A Pirate's Life

Pirates! The very word summons images of gold, sword fights, and endless adventures on the high seas. But who were they really?

Pirates were outlaw sailors who attacked others' ships, stealing the crew's cargo. **(1)** A lucky pirate might have captured gold and silver, *exported* from the Americas, on its way to Spain. More often, though, pirates seized grain, molasses, or other goods. **(2)** They usually took only the *portable* goods from the hold of the ship, but they sometimes seized entire ships as well.

Pirates caused terror around the world. Corsairs were pirates who operated in the Mediterranean and in the Indian Ocean, along the coast of Africa. Several types of pirates worked in the Americas. Buccaneers operated in the Caribbean, mainly from present-day Haiti and the Dominican Republic. Marroners, who also terrorized this area, were deserters from the Spanish army, and escaped black slaves who became pirates.

Some pirates became infamous, due to their bold deeds. **(3)** Maurycy Beniowski took part in a Polish uprising against Russia and was subsequently *deported* to Siberia as punishment. He escaped from Siberia and traveled to Madagascar, where he became a pirate. Declaring himself "King of Madagascar," he had a long career, illegally raiding ships.

(4) Anne Bonny was a famous female pirate whose *deportment* was of some concern to her wealthy family. **(5)** Her father wanted her to *comport* herself like a lady and marry a rich man. Instead, Bonny married a pirate. Once, at a party, another lady insulted her. In response, Bonny attacked her, knocking out two of the lady's teeth. **(6)** For such *insupportable* behavior, Bonny was thrown out of polite society. So she took up pirating and earned a fearsome reputation.

One of the most infamous pirates was Francis Drake. He was a privateer, a pirate who received orders from his government to attack the ships of other nations. Drake stole an astonishing amount of gold and silver from Spanish ships. **(7)** This treasure was then *imported* into England. Queen Elizabeth I received most of it, but what was left was enough to make Drake a very wealthy man.

If a pirate's life seems like all fun and adventure, think again. Piracy was not only extremely dangerous, it could also be very tedious. **(8)** For every hour they spent *disporting* themselves at parties or gazing at their stolen treasure, there were many more hours of boring work while sailing and cleaning their ships. **(9)** When traveling on rivers and lakes, their illegally obtained cargo often required *portage*. For all this effort, the common pirate got only a tiny fraction of the treasure; the captain and officers took most of it.

Pirates are much less common today than they once were. But there are other types of modern piracy. You may have heard of software piracy or pirated music. **(10)** Or perhaps you have read stories of business people who stole their companies' funds to increase their own *portfolios*. Like the piracy of old, these illegal, get-rich schemes bring nothing but trouble and usually land the culprits in jail.

Each sentence below refers to a numbered sentence in the passage. Write the letter of the choice that gives the sentence a meaning that is closest to the original sentence.

___d___ **1.** A lucky pirate might have captured gold and silver, _____ from the Americas, on its way to Spain.
    a. brought in   **b.** carried easily   **c.** stolen   **d.** sent out

___b___ **2.** They usually took only the _____ goods from the hold of the ship.
    a. valuable   **b.** easily carried   **c.** practical   **d.** foreign

___a___ **3.** Maurycy Beniowski took part in a Polish uprising against Russia and was subsequently _____ to Siberia as punishment.
    a. forced out   **b.** not tolerated   **c.** carried out   **d.** brought in

_____a_____ **4.** Anne Bonny was a famous female pirate whose _____ was of some concern to her wealthy family.
    a. behavior   **b.** marriage   **c.** bringing in items   **d.** violence

_____b_____ **5.** Her father wanted her to _____ herself like a lady and marry a rich man.
    a. entertain   **b.** conduct   **c.** pretend   **d.** dress

_____a_____ **6.** For such _____ behavior, Bonny was thrown out of polite society.
    a. unbearable   **b.** type of behavior   **c.** criminal   **d.** easily

_____b_____ **7.** This treasure was then _____ into England.
    a. smuggled   **b.** brought   **c.** forced   **d.** amassed

_____d_____ **8.** For every hour they spent _____ themselves, there were many more hours of boring work.
    a. carrying   **b.** stealing   **c.** conducting   **d.** entertaining

_____a_____ **9.** When traveling on rivers and lakes, their illegally obtained cargo often required _____.
    a. carrying   **b.** hiding   **c.** repairs   **d.** entertainment

_____c_____ **10.** Business people have stolen their companies' funds to increase their own _____.
    a. risk of being fired   **b.** job position   **c.** financial investments   **d.** ability to be carried

Indicate whether the statements below are TRUE or FALSE according to the passage.

_____T_____ **1.** Pirates came from many different backgrounds.

_____T_____ **2.** Some pirates' robberies were approved by their governments.

_____T_____ **3.** Today, the term *piracy* refers to many types of stealing, not just that done at sea.

FINISH THE THOUGHT

Complete each sentence so that it shows the meaning of the italicized word.

1. The woman was *deported* because _____ Answers wil vary. _____

_____

2. Because your behavior is *insupportable*, _____ Answers will vary. _____

_____

WRITE THE DERIVATIVE

Complete the sentence by writing the correct form of the word shown in parentheses. You may not need to change the form that is given.

__disporting__   **1.** The children were in the playroom, _____ themselves with puzzles and board games. (*disport*)

__insupportable__   **2.** Carrying a heavy backpack up a mountain would be _____. (*insupportable*)

deportment

3. In Victorian England, wealthy girls often took lessons in etiquette and _____. (*deportment*)

portable

4. I bought this video camera because it is _____. (*portable*)

deportations

5. Throughout European history, there were _____ of citizens who did not practice the established religion of the government. (*deport*)

portage

6. We needed to organize the _____ of the supplies and boats to the next river. (*portage*)

comported

7. Everyone admired the way the politician _____ himself after he admitted defeat in the election. (*comport*)

exporter

8. Ms. McManis is an _____ of fine jewelry. (*export*)

portfolios

9. As an investment banker, Dominic manages the _____ of many wealthy businesspeople. (*portfolio*)

importation

10. The government has limits on the _____ of certain products. (*import*)

FIND THE EXAMPLE

Choose the answer that best describes the action or situation.

c   **1.** Something small children are likely to do to *disport* themselves
     a. study history   **b.** cook dinner   **c.** play dress-up   **d.** play chess

d   **2.** Of the following items, the one that is the most *portable*
     a. sofa   **b.** refrigerator   **c.** television   **d.** cell phone

c   **3.** A person who is *deported* from America might then go to this city
     a. Chicago   **b.** Los Angeles   **c.** London   **d.** Houston

b   **4.** Something America does NOT *import*
     a. chocolate   **b.** parents   **c.** clothes   **d.** cars

a   **5.** How one should *comport* oneself in an emergency situation
     a. stay calm   **b.** scream and run   **c.** panic   **d.** don't think

c   **6.** Something America does NOT *export*
     a. cars   **b.** wheat   **c.** schools   **d.** food

c   **7.** Something that the average student would find *insupportable*
     a. daily homework   **b.** weekly quizzes   **c.** twice daily tests   **d.** monthly exams

d   **8.** Someone who might carry a *portfolio* to work every day
     a. plumber   **b.** receptionist   **c.** nurse   **d.** artist

a   **9.** Where *portage* takes place
     a. on land   **b.** in a boat   **c.** on an airplane   **d.** underwater

b   **10.** An example of likely *deportment* at a comedy show
     a. crying   **b.** laughing   **c.** hopping   **d.** running

The Roots -clam- and -voc-

WORD LIST

claimant	clamor	declaim	disclaim	evocative
invoke	reclaim	revoke	vocation	vouch

The Latin roots *-clam-* and *-voc-* are the foundation of many English words. In Latin, the word *clamare* means "to cry out." A person who *proclaims* something calls it out publicly and officially; to *exclaim* is to cry out in surprise or with emotion. The Latin verb *vocare* means "to call out." The common words *voice* and *vocal* come from this word root. In this lesson, you will study words derived from these roots and their related forms, such as *-claim-* and *vok-*.

Point out that, while some of these words are clearly related to the meaning of the roots (such as *clamor* and *invoke*), others have a less apparent relationship (such as *disclaim* and *reclaim*).

> *Claimant* is formed from the common word *claim*.

1. **claimant** (klā´mənt) *noun* from *clam*, "cry out"
   A person or party who makes a claim or demands a right
   • In the 1500s, both Spain and Portugal were **claimants** to the riches of South America.

2. **clamor** (klăm´ər) from *clam*, "cry out"
   a. *verb* To make a loud and continuous noise or outcry
      • The crowd **clamored** for the rock star to come out and say hello.
   b. *verb* To make continued demands
      • The public **clamored** for improvement in public transportation.
   c. *noun* A loud noise, or a strong demand
      • We could hardly stand the **clamor** of the birds in the pet shop.

   clamorous *adjective* A **clamorous** work environment can, over time, injure the hearing of musicians.

clamor

3. **declaim** (dǐ-klām´) *verb* from Latin *de-*, "intensely" + *clam*, "cry out"
   To speak loudly or dramatically
   • In no uncertain words, the candidate **declaimed** opposition to the war.

   declamatory *adjective* Patrick Henry's **declamatory** statement, "Give me liberty or give me death," helped inspire the American Revolution.

   declamation *noun* The senator's **declamation** was, "No increase in taxes!"

4. **disclaim** (dǐs-klām´) *verb* from Latin *dis-*, "reversal of" + *clam*, "cry out"
   To deny; to state that you have no responsibility for something
   • The politician **disclaimed** any involvement with the scandal.

   disclaimer *noun* The producers of the show issued a **disclaimer** stating that any references to actual people were completely accidental.

5. **evocative** (ĭ-vŏk´ə-tĭv) *adjective* from Latin *e-*, "out" + *voc*, "call out"
Having the power to bring forth or produce
• Smells are often **evocative** of memories.

evoke *verb* The taste of cookies **evokes** images of my mother baking.

6. **invoke** (ĭn-vōk´) *verb* from Latin *in-*, "in" + *voc*, "call out"
To call on for help or protection
• As floodwaters rose, the country **invoked** the help of its neighbors.

invocation *noun* A prayer
• The priest gave the **invocation** at the dinner.

7. **reclaim** (rĭ-klām´) *verb* from Latin *re-*, "back" + *clam*, "cry out"
a. To make usable or better
• The country **reclaimed** much of its desert land for farming.
b. To recover something, or to demand that something be returned
• Gabbie **reclaimed** her lost dog at the pound.

reclamation *noun* The government encourages the **reclamation** of old strip-mining sites for use as park land.

reclaimable *adjective* American chestnut wood now exists only in **reclaimable** form; it is found only in structures built many years ago.

8. **revoke** (rĭ-vōk´) *verb* from Latin *re-*, "back" + *voc*, "call out"
To cancel or reverse
• Mrs. Martin **revoked** Joe's library privileges because he had failed to return so many books.

revocation *noun* Some years ago, Russia issued a **revocation** of a law requiring citizens to carry identity cards.

revocable *adjective* A drivers license is **revocable;** it can be taken away for breaking laws.

9. **vocation** (vō-kā´shən) *noun* from *voc*, "call out"
A profession or an occupation
• After serving six summers as a camp counselor, Anita decided to choose teaching as her **vocation.**

vocational *adjective* Some states offer **vocational** training for ex-convicts.

> A *vocation* is sometimes said to be "a calling."

10. **vouch** (vouch) *verb* from *voc*, "call out"
To give a guarantee or an assurance
• I can **vouch** that my friend is telling the truth.

voucher *noun* Proof that something has been paid for or given
• The state issued **vouchers** that enabled working-class families to receive free meals.

WORD ENRICHMENT

From *c* to *k*

Note that when two of the lesson words are changed from verb to adjective form, the *k* becomes a *c*: *Evoke* becomes *evocative*, and *revoke* becomes *revocable*. With *revoke*, the noun form—*revocation*—undergoes the same change.

WRITE THE CORRECT WORD

Write the correct word in the space next to each definition.

_____declaim_____ 1. to speak dramatically

_____vouch_____ 2. to give a guarantee

_____clamor_____ 3. loud noise

_____invoke_____ 4. to call upon

_____revoke_____ 5. to cancel

_____claimant_____ 6. a person who demands a right

_____evocative_____ 7. able to bring out or produce

_____reclaim_____ 8. to recover something

_____vocation_____ 9. a profession

_____disclaim_____ 10. to deny

COMPLETE THE SENTENCE

Write the letter for the word that best completes each sentence.

___a___ 1. Makenzie hoped she would be able to _____ her luggage that had been lost by the airline.
    a. reclaim   **b.** invoke   **c.** disclaim   **d.** vouch

___c___ 2. Because the students protested, the school administration was forced to _____ its new policies.
    a. clamor   **b.** reclaim   **c.** revoke   **d.** vouch

___b___ 3. Harold _____ the help of his friends to find his lost essay.
    a. reclaimed   **b.** invoked   **c.** revoked   **d.** disclaimed

___a___ 4. Muhammad's kindness and patience led him to nursing, his current _____.
    a. vocation   **b.** claimant   **c.** clamor   **d.** declamation

___d___ 5. The smell of a new box of crayons is _____ of my childhood.
    a. revocable   **b.** declamatory   **c.** clamorous   **d.** evocative

___d___ 6. I can _____ for Stephanie's dependability.
    a. reclaim   **b.** declaim   **c.** disclaim   **d.** vouch

___c___ 7. Boyd _____ all responsibility for the accident.
    a. invoked   **b.** clamored   **c.** disclaimed   **d.** declaimed

___a___ 8. The pamphlet _____ against the wasteful spending of our society.
    a. declaims   **b.** revokes   **c.** vouches   **d.** disclaims

___b___ 9. The _____ insisted that the property was rightfully hers.
    a. evoker   **b.** claimant   **c.** disclaimer   **d.** vocation

___b___ 10. After the managers cut their workers' wages, they faced the _____ of the angry employees.
    a. vocation   **b.** clamor   **c.** claimant   **d.** voucher

Challenge: I can _____ that the _____ has a right to this house.

___b___   **a.** declaim...vocation   **b.** vouch...claimant   **c.** disclaim...invocation

The Teenagers of Doo-wop

(1) In the 1950s and 1960s, as today, urban areas rang with the *clamor* of traffic and crowds. But some city neighborhoods also echoed with music. In schools, clubs, and even on street corners, teenagers were creating a new music called "doo-wop." Doo-wop originated in African-American neighborhoods in cities such as New York, Los Angeles, Detroit, Baltimore, and Chicago—and it changed music history in America. **(2)** *Evoking* the sounds of rhythm and blues, groups backed up a lead singer with tight harmony and smooth sounds.

Groups such as the Flamingos, the Robins, the Cadillacs, and the Impalas practiced around the clock. Since the music relied more on voices than on instruments, groups could rehearse anywhere, anytime. As this singing spread, groups came to know each other's music quite well. **(3)** One time, the Crickets needed a singer, so they simply *invoked* the aid of a member of another band, who easily performed the material. **(4)** New songs were played at parties, and groups competed at local community centers, where one group would be *declaimed* the winner by the judges. A member of Baby Jane and the Rockabyes remembers that, as they sang on a corner, a stranger came up to tell them about a talent show. They auditioned and ended up winning first prize.

Enthusiasm and talent soon led to recordings. The record industry of the 1950s was segregated into the African-American rhythm-and-blues market and the white mainstream pop market. Initially, the doo-wop recordings were categorized as rhythm and blues. But in 1954, the Chords' hit "Sh-Boom" crossed over to the pop charts. From then on, doo-wop hits appeared on the pop charts regularly. The music of urban youth had become mainstream. By the late 1950s, the doo-wop sound dominated the radio, with songs like "Who Put the Bomp" and "Come Go with Me."

Unfortunately, many of the groups made little money from their hits. Lacking business knowledge, the singers were persuaded to sign contracts for little pay. Label owners often claimed copyrights for the songs by listing themselves as the composers. **(5)** Or, they persuaded the young singers to *disclaim* their rights. **(6)** The label owners told the young singers that DJs would be more likely to play the songs on the radio if a well-known music label *vouched* for the quality of the music. The expenses for tours were often deducted from the singing groups' paychecks. **(7)** If they complained, they risked having their contracts *revoked.*

Later, as adults, many singers regretted how they had handled business matters in their youth. **(8)** But the contracts they had signed left them in a poor position to be *claimants* in lawsuits. **(9)** Years later, in an effort to *reclaim* what they felt was rightfully theirs, some rereleased recordings of their songs.

(10) Some doo-wop singers went on to make music their long-term *vocation.* Arthur Crier, a member of the Halos, had a distinguished career, singing, writing, and producing songs. Others pursued different paths. But the echoes of these young artists are still heard in the popular music of today.

Each sentence below refers to a numbered sentence in the passage. Write the letter of the choice that gives the sentence a meaning that is closest to the original sentence.

_____a_____ **1.** In the 1950s and 1960s, urban areas rang with the _____ of traffic and crowds.
    a. noise   **b.** music   **c.** job   **d.** denial

_____b_____ **2.** _____ the sounds of rhythm and blues, groups backed up a lead singer.
    a. Trying to imitate   **b.** Calling to mind   **c.** Defying   **d.** Admiring

_____c_____ **3.** One time, the Crickets needed a singer, so they simply _____ the aid of a member of another band.
    a. needed   **b.** refused   **c.** called upon   **d.** borrowed

_____d_____ **4.** One group would be _____ the winner by the judges.
    a. allowed to be   **b.** guaranteed to be   **c.** hoping to be   **d.** announced loudly as

_____c_____ **5.** Or, they persuaded the young singers to _____ their rights.
  a. recover   **b.** cancel   **c.** give up   **d.** claim again

_____b_____ **6.** The label owners told the young singers that DJs would be more likely
  to play the songs on the radio if a well-known music label _____ the quality
  of the music.
  a. called upon   **b.** guaranteed   **c.** claimed loudly   **d.** denied

_____a_____ **7.** If they complained, they risked having their contracts _____.
  a. canceled   **b.** increased   **c.** read aloud   **d.** made legal

_____d_____ **8.** But the contracts they had signed left them in a poor position to be _____
  in lawsuits.
  a. noisy complainers   **c.** real musicians
  b. ones with authority   **d.** people who demand rights

_____a_____ **9.** Years later, in an effort to _____ what they felt was rightfully theirs, some
  rereleased recordings of their songs.
  a. take back   **b.** call upon   **c.** damage   **d.** make money

_____c_____ **10.** Some doo-wop singers went on to make music their long-term _____.
  a. guarantee   **b.** right   **c.** career   **d.** noise

Indicate whether the statements below are TRUE or FALSE according to the passage.

_____F_____ **1.** Doo-wop music was invented in suburban or rural neighborhoods.

_____T_____ **2.** Doo-wop originated in urban neighborhoods.

_____T_____ **3.** Many record labels took advantage of the young and inexperienced
  doo-wop artists.

WRITING EXTENDED RESPONSES

When they were older, some doo-wop artists sued record companies
that the artists claimed had stolen their rightful earnings. Think about
how the musicians had been treated. Then, in a persuasive essay, explain
your opinion as to whether they had been treated fairly or unfairly. Your
essay should be at least three paragraphs long and contain at least two
well-supported points. Use at least three lesson words in your essay and
underline them.

WRITE THE DERIVATIVE

Complete the sentence by writing the correct form of the word shown in
parentheses. You may not need to change the form that is given.

_____disclaimer_____ **1.** Many consumer products come with a _____ stating that the company is
  not responsible for any damages that result from improper use of the product.
  (*disclaim*)

_____declamatory_____ **2.** Many thought that the leader's _____ speech was insincere. (*declaim*)

clamorous	**3.** I had a headache after the _____ birthday party. (*clamor*)
vocational	**4.** Melanie wanted to go to a _____ school. (*vocation*)
reclamation	**5.** The _____ of the marsh involved intense efforts to drain and fertilize the soil. (*reclaim*)
evokes	**6.** I can tell that this song _____ strong memories for Grandma. (*evocative*)
voucher	**7.** This _____ serves as a record of my payment. (*vouch*)
revoked	**8.** The company _____ its policy of allowing employees to bring pets to work after people with allergies complained. (*revoke*)
invocations	**9.** The Aztecs uttered _____ to their gods to ask for good harvests. (*invoke*)
claimant	**10.** The _____ argued that the painting was rightfully hers. (*claimant*)

FIND THE EXAMPLE

Choose the answer that best describes the action or situation.

d **1.** Something that a politician would probably *disclaim*
  a. great new bill
  b. successful campaign
  c. chips and salsa
  d. involvement in a scandal

d **2.** Someone who is most likely to be *invoked* by a poor swimmer
  a. a police officer **b.** a firefighter **c.** a pet **d.** a lifeguard

c **3.** A good *vocation* for someone who loves the outdoors
  a. mechanic **b.** senator **c.** park ranger **d.** museum guide

a **4.** A smell that is most *evocative* of the beach
  a. seaweed **b.** pine **c.** pickles **d.** fruit

b **5.** Most likely to be said by someone who is *vouching* for something
  a. I'm not sure… **b.** I promise… **c.** Well, um… **d.** What do you think…

d **6.** Something a *claimant* would be likely to say
  a. It's too noisy! **b.** I feel sick. **c.** I am uncertain. **d.** That is mine.

c **7.** A place you would most likely hear a *clamor*
  a. a library **b.** a hospital **c.** a football game **d.** an office building

a **8.** A reason why a parent might *revoke* a child's privileges
  a. for poor behavior **b.** for good grades **c.** as a vacation treat **d.** for helping with chores

b **9.** Something an animal-rights activist might *declaim* against
  a. vegetarianism **b.** eating meat **c.** adopting pets **d.** humane treatment

d **10.** A way to *reclaim* garbage
  a. bring it to a dump **b.** toss it from window **c.** bury it **d.** recycle it

Prefixes, Roots, and Suffixes

Number Prefixes

The number prefixes that come from both Greek and Latin form thousands of English words. They are particularly useful in the sciences. These prefixes are fairly easy to learn, since they follow a pattern. Here, each prefix appears with a word that contains it.

Prefix	Meaning	Origin	Word, Word Meaning
uni-	one	Latin	unicycle, "pedaling machine with one wheel"
mono-	one	Greek	monopoly, "control by one person or company"
bi-	two	Latin	bicycle, "pedaling machine with two wheels"
di-, du-	two	Greek	duplex, "apartment with two floors"
tri-	three	Greek, Latin	tricycle, "pedaling machine with three wheels"

To help you practice the number prefixes from one to three, fill in the blanks in this exercise.

Something that is *unidirectional* goes in _____ one _____ direction.

A train traveling on a *monorail* goes on _____ one _____ rail.

When we *bisect* a circle, we divide it into _____ two _____ parts.

There are _____ two _____ people in a *duet*.

A *tripod* has _____ three _____ legs.

Practice

You can combine the use of context clues with your knowledge of these prefixes to make intelligent guesses about the meanings of words. All of the sentences below contain a word formed with a number prefix for "one," "two," or "three." Read the sentences and write down what you think the word in italics means. Then check your definition with the one you find in the dictionary, remembering to choose the definition that best fits the sentence.

1. The *monochromatic* room was decorated in subtle shades of gray.

   My definition _____ having different shades of one color _____

   Dictionary definition _____ having a single color _____

2. The author wrote a *trilogy* of books about President Johnson.

   My definition _____ set of three _____

   Dictionary definition _____ a group of three related literary works _____

3. The United States has a *bicameral* Congress. (The Latin word *camera* means "chamber.")

My definition _____, _____ two part _____

Dictionary definition _____ composed of two legislative branches _____

4. This can opener serves a *dual* purpose; it also opens bottles.

My definition _____ two-part; two; double _____

Dictionary definition _____ double _____

5. The amoeba is a *unicellular* animal.

My definition _____ one cell _____

Dictionary definition _____ having a single cell _____

6. Jonah carefully *trisected* the sandwich so that he and his friends each had an equal portion.

My definition _____ cut into three parts _____

Dictionary definition _____ to divide into three equal parts _____

Review Word Elements

Reviewing word elements helps you to remember them and use them in your reading. Below, write the meaning of the word elements you have studied. Each one appears italicized in a word.

Word	Word Element	Type of Element	Meaning of Word Element
*re*bound	*re-*	prefix	back
*voc*al	*voc*	root	voice
*port*able	*port*	root	carry
con*duct*	*duct*	root	lead
re*gen*erate	*gen*	root	birth; beginning; type
*co*worker	*co-*	prefix	together
dis*rupt*	*rupt*	root	break
de*claim*	*claim, clam*	root	cry out
re*pulse*	*pel, pul*	root	strike; thrust
*frag*mentary	*fract, frag*	root	break

Buildings and Structures

WORD LIST

abode	annex	cloister	edifice	excavate
masonry	prefabricate	rotunda	trellis	turret

The words in this lesson apply to buildings and other structures. Some of the creations that these words describe are practical, while others are more decorative, but all are important to know.

Ask students which of these structures they have seen. Where do they remember seeing these things?

1. **abode** (ə-bōd´) *noun* from Middle English *abod,* "a home"
   A home; a place where one lives
   • The young couple's little cottage was their first **abode.**

2. **annex** from Latin *ad-,* "to" + *nectere,* "to bind"
   a. *noun* (ăn´ĕks´) A building added on to a larger one; a secondary building near a main one
   • Some colleges have sports **annexes** just a short walk from the academic buildings.
   b. *verb* (ə-nĕks´) To add or attach, especially to a larger or more important thing
   • The town **annexed** the little village.

   annexation *noun* The nation's attempted **annexation** of its neighbor's land almost led to war.

annex

> Notice that when *annex* is a noun, the first syllable is accented, and when *annex* is a verb, the second is accented.

3. **cloister** (kloi´stər) *noun* from Latin *claustrum,* "enclosed place"
   a. *noun* A quiet, private place
   • Religious monks often live in **cloisters,** protected from the concerns of everyday life.
   b. *verb* To shut away from the outside world; to seclude
   • I **cloistered** myself in my room and studied for the exam.

> *Cloister* can also mean "a covered walk, open on one side, running along the outside wall of a building."

4. **edifice** (ĕd´ə-fĭs) *noun* from Latin *aedificare,* "to build"
   A building, especially one of grand size or design
   • The Supreme Court building is one of many famous **edifices** in Washington, D.C.

5. **excavate** (ĕk´skə-vāt´) *verb* from Latin *ex-,* "out" + *cavare,* "to hollow"
   To dig or hollow out
   • The county engineers will **excavate** a new tunnel for the train terminal.

   excavation *noun* Archaeological **excavations** of buried cities tell us much about the ancient past.

6. **masonry** (mā´sən-rē) *noun* from Old French *mason*, "house"
Stonework or brickwork
   • The front of the house was **masonry**, but the rest was made of wood.

   mason *noun* **Masons** came every spring to repair the stone walls, bridges, and walking paths of the estate.

7. **prefabricate** (prē-făb´rĭ-kāt´) *verb* from Latin *pre-*, "before"
+ *fabrere*, "to make"
To manufacture in advance, especially in large, standard sections that are easily shipped and assembled
   • The company **prefabricated** our home before we had even bought the land where it was going to be assembled.

   prefabrication *noun* The **prefabrication** of car engines greatly increased the speed of the assembly process.

8. **rotunda** (rō-tŭn´də) *noun* from Latin *rotundus*, "round"
A circular building, or a large circular room with a high ceiling
   • The queen waved at the crowd from the balcony of the **rotunda**.

9. **trellis** (trĕl´ĭs) *noun* from Latin *trillix*, "woven with three threads"
A crisscrossed framework of strips with open spaces in between, often used as an archway or a support for plants and vines
   • A pretty, rose-covered **trellis** arched over the pathway.

10. **turret** (tûr´ĭt) *noun* from Old French *torete*, "little tower"
A small tower or tower-shaped part of a building
   • A **turret** graced each of the main corners of the castle.

Turret can also refer to a rotating structure with guns mounted on it.

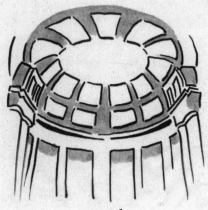
rotunda

trellis

turret

WRITE THE CORRECT WORD

Write the correct word in the space next to each definition.

excavate	**1.** to dig or hollow out		prefabricate	**6.** to make in advance
masonry	**2.** brickwork or stonework		rotunda	**7.** a circular building
abode	**3.** a home		annex	**8.** to add or attach
turret	**4.** a small tower		edifice	**9.** a grand building
cloister	**5.** a quiet, private place		trellis	**10.** a crisscrossed frame

WRITE THE CORRECT WORD

Write the letter for the word that best completes each sentence.

__c__ **1.** The Doge's Palace in Venice is a colorful marble _____.
   a. trellis   **b.** excavation   **c.** edifice   **d.** prefabrication

__b__ **2.** The nuns were _____, so they avoided catching the flu last year.
   a. excavated   **b.** cloistered   **c.** prefabricated   **d.** masons

__a__ **3.** Each time a guest entered his house the host said, "Welcome to my humble
   _____."
   a. abode   **b.** masonry   **c.** annex   **d.** trellis

__d__ **4.** The circular shape of the temple's golden _____ symbolizes the repeating cycle
   of life.
   a. trellis   **b.** cloister   **c.** abode   **d.** rotunda

__c__ **5.** Miners began to _____ the area, hoping to unearth valuable minerals.
   a. cloister   **b.** annex   **c.** excavate   **d.** prefabricate

__d__ **6.** We thought we'd have to build a doghouse ourselves, but fortunately we found
   one that was _____.
   a. excavated   **b.** annexed   **c.** cloistered   **d.** prefabricated

__a__ **7.** The _____ repaired the brick wall quickly and skillfully.
   a. mason   **b.** excavation   **c.** annex   **d.** rotunda

__d__ **8.** The library is planning to add a new _____ devoted to documentary films.
   a. abode   **b.** trellis   **c.** masonry   **d.** annex

__b__ **9.** The new white _____ will be covered with vines in no time.
   a. excavation   **b.** trellis   **c.** mason   **d.** prefabrication

__c__ **10.** This morning, I saw a hawk perched on the _____ of an old stone building.
   a. adobe   **b.** excavation   **c.** turret   **d.** prefabrication

Challenge: _____ of the site revealed some very old _____.

__b__   **a.** Prefabrication…abodes   **b.** Excavation…masonry   **c.** Cloistering…trellises

A Nation's Capital

Washington, D.C., is not only the seat of the U.S. federal government; it is also a city of charm and culture. Visitors can enjoy an amazing variety of musical performances, museums, art galleries, and historic sites. **(1)** Stately old homes with ivy-covered *trellises* adorn the city, too. Washington, D.C., is known for its beauty, culture, and political importance.

The city was actually built to be a capital. Before 1791, the federal government did not have a central location. Early Congresses met in various places, like New York City, Philadelphia, and Baltimore.

After Congress accepted the idea of establishing a permanent capital, President George Washington chose the area along the Potomac River as the site for the city that we now know as Washington, D.C. He selected well-known French designer Pierre Charles L'Enfant to plan the new city.

(2) This master designer wanted the president's *abode* to be a palace. **(3)** Washington, however, was strongly opposed to a castle with *turrets* and other features that suggested royalty. Instead, he thought the president's home should be more like a "fortress from which to guard against the tyranny of big government."

Benjamin Banneker, a well-known African-American mathematician and astronomer, had helped survey the area of the city-to-be. Later, when L'Enfant was taken off the project, the angry Frenchman took his plans with him. Banneker is credited with reproducing them entirely from memory.

The plans included a building on what was then called Jenkin's Hill. As L'Enfant had said earlier, the hill was "a pedestal waiting for a monument." A monument was indeed built there—a monument to democracy.

(4) This *edifice* is the U.S. Capitol, where federal laws are still made today.

(5) Architects had originally developed several plans for the Capitol, some of which included *cloistered* courtyards. Ultimately, though, construction followed Dr. William Thornton's design. **(6)** Thornton's original plan called for a dome-topped, central *rotunda* and two rectangular wings, one for each house of Congress. Washington approved this plan because of its "grandeur, simplicity, and convenience." **(7)** *Excavation* for the Capitol's foundation began in 1793. **(8)** Teams of *masons,* carpenters, and other builders worked on the project that became a symbol of the nation.

(9) Over the years, new wings and other *annexes* have been built. In 1855, workmen constructed a new dome. **(10)** Parts of the dome were *prefabricated* and then lifted to the top of the building by steam-powered cranes.

You can see this structure and many others if you take a walking tour of the city. You can also take a "virtual tour" online at *www.senate.gov/vtour/index.html.* But no matter how you see it, you will enjoy your tour of this charming city.

Each sentence below refers to a numbered sentence in the passage. Write the letter of the choice that gives the sentence a meaning that is closest to the original sentence.

___d___ **1.** Stately old homes with ivy-covered _____ adorn the city, too.
    a. quiet refuges   **b.** stone walls   **c.** additions   **d.** crisscrossed frame

___c___ **2.** This master designer wanted the president's _____ to be a palace.
    a. big building   **b.** gun tower   **c.** home   **d.** office

___b___ **3.** Washington was strongly opposed to _____ and other features that suggested royalty.
    a. stonework   **b.** towers   **c.** round roofs   **d.** frameworks

___a___ **4.** This _____ is the U.S. Capitol, where federal laws are still made today.
    a. grand building   **b.** refuge   **c.** extra room   **d.** round roof

c   **5.** Architects had originally developed plans which included _____ courtyards.
    a. dug-out   **b.** rounded   **c.** private   **d.** sculpted

d   **6.** Thornton's original plan called for a dome-topped, central _____.
    a. flowered frame   **b.** courtyard   **c.** stone pattern   **d.** round building

a   **7.** _____ for the Capitol's foundation began in 1793.
    a. Digging   **b.** Stonework   **c.** Funding   **d.** Planning

b   **8.** Teams of _____, carpenters, and other builders worked on the project that became a symbol of the nation.
    a. towermakers   **b.** stoneworkers   **c.** diggers   **d.** homebuilders

d   **9.** Over the years, new wings and other _____ have been built.
    a. living quarters   **b.** huge buildings   **c.** brick walls   **d.** added structures

c   **10.** Parts of the dome were _____ and then lifted to the top of the building by steam-powered cranes.
    a. dug out   **b.** attached   **c.** made in advance   **d.** secluded

Indicate whether the statements below are TRUE or FALSE according to the passage.

T   **1.** In the early days of the United States, Washington, D.C., was not the capital.

F   **2.** Pierre Charles L'Enfant supervised the creation of Washington, D.C., from start to finish.

F   **3.** George Washington wanted the new capital's buildings to be like a king's palace, to symbolize the strength of a huge, powerful government.

FINISH THE THOUGHT

Complete each sentence so that it shows the meaning of the italicized word.

1. My ideal *abode* would be _____ Answers will vary. _____

2. An example of an impressive *edifice* is _____ Answers will vary. _____

WRITE THE DERIVATIVE

Complete the sentence by writing the correct form of the word shown in parentheses. You may not need to change the form that is given.

excavation   **1.** Building a high-rise requires a large _____ for the foundation. (*excavate*)

trellises   **2.** The vine-covered _____ were a beautiful substitute for a tree's shade. (*trellis*)

Rotundas   **3.** _____ are my favorite architectural feature. (*rotunda*)

annexation   **4.** The restaurant's recent _____ of the former shoe store allowed it to expand the dining room. (*annex*)

abode   **5.** His _____ was just like him: simple, practical, and solid. (*abode*)

prefabrication   **6.** Partial _____ allows people without special skills to put complicated things together more easily. (*prefabricate*)

edifices   **7.** Seattle is a city of many impressive _____. (*edifice*)

mason   **8.** The _____ had bulging arm muscles, earned through years of hard, satisfying work. (*masonry*)

turrets   **9.** The design called for so many _____ that the building would have looked like a pincushion or a porcupine. (*turret*)

cloister   **10.** The wooded hillside is a perfect _____ for me. (*cloister*)

FIND THE EXAMPLE

Choose the answer that best describes the action or situation.

b   **1.** Something found in most American *abodes*
     a. elevators   **b.** furniture   **c.** towers   **d.** domes

a   **2.** Something made by a *mason*
     a. stone wall   **b.** wooden fence   **c.** flowerbed   **d.** sports car

d   **3.** Something you would be most likely to find in or near a *turret*
     a. packing crate   **b.** beach ball   **c.** jellyfish   **d.** stairs

a   **4.** One result of major *excavation*
     a. a large hole   **b.** a bigger building   **c.** prettier paths   **d.** space flight

c   **5.** Most likely to be *prefabricated*
     a. six-year-old   **b.** celery   **c.** mobile home   **d.** erector set

c   **6.** Most likely to be *annexed* by a nation
     a. boat   **b.** desk   **c.** island   **d.** sky

b   **7.** Area where you would be most likely to find *trellises*
     a. bus stop   **b.** botanical garden   **c.** taxicab   **d.** school locker

d   **8.** NOT an *edifice*
     a. a skyscraper   **b.** the Capitol   **c.** the Pentagon   **d.** a wooden shack

b   **9.** Something that has a shape similar to a *rotunda*
     a. train track   **b.** wheel   **c.** shoe box   **d.** pyramid

c   **10.** What people often hope to get by *cloistering* themselves
     a. danger   **b.** loud excitement   **c.** peace and quiet   **d.** diseases

Geography

WORD LIST

archipelago	chasm	latitude	longitude	meridian
panorama	peninsula	precipice	terrestrial	topography

How do earthquakes and volcanic eruptions take place? What causes tsunamis? How are mountains and canyons formed? All of these questions, and many more, can be answered by studying geography.

Ask students to draw informal sketches of at least five of the words on this list.

1. **archipelago** (är´kə-pĕl´ə-gō´) *noun* from Italian *arcipelage,* "a sea of islands"
   A large group of islands, or a sea containing a large number of islands
   • The Philippines **archipelago** consists of more than 7,000 islands in the Pacific Ocean.

2. **chasm** (kăz´əm) *noun* from Greek *khasma,* "a gash"
   A deep divide or rift
   • Over time, the river created a deep **chasm** in the stone.

3. **latitude** (lăt´ĭ-tōōd´) *noun* from Latin *latitude,* "width or breadth"
   a. The distance north or south of the equator, measured in degrees
      • Lines going horizontally around a globe mark **latitude.**
   b. Freedom from limits or rules
      • He gave his children greater **latitude** to run around on the farm than he gave them in the city.

   latitudinal *adjective* The **latitudinal** position of the island is 10° N.

4. **longitude** (lŏn´jĭ-tōōd´) *noun* from Latin *longitude,* "length"
   The distance east or west of the prime meridian, measured in degrees
   • The map lines that show **longitude** run north to south.

   longitudinal *adjective* The **longitudinal** position of the island is 38° E.

5. **meridian** (mə-rĭd´ē-ən) *noun* from Latin *meridies,* "midday"
   The lines on maps or globes that pass through the North and South Poles
   • The prime **meridian,** or 0° longitude, is an imaginary line that passes through Greenwich, England.

6. **panorama** (păn´ə-răm´ə) *noun* from Latin *pan-,* "all" + *horama,* "sight"
   A broad view spanning a large area
   • From the mountaintop, we viewed a **panorama** of snow-capped peaks, deep valleys, and icy rivers.

   panoramic *adjective* The professor had **panoramic** knowledge of Canadian history and could present a wide array of information to his classes.

archipelago

Meridians run north and south around the globe and are used to measure *longitude.*

Panorama can refer to a physical view or, more figuratively, to any comprehensive presentation.

©Great Source. DO NOT COPY

7. **peninsula** (pə-nĭn´sə-lə) *noun* from Latin *paene,* "almost"
   + *insula,* "island"
   A piece of land that projects into a body of water
   • When most Americans are asked to name a **peninsula,** they usually
     come up with Florida.

   peninsular *adjective* The geologist studied the **peninsular** landform.

8. **precipice** (prĕs´ə-pĭs) *noun* from Latin *praeceps,* "headlong"
   A steep cliff or overhang
   • A sturdy guardrail at the edge of the **precipice** protected tourists
     who were taking pictures.

   precipitous *adjective* Very steep
   • We walked slowly and carefully down the **precipitous** path.

9. **terrestrial** (tə-rĕs´trē-əl) *adjective* from Latin *terra,* "earth"
   Of the earth or land
   • A tortoise is a **terrestrial** turtle.

10. **topography** (tə-pŏg´rə-fē) *noun* from Greek *topos,* "place"
    + *-graphy,* "write"
    The physical features of a region, including mountains, plains,
    and rivers
    • As he was familiar with the **topography** of the islands, the captain
      could see that we were approaching Borneo.

    topographical *adjective* A **topographical** map would have been useful
    to the climbers.

ANALOGIES

**On the answer line, write the letter of the answer that best completes
each analogy. Refer to Lessons 27–29 if you need help with any of the
lesson words.**

_d_ 1. Skyscraper is to edifice as _____.
    a. hot is to ice   **c.** good is to evil
    b. water is to plumbing   **d.** expressway is to road

_a_ 2. Potter is to clay as _____.
    a. mason is to stone   **c.** map is to topography
    b. latitude is to longitude   **d.** precipice is to cliff

_b_ 3. Terrestrial is to land as _____.
    a. bird is to sky   **c.** revoke is to license
    b. aquatic is to water   **d.** panorama is to mountain

_c_ 4. Island is to archipelago as _____.
    a. vocation is to job   **c.** goose is to flock
    b. rain is to cloud   **d.** clamor is to noise

WRITE THE CORRECT WORD

Write the correct word in the space next to each definition.

latitude	1. freedom from rules	panorama	6. a broad view
longitude	2. the distance east or west from the prime meridian	meridian	7. an imaginary north-south line on a globe
archipelago	3. a group of islands	chasm	8. a deep rift or divide
terrestrial	4. of the earth	precipice	9. a steep cliff
peninsula	5. land almost totally surrounded by water	topography	10. physical features of a region

COMPLETE THE SENTENCE

Write the letter for the word that best completes each sentence.

a   1. _____ are often formed by volcanic eruptions that create lots of new islands.
    a. Archipelagos   **b.** Meridians   **c.** Latitudes   **d.** Panoramas

d   2. People with a fear of heights should avoid standing near the _____.
    a. archipelago   **b.** meridian   **c.** peninsula   **d.** precipice

c   3. As the family drove through Manitoba, they noticed that the _____ was very flat.
    a. chasm   **b.** longitude   **c.** topography   **d.** latitude

c   4. You can calculate how far east or west a place is if you understand _____.
    a. panorama   **b.** latitude   **c.** longitude   **d.** topography

b   5. _____ tells you the distance between any point on the globe and the equator.
    a. Longitude   **b.** Latitude   **c.** A meridian   **d.** A precipice

d   6. Korea is surrounded by water on three sides; it is a well-known _____.
    a. meridian   **b.** archipelago   **c.** precipice   **d.** peninsula

a   7. _____ upheavals, such as earthquakes, can endanger people.
    a. Terrestrial   **b.** Peninsular   **c.** Chasm   **d.** Meridian

c   8. From the hills of Los Angeles, one can see a spectacular _____ that includes the coast and the downtown area.
    a. topography   **b.** peninsula   **c.** panorama   **d.** precipice

a   9. We got dizzy when we peered into the deep _____.
    a. chasm   **b.** peninsula   **c.** meridian   **d.** archipelago

a   10. Although a _____ is an imaginary line, navigators use it to determine location.
    a. meridian   **b.** precipice   **c.** panorama   **d.** chasm

Challenge: The _____ of the islands in the _____ included hilly, volcanic rock formations.
c   **a.** chasm...meridian   **b.** panorama...precipice   **c.** topography...archipelago

Discovering Earth from Space

The ancient Greeks were fascinated by the study of our world. **(1)** Anxious to learn as much as they could about geography, they continually pushed their explorers to make the long, dangerous voyages beyond the *archipelago* of their home. They ventured into the Mediterranean Sea and also along the eastern shores of the Atlantic Ocean.

Today, we can learn the outlines of these places in a matter of moments. **(2)** Satellites transmit photographs of the earth's broadest seas, highest peaks, and deepest *chasms* to people all over the world.

(3) With computers and satellite technology, geographers can pinpoint the exact *latitude* of any feature of the earth, just by inputting a few pieces of data. **(4)** They can also determine the *longitudinal* position of any geographical feature. **(5)** They do this by noting the location east or west of the prime *meridian*.

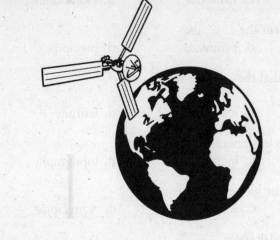

NASA, or the National Air and Space Administration, has created satellites that orbit the earth from 180 to 22,000 miles above sea level. This system of satellites is called the Earth Observing System, or EOS. **(6)** Launched in 1999, this small group of satellites continuously scans and observes the earth, tracking weather patterns, measuring pollution levels, and generating *topographical* maps. EOS also aids in forest fire detection, storm prediction, and the study of the ozone layer. EOS offers scientists an ability to understand our planet in a way that has never been possible before.

(7) Information on *terrestrial* features is not the only thing that scientists get from EOS data. Yes, researchers can view things such as the activity of volcanoes. But they can also track the movement of hurricanes and measure the quality of air. Additionally, they can monitor the ways humans affect the environment. This knowledge, integrating earth science, oceanography, atmospheric science, and biology, will ultimately benefit all humankind. This integrated approach is now known as Earth System Science. And EOS is key to giving us information we need to continue discovering and protecting our planet.

Satellite images of the earth are available to anyone with Internet access. **(8)** You can view the Florida *peninsula,* from which many satellites are launched. **(9)** Or you can pinpoint the locations—and even measure the altitudes—of the *precipices* of Nova Scotia's sea cliffs. **(10)** You can even take in *panoramic* views of the earth's surface as seen from space. Check out *http://earthobservatory.nasa.gov* to see for yourself!

Each sentence below refers to a numbered sentence in the passage. Write the letter of the choice that gives the sentence a meaning that is closest to the original sentence.

_____ a **1.** They continually pushed their explorers to make the long, dangerous voyages beyond the _____ of their home.
   a. group of islands   **b.** steep cliffs   **c.** deep divide   **d.** enclosed lands

_____ a **2.** Satellites transmit photographs of the earth's broadest seas, highest peaks, and deepest _____ to people all over the world.
   a. rifts   **b.** peaks   **c.** broad views   **d.** oceans

_____ d **3.** Geographers can pinpoint the exact _____ of any feature of the earth, just by inputting a few pieces of data.
   a. width   **b.** height   **c.** wind direction   **d.** distance from equator

_____ d **4.** They can also determine the _____ position of any geographical feature.
   a. north or south   **b.** group of islands   **c.** broad   **d.** east or west

_____d_____ **5.** They do this by noting the location east or west of the prime _____.
  a. equator   **b.** imaginary map   **c.** deep divide   **d.** line through the poles

_____b_____ **6.** Launched in 1999, this small group of satellites continuously scans and observes the earth, tracking weather patterns, measuring pollution levels, and generating _____ maps.
  a. weather   **b.** physical-feature   **c.** earthly river   **d.** satellite

_____c_____ **7.** Information on _____ features is not the only thing that scientists get from EOS data.
  a. aquatic   **b.** volcanic   **c.** land   **d.** sea

_____d_____ **8.** You can view the Florida _____.
  a. valley   **b.** plateau   **c.** land below a cliff   **d.** strip of land

_____a_____ **9.** You can pinpoint the locations—and even measure the altitudes—of the _____ of Nova Scotia's sea cliffs.
  a. steep overhangs   **b.** group of islands   **c.** volcanoes   **d.** deep valleys

_____b_____ **10.** You can even take in _____ views of the earth's surface as seen from space.
  a. detailed   **b.** broad   **c.** geographical   **d.** relaxed

Indicate whether the statements below are TRUE or FALSE according to the passage.

_____T_____ **1.** The ancient Greeks used the tools they had available to them to understand geography.

_____T_____ **2.** NASA launched EOS to help humans better understand our planet.

_____F_____ **3.** EOS can be visited by tourists easily.

WRITING EXTENDED RESPONSES

Suppose you were asked to defend the Earth Observing System from budget cuts that would discontinue the project. Write a persuasive essay explaining why the project is needed. Or, if you prefer, write an essay supporting the budget cuts. Whichever position you take, give at least two reasons that support it. Your essay should be at least three paragraphs long. Use at least three lesson words in your essay and underline them.

WRITE THE DERIVATIVE

Complete the sentence by writing the correct form of the word shown in parentheses. You may not need to change the form that is given.

_____Terrestrial_____ **1.** _____ navigation involves the use of a map and a compass. *(terrestrial)*

_____longitudinal_____ **2.** The _____ position of the lighthouse is 14° E. *(longitude)*

_____peninsular_____ **3.** The _____ form of the jetty protects the harbor from high seas and rough weather. *(peninsula)* __panoramic__   **4.** The book provides a _____ history of the sports and games people have played since the earliest recorded times. (*panorama*)

__chasms__   **5.** One of the largest _____ in the solar system can be found on Mars. (*chasm*)

__topographical__   **6.** The geologists checked the _____ map to determine the shape of the mesa. (*topography*)

__latitudinal__   **7.** Mr. Valdez asked the class to find the _____ coordinates of Miami and Minneapolis. (*latitude*)

__precipitious__   **8.** The new skier found herself at the top of a _____ expert slope. (*precipice*)

__meridians__   **9.** On the globe that he made, Miklos plotted several _____. (*meridian*)

__archipelago__   **10.** Indonesia is the largest _____ in the world. (*archipelago*)

FIND THE EXAMPLE

Choose the answer that best describes the action or situation.

___c___   **1.** Where you might see a *meridian*
   a. near the equator   **b.** in England   **c.** on a globe   **d.** on the ground

___d___   **2.** All lines of *latitude* can be described this way
   a. run north to south   **b.** visible from space   **c.** near the equator   **d.** parallel to the equator

___b___   **3.** A *terrestrial* mammal
   a. whale   **b.** bear   **c.** goose   **d.** dolphin

___a___   **4.** The *topography* of Antarctica
   a. snowy plains   **b.** flat desert   **c.** cold climate   **d.** tree-covered mountains

___b___   **5.** An example of a *peninsula*
   a. Colorado   **b.** Florida   **c.** California   **d.** Montana

___a___   **6.** A place an *archipelago* can be found
   a. in an ocean   **b.** in a desert   **c.** on a mountain   **d.** on farmland

___c___   **7.** Place from which it would be easiest to view a *panorama*
   a. inside a closet   **b.** a small window   **c.** the top of a hill   **d.** a basement

___a___   **8.** All lines of *longitude* can be described this way
   a. run north to south   **b.** touch England   **c.** visible from space   **d.** parallel to the equator

___b___   **9.** Something a person watching someone at the edge of a *precipice* would be most likely to say
   a. Look up there!   **b.** Stand back!   **c.** It's so funny!   **d.** It might erupt!

___a___   **10.** Something that is likely to cause a *chasm* in a relationship
   a. lack of trust   **b.** true love   **c.** geography books   **d.** shared values

Science and Technology

WORD LIST

alloy	buoyancy	celestial	coagulate	combustible
conflagration	dissection	distill	meteorology	saturate

Science and technology play a critical role in humans' health, standard of living, and lifespan. The words in this lesson can help you communicate about some of the amazing discoveries and developments that have lengthened our lives and made living easier.

1. **alloy** (ăl´oi´) *noun* from Latin *alligare,* "to bind to"
   A metal formed by combining one metal with another metal or element
   • Steel, an **alloy,** is often made by combining iron with carbon.

2. **buoyancy** (boi´ən-sē) *noun* from Spanish *boyante,* "to float"
   a. The ability to rise or float
      • The **buoyancy** of the waterproof camera brought it back to the surface.
   b. The ability to recover quickly from bad events; resiliency
      • Finn's **buoyancy** enabled him to recover quickly from the disappointment of not making the team.

   buoyancy

   Buoyancy can also mean "lightheartedness; cheerfulness."

   buoyant *adjective* Boats are **buoyant** and can float on the surface of water.

3. **celestial** (sə-lĕs´chəl) *adjective* from Latin *caelum,* "sky"
   Heavenly; related to the heavens or the sky
   • An appearance of the Northern Lights is often preceded by a shimmering **celestial** glow near the horizon.

   Celestial can also mean "inspiring and wonderful."

4. **coagulate** (kō-ăg´yə-lāt´) *verb* from Latin *com-,* "together" + *agere,* "to bring"
   To clot; to change from a liquid into a solid
   • Jake watched the scrambled eggs slowly **coagulate** in the hot frying pan.

5. **combustible** (kəm-bŭs´tə-bəl) *adjective* from Latin *combustus,* "consumed by fire"
   a. Able to catch fire easily
      • **Combustible** fumes rise from the open tank when a car is being filled with gas.
   b. Emotionally excitable
      • Great-Aunt Seely had a hard time controlling her **combustible** personality.

   combustion *noun* The **combustion** of the gasoline-soaked rags damaged the garage.

Remind students of common words that have the same roots as words in this lesson. For example, *celestial* has the same root as *ceiling; conflagration* and *flame* also contain a similar word element.

6. **conflagration** (kŏn´flə-grā´shən) *noun* from Latin *conflagrare,* "to burn up"
   Immense and destructive fire
   • In the strong winds, the grass fire became a **conflagration,** consuming everything in its path.

7. **dissection** (dĭ-sĕk´shən, dī-sĕk´shən) *noun* from Latin *dis-,* "apart" + *secare,* "to cut"
   The cutting apart for analysis
   • The marine lab received thirty of the jellyfish specimens for **dissection.**

   dissect *verb* The debate teams will **dissect** each other's arguments.

8. **distill** (dĭ-stĭl´) *verb* from Latin *de-,* "from" + *stillare,* "to drip"
   To purify a liquid by turning it to steam, then cooling it to a liquid again
   • The scientist **distilled** the water so that it would be pure enough to use for her experiment.

   distillation *noun* Salt water can be made drinkable through a process of **distillation.**

9. **meteorology** (mē´tē-ə-rŏl´ə-jē) *adjective* from Greek *meteros,* "high in the air" + *-logy,* "study of "
   The science dealing with the weather and atmospheric conditions
   • The Australian Bureau of **Meteorology** observes the strength of the global wind called El Niño.

   meteorologist *noun* Modern **meteorologists** use technology to give the most accurate weather forecasts possible.

   meteorological *adjective* Today's **meteorological** conditions make rainfall likely.

10. **saturate** (săch´ə-rāt´) *verb* from Latin *saturare,* "to fill"
    To soak, flood, or fill thoroughly
    • Water from the spill soon **saturated** the sponge.

    saturation *noun* When warm, moist air cools to its **saturation** point, water vapor condenses into water droplets, forming clouds.

> *Dissection* can refer to examining or analyzing something in detail, as in "In English class, we *dissected* the novel."

> *Distill* can also mean "to condense," as in "She *distilled* her argument down to one key point."

WORD ENRICHMENT

All filled up

The word *saturate* comes from the Latin verb *saturare,* "to fill." *Satisfied* and *sated,* or "being full of food," also contain this root.

The word *asset* comes from this root, too. An *asset* can be "a useful or valuable quality of a person"; it can also mean "a property or thing that one owns." At one time, *asset* meant "enough goods so that a person who died could have debts paid off." The French word *assez,* or "enough," is also related to the word *saturate.*

WRITE THE CORRECT WORD

Write the correct word in the space next to each definition.

distill **1.** to purify a liquid

dissection **2.** cutting apart

alloy **3.** a substance made by combining two metals

buoyancy **4.** ability to float

celestial **5.** relating to the heavens or the sky

combustible **6.** easily excited

saturate **7.** to completely soak

meteorology **8.** the science of atmospheric conditions

conflagration **9.** a huge, destructive fire

coagulate **10.** to change from liquid to solid

COMPLETE THE SENTENCE

Write the letter for the word that best completes each sentence.

d 1. Jared _____ the water he uses for his freshwater aquarium.
a. saturates   b. dissects   c. coagulates   d. distills

b 2. During the _____, many homes were completely destroyed.
a. buoyancy   b. conflagration   c. coagulation   d. dissection

a 3. If _____ materials collect in a storage area, they may cause a fire.
a. combustible   b. celestial   c. coagulated   d. saturated

a 4. The sauce has to be stirred constantly so that it will not _____.
a. coagulate   b. dissect   c. saturate   d. alloy

c 5. The _____ of the raft helped it bounce over the swirling rapids.
a. alloy   b. conflagration   c. buoyancy   d. meteorology

d 6. Jean studied _____ so that she could give accurate weather reports.
a. alloys   b. dissection   c. conflagration   d. meteorology

b 7. The mixture of metals in this _____ causes allergic reactions in many people.
a. buoyancy   b. alloy   c. combustion   d. meteorology

a 8. Noel was interested in shooting stars, comets, and other _____ phenomena.
a. celestial   b. buoyant   c. saturated   d. coagulated

d 9. Rain had _____ Zara's garden, drowning all her seedlings.
a. alloyed   b. combusted   c. coagulated   d. saturated

c 10. His _____ of every comment the teacher made was getting annoying.
a. coagulation   b. saturation   c. dissection   d. conflagration

Challenge: The presence of _____ materials in the woodpile was what started the _____.

c   a. celestial…dissection   b. buoyant…coagulation   c. combustible…conflagration

Witness to Pompeii

On August 24 in the year AD 79, seventeen-year-old Pliny the Younger was relaxing with relatives in the town of Misenium, on Italy's west coast. Suddenly, his mother noticed a horrible black cloud across the Bay of Naples, rising like a column over Pompeii. Realizing that Mount Vesuvius had erupted, Pliny's uncle, Pliny the Elder, set sail to help in this disaster. He tried to reach the city of Pompeii but couldn't land there. **(1)** Hot, thick ashes and large chunks of *coagulated* lava blocked the harbor.

Meanwhile, the column of black ash continued to rise to an estimated height of 66,000 feet! The column became a "mushroom cloud," which fell like rain to the earth. A huge river of melted rock poured over Pompeii, turning much of the city to stone. Those who escaped the lava flow were trapped by burning ashes and chunks of rock that rained down on the city. **(2)** Anything *combustible* immediately went up in flames. **(3)** People ran around wildly, trying to escape the *conflagration*. **(4)** Harmful sulfuric gas *saturated* the air. **(5)** This heavy gas was not *buoyant*, so it sank to the ground, suffocating some and poisoning others.

Pliny the Elder had landed at a town twenty miles away from the eruption, but even there, the lava rose so high that it started to block doors. He escaped outside, but, weakened by asthma, he collapsed and died.

Meanwhile, the horrors continued in the city of Pompeii. **(6)** *Meteorologists* have found that volcanic explosions sometimes cause earthquakes and tsunamis. It is believed that this happened in Pompeii. As the land was shocked by earthquakes, the sea was sucked back and then hurled at the beaches. This even changed the course of the Sarno River.

Pliny the Younger's letters reveal that the disaster spread even to where he was, a full seventy miles away. He describes seeing people running from place to place, calling out the names of missing relatives, trying to recognize their voices through the black clouds that turned day into night. Some prayed for deliverance. **(7)** Others, certain that the *celestial* powers had deserted them, thought they were witnessing the end of the world.

Eighteen hours later, it was over. Pompeii, a city of 20,000, was buried under twenty feet of rock and ash. Thousands were interred within their city for centuries.

Although written accounts such as Pliny the Younger's survived, the location of Pompeii was lost to history for many years. But in the 1800s, the city was rediscovered during archaeological excavations. Amazingly, the sudden lava flood had stopped life in its tracks, preserving in stone loaves of bread baking and people sleeping. **(8)** Roman murals and mosaic flooring still decorated the walls; bronze jewelry, made from an *alloy* of tin and copper, was found almost perfectly preserved on some victims.

(9) Today, the *dissection* of the stone data continues to reveal many scientific secrets. Geneticists are even studying the DNA of Pompeii's residents. **(10)** They will *distill* this genetic information so they can learn more about the traits of the ancient Romans. Still a site of archaeological investigation, Pompeii is the most complete record we have of life in ancient Roman times.

Each sentence below refers to a numbered sentence in the passage. Write the letter of the choice that gives the sentence a meaning that is closest to the original sentence.

_____ d **1.** Hot, thick ashes and large chunks of _____ lava blocked the harbor.
    a. purified   **b.** floating   **c.** oozing   **d.** hardened

_____ b **2.** Anything _____ immediately went up in flames.
    a. floating   **b.** able to burn   **c.** highly purified   **d.** in the sky

_____ a **3.** People ran around wildly, trying to escape the _____.
    a. huge fire   **b.** metal mixture   **c.** atmosphere   **d.** flammable material

_____ c **4.** Harmful sulfuric gas _____ the air.
    a. made solid   **b.** cut apart   **c.** filled   **d.** floated

___c___ **5.** This heavy gas was not _____, so it sank to the ground.
    a. able to soak   **b.** able to mix   **c.** able to float   **d.** able to burn

___d___ **6.** _____ have found that volcanic explosions sometimes cause earthquakes and tsunamis.
    a. School teachers   **c.** Those who float
    b. Ancient Romans   **d.** Those who study weather

___b___ **7.** Others, certain that the _____ powers had deserted them, thought they were witnessing the end of the world.
    a. atmospheric   **b.** heavenly   **c.** exploding   **d.** geological

___a___ **8.** Bronze jewelry, made from a(n) _____ of tin and copper, was found on some victims.
    a. mixture   **b.** melting   **c.** cutting apart   **d.** artistic carving

___d___ **9.** The _____ of the stone data continues to reveal many scientific secrets.
    a. related to weather   **b.** carved markings   **c.** ability to float   **d.** detailed examination

___d___ **10.** They will _____ this genetic information so they can learn more about the traits of the ancient Romans.
    a. study   **b.** set fire to   **c.** solidify   **d.** condense

Indicate whether the statements below are TRUE or FALSE according to the passage.

___T___ **1.** The volcanic eruption happened so quickly that many people didn't escape.

___F___ **2.** Pliny the Elder died in the lava flow that consumed Pompeii.

___F___ **3.** All evidence of what life was like in Pompeii was destroyed by the volcanic eruption.

FINISH THE THOUGHT

Complete each sentence so that it shows the meaning of the italicized word.

1. An example of something *combustible* is _____ Answers will vary.

2. A *buoyant* object _____ Answers will vary.

WRITE THE DERIVATIVE

Complete the sentence by writing the correct form of the word shown in parentheses. You may not need to change the form that is given.

___alloy___ **1.** Silver jewelry is often an _____ of silver and nickel. *(alloy)*

___distilled___ **2.** To cultivate their famous tulips, the Dutch often use water that has been _____ from seawater. *(distill)*

<u>dissect</u>   **3.** Many schools offer students alternatives so that they do not have to _____ frogs. *(dissection)*

<u>meteorologist</u>   **4.** The _____ predicted that the hurricane wouldn't hit our neighborhood until the evening. *(meteorology)*

<u>buoyant</u>   **5.** Many small children swim with vests that make them _____. *(buoyancy)*

<u>combustion</u>   **6.** Under certain conditions, _____ takes place spontaneously. *(combustible)*

<u>celestial</u>   **7.** The astronomer studied the _____ bodies through her telescope. *(celestial)*

<u>coagulate</u>   **8.** Adding gelatin to sugary liquid causes it to _____. *(coagulate)*

<u>saturation</u>   **9.** The flooding caused the complete _____ of her basement carpet. *(saturate)*

<u>conflagration</u>   **10.** Because of the flammable material used in the housing structures, the small fire soon became a full-blown _____. *(conflagration)*

FIND THE EXAMPLE

Choose the answer that best describes the action or situation.

<u>c</u>   **1.** Something that is *coagulated*
    a. helium gas   **b.** melted ice   **c.** a blood clot   **d.** a flowing river

<u>b</u>   **2.** Something that is *combustible*
    a. steel beams   **b.** gasoline   **c.** jewelry   **d.** seawater

<u>c</u>   **3.** Something you would NOT be able to do if your bath towel were *saturated*
    a. wash the dishes   **b.** brush your teeth   **c.** dry yourself off   **d.** find a washcloth

<u>d</u>   **4.** The material NOT likely to be part of an *alloy*
    a. zinc   **b.** carbon   **c.** iron   **d.** chocolate

<u>c</u>   **5.** The most likely effect of a *conflagration*
    a. hurricanes   **b.** an earthquake   **c.** ashes   **d.** a volcanic eruption

<u>d</u>   **6.** A phenomenon that someone who studies *meteorology* might focus on
    a. diseases   **b.** trees   **c.** ocean life   **d.** greenhouse effect

<u>a</u>   **7.** Something that is *buoyant*
    a. inflated balloon   **b.** metal hammer   **c.** large stone   **d.** bottle of nail polish

<u>b</u>   **8.** An instrument you would use to best see a *celestial* object
    a. microscope   **b.** telescope   **c.** prism   **d.** magnifying glass

<u>c</u>   **9.** Something that can be *distilled*
    a. rough stone   **b.** metal   **c.** crude oil   **d.** oxygen

<u>d</u>   **10.** Someone whose job it is to *dissect* films
    a. a TV actor   **b.** a scientist   **c.** a photographer   **d.** a movie critic

Prefixes, Roots, and Suffixes

Number Prefixes Continued

In the last skill feature, you learned about the Greek and Latin prefixes that mean "one," "two," and "three." This skill feature continues with other number prefixes. Some are specific numbers, and some are not.

Below, each number prefix is given with an example, its origin, and its meaning.

Prefix	Meaning	Origin	Word, Word Meaning
dec-, deca-	ten	Greek, Latin	decade, "period of ten years"
cent-	hundred	Latin	century, "hundred years"
ambi-, amphi-	both, around	Latin, Greek	ambidextrous, "able to use both hands" / amphitheater, "a round theater"
hemi-, semi-	half, partial	Greek, Latin	hemisphere, "half of the earth" / semisweet, "partially sweet"
ann-, enn-	year	Latin	annual, "each year"

Practice

You can combine the use of context clues with your knowledge of these prefixes to make intelligent guesses about the meanings of words. All of the sentences below contain a word formed with the prefixes you have just learned. Read the sentences and write down what you think the word in italics means. Then check your definition with the one you find in the dictionary, remembering to choose the definition that best fits the sentence.

1. I would like to buy a *semiprecious* stone to put in this ring.

   My definition ___rather precious; partially precious___

   Dictionary definition ___a gem that has value but is less rare than a precious stone___

2. Montana recently celebrated the *centennial* of its admission to the United States.

   My definition ___hundredth anniversary___

   Dictionary definition ___a hundredth anniversary or celebration of one___

3. Our *semiannual* meetings are held in January and July.

   My definition ___at the half-year mark___

   Dictionary definition ___occurring twice per year___

4. With the soft music, beautiful decorations, and wonderful lighting, the restaurant had a lovely *ambience*.

   My definition ___atmosphere___

   Dictionary definition ___atmosphere or mood___

5. The teacher asked the students to draw a *decagon*.

My definition _____ figure with ten sides _____

Dictionary definition ___ a geometric figure with ten sides and ten angles ___

6. The store employees prepared for the *semiannual* sale.

My definition _____ happening two times a year _____

Dictionary definition _____ occurring twice a year _____

7. The athlete was relieved when he completed all of the events in the *decathalon*.

My definition _____ competition with ten parts _____

Dictionary definition ___ athletic contest with ten different events ___

Review: Word Elements

Reviewing word elements helps you to remember them and use them in your reading. Below, write the meaning of the word elements you have studied. Each one appears italicized in a word.

Word	Word Element	Type of Element	Meaning of Word Element
*tri*angle	*tri-*	prefix	three
pro*pul*sion	*pel, pul*	root	strike; thrust
*voc*alize	*voc*	root	voice
*uni*form	*uni-*	prefix	one
ex*port*	*port*	root	carry
*co*worker	*co-*	prefix	together
*rupt*ure	*rupt*	root	break
*bi*sect	*bi-*	prefix	two
*du*al	*di-, du-*	prefix	two
*clam*or	*claim, clam*	root	cry out
con*duct*	*duct*	root	lead
*frag*mentary	*fract, frag*	root	break
*re*bound	*re-*	prefix	back
*gen*esis	*gen*	root	birth; beginning
*mono*arch	*mono-*	prefix	one

Contents

USING BONUS ACTIVITIES AND TESTS

For your convenience, the lesson **Tests** and **Bonus** activities that accompany *Vocabulary for Achievement*, Second Course, are available as reproducible masters in this section. Answers are printed in color on the front of each reproducible master for ease in locating.

This section also contains recordkeeping charts that may be reproduced for each of your classes. These will help you keep track of student progress on **lesson exercises, Bonus** activities, and **Tests.**

Tests

There are fifteen multiple-choice tests, each covering two consecutive lessons. This format ensures that students can demonstrate proficiency with a wider set of vocabulary words than is found in a single lesson.

Test formats resemble those of the lesson exercises. Each test is divided into two parts of ten items each, allowing for the testing of all words in the two lessons. Part A focuses on recognizing and recalling definitions, whereas Part B emphasizes placing words within the context of sentences.

Bonuses

Fifteen **Bonus** activities, each covering two consecutive lessons, offer students further opportunities for reinforcement and enrichment. These activities consist of crossword puzzles, word searches, sentence completions, scrambled words, and other word-game formats. Depending on classroom needs, use these activities as added practice, as reviews of previously mastered words, or as extra-credit assignments.

VOCABULARY FOR ACHIEVEMENT

Second Course

Student Record

Class Period _____

	Lesson 1 Exercises	Lesson 2 Exercises	Bonus: Lessons 1 & 2	Test: Lessons 1 & 2	Lesson 3 Exercises	Lesson 4 Exercises	Bonus: Lessons 3 & 4	Test: Lessons 3 & 4	Lesson 5 Exercises	Lesson 6 Exercises	Bonus: Lessons 5 & 6	Test: Lessons 5 & 6	Lesson 7 Exercises	Lesson 8 Exercises	Bonus: Lessons 7 & 8	Test: Lessons 7 & 8	Lesson 9 Exercises	Lesson 10 Exercises	Bonus: Lessons 9 & 10	Test: Lessons 9 & 10	Lesson 11 Exercises	Lesson 12 Exercises	Bonus: Lessons 11 & 12	Test: Lessons 11 & 12	Lesson 13 Exercises	Lesson 14 Exercises	Bonus: Lessons 13 & 14	Test: Lessons 13 & 14	Lesson 15 Exercises	Lesson 16 Exercises
1.																														
2.																														
3.																														
4.																														
5.																														
6.																														
7.																														
8.																														
9.																														
10.																														
11.																														
12.																														
13.																														
14.																														
15.																														
16.																														
17.																														
18.																														
19.																														
20.																														
21.																														
22.																														
23.																														
24.																														
25.																														
26.																														
27.																														
28.																														
29.																														
30.																														
31.																														
32.																														
33.																														
34.																														
35.																														

#	Bonus: Lessons 15 & 16	Test: Lessons 15 & 16	Lesson 17 Exercises	Lesson 18 Exercises	Bonus: Lessons 17 & 18	Test: Lessons 17 & 18	Lesson 19 Exercises	Lesson 20 Exercises	Bonus: Lessons 19 & 20	Test: Lessons 19 & 20	Lesson 21 Exercises	Lesson 22 Exercises	Bonus: Lessons 21 & 22	Test: Lessons 21 & 22	Lesson 23 Exercises	Lesson 24 Exercises	Bonus: Lessons 23 & 24	Test: Lessons 23 & 24	Lesson 25 Exercises	Lesson 26 Exercises	Bonus: Lessons 25 & 26	Test: Lessons 25 & 26	Lesson 27 Exercises	Lesson 28 Exercises	Bonus: Lessons 27 & 28	Test: Lessons 27 & 28	Lesson 29 Exercises	Lesson 30 Exercises.	Bonus: Lessons 29 & 30	Test: Lessons 29 & 30
1.																														
2.																														
3.																														
4.																														
5.																														
6.																														
7.																														
8.																														
9.																														
10.																														
11.																														
12.																														
13.																														
14.																														
15.																														
16.																														
17.																														
18.																														
19.																														
20.																														
21.																														
22.																														
23.																														
24.																														
25.																														
26.																														
27.																														
28.																														
29.																														
30.																														
31.																														
32.																														
33.																														
34.																														
35.																														

NAME ______________________________ DATE ____________________

BONUS: LESSONS 1 AND 2

(pages 1–12)

Use the clues to complete the crossword puzzle.

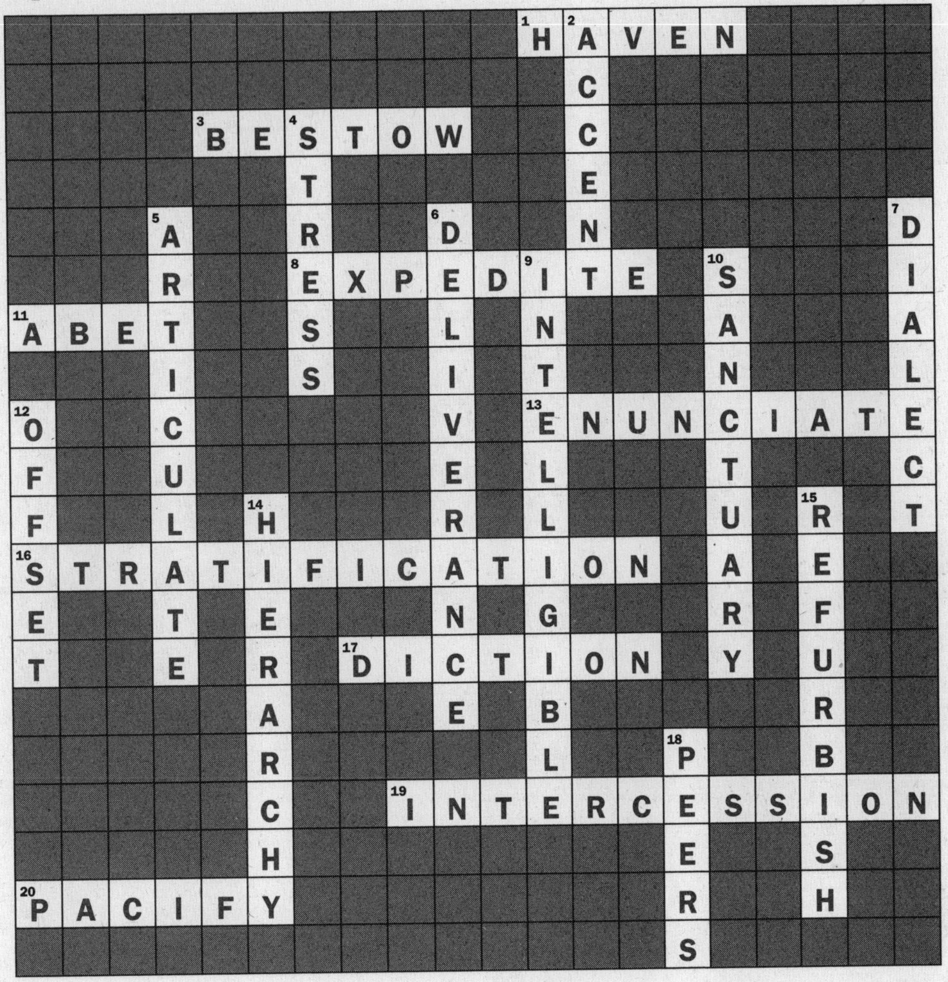

1 H A V E N
2 A C C E N T
3 B E S T O W
4 S T R E S S
5 A R T I C U L A T E
6 D E L I V E R A N C E
7 D I A L E C T
8 E X P E D I T E
9 I N T E L L I G I B L E
10 S A N C T U A R Y
11 A B E T
12 O F F S E T
13 E N U N C I A T E
14 H I E R A R C H Y
15 R E F U R B I S H
16 S T R A T I F I C A T I O N
17 D I C T I O N
18 P E E R S
19 I N T E R C E S S I O N
20 P A C I F Y

Across

1 A place of refuge or safety is also known as a(n) _______.

3 If you give or present something, you _______ it.

8 To speed up the progress of something

11 To _______ is to encourage or assist.

13 To state clearly

16 _______ is separation into different levels.

17 _______ is clearness of speech.

19 The mediation of a problem between others

20 To _______ someone is to calm his or her anger.

Down

2 To focus attention on is to _______.

4 Emphasis in speaking or music is _______.

5 When you _______, you express something clearly with words.

6 Rescue from slavery, capture, or danger

7 A unique form of language, spoken by people from a particular place

9 Something that is _______ is easily understood.

10 Any place of safety or protection

12 To make up for is to _______.

14 A group organized according to rank or status is a(n) _______.

15 To clean, renew, repair, or refresh all describe the word _______.

18 People who are equal in social standing or age

BONUS: LESSONS 1 AND 2

(pages 1–12)

Use the clues to complete the crossword puzzle.

Across

1 A place of refuge or safety is also known as a(n) _____.

3 If you give or present something, you _____ it.

8 To speed up the progress of something

11 To _____ is to encourage or assist.

13 To state clearly

16 _____ is separation into different levels.

17 _____ is clearness of speech.

19 The mediation of a problem between others

20 To _____ someone is to calm his or her anger.

Down

2 To focus attention on is to _____.

4 Emphasis in speaking or music is _____.

5 When you _____, you express something clearly with words.

6 Rescue from slavery, capture, or danger

7 A unique form of language, spoken by people from a particular place

9 Something that is _____ is easily understood.

10 Any place of safety or protection

12 To make up for is to _____.

14 A group organized according to rank or status is a(n) _____.

15 To clean, renew, repair, or refresh all describe the word _____.

18 People who are equal in social standing or age

TEST: LESSONS 1 AND 2

(pages 1–12)

Part A Choosing the Best Definition

On the answer line, write the letter of the best definition of the italicized word.

1. The people were grateful for their *deliverance* when the hurricane turned out to sea. 1. _____
   a. emergency supplies
   b. safe arrival
   c. rescue from danger
   d. takeout food

2. More than winning games, our coach *stresses* teamwork, good sportsmanship, and having fun. 2. _____
   a. believes in
   b. ridicules
   c. worries about
   d. emphasizes

3. Mr. Banderat was surprised by the number of *dialects* in the United States. 3. _____
   a. regional forms of language
   b. good speakers
   c. protected places
   d. immigrants

4. The woman *bestowed* a pearl necklace on her young niece. 4. _____
   a. dropped
   b. told a story about
   c. hid
   d. gave as a gift

5. Marco's score of 98 on today's test will help *offset* his low grade on the last test. 5. _____
   a. make up for
   b. eliminate
   c. forget about
   d. improve

6. The shipwrecked sailor was exhausted and barely *intelligible*. 6. _____
   a. thinking
   b. able to breathe
   c. alive
   d. able to be understood

7. Several senators worked to *expedite* emergency aid for the disaster victims. 7. _____
   a. pledge money for
   b. gain favor for
   c. speed up
   d. bring to public attention

8. The actor looked directly at the audience and *enunciated* his lines. 8. _____
   a. sang loudly
   b. pronounced clearly
   c. explained carefully
   d. remembered perfectly

9. This quiet island is a *haven* for vacationers who are used to cities, crowds, and noise. 9. _____
   a. refuge
   b. bore
   c. contrast
   d. shock

10. Your Aunt Brenna has a pretty voice and a charming *accent*. 10. _____
    a. personality
    b. style of pronunciation
    c. smile
    d. style of dress

TEST: LESSONS 1 AND 2

(pages 1–12)

Part B Choosing the Best Word

On the answer line, write the letter of the word that best completes the sentence.

11. A collection of birdhouses in my neighbor's yard provides a ———— for wild birds.
    a. sanctuary   **b.** dialect   **c.** hierarchy   **d.** stratum

    11. _____

12. Elsa, who wants to be a radio announcer, is working hard to improve her ————.
    a. intercession   **b.** peers   **c.** deliverance   **d.** diction

    12. _____

13. The team is ———— into star players, good players, and the rest of us, who rarely have a chance to play.
    a. expedited   **b.** offset   **c.** stratified   **d.** stressed

    13. _____

14. We chose our most ———— classmate to make the graduation speech.
    a. articulate   **b.** expeditious   **c.** pacified   **d.** hierarchical

    14. _____

15. A bank employee ———— the thieves by providing information about the security system.
    a. refurbished   **b.** abetted   **c.** enunciated   **d.** offset

    15. _____

16. Unlike most of his ————, Brian enjoys classical music.
    a. deliverance   **b.** dialect   **c.** accents   **d.** peers

    16. _____

17. When the other students refused to share the computer, Stuart asked Mr. Grogan to ———— on his behalf.
    a. intercede   **b.** stress   **c.** bestow   **d.** pacify

    17. _____

18. The superintendent of schools ranks above the school principals in the city's educational ————.
    a. haven   **b.** hierarchy   **c.** diction   **d.** sanctuary

    18. _____

19. The babysitter tried to ———— the tired, cranky child with food, but what the child needed was a nap.
    a. refurbish   **b.** enunciate   **c.** pacify   **d.** stratify

    19. _____

20. Tina plans to ———— her kitchen table by sanding and repainting it.
    a. abet   **b.** intercede   **c.** articulate   **d.** refurbish

    20. _____

BONUS: LESSONS 3 AND 4

(pages 13–18 and 21–26)

Use the following clues to identify the vocabulary words and write the words on the lines to the right. Then circle each vocabulary word in the word-search box below. The words may overlap and may read in any direction.

1. A(n) ———— is a trick. (9 letters)

2. False and harmful statements about someone (7 letters)

3. ———— is great physical or mental pain. (7 letters)

4. Governed by personal thoughts or feelings (10 letters)

5. Openly or boldly resisting authority (7 letters)

6. Open to advice or suggestion (8 letters)

7. One who is filled with joy or enthusiasm is ————. (9 letters)

8. Satisfaction (13 letters)

9. To be ———— is to be discontented or resentful. (11 letters)

10. Believed before one has full knowledge or experience (12 letters)

11. In low spirits; dejected (10 letters)

12. A favorable bias or prejudice toward something is ————. (10 letters)

1. deception
2. slander
3. anguish
4. subjective
5. defiant
6. amenable
7. exuberant
8. gratification
9. disgruntled
10. preconceived
11. despondent
12. partiality

Challenge

Locate and circle the eight additional vocabulary words in the word-search box.

forbearance
objective
partisanship
tolerate
blithe
congenial
desolate
disillusion

```
F O R B E A R A N C E K R N A Z Y E P
G R S P I H S N A S I T R A P E L D R
I T A L I F E E D A L S N D H E O I E
F I E S A N P H N O C G N T L D W S C
E C T X O N L A T G U O L B P E L I O
V A O A U E D E F I H J A H A L A L N
I T L G T B W E S P L N M S R T I L C
T O E B V C E H R Q E B O I T N N U E
C N R S D R Y R U M X U B U I U E S I
E T A L N O I T A C I F I T A R G I V
J I T I A B E M A N G A R G L G N O E
B A E P F E I V E V T R A T I S O N D
O Y C R D E S P O N D E N T T I C I J
S P O N T F D E S O L A T E Y D K N H
E V I T C E J B U S D E C E P T I O N
```

NAME _____ DATE _____

BONUS: LESSONS 3 AND 4

(pages 13–18 and 21–26)

Use the following clues to identify the vocabulary words and write the words on the
lines to the right. Then circle each vocabulary word in the word-search box below.
The words may overlap and may read in any direction.

1. A(n) _____ is a trick. (9 letters)

2. False and harmful statements about someone (7 letters)

3. _____ is great physical or mental pain. (7 letters)

4. Governed by personal thoughts or feelings (10 letters)

5. Openly or boldly resisting authority (7 letters)

6. Open to advice or suggestion (8 letters)

7. One who is filled with joy or enthusiasm is _____. (9 letters)

8. Satisfaction (13 letters)

9. To be _____ is to be discontented or resentful. (11 letters)

10. Believed before one has full knowledge or experience (12 letters)

11. In low spirits; dejected (10 letters)

12. A favorable bias or prejudice toward something is _____.
(10 letters)

1. _____
2. _____
3. _____
4. _____
5. _____
6. _____
7. _____
8. _____
9. _____
10. _____
11. _____
12. _____

Challenge
Locate and circle the eight additional vocabulary words in the word-search box.

forbearance
objective
partisanship
tolerate
blithe
congenial
desolate
disillusion

F	O	R	B	E	A	R	A	N	C	E	K	R	N	A	Z	Y	E	P
G	R	S	P	I	H	S	N	A	S	I	T	R	A	P	E	L	D	R
I	T	A	L	I	F	E	E	D	A	L	S	N	D	H	E	O	I	E
F	I	E	S	A	N	P	H	N	O	C	G	N	T	L	D	W	S	C
E	C	T	X	O	N	L	A	T	G	U	O	L	B	P	E	L	I	O
V	A	O	A	U	E	D	E	F	I	H	J	A	H	A	L	A	L	N
I	T	L	G	T	B	W	E	S	P	L	N	M	S	R	T	I	L	C
T	O	E	B	V	C	E	H	R	Q	E	B	O	I	T	N	N	U	E
C	N	R	S	D	R	Y	R	U	M	X	U	B	U	I	U	E	S	I
E	T	A	L	N	O	I	T	A	C	I	F	I	T	A	R	G	I	V
J	I	T	I	A	B	E	M	A	N	G	A	R	G	L	G	N	O	E
B	A	E	P	F	E	I	V	E	V	T	R	A	T	I	S	O	N	D
O	Y	C	R	D	E	S	P	O	N	D	E	N	T	T	I	C	I	J
S	P	O	N	T	F	D	E	S	O	L	A	T	E	Y	D	K	N	H
E	V	I	T	C	E	J	B	U	S	D	E	C	E	P	T	I	O	N

T4 **Bonus: Lessons 3 and 4**

©Great Source. Copying is permitted; see page ii.

TEST: LESSONS 3 AND 4

(pages 13–18 and 21–26)

Part A Choosing the Best Definition

On the answer line, write the letter of the best definition of the italicized word.

1. Isobel's *blithe* comments amused us on the long ride to the beach.
   a. mean-spirited   **c.** lighthearted
   b. accurate   **d.** thoughtful

   1. _____

2. Mr. Klein is strict but fair, and he would never *tolerate* cheating or lazy work.
   a. allow   **c.** discuss
   b. perform   **d.** criticize

   2. _____

3. Filled with *anguish,* Sean held the injured dog as Dad drove to the animal hospital.
   a. great longing   **c.** mental pain
   b. pity   **d.** hope

   3. _____

4. Matt felt *despondent* when he didn't make the baseball team, but he cheered up when he learned he could join the lacrosse team instead.
   a. furious   **c.** puzzled
   b. injured   **d.** depressed

   4. _____

5. Mom, who cooks most of our family's meals, showed great *forbearance* when my brother Joel decided to stop eating meat.
   a. annoyance   **c.** eagerness
   b. patience   **d.** support of a cause

   5. _____

6. The judge's *partiality* probably helped Mrs. Wheeler win the pie-baking contest.
   a. enthusiasm   **c.** favorable bias
   b. good taste   **d.** low spirits

   6. _____

7. Mary's *preconceived* ideas about college life will soon be put to the test.
   a. personal   **c.** favorable
   b. believed beforehand **d.** based on experience

   7. _____

8. A teacher's greatest reward is the *gratification* she feels when her students succeed.
   a. satisfaction   **c.** surprise
   b. pride   **d.** thrill

   8. _____

9. The *defiant* prisoner refused to eat the meals brought to him each day.
   a. impatient   **c.** excitable
   b. lonely and sad   **d.** resistant

   9. _____

10. If you ask Dad for a ride to the movies, I'm sure he will be *amenable.*
    a. willing   **c.** too busy
    b. angry   **d.** opposed

    10. _____

TEST: LESSONS 3 AND 4

(pages 13–18 and 21–26)

Part B Choosing the Best Word

On the answer line, write the letter of the word that best completes the sentence.

11. In skating competitions, the judges' decisions often seem _____ to me.
   a. disgruntled   **b.** defiant   **c.** despondent   **d.** subjective

11. _____

12. Speaking the truth, even if it's unpleasant, cannot be considered _____.
   a. anguish   **b.** partiality   **c.** slander   **d.** gratification

12. _____

13. Mr. and Mrs. Felipe have always been _____ neighbors, and I'm sorry to hear they are moving.
   a. preconceived   **b.** partisan   **c.** congenial   **d.** objective

13. _____

14. Many young players and fans became _____ when they heard reports of some professional athletes using illegal drugs.
   a. tolerated   **b.** disillusioned   **c.** defied   **d.** slandered

14. _____

15. After the fire, the once-beautiful valley was _____ and forbidding.
   a. amenable   **b.** despondent   **c.** desolate   **d.** exuberant

15. _____

16. Tim was punished for his _____ after he tried to blame someone else for breaking the neighbor's window.
   a. deception   **b.** congeniality   **c.** objective   **d.** forbearance

16. _____

17. _____ shoppers complained when they found that none of the advertised sale items were available.
   a. Blithe   **b.** Disgruntled   **c.** Desolate   **d.** Subjective

17. _____

18. People wear political buttons to show _____ for their favored candidate.
   a. deception   **b.** gratification   **c.** anguish   **d.** partisanship

18. _____

19. "Every field trip has an educational _____," the teacher told his class.
   a. objective   **b.** forbearance   **c.** partisanship   **d.** exuberance

19. _____

20. Feeling _____ about his new afterschool job, Leo called all his friends with the good news.
   a. congenial   **b.** defiant   **c.** exuberant   **d.** blithe

20. _____

NAME ______________________ DATE ______________

BONUS: LESSONS 5 AND 6

(pages 27–38)

Use the clues to complete the crossword puzzle.

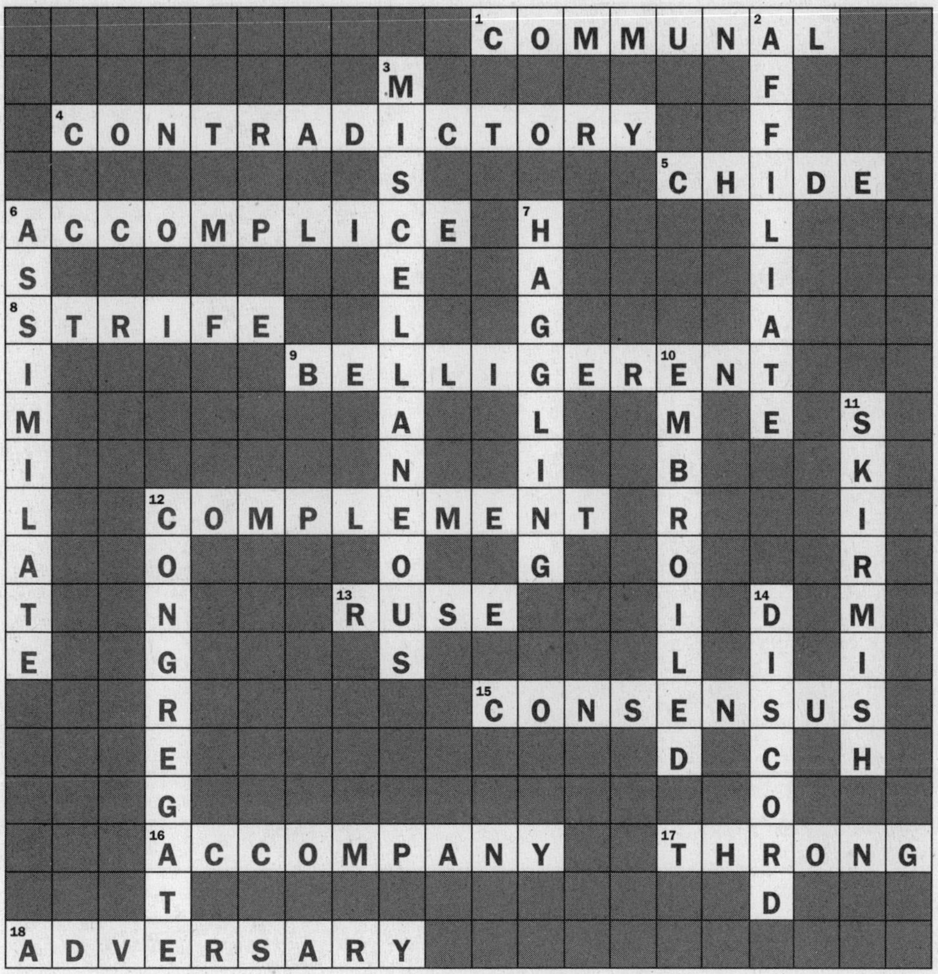

1 COMMUNAL
2 AFFILIATE
3 MISCELLANEOUS
4 CONTRADICTORY
5 CHIDE
6 ACCOMPLICE
6 ASSIMILATE
7 HAGGLING
8 STRIFE
9 BELLIGERENT
10 EMBROILED
11 SKIRMISH
12 COMPLEMENT
12 CONGREGATE
13 RUSE
14 DISCORD
15 CONSENSUS
16 ACCOMPANY
17 THRONG
18 ADVERSARY

Across

1 Something that is shared commonly by a group

4 If you are ______, you express the opposite of a statement.

5 To scold someone is to ______ them.

6 A person who helps another person carry out a crime

8 ______ is bitter conflict or struggle.

9 Hostile, aggressive, and quarrelsome

12 Something that completes or harmonizes with something else

13 A crafty trick intended to give a false impression

15 A general agreement among a group of people

16 To provide musical support for another musical part

17 A large crowd that is gathered densely together

18 An opponent or enemy is a(n) ______.

Down

2 To join or associate with a larger group is to ______ with them.

3 Things that are difficult to categorize can also be called ______.

6 To adopt or take on the traditions of the larger or surrounding group

7 Arguing or bargaining to get to favorable terms or a good price

10 To get ______ is to get involved in a conflict, argument, or confusion.

11 A minor battle can also be called a(n) ______.

12 To gather or come together

14 Lack of agreement or harmony is also known as ______.

BONUS: LESSONS 5 AND 6

(pages 27–38)

Use the clues to complete the crossword puzzle.

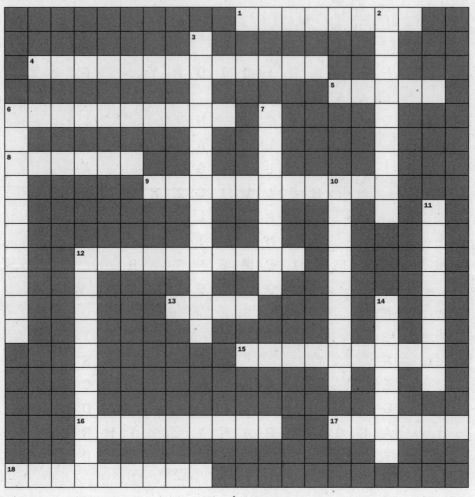

Across

1 Something that is shared commonly by a group

4 If you are _____, you express the opposite of a statement.

5 To scold someone is to _____ them.

6 A person who helps another person carry out a crime

8 _____ is bitter conflict or struggle.

9 Hostile, aggressive, and quarrelsome

12 Something that completes or harmonizes with something else

13 A crafty trick intended to give a false impression

15 A general agreement among a group of people

16 To provide musical support for another musical part

17 A large crowd that is gathered densely together

18 An opponent or enemy is a(n) _____.

Down

2 To join or associate with a larger group is to _____ with them.

3 Things that are difficult to categorize can also be called _____.

6 To adopt or take on the traditions of the larger or surrounding group

7 Arguing or bargaining to get to favorable terms or a good price

10 To get _____ is to get involved in a conflict, argument, or confusion.

11 A minor battle can also be called a(n) _____.

12 To gather or come together

14 Lack of agreement or harmony is also known as _____.

TEST: LESSONS 5 AND 6

(pages 27–38)

Part A Choosing the Best Definition

On the answer line, write the letter of the best definition of the italicized word.

1. My two best friends gave me *contradictory* advice, and I didn't know what to do.   **1.** _____
    a. sympathetic   **c.** dangerous
    b. opposite   **d.** unhelpful

2. For years, there was great *strife* between farmers and ranchers in the region.   **2.** _____
    a. suspicion   **c.** cooperation
    b. conflict   **d.** progress

3. Many of the newcomers blended in by *assimilating* with the residents.   **3.** _____
    a. outlawing   **c.** eliminating customs
    b. changing   **d.** adopting customs

4. Mona's *adversary* has won the tennis championship for the last three years.   **4.** _____
    a. instructor   **c.** relative
    b. opponent   **d.** teammate

5. The band will *congregate* at the town hall an hour before the parade begins.   **5.** _____
    a. practice   **c.** gather
    b. perform   **d.** dress

6. For lunch, French fries are the usual *complement* to a cheeseburger.   **6.** _____
    a. suitable addition   **c.** improvement over
    b. alternative   **d.** opposite

7. David found two coins among the *miscellaneous* objects in his desk drawer.   **7.** _____
    a. inexpensive   **c.** various
    b. useful   **d.** small

8. Most parents would *chide* their children for snacking just before a meal.   **8.** _____
    a. gather   **c.** ignore
    b. punish   **d.** scold

9. When the thief was caught, he refused to tell the police the names of his *accomplices*.   **9.** _____
    a. rivals   **c.** parents
    b. criminal partners   **d.** closest friends

10. *Discord* among team members makes winning more difficult.   **10.** _____
    a. missing practices   **c.** lack of agreement
    b. sorrow and sadness   **d.** fierce competition

TEST: LESSONS 5 AND 6

(pages 27–38)

Part B Choosing the Best Word

On the answer line, write the letter of the word that best completes the sentence.

11. If a customer gets _____ , you should call a security guard right away.
 a. miscellaneous **b.** communal **c.** complementary **d.** belligerent
 11. _____

12. Anyone who is _____ with the university is allowed to use the library and the computer lab.
 a. embroiled **b.** affiliated **c.** congregated **d.** haggled
 12. _____

13. Both soldiers and civilians were wounded in a _____ .
 a. skirmish **b.** complement **c.** strife **d.** consensus
 13. _____

14. A _____ of parents waits outside the kindergarten door at the close of school every day.
 a. discord **b.** ruse **c.** skirmish **d.** throng
 14. _____

15. It won't do you a bit of good to _____ about your grade in science class.
 a. embroil **b.** assimilate **c.** haggle **d.** contradict
 15. _____

16. At our family reunion, everyone enjoyed the _____ sing-along and pizza party.
 a. communal **b.** contradictory **c.** adversarial **d.** belligerent
 16. _____

17. Mrs. Singer will play the piano to _____ the eighth-grade chorus.
 a. chide **b.** haggle **c.** accompany **d.** affiliate
 17. _____

18. We need a convincing _____ to get Mom out of the house while we make her birthday cake.
 a. consensus **b.** ruse **c.** contradiction **d.** strife
 18. _____

19. A good babysitter doesn't get _____ in the children's disagreements.
 a. congregated **b.** miscellaneous **c.** accompanied **d.** embroiled
 19. _____

20. The class failed to reach a _____ about where to hold the end-of-year party.
 a. consensus **b.** discord **c.** complement **d.** throng
 20. _____

BONUS: LESSONS 7 AND 8

(pages 41–52)

Use the clues to spell out the vocabulary words on the answer blanks. Then identify the mystery person at the bottom of the page by writing the numbered letters on the lines with the corresponding numbers.

1. Weak or delicate
1. f r a i l (5)

2. Worthy of imitation; admirable
2. e x e m p l a r y (3)

3. Childish; immature
3. p u e r i l e (4)

4. A(n) _____ gives financial aid.
4. b e n e f a c t o r (7)

5. Just coming into existence; emerging
5. n a s c e n t (10)

6. An inexperienced person
6. f l e d g l i n g (13)

7. To _____ is to fix or correct.
7. r e c t i f y (14)

8. A(n) _____ group intends to help humans.
8. h u m a n i t a r i a n (2)(15)

9. Worthy of great respect because of age or dignity
9. v e n e r a b l e (12)

10. Courteous behavior; politeness
10. c i v i l i t y (9)

11. A(n) _____ meal is abundant and plentiful.
11. b o u n t i f u l (16)(8)

12. Unselfish concern for the welfare of others
12. a l t r u i s m (6)

13. Harmless; not dangerous to health
13. b e n i g n (11)

14. The medical study of the elderly
14. g e r i a t r i c s (1)(17)

T(1) H(2) O(16) M(15) A(5) S(17) E(3) D(13) I(14) S(17) O(16) N(10),

I(14) N(10) V(9) E(3) N(10) T(1) O(16) R(4) O(16) F(8) T(1) H(2) E(3)

L(12) I(14) G(11) H(2) T(1) B(7) U(6) L(12) B(7)

BONUS: LESSONS 7 AND 8

(pages 41–52)

Use the clues to spell out the vocabulary words on the answer blanks. Then identify the mystery person at the bottom of the page by writing the numbered letters on the lines with the corresponding numbers.

1. Weak or delicate

1. __ __ __ __ __
        ⁵

2. Worthy of imitation; admirable

2. __ __ __ __ __ __ __ __ __
          ³

3. Childish; immature

3. __ __ __ __ __ __ __
              ⁴

4. A(n) _____ gives financial aid.

4. __ __ __ __ __ __ __ __ __
       ⁷

5. Just coming into existence; emerging

5. __ __ __ __ __ __ __
                    ¹⁰

6. An inexperienced person

6. __ __ __ __ __ __ __ __ __
              ¹³

7. To _____ is to fix or correct.

7. __ __ __ __ __ __ __ __
              ¹⁴

8. A(n) _____ group intends to help humans.

8. __ __ __ __ __ __ __ __ __ __ __ __
       ²   ¹⁵

9. Worthy of great respect because of age or dignity

9. __ __ __ __ __ __ __ __ __
                          ¹²

10. Courteous behavior; politeness

10. __ __ __ __ __ __ __
              ⁹

11. A(n) _____ meal is abundant and plentiful.

11. __ __ __ __ __ __ __ __
        ¹⁶   ⁸

12. Unselfish concern for the welfare of others

12. __ __ __ __ __ __
                  ⁶

13. Harmless; not dangerous to health

13. __ __ __ __ __ __
               ¹¹

14. The medical study of the elderly

14. __ __ __ __ __ __ __ __ __ __
                          ¹   ¹⁷

__ __ __ __ __ __   __ __ __ __ __ __ ,
1 2 16 15 5 17   3 13 14 17 16 10

__ __ __ __ __ __ __ __   __ __   __ __ __
14 10 9 3 10 1 16 4   16 8   1 2 3

__ __ __ __ __   __ __ __ __
12 14 11 2 1   7 6 12 7

TEST: LESSONS 7 AND 8

(pages 41–52)

Part A Choosing the Best Definition

On the answer line, write the letter of the best definition of the italicized word.

1. Dad had an *amicable* talk with our new neighbors about sharing the driveway.
   a. unpleasant   **c.** important
   b. friendly   **d.** stern

   1. _____

2. The company held a party to celebrate Mr. Green's *longevity* as their president.
   a. great success   **c.** admirable behavior
   b. long time   **d.** fame

   2. _____

3. Although the colt looked *frail,* it soon grew into a swift and powerful runner.
   a. weak   **c.** young
   b. graceful   **d.** unattractive

   3. _____

4. Every newspaper article mentions the actor's great *altruism.*
   a. talent   **c.** courage
   b. performance   **d.** concern for others

   4. _____

5. Let's *indulge* ourselves today and order hot-fudge sundaes!
   a. treat with respect **c.** get help for
   b. act immaturely   **d.** give in to a desire

   5. _____

6. Eleven-year-old Lara often scolds her twin brother about his *puerile* jokes.
   a. childish   **c.** wicked
   b. not funny   **d.** old-fashioned

   6. _____

7. People who meet the famous author are often impressed by his *civility.*
   a. serious attitude   **c.** courteous behavior
   b. success   **d.** worthiness

   7. _____

8. "Your son Anthony is an *exemplary* student," said Mr. Ives.
   a. unusual   **c.** struggling
   b. thoughtful and caring   **d.** worthy of imitation

   8. _____

9. The tribal chief greeted his guests with a *benign* smile.
   a. kind and gentle   **c.** not real; artificial
   b. suspicious   **d.** joyful

   9. _____

10. Most of the preschoolers enjoy banging away on the teacher's *antiquated* typewriter.
    a. broken   **c.** noisy
    b. new   **d.** out-of-date

    10. _____

TEST: LESSONS 7 AND 8

(pages 41–52)

Part B Choosing the Best Word

On the answer line, write the letter of the word that best completes the sentence.

11. Most _____ teachers need a lot of support from their more experienced coworkers.
   a. venerable   **b.** fledgling   **c.** antique   **d.** benign

11. _____

12. A great _____ named Albert Schweitzer helped build hospitals in several African villages.
   a. longevity   **b.** frailty   **c.** humanitarian   **d.** civility

12. _____

13. Alicia worked all weekend to _____ her mother's mistake.
   a. rectify   **b.** indulge   **c.** venerate   **d.** antiquate

13. _____

14. Many dedicated people work in long-term care and other aspects of _____ .
   a. centenary   **b.** veneration   **c.** humanitarian   **d.** geriatrics

14. _____

15. Michaela's _____ behavior in the restaurant really embarrassed the rest of the family.
   a. amicable   **b.** infantile   **c.** nascent   **d.** frail

15. _____

16. The _____ poet autographed a copy of his newest book for me, along with hundreds of other people.
   a. puerile   **b.** bountiful   **c.** venerable   **d.** infantile

16. _____

17. The _____ insists that green tea is the secret to his long, healthy life.
   a. fledgling   **b.** philanthropy   **c.** altruism   **d.** centenarian

17. _____

18. A generous _____ donated two million dollars for a new library.
   a. indulgence   **b.** longevity   **c.** benefactor   **d.** civility

18. _____

19. With his _____ reading skills, the little boy was able to enjoy a Dr. Seuss book, *The Cat in the Hat.*
   a. nascent   **b.** geriatric   **c.** frail   **d.** altruistic

19. _____

20. The settlers had a barn dance to celebrate their _____ harvest.
   a. benign   **b.** bountiful   **c.** amicable   **d.** puerile

20. _____

BONUS: LESSONS 9 AND 10

(pages 53–58 and 61–66)

Unscramble the letters of each italicized vocabulary word and write the word on the answer line to the right.

1. The *edgaelte* who represented our class reported to us about the meeting she attended.

2. From the moment of its *onptoicenc,* the idea was well liked.

3. I picked up the dry cleaning first and *sqbsyeenutul* did my grocery shopping.

4. The scandal led to the president's *nieahmpecmt.*

5. It snowed *csseanitlny* for four days, making travel nearly impossible.

6. The *thaiaoritarun* ruler would not allow the formation of a congress.

7. Because the club meetings were held *usuianyeosltml,* he had to miss one of them.

8. His overly *llbirae* views were frowned upon by the new administration.

9. Lex enjoyed the *eilamevd* fair and spent most of her time watching the jousting.

10. The peasants in the king's *onnidomi* were unhappy with his decisions.

11. Usually dressed in odd clothing and loud colors, Callie surprised us by wearing a(n) *ncvorvtiasee* outfit.

12. The *ebdaelt* card arrived three weeks after Hannah's birthday.

13. I have three more months to use the card before my membership *eierpsx.*

14. Until he could afford to add more comforts, his new house remained rather *anrtspa.*

15. After a brief *petiers,* the group continued on its hike.

16. After a long war, the *aytntr* was finally overthrown.

17. We all found the president's *gulniuraa* address very moving.

18. The *ondtirau* of the play was much longer than we expected.

19. The *hnyacar* in the classroom prompted the principal to stop by.

20. My favorite paintings were all created during the *esrananceis.*

1. **delegate**

2. **conception**

3. **subsequently**

4. **impeachment**

5. **incessantly**

6. **authoritarian**

7. **simultaneously**

8. **liberal**

9. **medieval**

10. **dominion**

11. **conservative**

12. **belated**

13. **expires**

14. **Spartan**

15. **respite**

16. **tyrant**

17. **inaugural**

18. **duration**

19. **anarchy**

20. **Renaissance**

BONUS: LESSONS 9 AND 10

(pages 53–58 and 61–66)

Unscramble the letters of each italicized vocabulary word and write the word on the answer line to the right.

1. The *edgaelte* who represented our class reported to us about the meeting she attended.   1. _____

2. From the moment of its *onptoicenc*, the idea was well liked.   2. _____

3. I picked up the dry cleaning first and *sqbsyeenutul* did my grocery shopping.   3. _____

4. The scandal led to the president's *nieahmpecmt*.   4. _____

5. It snowed *csseanitlny* for four days, making travel nearly impossible.   5. _____

6. The *thaiaoritarun* ruler would not allow the formation of a congress.   6. _____

7. Because the club meetings were held *usuianyeosltml*, he had to miss one of them.   7. _____

8. His overly *llbirae* views were frowned upon by the new administration.   8. _____

9. Lex enjoyed the *eilamevd* fair and spent most of her time watching the jousting.   9. _____

10. The peasants in the king's *onnidomi* were unhappy with his decisions.   10. _____

11. Usually dressed in odd clothing and loud colors, Callie surprised us by wearing a(n) *ncvorvtiasee* outfit.   11. _____

12. The *ebdaelt* card arrived three weeks after Hannah's birthday.   12. _____

13. I have three more months to use the card before my membership *eierpsx*.   13. _____

14. Until he could afford to add more comforts, his new house remained rather *anrtspa*.   14. _____

15. After a brief *petiers*, the group continued on its hike.   15. _____

16. After a long war, the *aytntr* was finally overthrown.   16. _____

17. We all found the president's *gulniuraa* address very moving.   17. _____

18. The *ondtirau* of the play was much longer than we expected.   18. _____

19. The *hnyacar* in the classroom prompted the principal to stop by.   19. _____

20. My favorite paintings were all created during the *esrananceis*.   20. _____

TEST: LESSONS 9 AND 10

(pages 53–58 and 61–66)

Part A Choosing the Best Definition

On the answer line, write the letter of the best definition of the italicized word.

1. I have a gift certificate for the restaurant, but it *expires* tomorrow.
   a. begins to work
   b. is able to be used
   c. excludes
   d. comes to an end

   1. _____

2. Carrie hums *incessantly* when she is working on math problems.
   a. annoyingly
   b. quietly
   c. constantly
   d. secretly

   2. _____

3. A cool swim in the lake offers a wonderful *respite* from the afternoon heat.
   a. contrast
   b. relief
   c. improvement
   d. surprise

   3. _____

4. There was *anarchy* in the classroom when the teacher suddenly left the room.
   a. confusion
   b. absolute quiet
   c. obedience
   d. unacceptable conduct

   4. _____

5. Young children often have no *conception* of what other people think.
   a. reason for thinking about something
   b. understanding
   c. appreciation for something
   d. experience

   5. _____

6. Yashar has read five or six adventure stories set in *medieval* times.
   a. referring to the Middle Ages
   b. far in the future
   c. happening at the same time
   d. unknown or mysterious

   6. _____

7. It is a serious matter when Congress decides to *impeach* a president.
   a. elect
   b. accuse of improper conduct
   c. dismiss
   d. install in office

   7. _____

8. The senator retired after twelve years in office and *subsequently* wrote a book about his experiences.
   a. later
   b. previously
   c. slowly
   d. never

   8. _____

9. Most of the country's citizens hated and feared their *authoritarian* leader.
   a. relating to literature
   b. too proud
   c. demanding obedience
   d. long-lasting

   9. _____

10. Roberto was surprised to receive a *belated* birthday gift in the mail.
    a. unidentified
    b. costly
    c. unexpected
    d. late

    10. _____

TEST: LESSONS 9 AND 10

(pages 53–58 and 61–66)

Part B Choosing the Best Word

On the answer line, write the letter of the word that best completes the sentence.

11. Let's take shelter in the barn for the _____ of the thunderstorm.
   a. conservatism   **b.** duration   **c.** delegate   **d.** respite
   11. _____

12. Many senior citizens support the more _____ candidate because she wants to improve health care for the elderly.
   a. medieval   **b.** belated   **c.** inaugural   **d.** liberal
   12. _____

13. No one dared to speak a word against the _____ until he was finally overthrown.
   a. tyrant   **b.** dominion   **c.** anarchy   **d.** impeachment
   13. _____

14. When I turn fourteen, Dad plans to _____ the job of cutting the grass to me.
   a. inaugurate   **b.** impeach   **c.** delegate   **d.** expire
   14. _____

15. A three-ring circus has three _____ acts.
   a. conservative   **b.** belated   **c.** simultaneous   **d.** incessant
   15. _____

16. The camp's _____ routine requires rising at dawn every morning for a half-mile swim in the lake.
   a. simultaneous   **b.** Spartan   **c.** anarchic   **d.** liberal
   16. _____

17. During the 1830s, the chieftain's _____ extended for hundreds of miles in every direction.
   a. conception   **b.** dominion   **c.** renaissance   **d.** duration
   17. _____

18. Mrs. Tate is so _____ that she never wears pants in public; she wears dresses even for gardening!
   a. conservative   **b.** Spartan   **c.** authoritarian   **d.** liberal
   18. _____

19. U.S. presidents are elected in November and _____ in January.
   a. impeached   **b.** delegated   **c.** inaugurated   **d.** tyrannized
   19. _____

20. Many large cathedrals, or churches, were built in Europe during the _____.
   a. anarchy   **b.** delegate   **c.** impeachment   **d.** Renaissance
   20. _____

BONUS: LESSONS 11 AND 12

(pages 67–78)

Use the following clues to identify the vocabulary words and write the words on the lines to the right. Then circle each vocabulary word in the word-search box below. The words may overlap and may read in any direction.

1. To criticize mildly is to _____. (8 letters)

2. To _____ something is to puzzle it or confuse it. (8 letters)

3. An error in math or estimation (14 letters)

4. To _____ something is to speak evil of it. (6 letters)

5. A difficult or an unpleasant situation (11 letters)

6. If something is _____, it is wrong or out of proper order. (5 letters)

7. A person who looks nervous and confused is probably _____. (9 letters)

8. To _____ is to criticize severely. (7 letters)

9. If something causes injury or damage, it is _____. (9 letters)

10. To make fun of something or to ridicule (5 letters)

11. Something that is wrong, mistaken, or false (9 letters)

12. If someone is in danger, he or she is _____. (9 letters)

1. **admonish**

2. **bewilder**

3. **miscalculation**

4. **malign**

5. **predicament**

6. **amiss**

7. **flustered**

8. **censure**

9. **injurious**

10. **scoff**

11. **erroneous**

12. **imperiled**

Challenge

Locate and circle the eight additional vocabulary words in the word-search box.

misinterpret
alienate
detriment
faux pas
subvert
blunder
incapacitate
fallible

O	E	N	Y	T	I	O	N	B	S	U	O	E	N	O	R	R	E	L
D	S	U	B	V	E	R	T	L	D	P	B	E	W	I	L	D	E	R
E	G	I	A	C	E	N	S	U	R	E	T	A	N	E	I	L	A	U
R	N	M	L	U	F	L	U	N	A	D	T	E	R	N	R	S	X	I
E	R	P	U	O	I	R	G	D	V	D	W	R	C	D	E	C	P	N
T	N	E	M	A	C	I	D	E	R	P	M	A	I	Y	D	O	A	J
S	D	R	E	T	L	M	E	R	N	F	P	O	F	M	N	S	S	U
U	C	I	H	A	F	S	S	I	M	A	G	H	N	A	E	U	B	R
L	A	L	M	I	S	C	A	L	C	U	L	A	T	I	O	N	E	I
F	N	E	C	T	A	E	D	I	N	X	A	F	N	O	S	D	T	O
T	F	D	A	U	P	S	T	E	T	P	I	F	D	M	L	H	E	U
E	L	B	I	L	L	A	F	M	T	A	B	O	A	I	Z	J	Q	S
M	F	F	O	S	T	U	O	I	R	S	L	C	B	L	U	S	T	G
I	S	I	T	E	R	P	R	E	T	N	I	S	I	M	K	A	L	I

BONUS: LESSONS 11 AND 12

(pages 67–78)

Use the following clues to identify the vocabulary words and write the words on the lines to the right. Then circle each vocabulary word in the word-search box below. The words may overlap and may read in any direction.

1. To criticize mildly is to _____. (8 letters)

2. To _____ something is to puzzle it or confuse it. (8 letters)

3. An error in math or estimation (14 letters)

4. To _____ something is to speak evil of it. (6 letters)

5. A difficult or an unpleasant situation (11 letters)

6. If something is _____, it is wrong or out of proper order. (5 letters)

7. A person who looks nervous and confused is probably _____. (9 letters)

8. To _____ is to criticize severely. (7 letters)

9. If something causes injury or damage, it is _____. (9 letters)

10. To make fun of something or to ridicule (5 letters)

11. Something that is wrong, mistaken, or false (9 letters)

12. If someone is in danger, he or she is _____. (9 letters)

1. _____

2. _____

3. _____

4. _____

5. _____

6. _____

7. _____

8. _____

9. _____

10. _____

11. _____

12. _____

Challenge

Locate and circle the eight additional vocabulary words in the word-search box.

misinterpret
alienate
detriment
faux pas
subvert
blunder
incapacitate
fallible

O	E	N	Y	T	I	O	N	B	S	U	O	E	N	O	R	R	E	L
D	S	U	B	V	E	R	T	L	D	P	B	E	W	I	L	D	E	R
E	G	I	A	C	E	N	S	U	R	E	T	A	N	E	I	L	A	U
R	N	M	L	U	F	L	U	N	A	D	T	E	R	N	R	S	X	I
E	R	P	U	O	I	R	G	D	V	D	W	R	C	D	E	C	P	N
T	N	E	M	A	C	I	D	E	R	P	M	A	I	Y	D	O	A	J
S	D	R	E	T	L	M	E	R	N	F	P	O	F	M	N	S	S	U
U	C	I	H	A	F	S	S	I	M	A	G	H	N	A	E	U	B	R
L	A	L	M	I	S	C	A	L	C	U	L	A	T	I	O	N	E	I
F	N	E	C	T	A	E	D	I	N	X	A	F	N	O	S	D	T	O
T	F	D	A	U	P	S	T	E	T	P	I	F	D	M	L	H	E	U
E	L	B	I	L	L	A	F	M	T	A	B	O	A	I	Z	J	Q	S
M	F	F	O	S	T	U	O	I	R	S	L	C	B	L	U	S	T	G
I	S	I	T	E	R	P	R	E	T	N	I	S	I	M	K	A	L	I

TEST: LESSONS 11 AND 12

(pages 67–78)

Part A Choosing the Best Definition

On the answer line, write the letter of the best definition of the italicized word.

1. Researchers found that watching too much TV can be *detrimental* to young children.
   a. exciting; stimulating   **c.** without any benefit
   b. causing harm   **d.** not recommended

   1. _____

2. Mr. Levy *admonished* James for failing to bring in his homework.
   a. warned harshly   **c.** criticized mildly
   b. misunderstood   **d.** spoke evil of

   2. _____

3. The scientists' *miscalculation* caused one of the rockets to misfire.
   a. study   **c.** bad judgment
   b. wrong idea   **d.** math error

   3. _____

4. Arnold proved that even he is *fallible,* when he answered a question incorrectly.
   a. able to be wrong   **c.** dishonest
   b. reasonable   **d.** able to be careless

   4. _____

5. Calling Felice by her twin brother's name was my worst *faux pas* ever!
   a. lapse of memory   **c.** social mistake
   b. nightmare   **d.** injury

   5. _____

6. I *scoffed* at my little brother when he told that crazy story, but it turned out to be true!
   a. criticized   **c.** refused to listen
   b. made fun of   **d.** believed the opposite

   6. _____

7. The mayor held a press conference to apologize for his *erroneous* statement.
   a. confusing   **c.** wrong
   b. ill-timed   **d.** negative

   7. _____

8. All those holiday desserts and candies *subverted* my vow to lose some weight this year.
   a. undermined   **c.** enhanced
   b. reinforced   **d.** rewarded

   8. _____

9. We giggled at the child's *bewilderment* when her brother seemed to disappear.
   a. fright   **c.** grin
   b. confusion   **d.** shriek

   9. _____

10. "You have *maligned* my daughter by accusing her of cheating," stated Mrs. Ross.
    a. angered   **c.** embarrassed
    b. insulted   **d.** slandered

    10. _____

TEST: LESSONS 11 AND 12

(pages 67–78)

Part B Choosing the Best Word

On the answer line, write the letter of the word that best completes the sentence.

11. Juan was _____ for several weeks while both of his legs were in casts.
    a. admonished   **b.** maligned   **c.** incapacitated   **d.** scoffed

11. _____

12. When she became lost in the woods, Tonya found a way out of her _____ by retracing her footprints.
    a. subversion   **b.** faux pas   **c.** predicament   **d.** censure

12. _____

13. I always feel _____ when I have to meet a lot of new people at once.
    a. detrimental   **b.** flustered   **c.** erroneous   **d.** injurious

13. _____

14. Last year, two congressmen were _____ for mishandling public funds.
    a. subverted   **b.** imperiled   **c.** bewildered   **d.** censured

14. _____

15. When the detective _____ an important clue, his error almost allowed the criminal to escape.
    a. alienated   **b.** imperiled   **c.** admonished   **d.** misinterpreted

15. _____

16. Lifting weights can be _____ to young people whose muscles have not developed fully.
    a. erroneous   **b.** amiss   **c.** injurious   **d.** fallible

16. _____

17. "Multiplying instead of dividing was a common _____ on problem number two," the math teacher told her class.
    a. bewilderment   **b.** blunder   **c.** censure   **d.** incapacitation

17. _____

18. Icy road conditions and blinding snow will _____ drivers until the storm ends around midnight.
    a. imperil   **b.** admonish   **c.** scoff   **d.** alienate

18. _____

19. Toby _____ most of the people at the meeting by making rude comments.
    a. subverted   **b.** incapacitated   **c.** alienated   **d.** imperiled

19. _____

20. When Ms. Lemon walked into her office, she knew right away that something was _____.
    a. flustered   **b.** amiss   **c.** detrimental   **d.** fallible

20. _____

NAME ______________________ DATE ______________________

BONUS: LESSONS 13 AND 14

(pages 81–92)

Use the clues to complete the crossword puzzle.

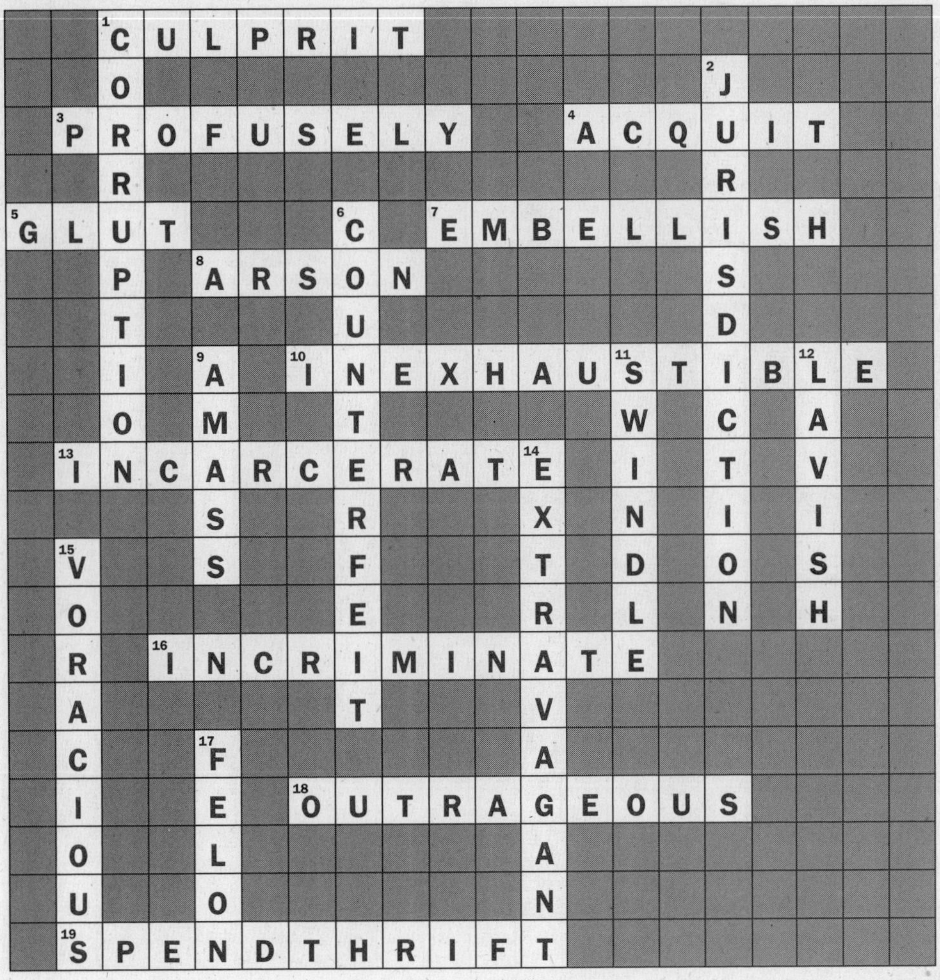

1 C U L P R I T
O 2 J
3 P R O F U S E L Y 4 A C Q U I T
R R
5 G L U T 6 C 7 E M B E L L I S H
P 8 A R S O N S
T U D
I 9 A 10 I N E X H A U 11 S T I B 12 L E
O M T W C A
13 I N C A R C E R A T 14 E I T V
S R X N I I
15 V S F T D O S
O E R L N H
R 16 I N C R I M I N A T E
A T V
C 17 F A
I E 18 O U T R A G E O U S
O L A
U O N
19 S P E N D T H R I F T

Across

1 A guilty person is a(n) ______.
3 Abundantly; generously
4 To declare not guilty
5 To eat beyond capacity
7 To add decorative details or ornaments
8 ______ is the crime of deliberately setting fire to something.
10 Something that is unlimited is ______.
13 To put in prison
16 To give evidence of guilt
18 Going beyond proper limits
19 A person who spends money wastefully

Down

1 Dishonesty or improper behavior in a person of authority
2 A(n) ______ is the extent of someone's authority.
6 Something that is ______ is made in fake imitation.
9 To gather or collect a large quantity is to ______.
11 To ______ someone is to cheat them out of money or property.
12 To ______ is to give in great abundance.
14 A person with expenses or efforts that are excessive is ______.
15 Extremely hungry for large amounts of food
17 A(n) ______ is a person who has committed a serious crime.

BONUS: LESSONS 13 AND 14

(pages 81–92)

Use the clues to complete the crossword puzzle.

Across

1 A guilty person is a(n) _____.

3 Abundantly; generously

4 To declare not guilty

5 To eat beyond capacity

7 To add decorative details or ornaments

8 _____ is the crime of deliberately setting fire to something.

10 Something that is unlimited is _____.

13 To put in prison

16 To give evidence of guilt

18 Going beyond proper limits

19 A person who spends money wastefully

Down

1 Dishonesty or improper behavior in a person of authority

2 A(n) _____ is the extent of someone's authority.

6 Something that is _____ is made in fake imitation.

9 To gather or collect a large quantity is to _____.

11 To _____ someone is to cheat them out of money or property.

12 To _____ is to give in great abundance.

14 A person with expenses or efforts that are excessive is _____.

15 Extremely hungry for large amounts of food

17 A(n) _____ is a person who has committed a serious crime.

TEST: LESSONS 13 AND 14

(pages 81–92)

Part A Choosing the Best Definition

On the answer line, write the letter of the best definition of the italicized word.

1. After his performance, Kevin's piano teacher praised him *profusely.*
   a. dishonestly
   b. hurriedly
   c. abundantly
   d. mildly

   1. _____

2. When Becky got home late, she made up an *outrageous* tale about a tornado.
   a. creative
   b. full of details
   c. quite funny
   d. beyond usual limits

   2. _____

3. "Okay, which one of you is the *culprit* who ate the cookies?" Aunt Ruth asked.
   a. trickster
   b. hungry person
   c. child
   d. guilty one

   3. _____

4. Clever thieves find many ways to *swindle* people.
   a. communicate with
   b. cheat
   c. make oneself useful
   d. locate

   4. _____

5. Jules knew the jacket was an *extravagance,* but he bought it anyway.
   a. something unlike all others
   b. poor decision
   c. excessive expense
   d. unpopular choice

   5. _____

6. Josh is a *voracious* reader of comic books.
   a. having a large appetite
   b. occasional
   c. unusually young
   d. secret

   6. _____

7. After a report on *corruption* in the police department, the chief of police resigned.
   a. dishonesty
   b. mistakes
   c. poor work
   d. criminals

   7. _____

8. Each year, the company treats all the employees to a *lavish* holiday party.
   a. fun-filled
   b. luxurious
   c. enjoyable
   d. loud and boisterous

   8. _____

9. The woman was *acquitted* after her husband confessed to committing the crime.
   a. sent to prison
   b. publicly humiliated
   c. left friendless
   d. declared not guilty

   9. _____

10. That five-year-old's energy seems to be *inexhaustible.*
    a. growing stronger
    b. fading quickly
    c. unlimited
    d. below average

    10. _____

TEST: LESSONS 13 AND 14

(pages 81–92)

Part B Choosing the Best Word

On the answer line, write the letter of the word that best completes the sentence.

11. After twenty-seven years, Grandpa had _____ a huge collection of license plates from all fifty states.   **11.** _____
    a. embellished   **b.** glutted   **c.** lavished   **d.** amassed

12. Randy _____ his sister when he told their parents what happened.   **12.** _____
    a. incarcerated   **b.** counterfeited   **c.** incriminated   **d.** swindled

13. The court's _____ includes all matters related to family conflicts and separation.   **13.** _____
    a. counterfeit   **b.** jurisdiction   **c.** acquittal   **d.** immoderation

14. During the movie, the girls _____ themselves on popcorn.   **14.** _____
    a. corrupted   **b.** glutted   **c.** embellished   **d.** acquitted

15. One of the sisters is a(n) _____, while the other has a bank account and saves every dime.   **15.** _____
    a. felony   **b.** luxury   **c.** incrimination   **d.** spendthrift

16. Tell me exactly what happened, and don't _____ the facts, please.   **16.** _____
    a. incriminate   **b.** acquit   **c.** embellish   **d.** swindle

17. Most people think _____ is a cruel and cowardly crime.   **17.** _____
    a. jurisdiction   **b.** arson   **c.** embellishment   **d.** luxury

18. The ten-dollar bill was so old and faded that it looked more _____ than real.   **18.** _____
    a. lavish   **b.** inexhaustible   **c.** voracious   **d.** counterfeit

19. If the man is found guilty, he will be _____ for a very long time.   **19.** _____
    a. incarcerated   **b.** corrupted   **c.** embellished   **d.** glutted

20. We all knew the accusations were false because Danny would never commit a _____.   **20.** _____
    a. felony   **b.** counterfeit   **c.** culprit   **d.** corruption

BONUS: LESSONS 15 AND 16

(pages 93–98 and 101–106)

Unscramble the letters of each italicized vocabulary word and write the word on the answer line to the right.

1. The entire platoon sadly attended the lieutenant's *ermintten*.
2. After the children *onceocdtc* the soup, they were hesitant to try it.
3. The camping site was so *ecuseldd* that they had trouble finding it.
4. The forward *eceteudx* the play perfectly and scored a goal.
5. The book was *anailualebv,* so he had to order it from another store.
6. The new *iradsinoatintm* was making many unexpected changes.
7. The spies *eidvsde* a plan to enter the building undetected.
8. Without her password, I couldn't *caescs* her computer.
9. While he was digging, Carlos *enethuard* an old clay pot.
10. Doctors Without Borders is an organization that *nerreds* medical services to people around the world.
11. William was puzzled by the *bcuoser* reference in the poem.
12. Devon thought the clip of the movie was *ntirngigui,* so she went to see it.
13. There was a small amount of soup left, and she tried to *paonortip* it fairly among the guests.
14. The forgotten *hceca* of candy attracted many ants.
15. We had to have a serviceperson come and *rvceataite* the cable after it stopped working.
16. Numerous customers complained about the telemarketers' *odgedg* efforts.
17. The birdwatcher searched all over the region for the *vueslie* bird.
18. The *evoeandr* to find gold in the stream didn't "pan out."
19. Though Kellyn thought her hat was *nocosuupisc,* no one seemed to notice it.
20. The team of *tromasnai* won an award for the cartoon movie.

1. **interment**
2. **concocted**
3. **secluded**
4. **executed**
5. **unavailable**
6. **administration**
7. **devised**
8. **access**
9. **unearthed**
10. **renders**
11. **obscure**
12. **intriguing**
13. **apportion**
14. **cache**
15. **reactivate**
16. **dogged**
17. **elusive**
18. **endeavor**
19. **conspicuous**
20. **animators**

BONUS: LESSONS 15 AND 16

(pages 93–98 and 101–106)

Unscramble the letters of each italicized vocabulary word and write the word on the answer line to the right.

1. The entire platoon sadly attended the lieutenant's *ermintten*.

 1. _____

2. After the children *onceocdtc* the soup, they were hesitant to try it.

 2. _____

3. The camping site was so *ecuseldd* that they had trouble finding it.

 3. _____

4. The forward *eceteudx* the play perfectly and scored a goal.

 4. _____

5. The book was *anailualebv,* so he had to order it from another store.

 5. _____

6. The new *iradsinoatintm* was making many unexpected changes.

 6. _____

7. The spies *eidvsde* a plan to enter the building undetected.

 7. _____

8. Without her password, I couldn't *caescs* her computer.

 8. _____

9. While he was digging, Carlos *enethuard* an old clay pot.

 9. _____

10. Doctors Without Borders is an organization that *nerreds* medical services to people around the world.

 10. _____

11. William was puzzled by the *bcuoser* reference in the poem.

 11. _____

12. Devon thought the clip of the movie was *ntirngigui,* so she went to see it.

 12. _____

13. There was a small amount of soup left, and she tried to *paonortip* it fairly among the guests.

 13. _____

14. The forgotten *hceca* of candy attracted many ants.

 14. _____

15. We had to have a serviceperson come and *rvceataite* the cable after it stopped working.

 15. _____

16. Numerous customers complained about the telemarketers' *odgedg* efforts.

 16. _____

17. The birdwatcher searched all over the region for the *vueslie* bird.

 17. _____

18. The *evoeandr* to find gold in the stream didn't "pan out."

 18. _____

19. Though Kellyn thought her hat was *nocosuupisc,* no one seemed to notice it.

 19. _____

20. The team of *tromasnai* won an award for the cartoon movie.

 20. _____

TEST: LESSONS 15 AND 16

(pages 93–98 and 101–106)

Part A Choosing the Best Definition

On the answer line, write the letter of the best definition of the italicized word.

1. Trying not to be *conspicuous,* I slipped quietly into my seat several minutes after the bell had rung.
   a. noticeable   **c.** clumsy
   b. noisy   **d.** rude

   1. _____

2. After the flood, food and supplies were *apportioned* to all the villages.
   a. put away   **c.** demonstrated
   b. allotted by plan   **d.** counted carefully

   2. _____

3. The principal will speak for the school *administration.*
   a. students   **c.** management
   b. parents   **d.** teachers

   3. _____

4. I helped set up our tent in a *secluded* campsite at the end of the trail.
   a. easy to find   **c.** beautiful
   b. popular   **d.** set apart

   4. _____

5. During the summer, Tara earned enough money to *reactivate* her membership at the gym.
   a. upgrade   **c.** pay for
   b. make active again   **d.** declare not active

   5. _____

6. The child's silly riddles *rendered* my friends hysterical with laughter.
   a. caused to become   **c.** mocked or made fun of
   b. disturbed   **d.** entertained

   6. _____

7. The students' *endeavor* to collect canned goods for the food bank has been enormously successful.
   a. contest   **c.** plot
   b. attempt   **d.** brief thought

   7. _____

8. Blue pens were *unavailable* at the corner store, so I bought some black ones.
   a. too expensive   **c.** not at hand
   b. plentiful   **d.** on sale

   8. _____

9. We were all *intrigued* by Mary's tales of foreign travel.
   a. astonished   **c.** embarrassed
   b. irritated   **d.** fascinated

   9. _____

10. We *concocted* a weird pizza topped with cheese, meatballs, and marshmallows.
    a. invented   **c.** imagined
    b. ordered   **d.** heated

    10. _____

TEST: LESSONS 15 AND 16

(pages 93–98 and 101–106)

Part B Choosing the Best Word

On the answer line, write the letter of the word that best completes the sentence.

11. Uncle Henry _____ a great camp stove from a large metal can.
    a. apportioned   **b.** rendered   **c.** intrigued   **d.** devised
    11. _____

12. Tina practiced over and over until she could _____ all three magic tricks perfectly.
    a. reactivate   **b.** access   **c.** execute   **d.** unearth
    12. _____

13. You can see from this film that the quality of computer _____ has greatly improved in the last few years.
    a. animation   **b.** endeavor   **c.** administration   **d.** obscurity
    13. _____

14. The body of an unknown soldier was _____ in the national cemetery.
    a. interred   **b.** administered   **c.** concocted   **d.** reactivated
    14. _____

15. Every afternoon, Max practiced shooting baskets with _____ determination.
    a. secluded   **b.** dogged   **c.** unavailable   **d.** elusive
    15. _____

16. You'll need your account number and some identification to _____ your bank records.
    a. inter   **b.** devise   **c.** access   **d.** endeavor
    16. _____

17. Mr. Kane keeps a(n) _____ of mints in the top desk drawer.
    a. execution   **b.** intrigue   **c.** cache   **d.** animation
    17. _____

18. Sal tried to remember her dream, but the longer she was awake, the more _____ it became.
    a. secluded   **b.** dogged   **c.** conspicuous   **d.** elusive
    18. _____

19. Do you know the story about the farmer who _____ a magic kettle as he was plowing his field one day?
    a. executed   **b.** unearthed   **c.** accessed   **d.** apportioned
    19. _____

20. The retired actor was famous in her youth, but now she lives in complete _____.
    a. obscurity   **b.** access   **c.** doggedness   **d.** intrigue
    20. _____

BONUS: LESSONS 17 AND 18

(pages 107–118)

Use the clues to spell out the vocabulary words on the answer blanks. Then identify the mystery person at the bottom of the page by writing the numbered letters on the lines with the corresponding numbers.

1. To intrude upon is to _____ .

2. To give concrete form to an idea

3. To enter into or go through something

4. Energetic; vigorous; quick moving

5. To _____ is to draw or trace an outline.

6. To swell or expand from internal pressure is to _____ .

7. Something that is _____ is calm, peaceful, and quiet.

8. Totally confused and lacking order

9. Still; without motion

10. Something that is in _____ is close or near.

11. Uneasy; impatient under restriction

12. The _____ of something are its boundaries or limits.

13. Boring repetition or sameness

14. _____ is swiftness or speedy motion.

1. i m p i n g e
   (8 under i)

2. e m b o d y
   (6 under b)

3. p e n e t r a t e
   (4 under e)

4. d y n a m i c
   (5 under m)

5. d e l i n e a t e
   (10 under i)

6. d i s t e n d
   (14 under t)

7. t r a n q u i l
   (13 under u)

8. c h a o t i c
   (1 under c)

9. s t a t i c
   (3 under c)

10. p r o x i m i t y
    (2 under x)

11. r e s t i v e
    (7 under r)

12. c o n f i n e s
    (12 under s)

13. m o n o t o n y
    (9 under o)

14. v e l o c i t y
    (11 under v)

C H R I S T O P H E R
3 1 7 8 12 14 9 4 1 11 7

C O L U M B U S ,
3 9 10 13 5 6 13 12

E X P L O R E R
11 2 4 10 9 7 11 7

BONUS: LESSONS 17 AND 18

(pages 107–118)

Use the clues to spell out the vocabulary words on the answer blanks. Then identify the mystery person at the bottom of the page by writing the numbered letters on the lines with the corresponding numbers.

1. To intrude upon is to _____ .

1. __ __ __ __ __ __
             8

2. To give concrete form to an idea

2. __ __ __ __ __
           6

3. To enter into or go through something

3. __ __ __ __ __ __ __ __
      4

4. Energetic; vigorous; quick moving

4. __ __ __ __ __ __ __
                  5

5. To _____ is to draw or trace an outline.

5. __ __ __ __ __ __
           10

6. To swell or expand from internal pressure is to _____ .

6. __ __ __ __ __ __
              14

7. Something that is _____ is calm, peaceful, and quiet.

7. __ __ __ __ __ __ __
                 13

8. Totally confused and lacking order

8. __ __ __ __
      1

9. Still; without motion

9. __ __ __ __ __ __
                 3

10. Something that is in _____ is close or near.

10. __ __ __ __ __ __ __
              2

11. Uneasy; impatient under restriction

11. __ __ __ __ __
     7

12. The _____ of something are its boundaries or limits.

12. __ __ __ __ __ __ __
                    12

13. Boring repetition or sameness

13. __ __ __ __ __ __ __
                 9

14. _____ is swiftness or speedy motion.

14. __ __ __ __ __ __
     11

__ __ __ __ __ __ __ __ __ __ __
3   1   7   8   12 14 9   4   1   11 7

__ __ __ __ __ __ __ __ ,
3   9   10 13 5   6   13 12

__ __ __ __ __ __ __ __
11 2   4   10 9   7   11 7

TEST: LESSONS 17 AND 18

(pages 107–118)

Part A Choosing the Best Definition

On the answer line, write the letter of the best definition of the italicized word.

1. The plastic bag *distended* from the weight of its mysterious contents.   1. _____
   a. tore   c. rested
   b. expanded   d. dropped

2. When the game ended, fans rushed onto the field in a *chaotic* but joyful mob.   2. _____
   a. loud   c. confused and disorderly
   b. shocked   d. well-disciplined

3. On our weekend camping trip, I tried to ignore the *omnipresent* mosquitoes,   3. _____
   but it wasn't easy!
   a. biting   c. annoying
   b. unusually large   d. existing everywhere

4. We hiked all afternoon, enjoying the beauty and *tranquility* of the forest.   4. _____
   a. privacy and secrecy   c. majesty and grandeur
   b. peace and quiet   d. charm and attraction

5. How do scientists calculate the *velocity* of a rocket traveling in space?   5. _____
   a. speed   c. mileage
   b. direction   d. location

6. "We can't let *complacency* ruin our competitive edge," the coach told her team.   6. _____
   a. nervousness   c. defeat or loss
   b. self-satisfaction   d. petty arguments

7. The melting pot is a symbol that *embodies* our country's multicultural heritage.   7. _____
   a. contradicts or opposes   c. brings about or causes
   b. gives concrete form to   d. serves as a reminder

8. Most three-year-old children quickly become *restive* during a restaurant meal.   8. _____
   a. impatient   c. hungry
   b. overtired   d. annoying

9. "Stay within the *confines* of the schoolyard" was the rule during recess.   9. _____
   a. sight   c. boundaries
   b. activities   d. equipment

10. Our *dynamic* new counselor soon had everyone involved in an active game.   10. _____
    a. young   c. reckless
    b. dependable   d. energetic

TEST: LESSONS 17 AND 18

(pages 107–118)

Part B Choosing the Best Word

On the answer line, write the letter of the word that best completes the sentence.

11. The boys originally met because of the _____ of their houses, but they became friends because of shared interests.
    a. velocity   b. demarcation   c. proximity   d. tranquility

11. _____

12. Joe tried to hammer in the nail, but it would not _____ the thick steel door.
    a. impinge   b. gerrymander   c. delineate   d. penetrate

12. _____

13. Nothing moved on that hot, humid afternoon; even the flag remained _____ .
    a. static   b. dynamic   c. restive   d. omnipresent

13. _____

14. After four straight days of rain, Dad took us all to a movie to break the _____ .
    a. demarcation   b. complacency   c. monotony   d. boisterousness

14. _____

15. Some people think that the governor _____ the new voting districts in this county for his own benefit.
    a. distended   b. gerrymandered   c. confined   d. embodied

15. _____

16. That racket coming from Lucy's trombone is _____ on my ability to concentrate.
    a. impinging   b. tranquilizing   c. distending   d. delineating

16. _____

17. The equator is the line of _____ between the Northern and Southern Hemispheres.
    a. demarcation   b. velocity   c. tranquility   d. monotony

17. _____

18. For three decades, our congressman was a _____ supporter of civil rights.
    a. chaotic   b. tranquil   c. static   d. steadfast

18. _____

19. Will and John put tape across their bedroom floor to _____ separate areas for each of them.
    a. gerrymander   b. distend   c. delineate   d. penetrate

19. _____

20. Uncle Frank claimed he was getting a headache from the children's _____ .
    a. velocity   b. boisterousness   c. confines   d. complacency

20. _____

BONUS: LESSONS 19 AND 20

(pages 121–132)

Use the following clues to identify the vocabulary words and write the words on the lines to the right. Then circle each vocabulary word in the word-search box below. The words may overlap and may read in any direction.

1. A(n) _____ person is healthy, strong, and vigorous. (6 letters)

2. Something that lacks importance is _____ . (15 letters)

3. A sudden takeover that overthrows the existing power (4 letters)

4. A(n) _____ supporter is firm, steadfast, and loyal. (7 letters)

5. Clearly; unquestionably; without a doubt (11 letters)

6. To survive without damage is to _____ . (9 letters)

7. High status (8 letters)

8. To set up a barrier that prevents exit or entrance (8 letters)

9. Someone who thinks about things of little importance is _____ . (5 letters)

10. Something _____ is near the surface. (11 letters)

11. The most important thing is _____ . (9 letters)

12. Not easily changed; relatively permanent (6 letters)

1. robust
2. inconsequential
3. coup
4. staunch
5. indubitably
6. withstand
7. prestige
8. blockade
9. petty
10. superficial
11. paramount
12. stable

Challenge

Locate and circle the eight additional vocabulary words in the word-search box.

eminence
indestructible
martial
momentous
omnipotent
vulnerability
indispensable
noteworthy

```
W  L A I C I F R E P U S  I  U K I N P  I
T  I  S T A U N C H  A X N N M A T R S  N
N  M  T Y B Z G O P B D I D O S E D T A  D
U  O  E R H S D B W I L J U U S M N A D  E
O  M  D E W T F Y S C H R B T Y O A D S  S
M  E  A E Q A R P V E O O I M U S T L T  T
A  N  K S U J E O B C R G T R T M S N R  R
R  T  C M T N K E W N E Z A A V L H U U  U
A  O  O O S V U L N E R A B I L I T Y  C
P  U  L A U I B R E N T L L R P U I O  T
G  S  B L B P A D N I E O Y F E S W M I  I
I  L  T L A I T R A M V Y N T T C P R B
E  P  O I N C O N S E Q U E N T I A L L
W  T R Y T N E T O P I N M O Y X B N E
```

BONUS: LESSONS 19 AND 20

(pages 121–132)

Use the following clues to identify the vocabulary words and write the words on the lines to the right. Then circle each vocabulary word in the word-search box below. The words may overlap and may read in any direction.

1. A(n) _____ person is healthy, strong, and vigorous. (6 letters)

2. Something that lacks importance is _____ . (15 letters)

3. A sudden takeover that overthrows the existing power (4 letters)

4. A(n) _____ supporter is firm, steadfast, and loyal. (7 letters)

5. Clearly; unquestionably; without a doubt (11 letters)

6. To survive without damage is to _____ . (9 letters)

7. High status (8 letters)

8. To set up a barrier that prevents exit or entrance (8 letters)

9. Someone who thinks about things of little importance is _____ . (5 letters)

10. Something _____ is near the surface. (11 letters)

11. The most important thing is _____ . (9 letters)

12. Not easily changed; relatively permanent (6 letters)

1. _____

2. _____

3. _____

4. _____

5. _____

6. _____

7. _____

8. _____

9. _____

10. _____

11. _____

12. _____

Challenge

Locate and circle the eight additional vocabulary words in the word-search box.

eminence
indestructible
martial
momentous
omnipotent
vulnerability
indispensable
noteworthy

W	L	A	I	C	I	F	R	E	P	U	S	I	U	K	I	N	P	I
T	I	S	T	A	U	N	C	H	A	X	N	N	M	A	T	R	S	N
N	M	T	Y	B	Z	G	O	P	B	D	I	D	O	S	E	D	T	D
U	O	E	R	H	S	D	B	W	I	L	J	U	U	S	M	N	A	E
O	M	D	E	W	T	F	Y	S	C	H	R	B	T	Y	O	A	D	S
M	E	A	E	Q	A	R	P	V	E	O	O	I	M	U	S	T	L	T
A	N	K	S	U	J	E	O	B	C	R	G	T	R	T	M	S	N	R
R	T	C	M	T	N	K	E	W	N	E	Z	A	A	V	L	H	U	U
A	O	O	O	S	V	U	L	N	E	R	A	B	I	L	I	T	Y	C
P	U	L	A	U	I	B	R	E	N	T	L	L	R	P	U	I	O	T
G	S	B	L	B	P	A	D	N	I	E	O	Y	F	E	S	W	M	I
I	L	T	L	A	I	T	R	A	M	V	Y	N	T	T	C	P	R	B
E	P	O	I	N	C	O	N	S	E	Q	U	E	N	T	I	A	L	L
W	T	R	Y	T	N	E	T	O	P	I	N	M	O	Y	X	B	N	E

TEST: LESSONS 19 AND 20

(pages 121–132)

Part A Choosing the Best Definition

On the answer line, write the letter of the best definition of the italicized word.

1. That was *indubitably* the best movie I have ever seen.   1. _____
   a. unfortunately   c. probably
   b. unfairly   d. without doubt

2. Mr. Lupine could not *withstand* the temptation to eat a big piece of apple pie.   2. _____
   a. understand or explain   c. resist successfully
   b. agree to   d. share

3. Without a *stable* income, it's difficult to plan or follow a budget.   3. _____
   a. large enough; adequate   c. above average
   b. growing   d. relatively permanent

4. In Egypt, the pharaoh was an *omnipotent* ruler with thousands of slaves at   4. _____
   his command.
   a. fortunate   c. all-powerful
   b. cruel   d. selfish

5. This extra large pan is *indispensable* for roasting the turkey on Thanksgiving Day.   5. _____
   a. workable   c. useful
   b. essential   d. not needed

6. Deciding to go to college was a *momentous* decision for Harry.   6. _____
   a. very important   c. well-intentioned
   b. quickly made   d. hopeful

7. Because of the professor's *eminence*, hundreds of people came to hear his lectures.   7. _____
   a. books and writing   c. fame and distinction
   b. great wealth   d. research

8. The nurse put a bandage on the *superficial* wound and said, "You'll be just fine!"   8. _____
   a. caused by an accident   c. relating to the face
   b. painful   d. near the surface

9. Mrs. Stewart chose the family-room rug for its *indestructibility*.   9. _____
   a. inability to be destroyed   c. fashionable style
   b. attractiveness   d. fair price

10. Mike and Tim showed their *pettiness* when they divided the dirty dishes into equal   10. _____
    piles before washing them.
    a. bad manners   c. cleverness
    b. concern with unimportant things   d. concern with order and organization

TEST: LESSONS 19 AND 20

(pages 121–132)

Part B Choosing the Best Word

On the answer line, write the letter of the word that best completes the sentence.

11. To break the ice, Keri made a silly and _____ comment about the weather.
    a. momentous   **b.** inconsequential   **c.** noteworthy   **d.** indispensable
11. _____

12. The chief surgeon held a position of great _____ in the county hospital.
    a. prestige   **b.** indestructibility   **c.** coup   **d.** blockade
12. _____

13. Karate is just one of many types of _____ arts.
    a. staunch   **b.** robust   **c.** martial   **d.** stable
13. _____

14. During the war, a _____ along the coast caused shortages of raw materials and textiles.
    a. prestige   **b.** vulnerability   **c.** pettiness   **d.** blockade
14. _____

15. Getting plenty of rest on the night before a test is of _____ importance.
    a. indestructible   **b.** paramount   **c.** inconsequential   **d.** superficial
15. _____

16. Many parents are concerned about their children's _____ to television advertising.
    a. vulnerability   **b.** eminence   **c.** indestructibility   **d.** pettiness
16. _____

17. My grandfather, a _____ seventy-year-old, plays tennis regularly, three times a week.
    a. martial   **b.** paramount   **c.** robust   **d.** chaotic
17. _____

18. The rebels' successful _____ toppled the government and allowed them to install a new leader.
    a. pettiness   **b.** coup   **c.** eminence   **d.** prestige
18. _____

19. The former congresswoman was a human rights activist and a _____ feminist.
    a. staunch   **b.** momentous   **c.** complacent   **d.** paramount
19. _____

20. In his _____ study, Professor Ames showed that students who watch a lot of television have lower grades than students who don't.
    a. stable   **b.** omnipotent   **c.** robust   **d.** noteworthy
20. _____

BONUS: LESSONS 21 AND 22

(pages 133–138 and 141–146)

Use the clues to complete the crossword puzzle.

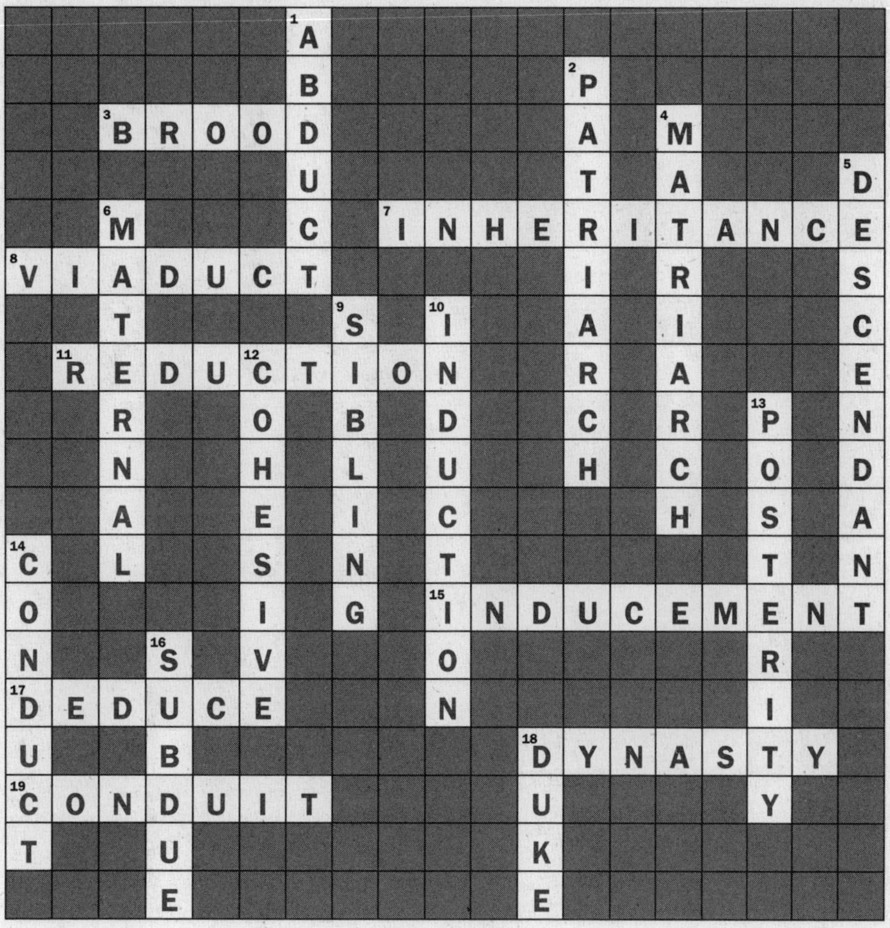

The crossword grid contains the following filled-in answers:

- 1 Down: ABDUCT
- 2 Down: PATRIARCH
- 3 Across: BROOD
- 4 Down: MA (MATRON)
- 5 Down: DESCENDANT
- 6 Down: MATERNAL
- 7 Across: INHERITANCE
- 8 Across: VIADUCT
- 9 Down: SIBLING
- 10 Down: INDUCTION
- 11 Across: REDUCTION
- 12 Down: COHESIVE
- 13 Down: POSTERITY
- 14 Down: CONDUCT
- 15 Across: INDUCEMENT
- 16 Down: SUBDUE
- 17 Across: DEDUCE
- 18 Across: DYNASTY
- 19 Across: CONDUIT

Across

3 To worry; to think negatively

7 Property or money willed to a person is a(n) _____.

8 A structure of spans and arches carrying a road or railroad

11 The amount something is lessened is a(n) _____.

15 A(n) _____ is an incentive.

17 To reach a conclusion through logical reasoning

18 A series of rulers in the same family is a(n) _____.

19 A(n) _____ is a pipe or channel for transporting fluids.

Down

1 To _____ is to kidnap.

2 A(n) _____ is a man who is the head of a family or group.

4 A highly respected older woman is a(n) _____.

5 A(n) _____ is an individual who can be traced back to one ancestor.

6 Referring to a mother or motherhood

9 A brother or sister

10 Placement or entry into a club or an office

12 Things that stick together are _____.

13 Future generations

14 The way a person acts is his or her _____.

16 To _____ is to conquer or bring under control.

18 A nobleman of the highest rank besides prince or king is a(n) _____.

BONUS: LESSONS 21 AND 22

(pages 133–138 and 141–146)

Use the clues to complete the crossword puzzle.

Across

3 To worry; to think negatively

7 Property or money willed to a person is a(n) _____.

8 A structure of spans and arches carrying a road or railroad

11 The amount something is lessened is a(n) _____.

15 A(n) _____ is an incentive.

17 To reach a conclusion through logical reasoning

18 A series of rulers in the same family is a(n) _____.

19 A(n) _____ is a pipe or channel for transporting fluids.

Down

1 To _____ is to kidnap.

2 A(n) _____ is a man who is the head of a family or group.

4 A highly respected older woman is a(n) _____.

5 A(n) _____ is an individual who can be traced back to one ancestor.

6 Referring to a mother or motherhood

9 A brother or sister

10 Placement or entry into a club or an office

12 Things that stick together are _____.

13 Future generations

14 The way a person acts is his or her _____.

16 To _____ is to conquer or bring under control.

18 A nobleman of the highest rank besides prince or king is a(n) _____.

TEST: LESSONS 21 AND 22

(pages 133–138 and 141–146)

Part A Choosing the Best Definition

On the answer line, write the letter of the best definition of the italicized word.

1. The lioness protected her young with a fierce *maternal* instinct.
   - a. motherly
   - b. untamed
   - c. forceful
   - d. shallow

   1. _____

2. Colombian rebels *abducted* an American businessman in Bogota last year.
   - a. cheated
   - b. kidnapped
   - c. assisted
   - d. wounded

   2. _____

3. Their beautiful family mansion was turned into a public museum for *posterity*.
   - a. special guests
   - b. royalty
   - c. future generations
   - d. members

   3. _____

4. The members of the hockey team had formed a *cohesive* group by the end of the season.
   - a. brotherly
   - b. fun-loving
   - c. popular
   - d. sticking together

   4. _____

5. Mom saw the crumbs on the table and *deduced* that the children had been snacking.
   - a. complained
   - b. worried
   - c. concluded
   - d. doubted

   5. _____

6. At the yearly reunion, both the young and the old paid their respects to the family *matriarch*.
   - a. female head of a family
   - b. breadwinner
   - c. newest member
   - d. godfather

   6. _____

7. My friend Elaine tells wonderful stories of growing up in a house with seven *siblings*.
   - a. business partners
   - b. parents
   - c. sisters or brothers
   - d. pets

   7. _____

8. The offer of a ride to the mall was all the *inducement* Kara needed to finish her chores.
   - a. warning
   - b. excuse
   - c. thanks
   - d. persuasion

   8. _____

9. It took a long time for the man to *subdue* his guard dogs.
   - a. catch up to
   - b. bring under control
   - c. put on a leash
   - d. make apologies for

   9. _____

10. Hiring extra teachers resulted in a *reduction* in the size of many classes.
    - a. making less good
    - b. slight change
    - c. making smaller
    - d. increase

    10. _____

TEST: LESSONS 21 AND 22

(pages 133–138 and 141–146)

Part B Choosing the Best Word

On the answer line, write the letter of the word that best completes the sentence.

11. Many proud parents attended the ———— ceremony of the school's Honor Society.
  a. abduction   **b.** induction   **c.** viaduct   **d.** reduction

  11. _____

12. Tracy ———— the visitors to the principal's office.
  a. abducted   **b.** descended   **c.** subdued   **d.** conducted

  12. _____

13. The young couple received a small ————, which they put aside to buy a house someday.
  a. duchy   **b.** brood   **c.** inheritance   **d.** conduit

  13. _____

14. With his family gathered around him, the ———— began to speak.
  a. posterity   **b.** matriarch   **c.** conduct   **d.** patriarch

  14. _____

15. Members of the T'ang ———— ruled ancient China from 618 to 907.
  a. dynasty   **b.** induction   **c.** sibling   **d.** deduction

  15. _____

16. Darryl tended to ———— for hours whenever the team lost a game.
  a. deduce   **b.** brood   **c.** conduct   **d.** subdue

  16. _____

17. The bicyclists rode under the ———— on their way to the last leg of the race.
  a. viaduct   **b.** inducement   **c.** brood   **d.** descendant

  17. _____

18. An underground ———— carries the oil to a processing plant hundreds of miles away.
  a. cohesion   **b.** dynasty   **c.** descent   **d.** conduit

  18. _____

19. Mr. Lattimer hoped his ———— would love and care for the farm he had spent a lifetime building.
  a. descendants   **b.** induction   **c.** inheritance   **d.** conduct

  19. _____

20. The soldiers were loyal to the ————, who rewarded them handsomely.
  a. viaduct   **b.** posterity   **c.** duke   **d.** reduction

  20. _____

BONUS: LESSONS 23 AND 24

(pages 147–158)

Use the following clues to identify the vocabulary words and write the words on the lines to the right. Then circle each vocabulary word in the word-search box below. The words may overlap and may read in any direction.

1. A strong urge or drive (7 letters)
2. To ——— is to officially cancel. (6 letters)
3. When something ———, it becomes worse. (11 letters)
4. To urge to action is to ———. (5 letters)
5. To bring into existence (8 letters)
6. The beginning of something is its ———. (7 letters)
7. Having the power to attract or arouse interest (9 letters)
8. To hit repeatedly is to ———. (4 letters)
9. Something ——— is general and not specific. (7 letters)
10. A family tree is a(n) ———. (9 letters)
11. To replace by growing new tissue (10 letters)
12. To cause feelings of disgust or disapproval (7 letters)

1. impulse
2. repeal
3. degenerates
4. impel
5. engender
6. genesis
7. appealing
8. pelt
9. generic
10. genealogy
11. regenerate
12. repulse

Challenge
Locate and circle the five additional vocabulary words in the word-search box.

pulsate
progeny
compel
gentry
propulsion

```
A D U W G E H E G K E R A T I E M P E
P R S J F H N A F P J B S D F M A I T
E Y U D E G E N E R A T E S G G P C A
L R Y K E A G L R O I L A E P E R E S
B T A N H X L N T P B M O Z M N R P L
E N D Z Y U Y E I U R S N C T E G P U
C E C D P V A T E L I O H D G A O E P
R G O E R H G D I S A R G E S L Y N E
W I M P U L S E E I G E N E K O H E A
O X P L Q P F N W O P E P L N G I G N
D C E Y K I E E P N R F G P J Y B O F
R E L R T G S L Q A N E H V A W A F P
E N C E B W K P T T R E P U L S E G S
C I R E N E G E A M P O I K A D T H J
```

BONUS: LESSONS 23 AND 24

(pages 147–158)

Use the following clues to identify the vocabulary words and write the words on the lines to the right. Then circle each vocabulary word in the word-search box below. The words may overlap and may read in any direction.

1. A strong urge or drive (7 letters)

2. To _____ is to officially cancel. (6 letters)

3. When something _____, it becomes worse. (11 letters)

4. To urge to action is to _____. (5 letters)

5. To bring into existence (8 letters)

6. The beginning of something is its _____. (7 letters)

7. Having the power to attract or arouse interest (9 letters)

8. To hit repeatedly is to _____. (4 letters)

9. Something _____ is general and not specific. (7 letters)

10. A family tree is a(n) _____. (9 letters)

11. To replace by growing new tissue (10 letters)

12. To cause feelings of disgust or disapproval (7 letters)

1. _____

2. _____

3. _____

4. _____

5. _____

6. _____

7. _____

8. _____

9. _____

10. _____

11. _____

12. _____

Challenge

Locate and circle the five additional vocabulary words in the word-search box.

pulsate
progeny
compel
gentry
propulsion

A	D	U	W	G	E	H	E	G	K	E	R	A	T	I	E	M	P	E
P	R	S	J	F	H	N	A	F	P	J	B	S	D	F	M	A	I	T
E	Y	U	D	E	G	E	N	E	R	A	T	E	S	G	G	P	C	A
L	R	Y	K	E	A	G	L	R	O	I	L	A	E	P	E	R	E	S
B	T	A	N	H	X	L	N	T	P	B	M	O	Z	M	N	R	P	L
E	N	D	Z	Y	U	Y	E	I	U	R	S	N	C	T	E	G	P	U
C	E	C	D	P	V	A	T	E	L	I	O	H	D	G	A	O	E	P
R	G	O	E	R	H	G	D	I	S	A	R	G	E	S	L	Y	N	E
W	I	M	P	U	L	S	E	E	I	G	E	N	E	K	O	H	E	A
O	X	P	L	Q	P	F	N	W	O	P	E	P	L	N	G	I	G	N
D	C	E	Y	K	I	E	E	P	N	R	F	G	P	J	Y	B	O	F
R	E	L	R	T	G	S	L	Q	A	N	E	H	V	A	W	A	F	P
E	N	C	E	B	W	K	P	T	T	R	E	P	U	L	S	E	G	S
C	I	R	E	N	E	G	E	A	M	P	O	I	K	A	D	T	H	J

TEST: LESSONS 23 AND 24

(pages 147–158)

Part A Choosing the Best Definition

On the answer line, write the letter of the best definition of the italicized word.

1. When he could not find the key to his bike lock, Anthony was *compelled* to leave his bike in the bike rack and walk home.
   - **a.** upset
   - **b.** relieved
   - **c.** forced
   - **d.** allowed

   1. _____

2. Road conditions will continue to *degenerate* until funding for repairs becomes available.
   - **a.** stay exactly the same
   - **b.** become worse
   - **c.** improve a bit at a time
   - **d.** be energized

   2. _____

3. Mrs. Taylor wanted to learn about African violets, but the information in her gardening book was too *generic*.
   - **a.** advanced
   - **b.** not specific
   - **c.** old-fashioned
   - **d.** brief

   3. _____

4. All of the former president's *progeny* attended a memorial program at the presidential library.
   - **a.** colleagues
   - **b.** staff
   - **c.** children
   - **d.** supporters

   4. _____

5. Working in his basement one evening, Mr. Morris had the *genesis* of an idea, which he later developed into a successful invention.
   - **a.** conclusion
   - **b.** outgrowth
   - **c.** explanation
   - **d.** beginning

   5. _____

6. His three hungry children and a lack of money *impelled* the man to find a second job.
   - **a.** begged
   - **b.** motivated
   - **c.** committed
   - **d.** invited

   6. _____

7. In the past, fox hunting was a popular pastime among the English *gentry*.
   - **a.** peasants
   - **b.** people who came before
   - **c.** citizens
   - **d.** high social class

   7. _____

8. We had a hard time choosing from the many *appealing* items on the menu.
   - **a.** ordinary
   - **b.** inexpensive
   - **c.** attractive
   - **d.** competing

   8. _____

9. As the crowd became quiet, Mona had a sudden *impulse* to giggle.
   - **a.** wish
   - **b.** weird dream
   - **c.** strong urge
   - **d.** opportunity

   9. _____

10. The school committee considered *repealing* the outdated dress code.
    - **a.** canceling
    - **b.** modifying
    - **c.** starting up
    - **d.** reviewing

    10. _____

TEST: LESSONS 23 AND 24

(pages 147–158)

Part B Choosing the Best Word

On the answer line, write the letter of the word that best completes the sentence.

11. At the dinner table, Miss Scarlett was _____ by the manners of the other guests.
    a. pelted   **b.** repulsed   **c.** appealed   **d.** regenerated

11. _____

12. I thought the darkened room was empty until I heard a loud _____ of laughter.
    a. peal   **b.** progeny   **c.** impulse   **d.** propulsion

12. _____

13. In humans, a broken bone can mend, but a lost limb cannot _____.
    a. degenerate   **b.** repulse   **c.** regenerate   **d.** pulsate

13. _____

14. Each _____ is well represented on the student council.
    a. gentry   **b.** pulse   **c.** genesis   **d.** gender

14. _____

15. Flashing lights _____ on stage, the crowd quieted down, and at last, the band began to play.
    a. pulsated   **b.** repealed   **c.** pealed   **d.** impelled

15. _____

16. Mark sat in the rear and worked the pedals to provide _____ for our paddleboat.
    a. compulsion   **b.** progeny   **c.** propulsion   **d.** impulse

16. _____

17. Those kids _____ me with snowballs, and now I am soaking wet!
    a. pealed   **b.** impelled   **c.** pelted   **d.** engendered

17. _____

18. Doctors do not know the cause of the newborn's _____ heart defect.
    a. congenital   **b.** generic   **c.** degenerate   **d.** appealing

18. _____

19. The public library offers a class to help people who are interested in researching their _____.
    a. peal   **b.** genealogy   **c.** gentry   **d.** propulsion

19. _____

20. Dad's handling of the motorboat did not _____ confidence among the passengers.
    a. pulsate   **b.** degenerate   **c.** repeal   **d.** engender

20. _____

BONUS: LESSONS 25 AND 26

(pages 161–172)

Unscramble the letters of each italicized vocabulary word and write the word on the answer line to the right.

1. The *truperu* in the dam caused a countywide evacuation.

2. William was constantly *srtiiupndg* the class with his jokes.

3. Melanie left her *rbptaole* CD player on the bus.

4. I *ecortmpod* myself differently at the dance than I did at the sports game.

5. *sgmferant* of the ripped paper flew in all directions when the wind blew.

6. When the children found an old ball, they *iedpsrtod* themselves by playing a game of kickball.

7. Shelby is very proud of her extensive writing *polioortf*.

8. After the football team *ouetrd* its rivals, there was a huge celebration.

9. The *arictufos* dog barked through the entire movie, making it impossible to hear anything.

10. The store was well known for carrying hard-to-find *xopesrt* from Africa.

11. The prism *rcteaefrd* rainbows of light around the room.

12. The inspector carefully examined the *empirtod* goods on the ship.

13. Karen's *ctifrinaon* of school rules resulted in three days of detention.

14. After a trial proved him guilty, the international thief was *erdteodp* to his homeland.

15. Calvin found the cold weather *pinlepsuabort* and moved further south.

16. The *pbartu* ending to the play left the audience confused.

17. The clerk's *rtndoepmet* earned him an early promotion.

18. The boats made easy *orgpeta* when we got out of the river to avoid the rapids.

19. The *rftoracrey* cat simply wouldn't obey its owner's commands.

20. The previously silent classroom *ruteped* with motion when the bell rang.

1. rupture
2. disrupting
3. portable
4. comported
5. Fragments
6. disported
7. portfolio
8. routed
9. fractious
10. exports
11. refracted
12. imported
13. infraction
14. deported
15. insupportable
16. abrupt
17. deportment
18. portage
19. refractory
20. erupted

BONUS: LESSONS 25 AND 26

(pages 161–172)

Unscramble the letters of each italicized vocabulary word and write the word on the answer line to the right.

1. The *truperu* in the dam caused a countywide evacuation. 1. _____

2. William was constantly *srtiiupndg* the class with his jokes. 2. _____

3. Melanie left her *rbptaole* CD player on the bus. 3. _____

4. I *ecortmpod* myself differently at the dance than I did at the sports game. 4. _____

5. *sgmferant* of the ripped paper flew in all directions when the wind blew. 5. _____

6. When the children found an old ball, they *iedpsrtod* themselves by playing a game of kickball. 6. _____

7. Shelby is very proud of her extensive writing *polioortf*. 7. _____

8. After the football team *ouetrd* its rivals, there was a huge celebration. 8. _____

9. The *arictufos* dog barked through the entire movie, making it impossible to hear anything. 9. _____

10. The store was well known for carrying hard-to-find *xopesrt* from Africa. 10. _____

11. The prism *rcteaefrd* rainbows of light around the room. 11. _____

12. The inspector carefully examined the *empirtod* goods on the ship. 12. _____

13. Karen's *ctifrinaon* of school rules resulted in three days of detention. 13. _____

14. After a trial proved him guilty, the international thief was *erdteodp* to his homeland. 14. _____

15. Calvin found the cold weather *pinlepsuabort* and moved further south. 15. _____

16. The *pbartu* ending to the play left the audience confused. 16. _____

17. The clerk's *rtndoepmet* earned him an early promotion. 17. _____

18. The boats made easy *orgpeta* when we got out of the river to avoid the rapids. 18. _____

19. The *rftoracrey* cat simply wouldn't obey its owner's commands. 19. _____

20. The previously silent classroom *ruteped* with motion when the bell rang. 20. _____

TEST: LESSONS 25 AND 26

(pages 161–172)

Part A Choosing the Best Definition

On the answer line, write the letter of the best definition of the italicized word.

1. Today's flight was canceled due to a *rupture* in the lining of the hot-air balloon.
   a. defeat   c. collection
   b. suddenness   d. break

   1. _____

2. During a TV interview, the young musician *comported* herself with quiet confidence.
   a. described   c. behaved
   b. performed   d. praised

   2. _____

3. In some schools of long ago, young ladies took classes to learn proper *deportment*.
   a. personal conduct c. style and fashion
   b. occupations   d. household skills

   3. _____

4. If you put a penny in a glass of water, you can see how the glass *refracts* the light and changes the apparent size of the penny.
   a. creates   c. brightens
   b. bends   d. reflects

   4. _____

5. The three brothers in the back seat became *fractious* after the first two hours of riding in the car.
   a. contagious   c. disobedient
   b. irritable   d. hungry

   5. _____

6. Mrs. Rahman's children ran into the room and *disrupted* the parents' meeting.
   a. entertained   c. observed
   b. participated in   d. threw into confusion

   6. _____

7. Halfway down the river, a steep waterfall made *portage* of the kayaks necessary.
   a. the abandoning   c. the carrying
   b. the guiding   d. the separating

   7. _____

8. Several *refractory* workers challenged their boss's orders, and then went on strike.
   a. stubborn   c. lazy
   b. skilled   d. experienced

   8. _____

9. U.S. leaders want to decrease the amount of oil we *import* each year.
   a. have need of   c. take from the ground
   b. send out of the country d. bring into the country

   9. _____

10. Lora set up her *portable* sewing machine on the dining-room table.
    a. often used   c. easily carried
    b. precious   d. brand-new

    10. _____

TEST: LESSONS 25 AND 26

(pages 161–172)

Part B Choosing the Best Word

On the answer line, write the letter of the word that best completes the sentence.

11. When the children's whining became ———, Mrs. Sumner sent them to bed.
    a. abrupt   **b.** insupportable   **c.** portable   **d.** fragmentary

    11. _____

12. Any ——— of school rules will result in disciplinary action.
    a. deportment   **b.** rupture   **c.** infraction   **d.** eruption

    12. _____

13. This new factory will ——— cheese to many countries around the world.
    a. disrupt   **b.** comfort   **c.** refract   **d.** export

    13. _____

14. Eleanor overheard ——— bits of our conversation, but I don't think she knows our secret.
    a. portable   **b.** refractory   **c.** fractious   **d.** fragmentary

    14. _____

15. The general's well-trained forces ——— the small, disorganized group of rebel soldiers.
    a. erupted   **b.** disported   **c.** routed   **d.** refracted

    15. _____

16. Every student must prepare a ——— for the teachers to evaluate at the end of the term.
    a. rupture   **b.** portfolio   **c.** portage   **d.** deportation

    16. _____

17. The film's ——— end was caused by a sudden power failure.
    a. abrupt   **b.** fragmentary   **c.** portable   **d.** refractory

    17. _____

18. The carefree teenagers ——— themselves happily all afternoon on the sunny beach.
    a. disported   **b.** routed   **c.** refracted   **d.** imported

    18. _____

19. During the volcano's most recent ———, ash traveled hundreds of miles through the air.
    a. import   **b.** deportment   **c.** rout   **d.** eruption

    19. _____

20. An immigrant who enters the country without a valid passport may be ———.
    a. deported   **b.** disrupted   **c.** comported   **d.** ruptured

    20. _____

BONUS: LESSONS 27 AND 28

(pages 173–178 and 181–186)

Use the clues to complete the crossword puzzle.

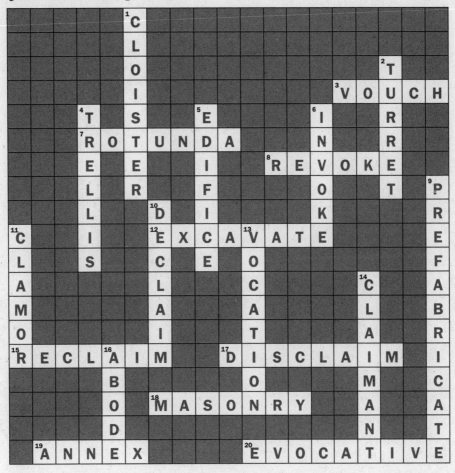

Across

3 To give a guarantee or an assurance

7 A circular building, or a large circular room with a high ceiling

8 To _____ is to cancel or reverse.

12 To dig or hollow out is to _____.

15 To _____ is to make usable or better.

17 To deny; to state that you have no responsibility for something

18 _____ is stonework or brickwork.

19 To add or attach is to _____.

20 Something that brings back memories is _____.

Down

1 A(n) _____ is a quiet, private place.

2 A(n) _____ is a small tower or tower-shaped part of a building.

4 A crisscrossed framework of strips with open space between

5 A building, especially one of grand size and design

6 To _____ is to call on for help or protection.

9 To _____ is to manufacture in advance.

10 To speak loudly or dramatically

11 To make a loud and continuous noise or outcry

13 A profession or an occupation is also known as a(n) _____.

14 A person who makes a claim or demands a right is a(n) _____.

16 A home can also be called a(n) _____.

BONUS: LESSONS 27 AND 28

(pages 173–178 and 181–186)

Use the clues to complete the crossword puzzle.

Across

3 To give a guarantee or an assurance

7 A circular building, or a large circular room with a high ceiling

8 To _____ is to cancel or reverse.

12 To dig or hollow out is to _____.

15 To _____ is to make usable or better.

17 To deny; to state that you have no responsibility for something

18 _____ is stonework or brickwork.

19 To add or attach is to _____.

20 Something that brings back memories is _____.

Down

1 A(n) _____ is a quiet, private place.

2 A(n) _____ is a small tower or tower-shaped part of a building.

4 A crisscrossed framework of strips with open space between

5 A building, especially one of grand size and design

6 To _____ is to call on for help or protection.

9 To _____ is to manufacture in advance.

10 To speak loudly or dramatically

11 To make a loud and continuous noise or outcry

13 A profession or an occupation is also known as a(n) _____.

14 A person who makes a claim or demands a right is a(n) _____.

16 A home can also be called a(n) _____.

TEST: LESSONS 27 AND 28

(pages 173–178 and 181–186)

Part A Choosing the Best Definition

On the answer line, write the letter of the best definition of the italicized word.

1. The builder brought in heavy equipment to *excavate* a site for the basement.
  a. fill in   **c.** repair
  b. build   **d.** dig
                                            1. _____

2. The man *invoked* his rights under the Fifth Amendment and refused to answer the policeman's questions.
  a. canceled   **c.** remembered
  b. called on for protection   **d.** shouted about angrily
                                            2. _____

3. Sarah was *cloistered* in her room, thinking about a big decision she had to make.
  a. secluded   **c.** waiting
  b. confined   **d.** pacing
                                            3. _____

4. The old song, "When I Was Seventeen," is *evocative* of my teenage years.
  a. improving; making better   **c.** typical
  b. having importance or influence   **d.** bringing back memories
                                            4. _____

5. The old stone *edifice* is now crumbling and in great need of repair.
  a. chimney   **c.** building
  b. fence   **d.** statue
                                            5. _____

6. As soon as Mrs. Wiggin walked in, her children began to *clamor* for a snack.
  a. hope   **c.** grab
  b. demand loudly   **d.** negotiate
                                            6. _____

7. Mr. Minelli hired a skilled craftsman to repair the *masonry* around the fireplace.
  a. wooden trim   **c.** bookcase
  b. corners   **d.** stonework
                                            7. _____

8. Mary wanted to live in an old-fashioned house and have her bedroom in a *turret*.
  a. dome   **c.** tower
  b. basement   **d.** porch
                                            8. _____

9. On that cold winter night, they were grateful to have a warm, cozy *abode*.
  a. meal   **c.** fireplace
  b. coat   **d.** home
                                            9. _____

10. We walked under a charming *trellis* covered with flowering vines.
  a. old bridge   **c.** tree house
  b. circular building   **d.** crisscrossed framework
                                            10. _____

TEST: LESSONS 27 AND 28

(pages 173–178 and 181–186)

Part B Choosing the Best Word

On the answer line, write the letter of the word that best completes the sentence.

11. In his role as Abraham Lincoln, Tim _____ his lines on the White House steps.
    a. clamored   **b.** declaimed   **c.** vouched   **d.** disclaimed

11. _____

12. The main character of the movie is the _____ to a large fortune, but it isn't until the very end that you find out whether he receives any of the money or not.
    a. annex   **b.** turret   **c.** claimant   **d.** clamor

12. _____

13. The new house was _____, and we all watched sections of it arriving on huge flatbed trucks.
    a. declaimed   **b.** clamored   **c.** prefabricated   **d.** evoked

13. _____

14. If he gets another speeding ticket this year, his driver's license will be _____.
    a. revoked   **b.** reclaimed   **c.** invoked   **d.** cloistered

14. _____

15. All tours of the Capitol building begin in the _____.
    a. masonry   **b.** rotunda   **c.** vocation   **d.** claimant

15. _____

16. Gloria got the job easily after the boss's daughter _____ for her.
    a. vouched   **b.** disclaimed   **c.** revoked   **d.** prefabricated

16. _____

17. For Dr. Inger, doing cancer research was a lifelong _____.
    a. edifice   **b.** turret   **c.** vocation   **d.** cloister

17. _____

18. Not many people bother to come to the Lost and Found to _____ their lost items.
    a. invoke   **b.** declaim   **c.** clamor   **d.** reclaim

18. _____

19. The new _____ at the hospital will provide space for new doctors' offices and a new operating room.
    a. abode   **b.** annex   **c.** masonry   **d.** trellis

19. _____

20. The students _____ responsibility for breaking a table in the school cafeteria.
    a. disclaimed   **b.** vouched   **c.** excavated   **d.** annexed

20. _____

BONUS: LESSONS 29 AND 30

(pages 187–198)

Use the following clues to identify the vocabulary words and write the words on the lines to the right. Then circle each vocabulary word in the word-search box below. The words may overlap and may read in any direction.

1. Something that is _____ is heavenly. (9 letters)

2. To cut apart for analysis (7 letters)

3. A deep divide or rift (5 letters)

4. The ability to rise or float (8 letters)

5. A(n) _____ is a broad view spanning a large area. (8 letters)

6. Something that catches fire easily is _____. (11 letters)

7. To soak, flood, or fill thoroughly is to _____. (8 letters)

8. To clot, or to change from a liquid to a solid (9 letters)

9. A strip of land that projects into a body of water is a(n) _____. (9 letters)

10. A steep cliff or overhang above a sheer drop is a(n) _____. (9 letters)

11. A large group of islands (11 letters)

12. The distance north or south of the equator (8 letters)

1. _____ **celestial** _____

2. _____ **dissect** _____

3. _____ **chasm** _____

4. _____ **buoyancy** _____

5. _____ **panorama** _____

6. _____ **combustible** _____

7. _____ **saturate** _____

8. _____ **coagulate** _____

9. _____ **peninsula** _____

10. _____ **precipice** _____

11. _____ **archipelago** _____

12. _____ **latitude** _____

Challenge

Locate and circle the eight additional vocabulary words in the word-search box.

terrestrial
alloy
longitude
conflagration
distill
meteorology
topography
meridians

BONUS: LESSONS 29 AND 30

(pages 187–198)

Use the following clues to identify the vocabulary words and write the words on the lines to the right. Then circle each vocabulary word in the word-search box below. The words may overlap and may read in any direction.

1. Something that is _____ is heavenly. (9 letters)

1. _____

2. To cut apart for analysis (7 letters)

2. _____

3. A deep divide or rift (5 letters)

3. _____

4. The ability to rise or float (8 letters)

4. _____

5. A(n) _____ is a broad view spanning a large area. (8 letters)

5. _____

6. Something that catches fire easily is _____. (11 letters)

6. _____

7. To soak, flood, or fill thoroughly is to _____. (8 letters)

7. _____

8. To clot, or to change from a liquid to a solid (9 letters)

8. _____

9. A strip of land that projects into a body of water is a(n) _____. (9 letters)

9. _____

10. A steep cliff or overhang above a sheer drop is a(n) _____. (9 letters)

10. _____

11. A large group of islands (11 letters)

11. _____

12. The distance north or south of the equator (8 letters)

12. _____

Challenge

Locate and circle the eight additional vocabulary words in the word-search box.

terrestrial
alloy
longitude
conflagration
distill
meteorology
topography
meridians

C	O	N	F	L	A	G	R	A	T	I	O	N	T	L	L	O	Y	M
E	E	A	R	U	T	S	P	I	C	R	A	E	O	N	A	P	T	E
L	P	D	Y	C	N	A	Y	O	U	B	R	Y	A	U	B	C	C	T
E	E	P	I	S	E	C	T	W	Q	R	C	E	L	O	H	O	E	E
S	C	O	A	G	U	L	A	T	E	S	H	T	U	A	Y	M	S	O
T	I	S	M	N	K	C	N	S	S	M	I	A	S	N	E	B	S	R
I	P	A	D	W	O	I	T	I	A	F	P	M	N	C	D	U	I	O
A	I	M	L	D	J	R	F	L	T	G	E	L	I	E	U	S	D	L
L	C	E	R	L	I	Q	A	L	U	R	L	U	N	L	T	T	L	O
D	E	T	M	A	O	U	E	M	R	T	A	G	E	E	I	I	A	G
U	R	R	L	O	L	Y	H	P	A	R	G	O	P	O	T	B	I	Y
T	P	F	L	A	G	R	E	P	T	I	O	N	C	S	A	L	R	S
S	N	A	I	D	I	R	E	M	E	P	O	T	I	T	L	E	T	R
I	S	U	B	I	L	O	N	G	I	T	U	D	E	I	A	T	E	R

TEST: LESSONS 29 AND 30

(pages 187–198)

Part A Choosing the Best Definition

On the answer line, write the letter of the best definition of the italicized word.

1. The *topography* of the area consists of rolling hills and small lakes.
   a. attraction
   b. physical features
   c. history
   d. problem or disadvantage

   1. _____

2. Stir the liquid ingredients until the mixture *coagulates* into a soft mass.
   a. separates
   b. cleans out
   c. expands
   d. becomes solid

   2. _____

3. Ghana, in western Africa, lies directly south of England, and at the same *longitude*.
   a. distance north or south of the equator
   b. continent or land mass
   c. distance east or west of the prime meridian
   d. section of a map or globe

   3. _____

4. Mrs. Koperniak kept her children well back from the edge of the *precipice*.
   a. large fire
   b. group of islands
   c. steep cliff
   d. deep water

   4. _____

5. In science class, students began the *dissection* of a frog in the biology lab.
   a. sketching or diagramming
   b. cutting apart for analysis
   c. intense study
   d. healing

   5. _____

6. The laundry left hanging on the line during the storm was *saturated*.
   a. wrinkled
   b. ruined
   c. muddied
   d. soaked

   6. _____

7. Some hikers rested on the mountain's highest peak, marveling at the *panorama*.
   a. broad view
   b. great accomplishment
   c. steep cliffs
   d. weather and climate

   7. _____

8. Oily rags are *combustible* and should be disposed of in closed metal containers.
   a. likely to remain wet
   b. no longer useful
   c. able to catch fire easily
   d. stained; dirty

   8. _____

9. Andrea plans to study *meteorology* at the university.
   a. the science of weather
   b. the science of life forms
   c. the science of medicine
   d. the science of landforms

   9. _____

10. We walked along the beach and out onto the narrow *peninsula*.
    a. high land with a steep drop
    b. one or more islands
    c. land with water on three sides
    d. small inlet or bay

    10. _____

TEST: LESSONS 29 AND 30

(pages 187–198)

Part B Choosing the Best Word

On the answer line, write the letter of the word that best completes the sentence.

11. Brass is a well-known _____ made of copper and zinc. **11.** _____
    a. distillation   **b.** alloy   **c.** topography   **d.** buoyancy

12. Last night, I dreamed about escaping my _____ life and learning to fly! **12.** _____
    a. combustible   **b.** celestial   **c.** terrestrial   **d.** buoyant

13. At _____ close to the equator, the climate is always hot. **13.** _____
    a. panoramas   **b.** meridians   **c.** longitudes   **d.** latitudes

14. You must _____ the water to purify it before using it in this science experiment. **14.** _____
    a. saturate   **b.** dissect   **c.** coagulate   **d.** distill

15. Tom peered down into the deep _____ , where he saw a rushing river. **15.** _____
    a. archipelago   **b.** chasm   **c.** peninsula   **d.** alloy

16. Some of the _____ events this month include a meteor shower and a partial eclipse of the moon. **16.** _____
    a. topographical   **b.** celestial   **c.** combustible   **d.** terrestrial

17. Many of the islands in the _____ are underwater during high tide. **17.** _____
    a. meridian   **b.** dissection   **c.** precipice   **d.** archipelago

18. Firefighters came from several surrounding states to help fight the _____ . **18.** _____
    a. conflagration   **b.** panorama   **c.** meteorology   **d.** longitude

19. Luckily, the oar's _____ kept it afloat until I could maneuver the boat around to reach it. **19.** _____
    a. chasm   **b.** topography   **c.** buoyancy   **d.** saturation

20. Look at the globe, find the North Pole, and follow a _____ all the way to the South Pole. **20.** _____
    a. meridian   **b.** chasm   **c.** conflagration   **d.** latitude

Answer Key

TEST: LESSONS 1 & 2

Part A	Part B
1. c	11. a
2. d	12. d
3. a	13. c
4. d	14. a
5. a	15. b
6. d	16. d
7. c	17. a
8. b	18. b
9. a	19. c
10. b	20. d

TEST: LESSONS 7 & 8

Part A	Part B
1. b	11. b
2. b	12. c
3. a	13. a
4. d	14. d
5. d	15. b
6. a	16. c
7. c	17. d
8. d	18. c
9. a	19. a
10. d	20. b

TEST: LESSONS 3 & 4

Part A	Part B
1. c	11. d
2. a	12. c
3. c	13. c
4. d	14. b
5. b	15. c
6. c	16. a
7. b	17. b
8. a	18. d
9. d	19. a
10. a	20. c

TEST: LESSONS 9 & 10

Part A	Part B
1. d	11. b
2. c	12. d
3. b	13. a
4. a	14. c
5. b	15. c
6. a	16. b
7. b	17. b
8. a	18. a
9. c	19. c
10. d	20. d

TEST: LESSONS 5 & 6

Part A	Part B
1. b	11. d
2. b	12. b
3. d	13. a
4. b	14. d
5. c	15. c
6. a	16. a
7. c	17. c
8. d	18. b
9. b	19. d
10. c	20. a

TEST: LESSONS 11 & 12

Part A	Part B
1. b	11. c
2. c	12. c
3. d	13. b
4. a	14. d
5. c	15. d
6. b	16. c
7. c	17. b
8. a	18. a
9. b	19. c
10. d	20. b

TEST: LESSONS 13 & 14

Part A	Part B
1. c	11. d
2. d	12. c
3. d	13. b
4. b	14. b
5. c	15. d
6. a	16. c
7. a	17. b
8. b	18. d
9. d	19. a
10. c	20. a

TEST: LESSONS 19 & 20

Part A	Part B
1. d	11. b
2. c	12. a
3. d	13. a
4. c	14. d
5. b	15. b
6. a	16. a
7. c	17. c
8. d	18. b
9. a	19. a
10. b	20. d

TEST: LESSONS 15 & 16

Part A	Part B
1. a	11. d
2. b	12. c
3. c	13. a
4. d	14. a
5. b	15. b
6. a	16. c
7. b	17. c
8. c	18. d
9. d	19. b
10. a	20. a

TEST: LESSONS 21 & 22

Part A	Part B
1. a	11. b
2. b	12. d
3. c	13. c
4. d	14. d
5. c	15. a
6. a	16. b
7. c	17. a
8. d	18. d
9. b	19. a
10. c	20. c

TEST: LESSONS 17 & 18

Part A	Part B
1. b	11. c
2. c	12. d
3. d	13. a
4. b	14. c
5. a	15. b
6. b	16. a
7. b	17. a
8. a	18. d
9. c	19. c
10. d	20. b

TEST: LESSONS 23 & 24

Part A	Part B
1. c	11. b
2. b	12. a
3. b	13. c
4. c	14. d
5. d	15. a
6. a	16. c
7. d	17. c
8. c	18. a
9. c	19. b
10. a	20. d

TEST: LESSONS 25 & 26

Part A	Part B
1. d	11. b
2. c	12. c
3. a	13. d
4. b	14. d
5. b	15. c
6. d	16. b
7. c	17. a
8. a	18. a
9. d	19. d
10. c	20. a

TEST: LESSONS 27 & 28

Part A	Part B
1. d	11. b
2. b	12. c
3. a	13. c
4. d	14. a
5. c	15. b
6. b	16. a
7. d	17. c
8. c	18. d
9. d	19. b
10. d	20. a

TEST: LESSONS 29 & 30

Part A	Part B
1. b	11. b
2. d	12. c
3. c	13. d
4. c	14. d
5. b	15. b
6. d	16. b
7. a	17. d
8. c	18. a
9. a	19. c
10. c	20. a